Infamous Scribblers

INFAMOUS SCRIBBLERS

The Founding Fathers and the Rowdy Beginnings of American Journalism

ERIC BURNS

PUBLICAFFAIRS

NEW YORK

BOOK DESIGN AND COMPOSITION BY JENNY DOSSIN
TEXT SET IN ADOBE CASLON

Library of Congress Cataloging-in-Publication Data
Burns, Eric.
Infamous scribblers : the Founding Fathers and the
rowdy beginnings of American journalism / Eric Burns.
p. cm.
Includes bibliographical references and index.
ISBN-13: 978-1-58648-334-0
ISBN-10: 1-58648-334-X
1. Journalism—United States—History—18th Century.
2. American newspapers—History—18th Century. I. Title
PN4861.B87 2006
071'.309033—dc22
2005053542

FIRST EDITION

1 3 5 7 9 10 8 6 4 2

TO

Dianne Wildman

FOR 25 YEARS OF INDISPENSABILITY

CONTENTS

✵

Part I: The Role of Authority

Part II: The Approach of War

Part III: The Tumult of Peace

A NOTE TO READERS

❁

EIGHTEENTH-CENTURY ENGLISH is a notoriously whimsical language, especially as it appears in newspapers. It is as if printers thought of their pieces of type as toys and were determined to play with as many as possible, as often as possible, on their pages. And so capital letters pop up where they are least expected. Italics materialize where they had seldom materialized before and have not shown themselves since. Commas and colons and semicolons seem sprinkled between the words, rather than placed with a purpose. The spelling is recognizable but sometimes requires the author who reproduces it to use an explanatory "[sic]," which means, "Don't blame me; it was like this when I found it." And then there is the occasional sentence that runs on so long and so ornately that the modern reader finds himself smiling and catching his breath at the same moment—the whole toy chest dumped onto the printing press at once.

Because of these flights and variations, a number of historians who write about the colonial era "translate" as they go along, rendering a passage in more modern form, rooting out at least some of the idiosyncrasies.

I have decided not to. It seems to me that altering the language of the Founding Fathers and their contemporaries as well as those who immediately preceded them would be presumptuous, or worse, counterproductive. Why edit the charm and authenticity from another era's journalism? Why not declare it a national treasure and preserve it as originally constructed? Why not embrace the differences, however small, between yesterday and today?

In a few cases, though, I have been thwarted. I have had to rely on secondary sources that provided their citations in already translated form. These passages, along with those of the vast majority of the quoted material that comes from primary sources—the newspapers and other publications of the period—are identified in the notes at the end of this book.

About my own use of capital letters: The words Federalist and Republican are almost always capitalized when they refer to our nation's first two political parties—or more precisely, to the two groups that were the forerunners of our modern two-party system. In the following pages, I use the terms more generically, lowercased. My federalist is someone who believed in a strong central government and close ties with Britain but did not necessarily attend meetings to promote those goals. My republican, similarly free of membership obligations, insisted that power should reside primarily with the states and that France was a more natural ally for the United States than the motherland.

I use the terms federalist and republican, in short, as I might use the words liberal and conservative if I were writing about the present—to refer to individuals and their ideas, not organized movements and their battle plans. It is not as small a distinction as it might seem; later in the book, I will refer to republican newspapers well before the existence of the Republican Party.

I should also point out as I begin that early American papers had a habit of changing their names from time to time, sometimes to signify new ownership, sometimes to announce a new editorial philosophy by the old owners, sometimes to signal the desire for a fresh start or a more successful venture. A "gazette" added a "country journal" to its masthead for a few months or years; a "journal" added a "commercial advertiser" or "general advertiser" or a "marine intelligencer." One publication even tacked on "A Lady's and Gentleman's Miscellany," even though its prose was often unsuitable for either of the title characters.

For the sake of convenience, both yours and mine, I refer to the publications in almost all cases by their most basic titles.

ERIC BURNS, *Westport, Connecticut*

INFAMOUS SCRIBBLERS

❁

Inappropriate Behavior

I T WAS THE BEST OF TIMES, it was the worst of journalism—and it is no small irony that the former condition led
directly to the latter, that the golden age of America's founding was also the gutter age of American reporting, that the most
notorious of presses in our nation's history churned out its copy on
the foothills of Olympus. The Declaration of Independence was literature, but the *New England Courant* talked trash. The Constitution of the United States was philosophy; the *Boston Gazette* slung
mud. The *Gazette of the United States* and the *National Gazette* were
conceived as weapons, not chronicles of daily events; the two of
them stood masthead to masthead, firing at each other, without
ceasing, without blinking, without acknowledging the limitations of
veracity. Philadelphia's *Aurora* was less a celestial radiance than a
ground-level reek, guilty of "taking a line that would have been
regarded as treasonable in any later international conflict." And
Porcupine's Gazette, the *Aurora's* sworn foe, was as barbed as its
namesake.

There were, of course, exceptions. Some journalism of the colonial era was cordial: Benjamin Franklin's pieces, especially in the
Pennsylvania Gazette, were witty and insightful and, more often
than not, absent of malice in any form.

Some journalism was thoughtful: Alexander Hamilton, James
Madison, and John Jay collaborated on *The Federalist Papers*, first
published in New York's *Independent Journal*, and they were as
scholarly a collection of essays as has ever appeared in an American
newspaper. Thomas Paine wrote with fiery perception, John
Adams with a stiff-collared eloquence, and John Dickinson, the

so-called Pennsylvania Farmer, with a lawyer's sharply reasoned clarity.

Some journalism was courageous: John Peter Zenger did not write at all but was a publisher of such uncommon and unwavering principle that he would blaze a trail for all who followed.

Some journalism was soporific: John Campbell produced so lifeless and irrelevant a paper for the citizenry of Boston that had it not started early, lasted long, and begun the most disreputable of all forms of American advertising, it would not even be remembered today.

And some journalism was obsequious: on the occasion of George Washington's sixty-sixth birthday, the *Pittsburgh Gazette* joyfully referred to the "sublime terms" in which he was being feted, remarking on the "radiance of his virtue and intelligence." It was as if the *Gazette* were doing penance for the censures it pronounced on others more commonly.

But Sam Adams was not an exception; it was he who slung the mud from the offices of the *Boston Gazette*, a warmonger in journalist's attire, a man even more devious outside the print shop than within. James Rivington, of *Rivington's New-York Gazetteer*, seemed seldom to meet an issue with two sides. John Fenno's *Gazette of the United States* almost never acknowledged a republican with a good idea. The republican Philip Freneau might have been the leading poet of the era, but his *National Gazette* could wound as seriously in prose. Benjamin Franklin Bache, Ben Franklin's grandson, seemed at times more intent on vilifying than informing in the pages of his *Aurora*. Bache's great-uncle, James Franklin, would not allow the truth to block the flow of his vitriol from the *New England Courant*. James Thomson Callender, who wrote for several papers, might as well have thrust his pen into the soft tissue of his subjects as written about them. Like Callender, William Cobbett, of *Porcupine's Gazette*, ran afoul of authority on two continents.

And Hamilton was not always scholarly, especially not when writing for Fenno's *Gazette* about the devil, who he believed had been incarnated as Thomas Jefferson.

❀

PERHAPS, THEN, they were not the best of times. Perhaps they were too divisive, too uncertain. Perhaps they only seem the best in retrospect, to generations who live in the country that those times produced, under the laws they established and the rights they defined and the liberties they so carefully prescribed.

But in many ways the men and women who settled the New World were the best of people. Surely not the type to print lies in their newspapers when the truth was insufficiently compelling or contradictory to their causes; to smear sex scandals across their pages or raise invective to levels previously unknown outside a cockfighting den. Not the type to confuse hyperbole with fact or scatology with analysis; to be ill informed or uninformed or misinformed; to correct their mistakes rarely and grudgingly; to inflate a peccadillo into a crime; to condemn a lapse of judgment with a sentence of perdition; to encourage violence against those who disagreed with their views.

Yet they did it all, these best of people, all of it and more, time and again over the course of many decades, an incendiary press somehow becoming the basis of a humane and enduring society.

❀

THE MEN AND WOMEN who settled the New World were, to begin with, God-fearing. Many of them had left their homes in England for the sole purpose of worshipping as they pleased rather than as the Anglican Church decreed; those who took up residence in Massachusetts, New Jersey, Maryland, and Pennsylvania referred to their colonies as "plantations of religion." They went to services on Sunday and said their prayers at home every other day of the week. They treated the Bible as if it were an instruction manual. And later, their rigorously nurtured and continuously exhibited faith would provide the underpinnings for rebellion, "a moral sanction for opposition to the British—an assurance to the average American that revolution was justified in the sight of God."

The men and women who settled the New World were devoted to family, believing it was, in Benjamin Franklin's phrase, the "sacred cement of all societies." Some years earlier, the clergyman Cotton Mather had chosen a different metaphor. "*Families* are the *Nurseries* of all Societies," he stated in 1693, "and the First Combinations of mankind." It was uncommon for a Franklin and a Mather to agree like this, and their most famous quarrel would be one of the most disreputable landmarks of early American journalism.

The men and women who settled the New World were well educated, and the family was a nursery for learning too, as the mother and father would teach their children the basics of reading, writing, and arithmetic.

If the parents were unable to do so, either because their days were too busy or their educational backgrounds too deficient, they would send their boys and girls to someone in the neighborhood, "usually an indigent widow," who would provide the lessons in her home. Dame schools, these casual institutions were called, and the most promising of the boys who attended them would later move on to an academy, where the approach was not casual in the least. They would study Latin, learning the language so they could read the word of God in its early versions, and learning the culture of ancient Greece and Rome so they could absorb lessons of leadership, valor, and proper governance. They would also take up philosophy, rhetoric, and mathematics. They would emerge from the academy—if all went according to plan—pious, thoughtful, and articulate.

Some of them would go on to more advanced work. Harvard was founded in 1636, the College of William and Mary in 1693, and Yale in 1701. Between 1746 and 1769, six more institutions of higher learning came into being, including schools now known as Princeton, Columbia, and Rutgers.

The men and women who settled the New World were literate, even those who did not go to dame schools and colleges. In *Amusing Ourselves to Death: Public Discourse in the Age of Show Business*, Neil Postman reckons that "between 1640 and 1700, the literacy rate for men in Massachusetts and Connecticut was somewhere between 89 percent and 95 percent." The rate for women in the same colonies "is estimated to have run as high as 62 percent in the years 1681–1697."

With the ability to read came the passion to be enlightened. In the next century, Thomas Jefferson would refer to his books as "mental furniture" and would complain when the "enormities of the times" took him away from "the delightful pursuit of knowledge." John Adams said that those same enormities had removed him too often from his family and gardens and fields. "But above all," he wrote, "except the Wife and Children I want to see my Books." As a child, Adams was seldom without his copy of Cicero's *Orations*; as an adult, he would sometimes carry *Don Quixote* in his saddlebag, and he once sailed to Europe with Molière's *Amphitryon* as companion. James Madison, who would succeed Jefferson as president, was as well acquainted with Aristotle and Demosthenes, John Locke and David Hume, John Milton and Jonathan Swift as he was with many of his contemporaries. Alexander Hamilton "read a considerable amount of philosophy, including Bacon, Hobbes, Montaigne, and Cicero. He also perused histories of Greece, Prussia, and France," even though such titles were "hardly light fare after a day of demanding correspondence for [General George] Washington," whom Hamilton served as secretary during the Revolutionary War. Washington himself prepared to lead the Continental army by studying "five books—military." Young Benjamin Franklin read so much, and found reading so meaningful, that he determined to encourage the experience in others. He was not surprised when, several years later, after he organized America's first subscription library in Philadelphia, people in other cities, towns, and villages formed their own.

The men and women who settled the New World appreciated painting no less than literature, with homegrown artists like Benjamin West and John Singleton Copley becoming famous not only in the colonies but in Europe as well. West's renderings of historical and religious themes and Copley's portraits were regarded as instant treasures by people who paid large sums to commission them. And Americans were no less admiring of other arts—including the creations that Henry William Stiegel fashioned of glass, Paul Revere of silver, and landscape gardener Henry Lauren of the Almighty's own expanses.

The men and women who settled the New World were equally fond of music. Some belonged to glee clubs that met once a month, if not more often, either to sing among themselves or to perform publicly. When Hamilton's daughter sang at social gatherings, he accompanied her on the pianoforte. At gatherings of his own, Jefferson played the violin while his wife and daughter played the harpsichord and pianoforte. Franklin dabbled with the violin as well as the harp and harmonica, or, as it was known at the time, the armonica. The latter's tones were not what he wanted them to be, however, so America's leading inventor fashioned his own, an instrument that was, at least in one of its later models, five feet long. It turned out to be such an improvement on its predecessors that both Beethoven and Mozart are said to have written pieces for it.

But Americans did not just listen to music. Sometimes they rose from their chairs and danced to it. The minuet was a particular favorite; for the male it involved "the graceful motion of the arms, the giving of your hand, and the putting on and pulling off your hat genteelly." Washington went to dancing school when he was fifteen, and for the next four decades delighted in the occasional turn or two around the floor. To Jefferson, dancing was "healthy exercise, elegant and very attractive for young people."

The men and women who settled the New World, these unlikeliest of candidates for developing a press that libeled and exaggerated and berated; a press that specialized in "foul-mouthed impertinence," dismissing Hamilton as "Tom S**t," for instance; a press whose editors often referred to the editors of competing journals as demagogues, traitors, and madmen, in one case recommending that a fellow not be spit upon in the street because it would be a waste of good saliva; a press that had no qualms about accusing its foes of blasphemy or bastardy or the taint of Negro blood—these early American colonists were nevertheless forgiving sorts. They forgave drunken men their loutishness and rambunctious boys their vandalism and even, on occasion, promiscuous women their adultery. In the latter case, offenders were usually allowed to marry without either legal sanction or public opprobrium.

The first American settlers were hardworking. They cleared forests, harvested fields, erected homes, built roads, raised animals, made their own clothes and furniture and farm implements; they built ships, ran businesses, traded with foreign lands, devised new institutions, put new customs into effect and discarded old ones. They created a homeland, in other words, where only a few generations earlier there had been a wilderness so foreign and distant that it had not even been mapped, much less understood.

The first settlers were charitable. They would provide lodging in their homes for orphans, the elderly, and others in their midst who might be in need; for orphans they would try to arrange an apprenticeship or some other form of gainful occupation. They would help their neighbors erect barns and plant crops and, through moneys collected in churches and by various secular agencies, would see to it that almshouses were constructed for the poor of their towns and villages.

It was mass calamities, however, which evoked the most dramatic exhibitions of benevolence, erasing provincial and ethnic lines to unite the colonists in a single overarching effort. The Charleston [South Carolina] fire of 1740 brought gifts for relief from as far off as Massachusetts. The Boston fire twenty years later merely repeated the story on a larger scale.

The first settlers were fair-minded. Some colonies passed laws to forbid traders from making excess profits, while others legislated against idleness, believing that an able-bodied man who refused to work was a burden on every other member of the community.

The first settlers were gregarious. They assembled at fairs where they traded livestock and baked goods, raced with one another, wrestled one another, and even, on especially festive occasions, chased a greased pig around a pasture. In more urban locales, they formed social clubs that met at churches and taverns and private homes, where they talked about philosophy and astronomy, offered advice and assistance to young people seeking vocation, and plotted the community's future.

The first settlers were well mannered on the street, acknowledging one another graciously as they passed, gentlemen tipping their hats to ladies and ladies smiling and nodding in return.

They were well mannered in shops, patient with clerks, slow to complain about merchandise that did not meet their standards or was not available at all.

They were well mannered at meals, making up for a dearth of utensils with a multitude of napkins. And they practiced other forms of etiquette, both at table and elsewhere, that they learned in such highly regarded manuals of the time as *The Boke of Nurture* and *The Boke of Curtseye*.

They dressed well.

They coiffed themselves meticulously.

They wrote neatly, believing that penmanship was a virtue as much as a skill.

They were modest, not given to self-promotion, garish display, or competitive excess.

They were patient and understanding, kind-hearted and devout, trustworthy and dignified and mutually supportive.

You would never have known it from their newspapers.

❀

IT SEEMS AN IDEALIZED PORTRAIT. It is certainly a selective one, ignoring such rampant and unconscionable practices of eighteenth-century America as slavery, the subjugation of women, and hostility toward the natives who had settled the land long before the Europeans even knew it existed. These are serious matters, but they are for other books to discuss, books whose goals are different from this one.

It is also a selective portrait because it is more true of the upper classes than the lower, who "were very rough and disorderly in colonial times, and spent a large part of their time drinking, gambling, and fighting at taverns and at elections." These were men and women who did not enjoy the minuet, did not stockpile napkins, did not know Plutarch and Bunyan, Milton and Swift. And, in a few cases, they were people who behaved criminally, preferring to accost a stranger in a dark, private place and relieve him of his valuables than to meet their fellows at the fair to pursue a well-oiled farm animal.

But it was the upper classes who set the tone for early American society, they who left the legacy, and, more to the point of the present volume, they who wrote the initial histories as well as the journalism that was their first draft. It was they who could afford printing presses and the other start-up costs of a new business. It was they who could spend the money to advertise in the papers. It was they who owned the land and cast the votes and, believing that the future was their possession no less than the present, set about expressing their views and influencing their countrymen through newspapers. And it was they, at least at the outset, who made up a majority of the readers.

One can only speculate, then, about why there was such a contrast between the values of the budding nation and the tone of its reporting. Why did one newspaper dismiss a competing journal as a collection of "incendiary, prostituted, hireling scriblers [sic]"? Why did another paper write, "If ever a nation was debauched by a man, the American nation has been debauched by [George]

Washington"? And why, when the editor of that paper died, which he did before reaching the age of thirty, did a pro-Washington paper gloat over his passing, declaring that "[t]he memory of this scoundrel cannot be too highly execrated"?

One reason is that there was no tradition at the time of an impartial press, either in the colonies or in Europe. In fact, insofar as there was a tradition in journalism at all, it favored bias; newspapers were printed either to indulge the whims of the owner or to serve the political causes with which he had aligned himself. If you told a man he had a civic duty to report the news objectively, he would have asked what duty the artisan had, or the ironworker or the shipbuilder or the farmer. These were men who did their jobs, nothing more; so was he. His newspaper was a business, and the news to him was the same thing that silver was to Paul Revere or glass to Henry William Stiegel—which is to say a product of his own manufacture, to be molded into whatever shape he thought would be most pleasing to his customers and thus most profitable to him.

Besides, the newspaperman would likely have thought that he *was* doing his duty to society by giving voice to the ideas in which he so ardently believed. In modern terms, we would say that he put his money where his mouth was. It would not have made sense to him to spend that money to encourage a contrary set of opinions or to muffle his own.

Some papers claimed to be different. The *Salem* [Massachusetts] *Gazette* boasted that it was "*Influenced neither by* COURT *or* COUNTRY," and, further, that it presented "*the most impartial accounts of the transactions of the present times.*" However, its pro-British leanings on the eve of the Revolution were obvious. The *Pennsylvania Ledger* swore that it was "Free and Impartial," but its disdain for the motherland was equally apparent.

More typical, though, was a paper like *Porcupine's Gazette*, which published a statement of purpose in its first issue. "Professions of impartiality I shall make none," wrote editor William Cobbett, who then went on to prove it by describing his competitor Benjamin Franklin Bache as a "crafty and lecherous old hypocrite."

But the colonial press was not merely partisan; as Cobbett demonstrates, it was at times vile, crude, unjust, more of a blight on the communities to which it reported than a service, a means of inciting more than informing. One continues, then, to search for an explanation for the quality of journalism in days long past . . .

. . . And muses on an era far more violent than our own, an era in which ignorance led to fear, and fear in turn to cruelty. When men do not understand, they do not behave compassionately toward those who differ from them. And so European nations warred against one another often and sometimes randomly in the seventeenth and eighteenth centuries; the religion that was so important to the colonists insisted on draconian penalties for heresy; and secular officials were no less severe in their reactions to even minor offenses: death or dismemberment for stealing an animal or a purse or possibly even a loaf of bread. Perhaps the underlying harshness of the times could not help but erupt in print. Perhaps Americans found in journalism a release from the amenities that bound them in other circumstances. Perhaps those amenities were, at least to some extent, a veneer.

And perhaps, and most likely, the colonists concluded that there was simply too much at stake in those days for the luxury of restraint. They had come to America to be governed more compassionately than they were in Europe. They had come to worship more freely. They had come to make decisions for themselves, not to accede to those who did not have their best interests in mind. When these freedoms were challenged by various policies of the Crown, Americans roared with the indignation of those for whom freedom is new and therefore especially prized.

And when, some years later, they took up arms to win their independence, the stakes got even higher and the odds of unbiased reporting correspondingly lower. Then the stakes got higher still, for the end of the war was the beginning of a nation, and a war of a different kind broke out among the victors over the form that nation should take. What would the provisions of the new government be? What would it allow and disallow? Who should have the authority to make decisions of this magnitude? Who would enforce them? What was the proper relationship between the individual and society, between governed and governor, between the Almighty and mortals in matters of state?

Such momentous questions. Such a variety of possible answers. Surely it seemed to most Americans a time for decisiveness more than congeniality, for directness of expression more than niceties of locution. Even a peaceful man will take up arms if he is pushed far enough; even a civilized people will dip their pens in venom if they believe their very civilization is in peril.

And, as the *Connecticut Bee* acknowledged in 1800, it was sometimes necessary, under conditions like these, for a newspaper to concede that truth was not always as important as expediency.

> Here various news we tell, of love and strife,
> Of peace and war, health and sickness, death and life,
> Of loss and gain, of famine and of store,
> Of storms at sea, and travels on the shore,
> Of prodigies, and portents seen in air,
> Of fires, and plagues, and stars with blazing hair,
> Of turns of fortune, changes in the state,
> The fall of fav'rites, projects of the great,
> Of old mismanagements, taxations new,
> *All neither wholly false, nor wholly true.*

❀

IF, SOMEHOW, THE MEN AND WOMEN who settled the New World could rise from their graves and return to us today, if they could step into our legislative chambers and listen to the deliberations of those we have chosen to represent us, they would be pleased that we have paid such careful heed to their instructions—

among other things, that we have followed the rules of parliamentary debate, kept the three branches of government checking and balancing one another to the best of our ability, maintained the peaceful transfer of power after our elections, and made of the Bill of Rights a set of secular commandments.

But if they were to step outside those chambers and pick up our newspapers and magazines, if they were to watch our television newscasts and listen to the verbal butcheries on our opinion programs on all-news cable and talk radio, even the loudest of them, even the coarsest, the most mean-spirited—if, under some marvelous set of circumstances, the citizens of the eighteenth century could find a way to make themselves media-savvy in the first decade of the twenty-first century, they would be startled by, and perhaps not altogether approving of, the extent to which we have tamed the wildly inglorious impulses of their journalism.

I

THE ROLE OF AUTHORITY

❁

CHAPTER ONE

The End
of the Beginning

Numb. 1.

PUBLICK OCCURRENCES

Both FORREIGN and DOMESTICK.

Boſton, Thurſday Sept. 25th. 1690.

IT is deſigned, that the Countrey ſhall be furniſhed once a moneth (or if any Glut of Occurrences happen, oftener,) with an Account of ſuch conſiderable things as have arrived unto our Notice.

In order hereunto, the Publiſher will take what pains he can to obtain a Faithful Relation of all ſuch things; and will particularly make himſelf beholden to ſuch Perſons in Boſton whom he knows to have been for their own uſe the diligent Obſervers of ſuch matters.

That which is herein propoſed, is, Firſt, That Memorable Occurrents of Divine Providence may not be neglected or forgotten, as they too often are. Secondly, That people every where may better underſtand the Circumſtances of Publique Affairs, both abroad and at home; which may not only direct their Thoughts at all times, but at ſome times alſo to aſſiſt their Buſineſſes and Negotiations.

Thirdly, That ſome thing may be done towards the Curing, or at leaſt the Charming of that Spirit of Lying, which prevails amongſt us, wherefore nothing ſhall be entered, but what we have reaſon to believe is true, repairing to the beſt fountain for our Information. And when there appears any material miſtake in any thing that is collected, it ſhall be corrected in the next.

Moreover, the Publiſher of theſe Occurrences is willing to engage, that whereas, there are many falſe reports, maliciouſly made, and ſpread among us,

from them, as what is in the For... gone for Canada; made them thi... impoſſible for them to get well ... Affairs of their Husbandry at th... year, yet the Seaſon has been ... favourable that they ſcarce fi... the many hundreds of hands, ... from them; which is looke... ciful Providence.

While the barbarous In... about Chelmsford, there ... the beginning of this m... then belonging to a ma... of them aged about ele... bout nine years, both ... be fallen into the ha...

A very Tragical ... ver-Town, the begin... Old man, that was ... Moroſe Temper, ... joyed the reputa... Man, having n... Devil took a... which he the... cretion and ... port of his ... with an in... come to v... very care... kept a f... himſelf ... from ...

*T*HE NEW WORLD'S first permanent settlement of English-men, and a very few women, was established on the swampy, bug-bedeviled peninsula of Jamestown, Virginia, in 1607. It did not have a newspaper. It did not even have a printing press. No one seemed to mind.

Nor were there any newspapers in Britain at the time, at least not as we know them today. Instead, as Peter Ackroyd tells us, there was

> the broadside, a sheet printed on one side which bore the latest news and the newest sensations. From the earliest years of the sixteenth century this was the language of the street—"Sir Walter Raleigh His Lamentations! . . . Strange News from Sussex. . . . No Natural Mother But a Monster . . ."

These tabloid-tinted tales were the beginning of print journalism in the English-speaking world.

There was also a form of broadcast journalism, in the person of "running patterers"—young men with resonant voices and muscular calves who dashed from one end of London to the other and shouted out the day's occurrences. Sometimes they would stop, collect their breath, and then "take up positions in different parts of the street and pretend to vie with each other for attention, thus heightening interest in the latest crime, murder, elopement or execution." A century later, the French would, with all disrespect intended, call these stories "public noises." Those who uttered them

were the predecessors of television news anchors, the "sitting patterers" of today.

People liked to hear about elopements. But then as now, crime
made better copy than romance. In 1605, a London broadside told
of "the 'pitilesse' Sir John Fites, 'thirstie of bloud,' who had just finished killing a man and stabbing that man's wife when he ran upon
his own bloody sword." The account goes on to say that the mur-
derer, apparently repentant, hoped for his own demise; he wanted
his heart to "Split, split, and in this onely wound die: That I thy
owner may not live, to heare the honour of my credite stayned with
these odious actes."

Journalism was more than a century and a half old when Sir
John went on his rampage, and it had not begun nobly. The world's
first broadside to relate the events of the day seems to have been
the work of a "Renaissance blackmailer and pornographer," the
Italian Pietro Aretino, who set up shop a few years after the invention of movable type. Aretino could have done something con-
structive with his little publication. He could have written about
Florence under the Medicis becoming the center of art and hu-
manism in the Western world. He could have written about the
founding of the University of Palermo, which would soon be a
major institution for the advancement of learning. He could have
written about Francesco Sforza, who had recently been named
Duke of Milan and proceeded to show up at social events accompanied by a patterer of his very own, a man who would sing out
poetry the duke had written himself, rhymes whose subject was
not the news of the day but the virtues of the poet.

Aretino did none of this. Instead, he "produced a regular series
of anticlerical obscenities, libelous stories, public accusations, and
personal opinion." The opinion was boldly, and often vulgarly, expressed. It was also for sale, with Aretino running a kind of protection racket on those who were the subjects of his stories: pay what
he asked and he praised you; refuse and you were slathered with
abuse. Either way, you were a commodity for him; he would tell

the tale that suited him best and profit from you as much as he could.

But few people in Renaissance Italy read Aretino's rag, and it did not stay in business long. Few people read the British broadsides of the early seventeenth century; they, too, were ephemeral in duration and impact. It was not that Europeans disliked these nascent attempts at journalism; more fundamentally, they did not understand the reason for them, living as they did in a world in which news could not thrive as a commodity because it barely existed as a concept. How could it? The Almighty was what mattered to men and women in ages past, but they could speak to Him directly. Their families were what mattered to them, but husbands and wives and sons and daughters lived in the same room. Their livelihood was what mattered to them, but they tended their shops or worked their fields from dawn until sunset, husbands and wives and sons and daughters together by day as well as by night.

In other words, what mattered to a person in the sixteenth and early seventeenth centuries was what happened to him and to those closest to him between one sunrise and the next, on his own plot of land or in his own place of business, and in the company of his own kinfolk and perhaps hired workers. But he could see that for himself. He could interpret it for himself. No intermediary was required to give voice or meaning to the events in his life. As for the events that were not in his life, those that occurred in the lives of other people in other places, of what possible interest could they be to him? The idea that a human being could be instructed or amused by the fortunes of a stranger was as foreign to a European back then as a land across the sea. The world outside one's immediate ken was a place of mystery, not a source of enlightenment.

Occasionally there was something from afar that a person needed to know. There might be an edict from the king ordering his subjects to provide an even greater share of their harvest to the royal granaries. There might be a ruling that taxes were to be increased to help pay for a war or for yet another lordly extravagance of some sort. There might be a declaration from a religious leader that the rituals or tenets of faith had been altered, or perhaps that more money was required by the church as well as the state. Any of these would be news.

But this kind of thing did not happen often, and was so unwelcome when it did that it did not inspire an interest in the wider world. On the contrary: better ignorance than tidings that brought even more hardship to an individual than was already his lot.

But even if the news *had* been relevant to men and women of an earlier age, they would not have had time for it—which was, of course, a further reason for their indifference. They led the same kinds of lives as the first American colonists, lives of toil and repetition. They fed and milked and slaughtered their animals. They cleared and plowed their fields and dammed their streams. They spun fabric and built shelters. They prepared food and cooked meals and mended fences. They cleaned and repaired and maintained houses and barns and outbuildings. They prayed to a strict and sometimes capricious God, wanting to please, and He was ever watching, ever judging.

Which is all to say that they led the kinds of lives even a greed-besotted, hedge fund–managing workaholic of the early twenty-first century would have found punishing, every minute of every hour accounted for, every second of every minute. And journalism, which requires an appreciation of events beyond the personal, the easily observable, is to some extent a function of leisure. Not much of it existed when Aretino first inked up his press.

In the New World, leisure would not make an appearance until the eighteenth century, and then for only a few: the more successful manufacturers and shopkeepers, the wealthier men of trade, and the owners and managers of large farms and plantations. In some of their spare time, some of the hours or minutes not already allotted to Bible study or letter writing or the mastery of a musical instrument, these men and their families began to read newspapers. They were not only the first Americans to have time for journalism; they were the first to sense that knowledge might be power or profit, or that it might at least ease some of their apprehensions about the people and places they did not know.

As the century progressed and relations with Britain grew strained and argumentative and then worse, the colonists read even more and began to debate what they had read with others, sharing not only their opinions but the newspapers themselves, passing their own copies along to friends, urging them to consider this particular point, to see the fallacy of that one. What was Parliament thinking about now? How would the colonies be affected? How would the colonies respond? Who was meeting where, and when, and what steps might be taken as a result? In the buildup to war, the irrelevance of journalism became a thing of the past; urgency, even more than leisure, was driving Americans to learn the day's happenings.

Even so, the news was seldom immediate, which is another reason people did not easily warm to it. As Will Durant pointed out, this was not all bad. "Medieval man could eat his breakfast," he wrote, "without being disturbed by the industriously collected calamities of the world; or those that came to his ken were fortunately too old for remedy." The same was true for the early settlers of Jamestown.

And it would remain true for decades to come. The news from Europe was a plodding traveler, a victim of distance and terrain, taking anywhere from a day to a month to make its way from its point of origin to a seaport, then another six to eight weeks to cross the Atlantic. Once it arrived in the New World, in either printed or oral form, it had to be fetched or overheard by a printer, who then returned to his shop, set the information in type for the next issue of his journal, and distributed it to subscribers, some of whom lived so far away, and were so isolated by rivers and forests and mountains, that the paper did not reach them for another week or two.

Domestic news did not cover ground any faster; it could also take six to eight weeks for reports of an event to journey from the East Coast to settlements near the Mississippi River, and then several days more for the customer to receive them from the print shop. By the time Americans learned of a proposal, it had become law; by the time they learned of a peace treaty, an unnecessary battle had been fought; by the time they learned of a death, the poor fellow had been buried and his soul had either risen or descended and his widow had remarried. Journalism would, in fact, be a dilatory matter—history more than current affairs—until the telegraph came into use in the 1840s and "threatened to overwhelm its users with information and insist on their rapid response."

But we are getting ahead of our story.

❖

FOR THE PRINTER who thought about publishing a newspaper in colonial times, or the man of means who thought about financing the printer, there was a further disincentive to journalism. Put simply, there were not enough customers—too few English speakers in America, too few towns and villages that were too widely scattered to allow for news to be gathered efficiently and a paper to be distributed economically. In addition, as historian of journalism Sidney Kobre points out, "[t]rade, commerce and industry were undeveloped. Settlers for a long time made their own clothes and furniture and raised their own foodstuffs. Advertising would not have been profitable, especially since money was scarce and the general income level low."

But, in time, money would become less scarce, and people would begin to purchase goods as well as produce them. It would not take much time, either: the colonies, not yet a country, grew more quickly than anyone had anticipated. By 1700, it is estimated, more than 300,000 people lived along the New World's Atlantic coast, and in cities like Philadelphia, Boston, and New York the populations were increasing even more rapidly than elsewhere. Most of the immigrants were from England, where there were not only more journals than there used to be, but also more journalists of serious inclination; Pietro Aretino, it seems, had left few heirs to vulgarity. The papers were now reporting such stories as Archduke Charles's becoming king of Spain, the English conquests of Gibraltar and Barcelona, and the union between England and Scotland to form Great Britain. And they reported on Tripoli gaining its independence, Russia and Turkey going to war, and the murder of Peter the Great and his son. It was hard news, not features; substance, not filler.

Accustomed to such publications in their old home, the Europeans in America were an eager audience for them in their new one.

As the colonies increased in population, they increased as well in prosperity. More Americans could afford to go into the newspaper business now than before, and more Americans could afford to buy newspapers. More Americans needed newspapers to learn about events that might influence their livelihoods: the latest shipping regulations, the latest import policies, the latest weather conditions that might affect agriculture, the latest mechanical innovations that might affect textile production, the latest proposals for taxation or fund-raising or the expansion of government services or control, the latest decisions of the Crown on all manner of colonial enterprise. And after a few more decades had passed, a postal service, which had for so long been more a hindrance to communication than an asset, was able to relay such news dependably.

As early as 1639, Massachusetts had attempted the delivery of mail on a regular basis. It was *ir*regular at best. The main problem was roads, which either did not exist or were so rocky, rutted, and circuitous that they were as much obstacle courses as lanes of conveyance. The mail was often delayed, sometimes lost, and sometimes delivered to the wrong place. "In the early days," Kobre writes, "if one wanted to get a letter to a relative or friend in another colony, he waited for a ship captain or a traveler passing through, perhaps a merchant sending a package or a cargo of goods. Sometimes, if it were urgent, one employed a friendly Indian to deliver a letter for him."

In January 1673, the Boston Post Road opened for the specific purpose of transporting letters, parcels, commercial goods, and newspapers from Boston to New York, a distance of 250 miles. A horse could travel it without breaking an ankle, and the rider without being thrown into a ravine as his mount stumbled. He could refresh himself by spending the night at an inn or stopping for dinner and libation at a tavern, and he could tend to his mount at any of several blacksmith shops along the way. The mail did not always arrive within two weeks, as promised, but it almost always got there eventually.

Not until the midway point of the following century, though, would postal service in the colonies become truly prompt, reliable, and inexpensive—not until Benjamin Franklin, a founding father of journalism no less than of the American republic, served in addition as parent to the post office.

There could, of course, be no news, not in the modern sense of the term, without presses on which to print it, and the first such machine did not appear in the New World until 1638, when Harvard College employed it to add to what was already the largest store of published material in the colonies. But by 1685, almost half a century later, the grand total of printing presses in the New World had risen to a mere four, and they were essentially what they had been in Gutenberg's time, which is to say cumbersome apparatuses that were as likely to break down as to grind out a story and that demanded of their operators a broad back more than sound news judgment, and manual dexterity more than a knack for layout and editing.

For the most part, they turned out Bibles, usually in English but occasionally in one of the Indian tongues. And they produced copies of sermons, laws, and official correspondence for the colonial government and the Crown, in addition to almanacs and poetry and songs.

But five years later, and more than eight decades after the first British expatriates had set foot in Jamestown, one of those presses would begin printing the first American newspaper. Its life would be short, turbulent, and unhappy.

❖

HISTORY DOES NOT HAVE MUCH TO SAY about Benjamin Harris, and when it refers to him at all, it seldom does so kindly. "He was a bigot and an opportunist," according to one historian; "a rabid anti-Catholic with an eye for the sensational," in the view of another. He had "mercury in his blood." He was dismissed by a contemporary as "the worst man in the world."

As a publisher in London, Harris had turned out a newspaper and a number of pamphlets, one of which was judged by the authorities to be seditious. He was arrested and sentenced to jail, serving a short time before being released. Then, acting as if he wanted to return to his confinement, he dashed back to the printing press and issued another pamphlet, this one called *English Liberties*—of which, in Harris's view, there were not nearly enough, and those that did exist were insufficiently promoted by the Crown. Before he could be arrested again, he came to the conclusion that his homeland was "an uneasy . . . place for an honest man," and he would dwell there no longer. He set sail for Boston, and in part because of that voyage, his new home would become the "cradle of journalism" in the future United States.

Boston was the largest urban center on the continent at the time, with a population approaching 7,000 and so much energy in the air that a person could feel a charge to the atmosphere the minute he stepped on shore. The city's shipbuilding industry had begun to thrive, as had its bankers and fishermen, its distillers and ropemakers, and its traders in rum, molasses, tobacco, and slaves.

In fact, merchants had now joined Puritan clerics as community leaders, causing the latter to scramble to their pulpits and, hoping to keep up with the times, make the case as best they could for Mammon, finding a path to salvation in commerce as well as piety. The wharves were teeming, the shops overflowing with goods and buyers—Boston seemed an ideal place for a new business of any kind, and in 1690, Harris started one. He rented a small wooden shack and became the first publisher of a newspaper in North America. "[I]t is safe to say," comments John Tebbel, who has written extensively on journalism's beginnings, that "no major American institution has been launched by so unworthy a pioneer."

Harris called his paper *Publick Occurrences both Foreign and Domestic.* The former he would lift from London journals brought to Boston by trading vessels; there were, after all, no copyright laws at the time. As for the latter, he would learn of them from friends, neighbors, tongue-waggers in the nearest tavern, and the occasional broadside turned out by a local publisher with an agenda of some sort. *Publick Occurrences* was four pages long, each page about six inches by ten inches. The first three pages contained two columns of news with a narrow margin between them; the fourth page was blank, so that readers could add items of their own and comment on the preceding items before sending the paper along to another reader. This made *Publick Occurrences* a source of interactive journalism a full three centuries before the Internet.

But it was also, at least to modern eyes, a jarring publication to behold. Each paragraph or two was a separate story, and there were neither breaks nor headlines between them, so that one account ran into the next without warning or context. No sooner did a reader learn that a sailor had made an escape from "*Indians* and *French*" than he discovered, in the very next line, that "The chief discourse of this month has been about the affairs of the Western Expedition against *Canada.*"

It made for an efficient use of paper—no wasted space, no large print, no fancy designs or insignias. For this reason, the *Publick Oc-*

currences style, with few modifications, would be the style of virtually all American journals during the colonial era.

Harris's first issue appeared on Thursday, September 25, 1690, the birthday of American journalism. It contained no news less than a month old, and its intentions, at least as Harris explained them, were honorable. His paper, the publisher told his readers in a front-page notice, would print "Memorable Occurrents of Divine Providence" as well as *"Circumstances of Publique Affairs . . . which may not only direct their thoughts at all times, but at some times also to assist their Businesses and Negotiations."* Further, Harris wrote, *Publick Occurrences* was being offered to the residents of Boston *"[t]hat some thing may be done toward* Curing, *or at least the* Charming, *of that* Spirit of Lying *which prevails among us; wherefore, nothing shall be entered but what we have reason to believe is true, repairing to the best foundations for our information."* If someone came to Harris with information that was *not* true, some "malicious Raiser of a false Report," the publisher would expose the person's dishonesty in the very next issue. *"It is Suppos'd that none will dislike this Proposal, but such as intend to be guilty of so villainous a Crime."*

Harris intended to publish his journal monthly. He would do so more often, he vowed, *"if any Glut of* Occurrences *happen."*

It sounds impressive, or at least respectable, and in fact *Publick Occurrences* started out that way, with the first story ever published by the paper reading as follows:

> The Christianized *Indians* in some parts of *Plimouth*, have newly appointed a day of Thanksgiving to God for his Mercy in supplying their extream and pinching Necessities under their late want of Corn, & for His giving them now a prospect of a very *Comfortable Harvest*. Their Example might be worth Mentioning.

So much for the mention. And so much for memorable occurrents of divine providence or stories that would assist the colonists in their businesses and negotiations. With story number two, *Publick Occurrences* began heading down a tawdrier trail—call it Aretino Alley—telling of "the kidnapping of two children by 'barbarous Indians lurking around Connecticut'; [and the] suicide by hanging of a citizen of 'Morose Temper.'" Harris also informed his readers that some Mohawk Indians—"miserable Salvages [sic]," he called them—had tortured and murdered the white men they took prisoner during a border war between the colonies and Canada. Of course, as we learn from further reading, there had been some provocation. The paper reported the testimony of "Two *English captives*" that a Captain Mason had "cut the faces, and ript the bellies of two *Indians*, and threw a third Over board in the sight of the *French*, who informing the other *Indians* of it, they have in revenge barbarously Butcher'd forty Captives of ours that were in their hands."

Harris was just getting revved up. Another story in the first edition of *Publick Occurrences* revealed that a Boston man had become despondent because of "having newly buried his wife." His friends kept a close eye on him, fearing a suicide attempt. "But one evening escaping from them into the Cow-house, they there quickly followed him, found him *hanging by a Rope*, which they had used to tye their *Calves* withal, he was dead with his feet near touching the Ground."

And then, most controversially, came one of the few foreign stories in the first Harris edition, a rumor, actually, about the king of France, said to be an immoral old reprobate who "used to lie with" his son's wife.

Publick Occurrences seems to have been a modest success with readers. To colonial authorities, however, it was an affront. In particular, they objected to the accounts of the French monarch and the Mohawk Indian massacre; to put it mildly, the authorities "did not like [their] tone." Both stories seemed to be based on hearsay as opposed to verifiable fact; the colony's leaders did not like that either. Nor did they approve of the man who had printed the stories in the first place, Benjamin Harris, who had not only demonstrated such bad taste but, perhaps even worse, had refused to get a license for his paper, as the law required, prior to publication. He had been warned about the license several times, had been told, in so many words, that it was the government's prerogative to approve or disallow any commercial enterprise anywhere in the kingdom, and that this was especially true in the colonies, where distance from the Crown tended to encourage a certain uppitiness in people. And he had been told that it was even *more* especially true when the enterprise was a newspaper, since the news, as often as not, was a record of the government's actions, or at least had an effect on people's perception of government.

Harris would have none of it. He was not the type to go through proper channels, and in fact the very notion of a proper channel struck him as an imposition, an indignity, a denial of his rights as a citizen of the New World.

He was about to be denied even more. Four days after Bostonians got their hands on *Publick Occurrences*, the colonial government, with the support of Boston's Puritan clergy, published a document of its own.

> The Governour and Council having had the perusal of the said Pamphlet, and finding that therein is contained Reflections of a very high nature: As also sundry doubtful and uncertain Reports, do hereby manifest and declare their high Resentment and Disallowance of said Pamphlet, and Order that the same be Suppressed and called in.

It would not be un-suppressed. The first edition of the first American newspaper was also the last. Journalism in America was but a few days old, the ink barely dry on the pages and the printing press showing virtually no signs of wear, and already it had left readers gasping with its explicitness and politicians fuming with its impertinence.

❀

BENJAMIN HARRIS CURSED his fate and those who, in his view, had so arbitrarily brought it upon him. The historian Louis Solomon, speaking for the minority, takes his side. Harris "stands out," Solomon believes, "as the first in a long list of ornery, non-conforming, trouble-making newspapermen who have insisted on being free despite the consequences. Winners or losers, they are the pride of American journalism."

But Harris was an American journalist for the briefest time, not long enough to be an influence, positive or otherwise, on those who followed. He remained in Massachusetts for a few years after *Publick Occurrences* expired, running a coffeehouse and a bookstore; then, in 1694, he returned to England, where he started another paper, this one called the *Post*. An acquaintance of his named John Dunton was not impressed. Harris, he said, "is so far from having any dealings with Truth and Honesty, that his solemn word, which he calls as good as his bond, is a studied falsehood, and he scandalizes Truth and Honesty in pretending to write for it."

The *Post* lasted longer than Harris's previous venture did, but it won him no more friends and might have lost even more money. He "spent his last years as a querulous and unsuccessful editor and a vendor of 'the only Angelical Pills against all Vapours, Hysterick and Melancholy Fits' and other belauded patent medicines."

It had taken the American colonies eighty-three years to get their first newspaper. Another fourteen would pass until the second, and it would be a publication of a very different kind.

❁

CHAPTER TWO

Publishing
by Authority

ISTORIANS ARE NOT ENAMORED of John Campbell either, although for virtually the opposite reasons that they disdained his predecessor. Harris was bold, Campbell squeamish; Harris was a rebel, Campbell a bootlicker; Harris was a blackguard, Campbell a bore. In *History of Journalism in the United States*, George Henry Payne writes of Campbell that "[t]here is none of the spirit of Harris here" and goes on to characterize Campbell's spirit as "timid" and his journal "puny and uninteresting."

Other reviews of America's second newspaper are similarly unkind. It was "terse and drab." It was "designed more to survive than to excite." It was "a monument of dullness," Louis Solomon believes, and even "when it was very occasionally enlivened with stories like the slaying of pirate chief Blackbeard, a public whipping, or a suicide, Campbell found it necessary to apologize for printing them. He explained that they were intended to provide spiritual uplift." There is no indication that they had this effect on readers.

Apparently the man did not make a better impression than his publication; Campbell has been described as "Boston's sour-faced Scottish postmaster." But his visage does not matter nearly as much as his occupation.

The mail service might not have been much help to journalism at the dawn of the eighteenth century, but to be in charge of the post office, especially in a city the size of Boston, and especially when it was the only post office in the entire colony at the time, was to be ideally situated not only to learn the events of the day but also to send word of them across town and, with luck, even farther. Campbell did both. A sour face might have been his curse, but his attentiveness would make a career for him.

Campbell listened as people came to his place of business and opened their letters from abroad and read parts of them aloud. He listened as they opened their letters from other colonies and discussed the contents with the friends or family members who had accompanied them. And he kept listening as his patrons kept talking; in fact, he encouraged them to talk all the more, to have a seat and light a pipe and reveal the events of their own lives as well as those of their correspondents as they read aloud their mail.

Campbell asked his customers questions, told them to speak up. For the most part, they seemed pleased with his curiosity. The post office was an information exchange, a trading floor for facts and opinions, for comedy and tragedy and the lengthy accounting of daily routine.

After a time, Campbell began to take notes on the chitchat, his place of business thus becoming the first one of its kind in America with a recording secretary. Not long afterward, the notes turned into a newsletter, a single sheet that he continued to write by hand and that consisted, for the most part, of "shipping and governmental news and laws, although some local news such as births, deaths and social events appeared occasionally." It was hard work to assemble his catalog of events, but no expense to circulate; as postmaster, Campbell could mail his correspondence without charge. He might not have been the most notable newsman of his age, but his working conditions were the envy of all who followed: his sources came to him rather than the other way around; they provided the raw materials of his product without charge; he was able to dispatch the product to interested parties without spending so much as a penny; and his workspace was provided free by the colonial government. Overhead does not get any lower than this.

In 1704, four years after he began his note taking, Campbell decided to expand. Unable to fit all of his intelligence into the newsletter format, and perhaps suffering from the world's worst case of writer's cramp, he found himself a printing press and began turning out the *Boston News-Letter*, the first American paper to appear regularly and one that would go on to become the longest-running publication of the entire colonial era. Campbell himself remained in charge for almost two decades; the *News-Letter* would outlive him by more than half a century and provide an invaluable record of its time. It would report on the Molasses Act and the Stamp Act and the Townshend Acts and the Intolerable Acts, on the Boston Massacre and the Boston Tea Party, and on all the other points of contention between the colonists and the British that would lead to equally contentious journalism and, eventually, to war.

❀

IF *PUBLICK OCCURRENCES* was the *National Enquirer* of its day, the *Boston News-Letter* was the *Congressional Record*, sluggish but trustworthy. Which is not to say that the two journals were totally dissimilar; like Harris before him and almost every journalist of the eighteenth century afterward, Campbell pilfered news from abroad. The first story in his first issue was a summary of what he had learned in "Letters from great *Poland*." The second told of an internal disturbance of no great significance in Sweden. The third relied for its intelligence on "Letters from *Turkey*." And whereas *Publick Occurrences* had a fondness for royal incest, the *News-Letter* reported more sedately, if less interestingly, on the Crown's decision to transfer "Popish ministers from France to Scotland."

Both papers, however, were victims of the time lag. In Campbell's case, absent-mindedness seems to have exacerbated the problem. No sooner did he receive the account of the Popish ministers, for example, than he set it aside and forgot it. By the time he happened across it again and finally got around to setting it in print, almost five months had passed, meaning that the information took more than twice as long to reach his readers as it would have if it had been included in a letter from a relative in England.

Campbell kept up with the shipping news in his journal, often in a manner that calls to mind the cool insider tones of a gossip columnist relating the comings and goings of celebrity.

Philadelphia, May 3d. Last night arrived here *Parker* from *Boston*, and its [sic] said that *Darby* is arrived from the said Port at *Salem* in *New-Jersey*.

New York, May 7th. On the 4th, Instant his Excellency the Lord *Cornbury* returned hither from *Albany*, and to Morrow sets out for his Government of *New-Jersey*.

Also, as he had done in the newsletter, Campbell provided details of births and deaths and illnesses, of shop openings and barn raisings. He included the topics of forthcoming sermons and some highlights of sermons past. He told of court cases and accidents, petty pilferings and fires, including one in Newport, Rhode Island, that destroyed a shop and a house but would have done much more damage had it not been for "the great industry of our people," who fought the blaze tirelessly. And the *News-Letter* would register the proceedings of various governmental agencies and publish certain of their documents and proclamations in their entirety.

It sounds like a lot. It was not. As Frank Luther Mott writes in his survey of American journalism from 1690 to 1960, "The entire contents of one of [the *Boston News-Letter*'s] numbers would scarcely fill two columns of a modern newspaper."

❁

ON OCCASION, Campbell would render his stories even less engaging by writing his own introductions to them, like an after-dinner speaker so unaware of his own ineptitude that he begins ad-libbing to hold the podium longer. For instance, it was not enough for him to report on the reaction of England's Queen Anne to a speech she had heard in Parliament a few months earlier; Campbell included his own prefatory remarks: "The Humble Address of the House of Commons," he wrote, "Presented to Her Majesty . . . To which Her Majesty return'd Her most Gracious Answer, in the following words." This kind of gilded language was more common then than it is today; still, there must have been times when the yawns were as audible in Boston as the sounds of commerce and industry.

The *News-Letter* never had more than 300 subscribers, although such a tiny circulation may be as much a reflection of the novelty of journalism at the time, and on the fact that people had not yet found newspapers to be a necessity in their lives, as it is of the uninspiring nature of Campbell's story selection and prose. It may also be a reflection of the price, which was "twopence a copy, or twelve shillings a year, delivered. That it was considered a luxury is illustrated by the fact that Judge Sewall occasionally presented copies of it to the ladies on whom he called, somewhat as later and less serious gallants present boxes of candy."

Whatever the reason, John Campbell did not get rich. He barely got by. In the first few issues of his paper, he asked for help from advertisers; he had started out with a few, but knew he would need many to survive.

This News-Letter is to be continued Weekly; & all Persons who have any Houses, Lands, Tenements, Farms, Ships, Vessels, Goods, Wares or Merchandises to be Sold or Let; or Servants Run-away, or Goods Stole or Lost; may have the same inserted at a Reasonable Rate; from Twelve-pence to Five Shillings, & not to exceed: Who may agree with John Campbell Post-Master for the same.

Campbell also sought financial assistance from the Massachusetts legislature, which was happy to oblige. He was, after all, a much more cooperative fellow than Harris had been, having not only applied for and been granted a license for his journal, but having faithfully obeyed the license's primary requirement, which was to cede virtually all editorial control of the *News-Letter* to colonial officials. They let him know, sometimes directly, sometimes subtly, what to cover and what not to cover; what to praise and what to blame; whom to promote and whom to snub. In return, they allowed him to use the phrase "Published By Authority" on the front page.

Campbell could not have been prouder. To him, the words were a badge of good citizenship, a gold star, evidence that he, like the majority of Americans at the time, trusted the dictates of king and Parliament and was pleased to follow them. "Your Majesties most auspicious Reign," the *News-Letter* wrote on one occasion, "and Your tender regard to the general Welfare & Happiness of Your Subjects, justly require our utmost returns of duty and gratitude."

But to Daniel Boorstin, who speaks for most who have studied colonial journalism in recent times, Campbell acted more the lackey than the newsman. His delight in the approbation of British royalty, Boorstin writes, was a stain on his character, evidence that he was "under the thumb of the governor and his council," a place where no reporter should ever situate himself.

Even so, the Crown was wary of the *Boston News-Letter*. It was wary of all newspapers. They were something new in the world, these sources of information that did not issue directly from the palace, these chronicles of events that might not even be known to the king's advisers and had certainly not been approved by them— and what was new was ipso facto troubling. What was new could raise expectations, create doubt, encourage dissatisfaction. It could upset existing power structures by leading people to question them. At best, newspapers would require constant vigilance; at worst, they could turn on authorities, state their own opinions, make their own demands. They would become an adversary of government rather than an arm.

As early as 1671, Sir William Berkeley, the royal governor of Virginia, had expressed his fears of such a situation.

I thank God we have no free schools or printing, and I hope that we shall not have them these hundred years.

For learning has brought disobedience and heresy and sects into the world, and printing has divulged them and libels against the government. God keep us from them both.

God would keep them from the latter for only a few more decades.

❀

BEFORE LONG, advertisers began responding to the *Boston News-Letter* in greater numbers. Sometimes they were businessmen with products to sell, but more often, at least in the beginning, they were individuals hoping to retrieve misplaced items.

Lost on the 10. of April last off Mr. Shippen's Wharff in Boston. Two Iron Anvils, weighing between 120 and 140 pounds each: Whoever has taken them up, and will bring or give true Intelligence of them to John Campbell Post-master, shall have a sufficient reward.

Appearing in the same issue were an appeal for the return of "several sorts of mens Apparel, both Woollen & Linnen," which had apparently been stolen "by an Irish man, speaks bad English," and an ad for "a very good Fulling-Mill, to be Let or Sold." Future editions of the *News-Letter* would call attention to such missing articles as books, musical instruments, and even an animal or two; and they would promote the purchase of soaps and unguents, medicines and tools, unoccupied acreage and bargain fares for ocean crossings. It is not known how much Campbell charged for his ads, only that the paper was a bit more solvent as a result and the enterprise of journalism a bit more inviting to him. He might even have been able to hire, at least on a part-time basis, an assistant post office eavesdropper.

A few weeks later, however, Campbell began engaging in a less honorable, and ultimately more profitable, form of advertising. As he had hoped in his early solicitations, he heard from the owners of those "Servants Run-away," and he would hear from them in great numbers for years to come. One escaped slave was *"a young man named* William Rogers, *about 18 years of Age, of a middle Stature, fair fac'd, light coloured curl'd hair."* Rogers's master, a hatter in Boston named Abraham Blish, wanted the lad back; Campbell called special attention to Blish's plight with his use of italics. Rogers's plight does not seem to have concerned him.

The *Boston News-Letter* also heard from owners whose servants had stayed put but who were eager to move them. One had a young Negro man, handsome of appearance and fit of build, whom he wished to sell. The price was reasonable. He sent the details to the *News-Letter* and they were promptly set in type. Another reader offered "Two Negro Men and one Negro Woman & Child," and not only announced their availability in Campbell's paper but specified a time and place where they could be seen, examined, taken for a test run. Campbell even took out such an ad himself, wanting to sell the sixteen-year-old Negro girl who toiled for him. He told interested parties to visit him at his residence next to a Boston tavern; the girl would show herself and try to make an impression.

The slave trade had found an efficient new venue for carrying on business.

❁

THE *NEWS-LETTER* would in time have company. Other papers would come along, in Boston and elsewhere, and they would carry similar ads throughout the eighteenth century and well into the nineteenth. There was always someone for sale, always some commodities on the market, perhaps "a likely Negro Boy and Girl; the Boy 13 Years of Age, the Girl 9 or 10." And there was always someone trying to escape from his servitude, such as "a Negro Man Servant, named *Ned*, about 30 Years of Age, speaks good English and French," who was so highly prized by the two men who owned him that "[w]hoever shall take up said Run-away, and him safely convey to the said *Dean* and *Mason*, living in *New Boston*, shall have *five Pounds* old Tenor Reward, and all necessary Charges paid."

Sometimes, wanting more space to advertise his missing slaves than a newspaper could provide, an owner would pay the publisher for a broadside, a sheet of paper devoted solely to an explanation of his woes and a plea for assistance. It might be distributed with the paper; it might be distributed separately by the customer. In Virginia, in 1799, a fellow named Parke Goodall lost seven servants in one fell swoop; this, he decided, was a job for a broadside's big letters and boldface type.

> I have reason to suspect that the said slaves were stolen, or enticed to run away, on the night of Sunday the 20th of last month, by one William Lucas late of the county of Caroline, and that they have since been in his possession. . . . I will give to the taker up of each of the said Slaves, who shall be brought to my house in the city of Richmond, SIX DOLLARS for taking up, and six-pence for each mile, which he shall travel, in coming to the said house, from the place where such slave was taken up, and six-pence per mile for returning from thence to the same place.

Many colonial printers could not have set up shop in the first place, or could not have stayed in business as long as they did, without profiting from the sale or return of the human property of others.

❀

VYING WITH SLAVE OWNERS as the leading sponsors of the *Bos-*

ton News-Letter were "shippers who had room in their vessels for freight, the products of colonial farms, timberland and craftshops. Some of the merchants with cargos of molasses, Madeira wine or English-styled cloth to sell might advertise." John Campbell welcomed, and published, them all.

For fifteen years, the *Boston News-Letter* was the only paper in Massachusetts, or anywhere else in America, and as such was a unique forum for advertisers, especially as they came to realize that the paper's modest circulation figures were misleading. Perhaps Campbell *was* printing fewer than 300 copies a week, but that did not mean only 300 people saw them. A husband might pass his copy to his wife and older children, and might use it in teaching his younger children to read. The wife and children might share the copy with a friend. An employer might give his *News-Letter* to an employee, a shopkeeper to a customer, a clergyman to a penitent. The latest edition of the paper, left on a table in a tavern one morning, might be perused by a dozen or more people before evening. They were as likely to remember the ads as they were the stories, especially when *News-Letter* advertisers made outrageous claims— the kind of claims that suggested magical powers for their products, or even divine intervention. One of them, it has been noted, "offered a remedy so potent and versatile that it 'cures Cholick, Dry Belly-Ache, Consumption, Smallpox, Gravel, Melancholy,' and for good measure, 'Loss of Limbs.'" Campbell did not question the boast; it was revenue that concerned him, not veracity. And even though his newspaper evolved over the years from a struggling new business to a going concern to something approaching the status of local institution, money remained a concern.

In fact, after having published the *Boston News-Letter* for a decade and a half, Campbell was still not making as much as he had hoped. Most of his advertisers were prompt with their payments; some of his subscribers, however, were not. He wrote letters to them, sometimes dunned them in passing on the street or as they entered church on Sunday. He even entreated them in one of his issues, saying that for fifteen years he had kept his part of the bargain; he had "supplied them conscientiously with publick oc-curances [sic] of Europe and with those of these, our neighboring provinces, and the West Indies." The subscribers should do their part: pay their bills when they were due.

But Campbell ended his complaint contritely. He admitted that his readers had grounds for dissatisfaction of their own. Some-times, he said, events overwhelmed him and he would get a little behind; there was, after all, that five-month delay in the story about the new postings for Popish ministers. But more recently, he confessed, he had found himself even further in arrears; a few is-sues back, the *News-Letter* had printed a piece that was more than a year old at the time of its publication. He did not say how such a thing could have happened, or whether the story had even the slightest bit of relevance once it appeared in the paper. He said only that he would try to do better from now on.

❧

AT THE SAME TIME that the *Boston News-Letter* was monopoliz-ing colonial journalism, the press in England was becoming more and more diversified. Early in the eighteenth century, when the population of London was about half a million, newspaper circula-tion surpassed 40,000—not an impressive ratio by today's stan-dards but probably the best that London, or any other city, had known to date. Among the papers from which the people could choose were the *Daily Courant, General Remark, General Postscript, Tatler, Female Tatler, Postman, Postboy, Postboy Junior, Flying Post, Evening Post, Observator, London Gazette,* and *British Apollo*—most of which, as George Henry Payne observes, shared "the tendency to exalt the common good of society at the expense of special priv-ileges."

When the men and women who read these papers came to the New World, they were almost unfailingly disappointed with the supply and quality of reporting they found. Why were American not more interested in their world? Why was the world not being presented to them in a more thoughtful, engaging manner? Why was journalism not one of those thriving businesses in Boston or, a little later, in other colonial metropolises? Was it not apparent by now that man no longer lived in seclusion, that a journalist might be able to give him the education he had never received from a schoolmaster or a perspective on worldly matters that could not be provided by a clergyman?

The recent arrivals to America might have agreed with the succinct editorial that appeared in the *News-Letter* on the occasion of the paper's finally having encountered some competition, the *Boston Gazette*, which began life in December 1719 and would eventually become the most influential paper of its time. Wrote John Campbell about the *Gazette* on his own front page: "I pity the reader of the news paper; it is not fit reading for the people."

It was true. Of course, it was also true of the *News-Letter*, and equally applicable to almost all of their immediate successors, in Massachusetts and in other colonies. They were "small, simple, and bland affairs," writes historian Gordon S. Wood, "two to four pages published weekly and containing mostly reprints of old European news, ship sailings, and various advertisements, together with notices of deaths, political appointments, court actions, fires, piracies, and such matters."

And it was not just that the European news was old; it was sometimes so startlingly unrelated to the quotidian concerns of Americans as to seem humor rather than journalism. "It is hard to know," Wood goes on, "what colonial readers made of the first news item printed in the newly created *South Carolina Gazette* of 1732: 'We learn from Caminica, that the Cossacks continue to make inroads onto polish Ukrania.'" It is also hard to know what readers made of this item, lifted by a Boston paper from a publication abroad and reprinted proudly: "*Letters from Moscow advise, that the Danish Envoy Extraordinary, M. Westphalen, having shewn*

*his credentials to the Count Golofskin, Chancellor of the Russian Em-
pire, was receiv'd with all possible Marks of Respect. . . . "*

All of which goes to show that before they reached their full
bloom of insolence and unreliability, of vituperation and bluster
and bias—before, that is, American newspapers caused tempers to
flare and hostilities to deepen and men of dispassionate temperament to throw up their hands in frustration—they caused minds to
wander and eyelids to droop.

❖

OCCASIONALLY a paper would try to atone for the thumping tedi-
um of its story selection by offering some visual relief, a woodcut to
brighten the look of a page that otherwise, when seen from a distance, looked like a single sheet of gray. The first illustration ever to
appear in an American paper was a British flag that Campbell used
to gussy up the inaugural edition of the *Boston News-Letter*. In later
issues he might print a silhouette of a man in flight, calling attention to an ad for the return of a slave to his owner, or a drawing of a
wagon, signifying that a local store had received a new shipment of
merchandise. It was as innovative as Campbell ever got.

But circumstances conspired against innovation no less than did
unimaginative publishers. Paper, for instance, was both expensive
and difficult to obtain. The first paper mill in New England did
not open until 1728, and its output was so modest and deliveries so
random that many printers were unable to rely on it; they continued to produce their own. Even then, they needed the raw materials for papermaking, and sometimes had to seek help in procuring
them. Paper in those days was made from linen rags, and when
printers could not get enough of them by their own means, they
ran advertisements to solicit them, begging the women who read
their publications to donate the old rags that they used to clean
their homes. Sometimes readers cooperated; sometimes they did
not. In a few of the households, the napkins were made of linen;

today's edition of the *Boston News-Letter* might well have been yesterday's means of wiping the grease from hands and lips after a hearty meal.

Ink was another problem at the time, also costly to purchase and also manufactured on the premises in many a print shop. But it was not the same kind of ink in which a writer dipped his pen. Newspaper ink was messier and harder to handle, as thick as petroleum jelly; the stuff had to be shoveled into trays for use on the presses, not poured. It was also olfactorily challenging, its primary ingredient being a sooty and carbonaceous compound that smelled like the last stages of urban or vegetable decay and was known as lampblack. On occasion, a printer might have wished he could engrave his journal on a stone tablet rather than endure repeated whiffs of his homemade ink.

Type, too, was high in price and low in availability. Furthermore, typefaces wore out frequently, the "p's" losing their stems, the "b's" their peaks, the "m's" one or both of their humps. They had to be replaced, and until Americans learned to make type themselves, they had to import it from England, which sometimes took so long that newspapers either had to go on unintended hiatuses while they waited for delivery, or else hope that their readers could somehow decipher words put together with letters so crippled they looked like code.

But once a printer had collected his linen rags, held his breath and whipped up a new batch of ink, received his shipment of new type from abroad, and arranged it in his trays—what then? How was he to fill his pages? Where was he to find the names and dates, the numbers and events, the declarations of legislative bodies, and the records of the constabularies? Here, too, he had to worry about supply. Yes, he could lift some news from other papers. Yes, he could interview ship captains returning from voyages and soldiers returning from battle and travelers returning from journeys. And yes, he could ask people to read him their mail from distant shores or colonies. In fact, the *American Weekly Mercury* did so in print.

"We desire those Gentlemen that receive any Authentick Account of News from *Europe*, or other places," wrote editor Andrew Bradford, "which may be proper for this paper, that they will please favour Us with a Copy."

But most of the time the printer had to locate the news himself. He had no reporters to assist him. There was no such thing as an editorial staff. There were no stringers or freelancers or wire services. There were no copy boys or summer interns. There were no fact-checkers or ombudsmen or secretaries. In some cases there was not even an apprentice around to send on an errand. No wonder there were times when a newspaper simply could not live up to its name. In December 1728 the *Pennsylvania Gazette*, facing a dearth of events, published an article refreshing in its candor if not gripping in content.

> We have little News of Consequence at present, the *English* Prints being generally stufft with Robberies, Cheats, Fires, Murders, Bankruptcies, Promotions of some, and Hanging of others; nor can we expect much better till Vessels arrive in the Spring. . . . In the mean Time we hope our Readers will be content for the present, with what we can give 'em, which if it does 'em no Good, shall do 'em no Hurt. 'Tis the best we have, and so take it.

No wonder the story from Caminica about the Cossacks made it into print; it could be snipped right out of another publication. No wonder Campbell was eager to accept the preposterous claims about that magnificent cure-all medicament; it served as a filler for both his cash drawer and his columns.

The former was a concern for all printers in the eighteenth century. None of them made much of a living until Benjamin Franklin came along, and even then, the prosperous newspaper was the exception rather than the rule. There is the story of Thomas Fleet, publisher of the *Boston Evening-Post*, and a man who brought as much conscience as he could to the job. It was not always enough. "Criticized by an anti-Methodist for printing a sermon by John Wesley," Louis Solomon writes, "[Fleet] replied he'd done it because of 'the Prospect of getting a Penny by it, as I have by all that I print.'"

It is remarkable, given all of these difficulties with materials and staffing, all of these woes attending the accumulation of news in the days before printers could afford to hire enough help, and even more woes attending the distribution of papers in the days before efficient transportation existed, and with all of the reluctance shown by Americans to become news junkies—it is remarkable, given such trying circumstances, that newspapers were published at all in our nation's earliest days. It is remarkable that even a small portion of what newspapers related was accurate and pertinent and, as the Revolutionary War drew closer, thought-provoking and in some cases inspiring. It is remarkable, as a contemporary observer put it, that the colonial newspaper, with surprising frequency,

> Brings Men of Merit into public View; promotes a spirit of Enquiry; is favourable to Civil and Religious Liberty; a cheap vehicle of Knowledge and Instruction to the Indigent; and attended with numberless commercial Advantages.—The perusal requires but a short Recess from Business; and the annual Expence is so inconsiderable, that few can be deprived of enjoying it, through Apprehension of trespassing, either upon their Time or their Pockets.

The *New England Courant* brought a man of merit into public view, and did so on a number of occasions. And it promoted a spirit of inquiry into his beliefs. The man would much rather have been ignored.

CHAPTER THREE

Defying Authority

THE COURANT WAS THE FOURTH NEWSPAPER in Boston and the fourth in America, after *Publick Occurrences*, the *News-Letter*, and the *Gazette*, when it made its debut in the summer of 1721. It did not have a license, nor was it published by authority. It was not, in fact, even tolerant of authority in any of its conventional forms, and that may have been the very point of its existence.

Its editor, James Franklin, did not think much of the other three papers. In his first issue, he declared that "out of kindness to my Brother-writers," he would, on occasion, "be (like them) *very, very* dull, for I have a strong Fancy, that unless I am sometimes flat and low, this paper will not be very grateful to them." Franklin was especially contemptuous of John Campbell, accusing the *News-Letter* of being a "dull vehicle of intelligence"—this even though, on the same page, only a few lines away, Franklin vowed "that nothing shall here be inserted, reflecting on the clergy (as such) of whatever denomination, nor relating to affairs of government, and no trespass against Decency or good manner."

Campbell returned fire in the *News-Letter*, calling Franklin a "Jack of all Trades, and it would seem, Good at none," and it looked as if American journalism, nascent though it was, had begun its first intramural feud. But Franklin did not respond to Campbell, and Campbell did not bait him further; another seventy years would pass before two papers seemed as intent on bloodying each other in print as they did on publishing the adventures of the day. In the meantime, Franklin sought the blood of others; the

New England Courant quickly became "the first fighting, rebellious periodical in America, expressing colonial resentment against the current religious and political order."

In fact, Franklin started expressing resentment before it was even colonial in origin. His first few issues printed excerpts from *Cato's Letters*, a series of essays that had originally appeared in the *London Journal* and were "a searing indictment" of both church and state in early eighteenth-century England. Perhaps Franklin thought the articles spoke to the problems of America as well. Just as likely, he was fond of searing indictments no matter what their object. James Franklin seems to have thought of journalism less as a career than as an outlet for his rage, a rage whose source is not known but whose manifestations were powerful and plentiful and did not always make sense.

❀

THE MOST SERIOUS DISEASE of the age, as feared in colonial times as AIDS would be in the late twentieth century and in many cases as fatal, was smallpox. Its first symptoms were headache, backache, chills, fever, and sometimes vomiting. A few days later, with the symptoms having worsened, a rash would appear on various parts of the victim's body; after a few more days, the rash turned to blisters that usually filled with pus. In a week or two, if the person was still alive, the blisters fell off, leaving behind skin so severely pockmarked that it would never again look normal.

Smallpox seemed a particular curse in Massachusetts, where an outbreak in 1677 killed 12 percent of the population. The disease lingered through 1690 or so, when *Publick Occurrences* would report that it "is now very much abated. It is thought that far more have been sick of it than were visited with it, when it raged so much twelve years ago, nevertheless it has not been so mortal."

Smallpox returned, although in less deadly form, in 1702. Then, almost two decades later, around the time the *New England Courant* started publishing, it broke out again, a new strain of the virus having apparently arrived from the West Indies. Almost one out of every ten citizens of Boston at the time was dead within months. Those who lived would be scarred for the rest of their lives, not only physically but emotionally, always dreading news of the malady's next appearance, to which they would react with anxiety, prayer, and, as often as not, self-imposed quarantine.

There was no cure for smallpox once a person caught it. But some people were beginning to think it might be prevented. Among them were the Mathers, the leading family of New England in the early colonial period, men whose words were taken seriously no matter what the topic, no matter who the listener.

Increase Mather was a Congregationalist minister and a foe of "Profane and Promiscuous Dancing." Once the president of Harvard College, he had been removed from his position for extreme theological conservatism; he was, in other words, a bigot. "While displaying the neatness, carriage, and conduct of a gentleman," writes Kenneth Silverman, the biographer of Mather's son Cotton, "his behavior was grave: '*His very Countenance carried the Force of a Sermon with it.*'" Increase was especially zealous about requirements for church membership; he thought it should be limited to people of intelligence, probity, and breeding—that is, to people much like him.

Also a preacher, Cotton was no less devout and even more erudite than his father. He would write almost 400 books and pamphlets in his sixty-some years, among them an ecclesiastical history of New England, highly regarded at the time, called *Magnalia Christi Americana*. He produced biographies, elegies, religious tracts, and the long and well forgotten *Sailours Companion*, which "reprov[ed] smutty talk, masturbation, and sodomy" among men at sea. Cotton was something of a scientist, something of a linguist, and a figure of note in the Salem witch trials, although not the fundamentalist fanatic that some historians have led us to believe.

The younger Mather also became an expert on smallpox, beginning to study the disease after three of his children were stricken in 1702 and he helped nurse them to survival. More important than his research, though, was a piece of information he received from an unlikely source. One of the reverend's slaves had been inoculated against smallpox in Africa and swore by the treatment. He explained it, and the idea behind it, to his master.* Intrigued, Mather talked to other slaves, both in his household and elsewhere in Boston, and heard similar endorsements. Although doubtful at first, he soon began to believe. And then he began to preach, asserting the tenets of his new faith as avidly as he did those of the old. As Silverman tells us, Mather:

> . . . drew up an address, dated June 6, 1721, which was circulated in manuscript among local physicians, describing a *"Wonderful Practice"* lately come into use in some parts of the world. In fact, inoculation had been performed as folk medicine for centuries in Africa, India, China, and even in parts of Europe. . . . The first recorded inoculation in England had been performed only two months before Mather's address, in April 1721, having struck London almost simultaneously with the epidemic in Boston.

But Americans were not as trusting, or as willing to experiment, as others had been. Some of them thought Mather's advocacy of inoculation was evidence that he had lost his mind. Others feared he had lost his soul and, despite his protestations of faith, begun to do the devil's work. Among them was James Franklin. Having already gone back on his word not to "trespass against Decency or good manner" by flailing at John Campbell in print, Franklin now

---

*It was not inoculation as we understand the term today; the hypodermic needle would not be invented until the middle of the nineteenth century. One of the methods of the eighteenth, as undergone by John Adams some years later and probably common in Mather's time as well, is described by biographer James Grant. Adams, he writes, "received a prick on his left arm; into the wound was inserted a quarter-inch of infected thread. A piece of lint was applied to the scratch, on top of which a rag was pressed; all of this was secured by a bandage. Adams could come and go as he pleased."

began "reflecting on the clergy," and reflecting most adversely, thereby mocking another pledge.

❀

THE *NEW ENGLAND COURANT* was the first American paper to employ a staff of reporters—or rather, since it did not pay them, the first paper to allow young men to volunteer their time and their pens in the hope of making a name for themselves in the new and growing field of event retailing. They were known to some, not altogether favorably, as the *Courant* wits. One of them, John Checkley, was assigned by Franklin to proclaim inoculation ineffective and heretical and, further, to suggest that by advocating it Cotton Mather revealed himself to be not a benefactor of mankind, as Boston almost unanimously believed, but an avowed foe.

Checkley was only too happy to follow orders. He picked up his pen, dipped it into his inkwell, and berated the cleric for his arrogance and sanctimoniousness and woefully misguided notions of disease avoidance. Then he laid siege to the entire Puritan religious establishment of Boston, whose members, Checkley wrote, "by teaching and practicing what's Orthodox, pray hard against sickness, yet preach up the Pox!"

Another article in the same issue of the *Courant*, by yet another volunteer wit who had, for the nonce, set aside his humor, dismissed inoculation as "the practice of Greek old women" and referred to Mather and those who agreed with him as "profoundly ignorant of the matter." The following issue made inoculation seem as great a threat to public health as smallpox itself, warning that it might cause "Impostumations and Ulcers in the Viscera or Bowels, Groin, and other glandulous Parts, Loss of the Use of their Limbs, Swellings, &c. occasioning Death."

The *New England Courant*'s reporting frightened many a reader. It made them scornful of inoculation and skeptical of the Mathers. In fact, as far as some people were concerned, it cast doubt on all figures of authority, raising questions about both their wisdom and their intentions. It should not have done any of this. As biographer and historian H. W. Brands writes, "James Franklin knew next to nothing of the etiology of smallpox, but he knew he despised Mather for what James judged the eminent minister's smugness and inordinate influence over the life of Boston. If Mather advocated inoculation, the *Courant* must oppose it—and did."

The opposition came in waves, in article after article, issue after issue; for more than a year, Franklin ordered his minions of the print shop to mock, chastise, and condemn. They accused Mather, fairly, of having had no medical training. They accused him, unfairly, of wanting to send the entire population of Boston to its eternal reward well ahead of schedule. They asked, What foul perversion of thought could lead a person to believe that a disease could be prevented by injecting small amounts of the very same malady into an otherwise healthy human being?

The question was worth raising. It was, in fact, on virtually every Bostonian's mind at the time; to many, inoculation seemed more likely to spread smallpox than to eliminate it. But the manner in which Franklin and his wits did their asking, and answering, was extraordinary. Never before had a colonial newspaper gotten so personal, assailing so viciously a resident of the paper's own community for his ideas. Never before had disagreement become so public and hostile. Cotton Mather, once an almost unanimously respected man in his circles, was now a figure of controversy. James Franklin, once virtually unknown, became even more controversial.

The *News-Letter* and the *Gazette* reviled the *Courant's* editor, with Increase Mather writing in the latter that Franklin's journal was but a "wicked Libel." Cotton went on in the *News-Letter*, calling the *Courant* a "Notorious, Scandalous paper," a "Flagicious and Wicked Paper," a publication "full-freighted with Nonsense, Unmannerliness, Railery, Prophaneness, Immorality, Arrogancy, Calumnies, Lyes, contradictions, and what not, all tending to Quarrels and Divisions, and to Debauch and Corrupt the Minds and Manners of New England." Running into Franklin on the street one day, Cotton warned him that the man who dared speak ill of a preacher would face *"many Curses"* from his fellow citizens. According to Franklin, Mather continued, *"'The Lord will smite thro' the Loins of them that rise up against the Levites. I would have you consider of it, I have no more to say to you.'"*

In the next issue of the *Courant,* Franklin responded. "This heinous Charge and heavy Curse would have been more surprizing to me, if it had not come from one who is ever as groundless in his *Invectives* as in his *Panegyricks.*" He then accused Mather of trying "to make me an Object of *publick Odium.*"

To an extent, Mather succeeded. But he also succeeded in lining his foe's pockets. The *New England Courant* added forty new subscribers during its campaign against inoculation; the *News-Letter* and the *Gazette* held even for defending the practice. Call it a sign: the first indication that controversy would almost always outsell moderation on the American newsstand, that accuracy would seldom be a match for zestful falsehood.

❖

AT NO POINT did James Franklin advocate violence against Mather, either in the pages of the *Courant* or, as far as anyone knows, in private conversation. But in the midst of the controversy, someone who shared Franklin's views on inoculation threw a grenade of sorts, a concoction of gunpowder and turpentine, into the Mather residence. For some reason, it did not go off; Mather's life, and that of his nephew, a houseguest who had also made known his support of inoculation, was spared. It was not supposed to be. A note attached to the device read as follows: "COTTON MATHER, You Dog, Dam you: I'll inoculate you with this, with a Pox to you."

The note was the only clue that the bomb-thrower left behind. His identity was never learned.

❁

MATHER WAS, of course, right about the efficacy of inoculation, something his foes, and indeed the entire medical community of colonial times, were slow to admit. At the start, only one doctor in Boston, Zabdiel Boylston, seems to have agreed with Mather about smallpox prevention—so ardently, in fact, that he inoculated his own son. His fellow physicians thought him a fool. His neighbors feared for their safety. Even his wife wondered about so reckless a show of confidence in a procedure so little tested. An article in the *Courant* accused the doctor of deliberately trying to create an epidemic. He ended up creating more confidence in inoculation than had ever existed before. Boylston injected 286 people with the smallpox virus, and, according to historian J. C. Furnas, only 2 percent of them died. Of the thousands of other Bostonians who contracted smallpox at the same time without a physician's assistance, the mortality rate was 14 percent.

"Thanks be to GOD we have such a One [as Dr. Boylston] among us," wrote one of its readers to the *Boston Gazette*, "and that so many poor *Miserables* have already found the benefit of his gentle and dextrous hand."

The *New England Courant* had nothing to say about Dr. Boylston. In fact, from this point on, it had nothing further to say about smallpox. It had moved on to other stories.

❁

MANY YEARS LATER, Franklin's four-year-old nephew Francis, an uncommonly alert and cheerful child described as "precocious, curious, and special," would die of smallpox. He had not been inoculated, despite the mounds of evidence that had been gathered in the interim supporting the procedure, and the boy's father, Franklin's brother Benjamin, at the time a well-known citizen of Philadelphia and on his way to becoming perhaps the most famous resident of the Western world, blamed himself. He should have known better, he thought; an amateur scientist himself, and so prominent a one that William Pitt would one day compare him to Isaac Newton, Benjamin should have realized the wisdom of Mather's position and insisted that his son be inoculated. The boy's death was "a cruel blow," and some said Benjamin never got over it—those who heard him speak of it more than two decades later noticed a kind of sorrow in his voice that they had never heard before. Benjamin would, from the moment the boy took ill until the moment of his own passing, be a strong supporter of Cotton Mather's cause.

As far as anyone knows, Francis's uncle James, who had so strongly campaigned against inoculation, did not share his reaction to his nephew's death.

❀

IT WAS WITH JAMES FRANKLIN that the American tradition of the crusading journalist began, although far from honorably. His first crusade, against inoculation, was misguided. His second would land him in jail.

In the spring and summer of 1722, pirates began to raid commercial vessels along the New England coast, looting the cargoes and sometimes killing the crews. It is not clear whether a single ship was responsible or a whole fleet of them was taking turns in depredation, but either way the raids were a serious problem for a colony that depended on trade for much of its economic well-being. To some in Boston, the pirates seemed an epidemic no less threatening than smallpox had so recently been.

Franklin believed the authorities were lax in dealing with the problem. He scolded them for both tardiness and ineptitude. Part of the problem, he announced, was the captain who had been chosen to combat the pirates; Franklin found him insufficiently committed to the mission. "'Tis thought he will sail sometime this month," the *Courant* observed sarcastically, "if wind and weather permit."

At the same time, Franklin also began to rail against the attire of colonial officials, apparently needing yet another showcase for his irascibility, perhaps having concluded that the way the authorities dressed was somehow the cause of their inaction against the buccaneers. "This Pride of Apparel," said the *Courant*, "will appear the more foolish, if we consider that those airy Mortals who have no other Way of making themselves considerable but by gorgeous Apparel; draw afret them Crowds of Imitators, who . . . destroy by Example, and envy one another's Destruction."

The Massachusetts General Court had begun to chafe at Franklin when he refused to license his paper. It chafed all the more when he maligned so estimable a figure as Cotton Mather. Now that the *Courant* had made the government itself an object of public ridicule, claiming it was responsible for theft and murder on the high seas and ostentatious garb on land, it decided to take action. James Franklin was arrested and sent to jail, not to be released until he had issued a public apology and, furthermore, gotten a note from his doctor declaring that the incarceration was ruining his health—which, considering the state of agitation brought on by the General Court's action against him, it probably was.

Franklin's apprentice at the time was none other than young brother Benjamin, and James instructed him to run the *Courant* in his absence. As Benjamin later wrote in perhaps the most famous of all autobiographies, the experience was a thoroughly enjoyable one. "I had the Management of the Paper," Benjamin related, "and I made bold to give our Rulers some Rubs in it, which my Brother took very kindly, while others began to consider me in an unfavorable Light as a young Genius that had a Turn for Libeling and Satire."

But the young genius was soon to return to apprenticeship. After three weeks James was set free, and having quickly regained his health, he went back on his apology with equal haste. It should not have surprised the General Court, which he had continued to lambaste in the pages of the *Courant* even while behind bars, although not about piracy. Rather, Franklin decided to "Wonder on the Stupidity of many of my Countrymen"—meaning in particular those who had imprisoned him for speaking his mind—"who know little or nothing of the happy Constitution of an *English* government, and who are as unconcern'd to know the Liberties they enjoy thereby, as if it were a thing indifferent with them, whether they were protected by it, or otherwise." And then, to teach those countrymen a lesson about liberty, he told his apprentice to fill the rest of that day's paper with the Magna Carta, as if to say, this, *this*, is how the colony of Massachusetts should be governed, not to mention how the editor of the *New England Courant* should be treated.

Benjamin did as instructed.

By the beginning of 1723, James was in even deeper trouble with colonial officials, which by now had begun to seem his natural state. In a single issue of the *Courant*, he made a much unappreciated suggestion about the way Massachusetts should conduct its affairs with the motherland, then savaged the Crown-appointed governor for taking so passive a role in the colony's affairs and the local clergy for being hypocrites virtually any time they took a position on any issue. "They have the Blaze of a *high Profession*," the *Courant* declared, "when perhaps they are blacker than a Coal within."

And in the following issue came the next batch of deprecations—that the clergy were guilty of exhibiting toward the *Courant* "the highest Pitch of Malice" and that those who believed their defamations of the paper displayed "the greatest Ignorance."

The General Court had no choice but to strike again. Decreeing that the purpose of Franklin's journal was "to mock religion and bring it into disrespect," it ruled that "James Franklyn, the printer and publisher thereof, be strictly forbidden by this court to print or publish the New England Courant" unless he finally agreed to submit each issue for approval prior to publication—unless, that is, he agreed, as had the editors of Boston's other newspapers after *Publick Occurrences*, to publish by authority.

Franklin would not even consider such a thing; he would instead fret and fume and shake his fists at the heavens. Was it a matter of principle? Probably not. The Magna Carta example notwithstanding, Franklin had never been the type to analyze and theorize and extrapolate, to turn his mind to larger meanings, such as the role of a free press in an emerging society or the role of government, if any, in the operation of the press. Instead, he seems to have taken the court's action personally, concluding that an institution he did not respect and whose authority he did not acknowledge had taken it upon itself to punish him for infractions that he did not believe were infractions at all.

At first Franklin defied the court's order, continuing to publish, continuing to inflame. The court then set the sheriff on him, ordering that the *New England Courant* be shut down and its proprietor returned forthwith to jail. This time, the court intended, the publisher would remain behind bars regardless of his health or his willingness to utter an insincere apology.

It did not happen. Somehow Franklin got word of the sheriff's impending visit and, as hastily as he could, packed a bag and scampered into hiding. First, though, he made a deal with his apprentice: Benjamin would once again take over the *Courant*, and this time his name would even appear as publisher at the bottom of the last page.

BOSTON: Printed and sold by BENJAMIN FRANKLIN in Queen Street, where Advertisements are taken in.

It was a ruse, however, a means of deceiving the authorities; James would be, as he had been when previously imprisoned, as he had always been, the power behind the press. At least, that was the plan.

But it did not happen. Benjamin might still be but an apprentice in James's eyes, but he had already become too much the journalist to serve as a mouthpiece for someone else's views—even his brother's, or *especially* his brother's. As H. W. Brands tells us:

> The February 11, 1723, issue of the *Courant* explained that James Franklin had "entirely dropped the undertaking"; this was not quite true, but it grew truer by the week. With each issue the paper lost a little of James's character and took on more of Ben's. Where James swung his pen like a broadsword, Ben wielded a rapier. His satire was always light, never ponderous; it usually brought smiles to objective lips and must occasionally have turned up the corners of even Cotton Mather's mouth.

It would soon be time for the two brothers, different as journalists and even more different as human beings, to go the separate ways that seem to have been their destiny from the beginning.

CHAPTER FOUR

The Sounds of Silence Dogood

[Nᵒ 55

THE

New-England Courant.

From MONDAY August 13. to MONDAY August 20. 1722.

Neque licitum interea est meam amicam visere.

To the Author of the New-England Courant. [Nᵒ XI.

SIR,

ROM a natural Compassion to my Fellow-Creatures, I have sometimes been betray'd into Tears at the Sight of an Object of Charity, who by a bear Relation of hisCircumstances,seem'd to demand the Asistance of those about him. The following Petition represents in so lively a Manner the forlorn State of a Virgin well stricken in Years and Repentance, that I cannot forbear publishing it at this Time, with some Advice to the Petitioner.

To Mrs. Silence Dogood.

The Humble Petition of Margaret Aftercast,

SHEWETH,

" THAT your Petitioner being puff'd up in her younger Years with a numerous Train of Humble Servants, had the Vanity to think, that her extraordinary Wit and Beauty would continually recommend her to the Esteem of the Gallants; and therefore as soon as it came to be publickly known that any Gentleman addres'd her, he was immediately discarded.

" 2. THAT several of your Petitioners Humble Servants, who upon their being rejected by her, were, to all Apperance in a dying Condition, have since recover'd their Health, and been several Years married, to the great Surprize and Grief of your Petitioner, who parted with them upon no other ——— , but that they should die or run di-

themselves in a Method of Friendly Society; already publish'd for Widows, I conceive very proper Proposal for them, whereby Woman, upon full Proof given of her c Virgin for the Space of Eighteen Year Virginity from the Age of Twelve,) tuled to 500 *l.* in ready Cash.

BUT then it will be necessary to m ing Exceptions.

1. THAT no Woman shall be a Society after she is Twenty Five Y made a Practice of entertaining a ble Servants, without sufficient until she has manifested her Re under her Hand.

2. NO Member of the Soc before two credible Witnesses she has refus'd several good C Subscribing, shall be entitule comes of Age; that is to

3. NO Woman, who a has had the good Fortun ny Company with Enc bove the Space of one returning one half the first Offence; and up the Remainder.

To the Author

SIR,

A S it is very D the nature it in its various mate and radica like a subtil Po and operates t

The Effects and almost in but a very fe most under The Dise and Appe ty to to the Wo Nam ce Hum

" finding her self disap- former Adorers, Years past,

*T*HE APPRENTICESHIP, which was supposed to have brought the two Franklins closer together, had begun five years earlier, when Benjamin signed a document called an indenture, swearing to "readily obey" his brother. The indenture also required that the apprentice "shall not commit Fornication, nor contract Matrimony within the said Term: At Cards, Dice, or any other unlawful Game he shall not play. . . . He shall not . . . haunt Alehouses, Taverns, or Play-houses." Benjamin was, at the time he agreed to these terms, twelve years old.

In return, brother James agreed to "procure and provide for him sufficient Meat, Drink, Apparel, Lodging, Washing, fitting for an Apprentice, during the said Term," which, if all went as agreed, would last nine years.

Prior to this, as the eighth child of the mother and the fifteenth of the father of what we would today call a "blended" family, and one that Benjamin himself referred to as "obscure," he had led a much more carefree life. He swam in the Charles River, flew a kite without any premonition of electricity, dreamed of running away to sea, and, on one unfortunate occasion, "gave up all the coins in his pocket" for a whistle, which he blew delightedly until his siblings accused him of having paid four times what the item was worth. He did poorly in arithmetic in school, as well.

Benjamin went to school for two years, then spent the next two working in his father's soap and candle shop, where, as he later explained, he "was employed in cutting Wick for the Candles, filling the Dipping Mold, & the Molds for cast Candles, attending the Shop, going of Errands, &c." But he was not happy there. He had a "Bookish inclination," he admitted, and wanted to devote himself to it. He could not remember a time when he was not reading.

And he could not remember a time when he got along well with his brother. One of the reasons, certainly, was the age difference, James being nine years older than Benjamin. Another was the difference in dispositions; James was volatile, Benjamin more often than not sunny, easygoing. Yet another reason seems to have been the favoritism that their father showed for the younger son. When the boys argued, which they did often, and old Josiah Franklin was asked to intervene, he almost always sided with Benjamin, who, in his own words, "was either generally in the right, or else a better Pleader."

It was Josiah who had arranged the apprenticeship, and he was perhaps even more disappointed than his sons that it did not heal the breach between them. In fact, it made matters worse. "Tho' a Brother," Benjamin later wrote of James, "he considered himself as my Master, & me as his Apprentice; and accordingly expected the same Services from me as he would from another; while I thought he demean'd me too much in some he requir'd of me, who from a Brother expected more Indulgence. . . . I fancy his harsh and tyrannical Treatment of me, might be a means of impressing me with that Aversion to arbitrary Power that has stuck to me thro' my whole life."

Benjamin's duties as apprentice were many and varied and, at least at the outset, dreary. Let us imagine a typical day for him, a day that is ten hours long and begins with his arrival at the print shop shortly after dawn, one of six such days that make up his work week. He is the first one there. He unlocks the door, pushes it open, and tosses his coat on a peg on the wall. He slips on a leather apron, then checks the supply of ink for the day's work. If it is low, he mixes a new batch, blending the lampblack with tree sap and linseed oil and a few other ingredients and, if need be, holding his nose. Then he digs into the ink with a wooden spatula, slapping one lump after another of the stuff into a tray that resembles the tray a modern house painter uses with a roller. He sets the tray on a table next to the press.

Now he is ready to prepare the paper for printing. He removes the sheets one at a time from a huge stack on the counter just inside the front door and dips them into a vat of water, dampening them to open the fibers so that the ink will be more readily absorbed. The paper will still be damp when the words are applied later in the morning. The news does not come hot off the presses in colonial times; it comes moist.

By now Benjamin is no longer alone on the premises. James has joined him, as have two or three assistant printers, known as journeymen, and they have gotten into their own aprons and begun their duties. They are handling other sheets of paper, the smaller ones on which the stories for that week's edition of the *Courant*, and the letters to the editor, have been written. They are reading them carefully and setting the words in type as they do, one letter and one space and one punctuation mark at a time. The type goes into a long, narrow frame called a composing stick. Once the stick is filled with sentences, the pieces of type are slid off the stick onto a tabletop, where they are tied with string to hold them in place— little bars of prose awaiting those that will follow and give them context.

When all the sentences for a particular story have been assembled, they are fitted into a different kind of frame, this one known as a chase. To hold them together and to make sure the margins will be even, wooden wedges are pounded into the chase between the ends of the lines of type and the edges of the frame. Next the chase is locked into the printing press.

At this point, Benjamin grabs a couple of ink beaters, which are wood-handled devices approximately the size and shape of the bells that town criers carry, covered at the thicker ends with leather and sheep's wool. He holds one in his right hand, one in his left. He dips them into the tray he prepared earlier, coating them with ink, and then thumps them onto the type in the chase so that it in turn is coated with ink. But not too thickly; Benjamin knows that ink is expensive, and if he forgets, his brother is always ready to remind him. Many colonial newspapers were hard to read then and are even harder to read today on microfilm because the type is so light.

One of the journeymen now slips a piece of damp paper into a frame of its own, a tympan, which he positions in the press an inch or two above the type, ready to make contact. The hard work is now about to begin.

The press has a long, horizontal arm, which would be known in later years as a devil's tail. James or a journeyman or perhaps even Benjamin begins to pull the arm in a semicircle, forcing the press down onto the paper and printing the page. But the part of the press that does the actual pressing, the platen, is smaller than the sheet of newspaper, which means that the first tug on the arm prints only the top half of the page; a second is required for the bottom half after the paper's position has been shifted.

Still, a master printer like James Franklin can do a page in fifteen or twenty seconds, and most print shops, even at this early stage of American journalism, have more than one press. Eventually the more successful publishers will have four, and a few of them even more.

After the page is printed, it is peeled off the chase and, still damp, hung from a rack on the ceiling to dry, as if it is an article of clothing that has just been washed and must now be draped over a clothesline. By the time the men in the print shop have been working for a few hours, the ceiling racks are full, and sometimes the work has to stop, or at least proceed more slowly, until more space is available. It is Benjamin who makes it available, pulling down the pages when they are dry enough to handle and folding them into the latest issue of the *New England Courant*.

At the end of the day, Benjamin cleans the ink from the type with lye and puts the pieces back in their cases, the "a's" with the "a's," the "b's" with the "b's," and so on—chores that are tedious and exacting and very important. Then he cleans the ink beaters with, of all things, urine. Neither this author nor the experts on early American printing whom he has consulted know whether Benjamin took the beaters outside and sprayed them from his own midsection, or soaked them in a container that had been filled with urine during the day by the men in the shop.

Benjamin wipes off the press and sweeps the floors and counter-tops and machinery. If some ink is left over in the tray, he scrapes it back into a kind of wooden bin. He makes sure there is enough paper for tomorrow's print run, and stacks it neatly. Then he takes off his apron and puts on his coat, but he might still not be done with the day's tasks. Sometimes, Benjamin says, despite his weariness and aching muscles, he "was employ'd to carry the Papers thro' the Streets to the Customers," dropping off stacks of them at taverns and other places of business, and single copies at the homes of individual subscribers.

The latter assignment, although not his favorite, was the only one that paid; an apprentice received no salary, but his customers sometimes gave him tips. The money was important to Benjamin, and he would long remember the pleasure of receiving and saving it and then buying a book of his own instead of having to borrow one, or of treating himself to a pastry and beverage at the neighborhood bakeshop after work. Several years later, he himself would be the publisher of a newspaper, and in the first issue of each year, often in subtle and understated fashion, he would encourage those who read it to think kindly of the poor young men who, exhausted though they might have been from the day's labors, nonetheless brought the news to their doors at night.

"The New-Year verses of the printer lads, who carry about the Pennsylvania gazette to its customers."

Blyth Christmas, joyous Season, past,
And happy New Year come at last,
Our gentle MUSE's annual Lays,
Attend the Tribute of your Praise,
Whilst, far above all selfish Ends,
She seeks the Int'rest of her Friends,
Contented, if the Tale she sings
Or Profit, or Instruction, brings.

❁

THE PRINT SHOP was a dirtier place to work than Josiah Franklin's soap and candle shop, and far more taxing on a young man's body. But Benjamin was a hardy sort and quickly mastered the physical demands of the job. He was, in addition, an intelligent and inquisitive sort, able to learn the mental aspects with equal dispatch. As a result, he was able to make the first of his many contributions to American journalism: an elevation of its tone. A columnist more than a reporter, a man of letters more than a scribe of daily happenstance, he owed his skill to the men of letters he had so eagerly read as a child and continued to study as a young man. Among his favorite books were Burton's *Historical Collections*, Plutarch's *Lives*, and Daniel Defoe's *An Essay Upon Projects*, which, as Franklin biographer Walter Isaacson points out, "proposed for London many of the sort of community projects that Franklin would later launch in Philadelphia: fire insurance associations, voluntary seamen's societies to create pensions, schemes to provide welfare for the elderly and widows, academies to educate the children of the middle class, and (with just a touch of Defoe humor) institutions to house the mentally retarded paid for by a tax on authors because they happened to get a greater share of intelligence at birth just as the retarded happened to get less."

Two more books also made an impression on the young Franklin—in part because of the similarity of their titles. One was

Bonifacius: Essays to Do Good; the other, which would have infuriated his brother if he had ever seen it on Benjamin's shelf, was *Essays
to Do Good*, by none other than Cotton Mather.

But no author inspired the young Franklin as did the London
essayist Joseph Addison. Sometimes, in fact, the topic of Addison's
journalism was journalism itself. "It is my Custom in a Dearth of
News," Addison revealed in 1710,

> to entertain my self with those Collections of Advertisements
> that appear at the End of all our publick Prints. These I consider
> as Accounts of the News from the little World, in the same
> Manner that the foregoing Parts of the Paper are from the great.
> If in one we hear that a Sovereign Prince is fled from his Capital
> City, in the other we hear of a Tradesman who hath shut up his
> Shop, and run away. If in one we find the Victory of a General,
> in the other we see the Desertion of a private Soldier. I must
> confess, I have a certain Weakness in my Temper, that is often
> very much affected by these little Domestick Occurrences, and
> have frequently been caught with Tears in my Eyes over a
> melancholy Advertisement.

As this passage reveals, Joseph Addison did more than merely
write essays; he "perfected" the form. "His prose style," it has been
said, "was the model for pure and elegant English until the end of
the 18th century; his comments on manners and morals were widely influential in forming the middle-class ideal of a dispassionate,
tolerant, Christian world-citizen."

Addison's essays appeared in London journals called *The Tatler*
and *The Spectator*, and no textbooks were more important to the
self-education of Benjamin Franklin than these. He pored over
Addison's work daily, making it into a routine of intellectual calis-
thenics. In her volume on Franklin called *The Most Dangerous Man
in America*, Catherine Drinker Bowen says that he "reproduced
pages from memory, or turned them into verse and back again to

prose. He made notes of what he read, jumbled the notes like a pack of cards, and after some weeks reduced them to the best order he could before forming full sentences and completing the paper—anything to gain flexibility and enlarge his vocabulary. It was laborious work."

But fruitful. It helped to make Franklin a thinker as well as a writer, and he knew at the time he was proceeding in that direction and could not help but be proud of the accomplishment. As he put it himself in his *Autobiography*:

> By comparing my work afterwards with the original, I discover'd many faults and amended them; but I sometimes had the Pleasure of Fancying that in certain Particulars of small Import, I had been lucky enough to improve the Method or the Language and this encourag'd me to think I might possibly in time come to be a tolerable English Writer, of which I was extreamly ambitious.

That Joseph Addison was a master of English prose is indisputable. That he became Franklin's model of journalistic excellence is at least mildly ironic, although it would not be apparent for some time. Long after newspapers had become indispensable both to England and her New World colonies, and long after Franklin's own indispensability to American journalism had been established, Addison would write: "There is no Humour in my Countrymen, which I am more enclined to wonder at, than their general Thirst after News."

❁

IT WAS ONLY NATURAL that Franklin would want to show off his still-developing skills in the *Courant*. It was also natural that the publisher would disapprove. Know your place, was James's attitude toward his brother; you are a menial, not an intellectual, and you must set your heart on nothing more. For the first few months of his apprenticeship, Benjamin had no choice but to comply.

But even a colonial newspaper appearing once a week, occupying a mere two or four pages, and culling its material from any number of sources, sometimes ran short of material. And even a man already jealous of his younger brother must sometimes bend to exigencies. James soon decided that the *Courant* would be better off if he allowed his assistant to become a part-time apprentice wit, and Benjamin was determined to make the most of his opportunity.

It was customary in those days, at least on occasion, for a newspaper to complement its stories with some light verse on the same topic, and this was Benjamin's first journalistic assignment. He seems to have debuted in print with a few lines about the recently slain pirate Blackbeard, whose real name was Edward Teach.

> Will you hear of a bloody battle,
> Lately fought upon the seas,
> It will make your ears to rattle,
> And your admiration cease.
> Have you heard of Teach the Rover
> And his knavery on the main,
> How of gold he was a lover,
> How he loved all ill-got gain. . . .

Benjamin also wrote a ballad called "The Lighthouse Tragedy," which told the woeful tale of Captain Worthilake, who, despite being an able mariner, drowned at sea with his two daughters.

To their author, looking back as an older man, such poems were "wretched Stuff"—not challenging to write, not edifying to read, certainly not worthy of being reprinted in books almost three centuries later. But James had to admit that he liked them. The wits liked them too, and might even have congratulated their boss on being so closely related to so clever and versatile a young man as

Benjamin. James did *not* like that. He was torn between wanting his newspaper to be as successful as possible and wanting his brother to remain an anonymous printer rather than an applauded litterateur.

Benjamin, of course, much preferred the latter but knew all too well that he would continue to be the victim of his brother's reluctance. Subterfuge, he decided, was the only path he could take at present, and he took it with the merriest of steps.

One morning in the spring of 1722, James showed up at the print shop before Benjamin and found that an envelope had been slipped under the door the previous night. He picked it up and opened it. Inside was a letter to the editor from a person whose signature read Silence Dogood. It began somewhat presumptuously.

> It may not be improper in the first place to inform your readers, that I intend once a fortnight to present them, by the help of this paper, with a short epistle, which I presume will add somewhat to their entertainment.

At the time, James was in the midst of his inoculation battle with Cotton Mather and was feeling beleaguered: the Boston clergy were rebuking him, as were other supporters of the Mathers, and the *News-Letter* and the *Gazette* were tweaking him in print as often as their contributors could think of something nasty or belittling to say. Thus he was pleased that Mrs. Dogood—whoever she, or he, really was—thought enough of him to forward her musings to the *Courant*. He might have preferred something harder-hitting—an exposé of a short-weighting merchant or a diatribe on one of Boston's holier-than-thou elders—but any submission was a welcome one. James pulled out a chair and sat. Perhaps it was still dark enough outside that he needed to light a candle and hold the letter in its glare. He read more from Mrs. Dogood.

The lady was a widow, she claimed, "untainted with vice, free and unbiased." She "took a more than ordinary delight in reading ingenious books," which, she said, "enable[d] the mind to frame great and noble ideas." Among other things, she said, she was accomplished at "all sorts of needle-work," and enjoyed "spending my leisure time either in some innocent diversion with the neighbouring females, or in some shady retirement, with the best of company, *books*. Thus I past away the time with a mixture of profit and pleasure, having no affliction but what was imaginary, and created in my own fancy; as nothing is more common with us women, than to be grieving for nothing, when we have nothing else to grieve for."

There was something familiar about Mrs. Dogood's style, something in the tone, the choice of words, the way the phrases were assembled and laid into place, like blocks set perfectly atop one another to form a structure both solid and graceful. To the knowledgeable reader, which James Franklin was not, the writing echoed Addison. It should have. The elderly widow Dogood, prim in her notions yet confident in her ability to interest the *Courant* in them, was the paper's youthful apprentice.

James Franklin published the letter from Silence Dogood in its entirety on the front page of the *New England Courant* on April 2, 1722.

Between then and the following October, Benjamin wrote thirteen more essays under his feminine nom de plume. As Catherine Drinker Bowen muses, he had said "that he liked to do his writing in the printing house on Sunday, when the workmen were absent. We see him sitting alone among piles of rag paper, the heavy wooden press standing idle and waiting. He was at pains, of course, to disguise his hand."

But there was no pain, only pleasure, in his manipulation of the pen. Franklin's joy of expression was apparent in every sentence, even those that ran on, as several did, long enough so that memories of the beginning were dim when one finally reached the end.

I am apt to fancy, the reason [that good poetry was not to be expected in New England] is, not because our countrymen are altogether void of a poetical genius, nor yet because we have not those advantages of education which other countries have, but purely because we do not afford that praise and encouragement which is merited, when any thing extraordinary of this kind is produced among us: upon which consideration I have determined, when I meet with a good piece of New England poetry, to give it a suitable encomium, and thereby endeavor to discover to the world some of its beauties, in order to encourage the author to go on, and bless the world with more, and more excellent productions.

It was also a pleasure for Benjamin to listen to James and the others at the *Courant* try to guess Mrs. Dogood's real identity. She could not be the simple country woman she claimed to be, of that the wits were certain. Perhaps the writer was a man of the cloth known for the profundity of his sermons. Perhaps it was a man of the law known for the brilliance of his arguments. Or perhaps it was, in fact, a sixty-year-old widow, but educated, as so few American women were back then, in the best European schools. "[N]one were named," Franklin proudly stated, "but Men of some Character among us for Learning and Ingenuity."

Franklin became even prouder of himself and more confident in his abilities as a newspaperman when he managed the paper for the three weeks that James spent in jail. Mrs. Dogood purported to be unhappy about the sentence. "Without freedom of thought," she wrote in the *Courant*, as James sat stewing in his cell, "there can be no such thing as wisdom, and no such thing as public liberty without freedom of speech."

Upon James's release, Mrs. Dogood, who had by now firmly established the inappropriateness of her first name, lashed out at the Puritan establishment of Boston, which, in her view, was almost solely responsible for the woes of James Franklin. It was not so much an example of Benjamin's being loyal to his brother as it was of his being true to his own beliefs about the role of religion in the civil society.

It has been for some time a question with me, whether a commonwealth suffers more by hypocritical pretenders to religion, or by the openly profane? . . . 'Tis not inconsistent with charity to distrust a religious man in power, though he may be a good man; he has many temptations to propagate *public destruction* for *personal advantages* and security: and if his natural temper be covetous, and his actions often contradict his pious discourse, we may with great reason conclude, that he has some other design in his religion besides barely getting to heaven.

The Silence Dogood letters became a more and more popular feature of the *New England Courant.* They combine, if such a thing is possible, Addison's grace with Walter Lippmann's grasp of public policy and Erma Bombeck's knack for the right joke in the right place. But the writer was a youth, a mere sixteen years of age, short on experience despite his book learning and drollery, and he was beginning to run out of ideas. Furthermore, his brother was now suspecting Mrs. Dogood's true identity, and he was not pleased. When, in fact, Benjamin finally got around to confessing his authorship, which seems to have happened after the last of his epistles, James reacted with "fraternal tyranny." He believed, Benjamin later wrote, "probably with reason, that [the success of the letters] tended to make me too vain." James seems even to have taken a hand to Benjamin, punching him or slapping him, something he had done on previous occasions, even though its victim felt such behavior was "extreamly amiss."

The day the last letter from Silence Dogood appeared in the *Courant* might also have been the day Benjamin first knew that the apprenticeship would not run its full nine years, that he would eventually have to break its bonds and set out on his own.

❁

THE *NEW ENGLAND COURANT*'s chief claim to fame is that it was the first paper ever to publish Benjamin Franklin. But Walter Isaacson believes it has other distinctions, that it "ought to be remembered on its own as America's first fiercely independent newspaper, a bold, antiestablishment journal that helped to create the tradition of an irreverent press." James Franklin, Isaacson insists, "set an example by challenging, with bravery and spunk, Boston's ruling elite"; by so doing, he "was the most important journalistic influence on his younger brother."

Moreover, unless one was a member of that elite, which is to say a man of the cloth or a government official, the *Courant* was often a pleasure to read, which could not be said of its predecessors or contemporaries. One cannot imagine Benjamin Harris or John Campbell welcoming the widow Dogood to his pages.

Furthermore, thanks to the older brother, cranky and contrarian though he was, the *Courant* became a vital part of the community, which is also something that no other American paper had yet accomplished. People read James Franklin's news, talked about it, thought about it. Whatever the *Courant*'s faults, and they were many and notable, it offered journalism that mattered, journalism to which attention had to be paid. It had a prickly temperament and a sense of social purpose, and these two traits remain characteristics of the best American newspapers and broadcast outlets today.

As for Benjamin, most of his career in journalism, including his grandest achievements and his most lasting innovations, lay ahead of him. All he knew, as the autumn of 1723 approached and James had once again taken control of the *Courant* despite his numerous conflicts with the law, was that he had to get away from his brother, and that James, out of spite, not sorrow, wanted to prevent his departure. "When he found I would leave him," Benjamin later wrote, "he took care to prevent my getting Employment in any other Printing-House of the Town, by going round & speaking to every Master, who accordingly refus'd to give me work. I then thought of going to New York as the nearest place where there was a Printer: and I was the rather inclin'd to leave Boston, when I reflected that I had already made myself a little obnoxious to the governing Party; & from the arbitrary Proceedings of the Assembly in my Brother's Case it was likely I might if I stay'd soon bring myself into Scrapes."

But there would have been scrapes with James as well, and, in the long run, they would have been more harmful to Benjamin both personally and professionally than any disputes with the government.

And so it was that late in September 1723, Benjamin Franklin took his leave of the *New England Courant*, walking out of the print shop and down to Boston Harbor and booking passage on a sloop headed south. "I sold some of my Books to raise a little Money," he recounted, "Was taken on board privately, and as we had a fair Wind in three Days I found my self in New York near 300 miles from home, a Boy of but 17, without the least Recommendation to or Knowledge of any Person in the Place, and with very little Money in my Pocket."

Just as James would never publicly comment on the death of his nephew from smallpox, neither would he respond to the departure of his brother, except in the most indirect and utilitarian manner. A few days after Benjamin set sail for New York, James ran an ad in the *Courant*, a small one, thirteen words that gave no clue whatsoever to his feelings:

"James Franklin, Printer in Queen Street, wants a likely lad for an Apprentice."

CHAPTER FIVE

Science, Sex,
and Super Crown Soap

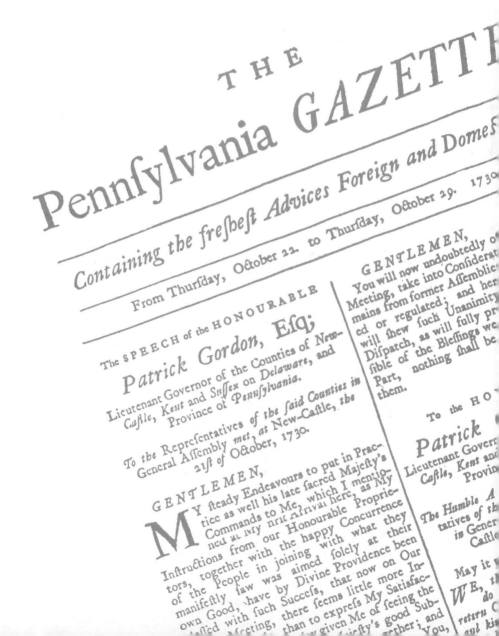

Numb. CII.

THE

Pennſylvania GAZETTE

Containing the freſheſt Advices Foreign and Domeſ

From Thurſday, October 22. to Thurſday, October 29. 1730.

The SPEECH of the HONOURABLE

Patrick Gordon, Eſq;

Lieutenant Governor of the Counties of New-
Caſtle, Kent and Suſſex on Delaware, and
Province of Pennſylvania.

To the Repreſentatives of the ſaid Counties in
General Aſſembly met, at New-Caſtle, the
21ſt of October, 1730.

GENTLEMEN,

MY ſteady Endeavours to put in Practice as well his late ſacred Majeſty's
Commands to Me, which I men:io-
ned at my firſt Arrival here, as My
Inſtructions from our Honourable Proprie-
tors, together with the happy Concurrence
of the People in joining with what they
manifeſtly ſaw was aimed ſolely at their
own Good, have by Divine Providence been
ſucceſs'd with ſuch Succeſs, that now on Our
Meeting, there ſeems little more In-
than to expreſs My Satisfac-

GENTLEMEN,
You will now undoubtedly of
Meeting, take into Conſiderat
mains from former Aſſemblie
ed or regulated; and her
will ſhew ſuch Unanimity
Diſpatch, as will fully pr
ſible of the Bleſſings we
Part, nothing ſhall be
them.

To the HO

Patrick
Lieutenant Govern
Caſtle, Kent and
Provin

The Humble A
tatives of
in Gener
Caſtle

May it
WE,
return
auk hi

*F*ROM NEW YORK, the colonies' third largest city, where he stayed long enough to learn that there were no opportunities for printers after all, Benjamin made his way to Philadelphia, the second largest. He has been described at the time as a "physically striking" young man, partly the result of all that working out over the years on his brother's printing press. He was "muscular, barrel-chested, open-faced, and almost six feet tall. He had the happy talent of being at ease in almost any company, from scrappy tradesmen to wealthy merchants, scholars to rogues."

But worldly goods were not among his attributes, and he was forced to enter Philadelphia in a most undistinguished manner.

> I was in my Working Dress, my best Cloaths being to come round by Sea. I was dirty from my Journey; my Pockets were stuff'd out with Shirts & Stockings; I knew no Soul, nor where to look for Lodging. I was fatigued with Travelling, Rowing & Want of Rest. I was very hungry, and my whole stock of Cash consisted of a Dutch Dollar and about a Shilling in Copper.

Six years later, long removed from his brother's shadow and no longer fatigued or hungry or poor, having served as a journeyman printer for a time and then sailed to London, worked in a print shop there, and returned to the colonies to open his own print shop, Benjamin Franklin became the owner, publisher, and editor of a newspaper called the *Pennsylvania Gazette*. He had yielded, as he said in the paper's first issue, to "several Gentlemen in this, and the

Neighbouring Provinces, [who] have given Encouragement to the Printer hereof to publish a Paper of Intelligence." And Philadelphia, indeed all of Pennsylvania, needed such a paper, Franklin believed, as the only other journal in town at the time "had so wretchedly performed, that it has been not only a Reproach to the Province, but such a Scandal to the very Name of Printing, that it may, for its unparallel'd Blunders and Incorrectness, be truly called *Nonsense in Folio*, instead of a Serviceable News-Paper."

It was an uncharacteristic display of animosity from Franklin, and when he continued it was in a more civil tone. Publishing a newspaper, he wryly explained to the readers of his initial issue,

is not so easy an Undertaking as many People imagine it to be. The Author of a *Gazette* (in the Opinion of the Learned) ought to be qualified with an extensive Acquaintance with Languages, a great Easiness and Command of Writing and Relating Things clearly and intelligibly, and in a few words; he should be able to speak of War both by Land and Sea; be well acquainted with Geography, with the History of the Time, with the several Interests of Princes and States, the Secrets of Courts, and the Manners and Customs of all Nations. Men thus accomplish'd are very rare in this remote Part of the World; and it would be well if the writer of these Papers could make up among his Friends what is wanting in himself.

In addition to Addison-inspired essays, which Franklin not only wrote himself but encouraged others to attempt, the *Pennsylvania Gazette* reported on crime and mishap, the deliberations of government both at home and abroad, and matters military, diplomatic, and economic—especially, in the latter case, concerning trade with other colonies and nations and the development of new colonial businesses. It reported on dogs who had drowned or run away from home. And it reported that the members of the Massachusetts legislature had refused to give the royal governor a pay raise; rather the lawmakers had insisted on "what *they think* their right, and that of the people they represent." The *Gazette* roared its approval.

Franklin wanted his paper to be the diary that Philadelphia kept of itself, but one that also recorded the events of the wider world, even though that world continued to yield its secrets slowly. Word from Europe still took two months to cross the Atlantic in fair weather, and as long as six in winter. Word from Boston, Philadelphia, and New York still took a similar time to get to the constantly-shifting western frontier. There was still nothing new about the news.

But simply printing the news was not enough for Franklin; he wanted to expand the very definition of the term. He wanted to report on "*Algebra*, or the Doctrine of Equations . . . *Analyticks*, or the Resolutions of Problems . . . *Architecture* . . . *Chronology*, or the Doctrine of Time . . . *Mechanicks* . . . *Mineralogy* . . . *Opticks* . . . *Perspective*, or the Projection of Points, Lines, Planes . . . [and] *Pneumaticks*, or the Consideration of the Air, its Weight, Density, Pressure, Elasticity, &c." The *Gazette* told of the latest developments in meteorology, for instance "that the material cause of thunder, lightning, and earthquakes, is one and the same." It reviewed the most recently published books from abroad. It did not just publish stories on government; it analyzed the ideas behind various forms and proposals for change. And it did not just publish stories on religion; it contrasted a belief in the Almighty with superstition, "a Monster which has introduced more Misery into the World, than all our natural Evils put together." More than anything else, Franklin said, he wanted to encourage his readers "to join the rationalists of the eighteenth century in pursuit of knowledge and exercise of reason."

❁

BUT FRANKLIN ALSO PURSUED PROFITS, and if he was not the first American newsman to realize the value of sex as a sales tool, he was certainly a pioneer in pushing back the borders of acceptability. The *Pennsylvania Gazette* contained more than its share of ribald tales: about a fellow "caught napping with another man's wife"; about a lust-riddled constable who "made an agreement with a neighboring female, to *watch* with her that night"; and about a wife who, the *Gazette* seemed pleased to relate, had changed her mind about her mate, twice:

> We are credibly informed, that the young woman who not long since petitioned the governor, and the assembly, to be divorced from her husband, and at times industriously solicited most of the magistrates on that account, has at last concluded to cohabit with him again. It is said the report of the physicians (who in form examined his *abilities*, and allowed him to be in every respect sufficient,) gave her but small satisfaction; whether any experiments *more satisfactory* have been tried, we cannot say; but it seems she now declares it as her opinion, that *George is as good as de best.*

Franklin was, as biographer Isaacson says, a "rather raunchy young publisher," and he did not let his marriage to Deborah Read at the age of twenty-four thwart his inclinations. She was older than he, unremarkable in appearance, Franklin's decided inferior both socially and intellectually. He would become a man of the world, of France and England even more than America; she, on the other hand, never left Philadelphia and in fact spent most of her days within the same few blocks. His mind was on a constant quest; hers, as harsh as it seems to say, in a permanent rut.

But she was kind, devoted, dependable. That Franklin was fond of her, there is no doubt. In 1742, he honored his wife in verse:

Of their Chloes and Phillisses Poets may prate
I sing my plain Country Joan
Now twelve Years my wife, still the Joy of my Life
Blest Day that I made her my own,

My dear Friends
Blest Day that I made her my own.

But his flirtations with women who were not so plain and not so country began—or, more likely, continued—a few days later. Would he have behaved with similar wantonness if he had married more suitably? Probably; Franklin seems to have had a genuine regard for marriage, but one that did not extend so far as adherence to the vows. As a result, he was able to conceive, or at least popularize, yet another journalistic innovation: the hoax.

Franklin had sired a son out of wedlock before marrying Deborah. He was thus sympathetic to the plight of both parents in such a situation, and out of that sympathy came the tale of a prostitute named Polly Baker, who had supposedly been brought before a court in Connecticut for having given birth not to one illegitimate child, but to *five*. She was as sassy a lass as she was prolific. She asked the court, "Can it be a crime (in the nature of things I mean) to add the number of the king's subjects, in a new country that really wants people?"

Later in her testimony, Franklin had Miss Polly explain that she was promiscuous because she was a strong believer in duty, "the Duty of the first and great Command of Nature, and of Nature's God, *Encrease and Multiply*. A Duty, from the steady Performance of which, nothing has ever been able to deter me; but for its Sake, I have hazarded the Loss of Publick Esteem, and frequently incurr'd Publick Disgrace and Punishment; and therefore ought, in my humble Opinion, instead of a Whipping, to have a Statue erected in my Memory." So saying, the defendant finished her testimony and the judges began to deliberate.

It did not take them long. They were so moved by Polly Baker's testimony that they found her innocent of all charges. In fact, her presentation even "induced one of her Judges to marry her the next Day." That was the story Franklin told.

In all likelihood, he did not expect people to take it literally;

rather, like Addison and others before him, he believed he was making a point, teaching a lesson, as did the Bible with its parables and such authors as Chaucer and Boccaccio with their tales of travelers and lovers and others. It was not the facts that were important in such writing, but the moral; it was not truth as niggling minds defined it, but Truth in the larger sense, as the cosmos recognized it.

Perhaps this explains why Polly Baker fascinated so many people for so long. Or perhaps it was simply the brazen lasciviousness of her confrontation with the authorities, and the fact that the details appeared in a newspaper—and newspapers did not usually recount stories of such a nature at the time. Regardless, the particulars of her appearance before the Connecticut court were first published in a London journal in 1747, then reprinted countless times in America and Britain in the following years and accepted as gospel by many a reader, at least a few of whom were men who must have longed to encounter in their own lives a woman with a devotion to duty just like Polly Baker's.

More than three decades would pass before Franklin admitted that this most clever of trollops had never drawn a mortal breath.

❀

BENJAMIN FRANKLIN made his readers smile more than any other journalist of the eighteenth century. It was the nature of the man, and, at least to a degree, it was the strategy he had developed to cope with his brother. It was also part of his journalistic strategy; he believed that if a story amused as well as informed, it would make a deeper and longer-lasting impression on readers. It would also be less likely to offend.

But it was Franklin's sense of purpose that made him so estimable a journalist, not his sense of humor. He was no less courageous than Benjamin Harris had been, and no less dubious of colonial authority than brother James. Unlike them, however,

Franklin had been a respected member of the community before becoming a publisher; the odds were slim, therefore, that governmental officials would consider legal action as a first recourse when the *Pennsylvania Gazette* found fault with them. And since its criticisms were usually written with wit rather than rancor, they did not have so bitter a sting; they were policy disputes more than personal attacks, and sometimes they were policy disputes couched as entertainment. Benjamin Franklin was serious about his humor.

But even when he was serious without it, he seldom inflamed either his subjects or his readers; he was too esteemed a figure, too widely known for a benevolent nature. Case in point: Pennsylvania had been founded by Quakers, among whose tenets was the repudiation of war. As a result, the colonial assembly had refused to create a militia, which, in Franklin's view, left his fellow citizens vulnerable to attack by any number of potential foes. He tried to convince the Quakers of their folly. He explained that pacifism was more admirable in theory than in practice; there were times, he said, when it would do more harm than good, and it was the kind of harm that would extend into future generations. It is unlikely that Franklin changed any minds among Pennsylvania's Quaker leadership, but he showed himself able to combine tact with boldness, a feat that few journalists of his or any other time have been able to manage.

Just as he did not shy from conflict, neither was he reluctant about self-promotion or the promotion of his ideas. Many of the scientific studies he published in the *Gazette* were intended to aid his own research. Many of the causes he publicized were those in which he had a personal interest: public sanitation, the creation of a fire department, improvement of the police department, better treatment for the mentally and physically ill, more opportunities for education.

The fire department was especially important to Franklin, as were efforts to prevent fires in the first place. So important, actually, that on one occasion the editor of the *Pennsylvania Gazette* wrote a letter to the editor of the *Pennsylvania Gazette* about the matter: to Benjamin Franklin, from Benjamin Franklin, referring to himself in this case as "A.A." The letter urged his fellow Philadelphians to be careful in winter, when they would warm their houses by carrying hot coals from room to room; the danger, Franklin said, was that "scraps of fire may fall into chinks and make no appearance till midnight; when your stairs being in flames, you may be forced (as I once was) to leap out of your windows and hazard your necks to avoid being over-roasted."

In his combination of virtues and skills and interests, Franklin was an original. In his choice of words, however, he could sometimes call others to mind, and for good reason. Plagiarism was not the vice in those days that it has since become; rather than being regarded as the theft of intellectual property and subjecting its perpetrator to legal sanctions, it was more commonly thought of as dipping into the vat of common wisdom. Franklin dipped frequently, especially for Poor Richard's almanacs. Seldom did he acknowledge his dipping; he was simply sampling the wares of others and appropriating those that best suited his purposes. He expected that others would do the same with his words, and the more it happened, the more flattered he would likely be.

On balance, Benjamin Franklin was as ethical a journalist as America produced in the eighteenth century. Yes, he deceived on occasion, but only because he thought it a better way to tell a story, and only because he believed his readers were sophisticated enough to know the ruse and understand that it served a deeper purpose. He never meant to impugn the integrity of those with whom he disagreed; he simply explained his views in such a manner that, more often than not, readers were likely to take his side, as Josiah Franklin had done long ago when his boys were arguing with each other. And Franklin never used his position to benefit at the expense of his own probity.

Once, in fact, he was offered a substantial amount of money to publish a piece in the *Gazette* that he believed to be "scurrilous and defamatory." He asked himself what to do. Then, as was his way, he took pen to paper and answered.

> To determine whether I should publish it or not, I went home in the evening, purchased a twopenny loaf at the baker's, and with the water from the pump made my supper; I then wrapped myself up in my great-coat, and laid down on the floor and slept till morning, when, on another loaf and a mug of water, I made my breakfast. From this regimen I feel no inconvenience whatever. Finding I can live in this manner, I have formed a determination never to prostitute my press to the purposes of corruption and abuse of this kind for the sake of gaining a more comfortable subsistence.

But Franklin did not have to worry about a comfortable subsistence. As a printer, he secured a number of lucrative contracts from both the colonial government and private citizens. And as a newspaperman, he made a significant amount of money from advertisers, in large part because, more than any other publisher of the time, he knew how to treat them. He solicited their business, listened to their concerns, advised them on the best ways to sell their products in print. Were the products "chemical and galenical medicines duly and honestly prepared, all at reasonable prices"? He knew how to make a reader's health seem dependent on them. Were they "two young likely Negro men, country born, bred up in a farm, and can do all manner of plantation work"? He knew, despite his reservations about slavery, how best to promote a transaction. Sometimes he advised his advertisers on what to write; sometimes he wrote the ads himself. He decided on the size and design of the type and figured out where best to place the ads in the paper.

With regard to the latter, it had been the custom in colonial America to segregate advertising, stuffing the pitches for goods and services into a ghetto on the back page. This, as Franklin pointed out, made it easy for readers to skip all the ads at once. He would make it harder. He would scatter the ads throughout the articles, and sometimes set them off with a white border, perhaps wasting paper but calling even more attention to the messages within.

And Franklin would give headlines to ads, thick and black and demanding to be noticed.

JUST IMPORTED, ANOTHER PARCEL OF SUPER CROWN SOAP

The man was a pragmatist. He knew the value of advertising to a newspaper, knew that it did not have to corrupt the content. He was the first American to make good money from journalism, and he did it with high spirits and an open mind. He delighted in running a print shop; it was his hobby as much as it was his vocation, a source of pleasure no less than a source of income, and a venture from which his subscribers seemed to take as much pleasure, and derive as much edification, as he did. His enthusiasm for the print shop was a childish one, even in adulthood, even after he had left the press behind for other pursuits; no matter how poorly brother James had treated him, he had never been able to diminish it.

In fact, in all the years that Franklin owned the *Pennsylvania Gazette*, he seems to have published only one item with reluctance, a single story out of hundreds upon hundreds of stories that not only saddened him but brought him torment, an article whose details he so wanted to withhold, not only from the public but, even more, from himself. It appeared on December 30, 1736.

UNDERSTANDING 'tis a current Report, that my Son Francis, who died lately of the Small Pox, had it by Inoculation; and it being desired to satisfy the Publick in that Particular . . . I do sincerely declare, that he was not Inoculated, but receiv'd the Distemper in the Common Way of Infection: and I suppose the

Report could only arise from its being my known Opinion, that Inoculation was safe and beneficial Practice; and from my having said among my Acquaintance that I intended to have my Child inoculated, as soon as he should have recovered sufficient strength from a Flux with which he had long been afflicted.

B. Franklin

❋

SO GREAT WERE FRANKLIN'S CONTRIBUTIONS to American journalism that he even made them while employed elsewhere. As co–deputy postmaster for the colonies in the mid–eighteenth century, he "drew up typically detailed procedures for running the service more efficiently, established the first home-delivery system and dead letter office, and took frequent inspection tours. Within a year, he had cut to one day the delivery time of a letter from New York to Philadelphia." Newspapers moved almost as fast, not only from New York to Philadelphia but up and down the entire East Coast. Now Boston could know what Charleston was thinking, Philadelphia could keep Richmond informed, New York could stay in touch with Baltimore. In fact, said Franklin, one of the main purposes of a postal system was "not to discourage the Spreading of Newspapers, which are on many Occasions Useful to Government and advantageous to Commerce and to the Publick." Franklin spread newspapers further by helping to create new ones, not only urging friends and in a few cases relatives to open print shops but also by investing in them. Many became successful, especially those whose owners followed Franklin's examples and took his advice. Like a modern media baron, he collected his share of the profits from them.

But newspapers were imperfect documents, and Franklin was perceptive enough not only to understand this but to explain the problems of journalism to his readers, asking for their forgiveness, or at least their understanding. In the summer of 1731, the *Pennsyl-*

vania Gazette presented an essay of Franklin's that has come to be known as "The Printer's Creed," and it is worth quoting at length.

Being frequently censur'd and condemn'd by different Persons for printing Things which they say ought not to be printed, I have sometimes thought it might be necessary to make a standing Apology for my self, and publish it once a Year, to be read upon all Occasions of that Nature. . . .

I request all who are angry with me on the Account of printing things they don't like, calmly to consider these following Particulars.

1. That the Opinions of Men are almost as various as their Faces; an Observation general enough to become a common Proverb, *So many Men so many Minds.*

2. That the Business of Printing has chiefly to do with Mens Opinions; most things that are printed tending to promote some, or oppose others.

3. That hence arises the peculiar Unhappiness of that Business, which other Callings are no way liable to; they who follow Printing being scarce able to do any thing in their way of getting a Living, which shall not probably give Offence to some, and perhaps to many; whereas the Smith, the Shoemaker, the Carpenter, or the Man of any other Trade, may work indifferently for People of all Persuasions, without offending any of them . . .

4. That it is unreasonable in any one Man or Set of Men to expect to be pleased with every thing that is printed, as to think that nobody ought to be pleased but themselves. . . .

7. That is it unreasonable to imagine Printers approve of every thing they print, and to censure them on any particular Thing accordingly; since in the way of their Business they print such great variety of Things opposite and contradictory.

8. That if all printers were determined not to print any Thing until they were sure it would offend no Body, there would be very little printed. . . .

10. I have heretofore fallen under the Resentment of Large Bodies of Men, for refusing absolutely to print any of their Party or Personal Reflections. In this Manner I have made my self many Enemies, and the constant Fatigue of denying is almost insupportable. But the Publick being unacquainted with all this, whenever the poor Printer happens either through Ignorance or much Persuasion, to do any thing that is generally thought worthy of Blame, he meets with no more Friendship or Favour on the above Account, than if there were no Merit in't at all.

But had it not been for the efforts of another man, someone far less celebrated than Benjamin Franklin, and far less skilled and visionary as a printer, colonial newspapers might never have played the role that they would soon begin to play in that most extraordinary of historical developments, the founding of the American republic.

CHAPTER SIX

The End of Authority

Numb. LXXIV

THE
New-York Weekly JOURNAL

Containing the freshest Advices, Foreign, and Domestick.

MUNDAY April 7th, 1735.

Sir.

IN my former I shewed, that allowing all that Mr. Murray wanted to prove, viz. That the Jurisdiction of the great Courts of England extend to New-York, the present supream Court of New-York, cannot exist lawfully, and exercise the same Powers which those Courts have; and I now further add, that no Ordinance of the Governor & Council, or even Act of the Legislature of this Province can give it the same Powers; because that cannot be done without destroying the Powers of the great Court of England, at least as relates to this Province: For, as I observed, both cannot have the same Powers at the same Time and in the same Place, and the Legisl.... in the same Place, and the Legisl.... of this province has no Kind of ... the great Courts or

and this must be with Respect Constitution: For if it be ta any other Sense, the Conclusio he draws from it will no The Word Fundamental co Foundation; so that when Thing is Fundamental of say, that that Thing is t on where on the other is b conceive that the Thin Foundation be taken ... ately perceive that t which is built upon down, and fall presume that any ceive how any o in England may Courts Establi without the l tution; and these Courts the Constit poses, but Proposition all his

*J*OHN PETER ZENGER'S CUSTOMERS were not always satisfied with his work. The documents he printed were sometimes sloppy, they complained: the lines uneven or the spacing off-center or the woodcuts too smudged to be discernible. His print shop was not a prosperous one; he could not afford the best equipment or a full complement of journeymen to assist him and, as a result, he would sometimes miss a deadline. That he became a true American hero, not only to his contemporaries but to journalists all the way up to the present, has less to do with Zenger himself than with the villain he would so publicly revile.

Enter William Cosby, royal governor of New York, who posed for a portrait at the time with his chin tucked in, his chest heaved out, and his lips pursed in a prissy kind of contemptuousness. He was, says John Tebbel, thoroughly unqualified for his position, "a lazy, lecherous, dissolute man who ruled by whim through a clique of sycophants."

But Cosby donned his black hat long before setting foot in New York; serving the Crown as governor of Minorca, one of the Balearic Islands off the eastern coast of Spain, he managed to make enemies among all classes of the population. "He was mean spirited," says Zenger biographer William Lowell Putnam, "a little military training had only taught him an affection for petty tyranny, and he was spiteful." Not to mention selfish, greedy, and as uncaring as could be about the lives and concerns of those he governed.

To make matters worse, Cosby was eventually caught with his

hands in the Minorcan treasury. He denied the charge, claiming to prize honesty above all other virtues, but no one believed him, and no one should have. He was forced to give up his position and leave the island immediately. When he did, it was with heavy valises and jingling pockets.

Rather than punishing him, though, the English ruler George II, who did not place a premium on integrity among his henchmen, assigned Cosby to New York. But it was a long trip, made all the longer by some personal business that Cosby had to address before setting off and, possibly, a stop he made en route. As a result, it took him six months to cross the Atlantic and report for his new posting. In the interim, with New York needing a chief executive, a man named Rip Van Dam was pressed into service. Cosby should have been grateful; Van Dam's presence had allowed him a longer absence. But he was not. No sooner did Cosby arrive in North America than he demanded that Van Dam pay him half the money he had made in his six months of service as governor, claiming that since the position was nominally Cosby's all that time, so were 50 percent of the proceeds.

Van Dam had never heard of such a thing, and refused to hear of it now; he told Cosby he was offended by both his venality and his thanklessness and would give him not so much as a penny. Cosby responded not only by suing Van Dam for the 50 percent but by ordering the chief justice of New York's court, Lewis Morris, to rule in the new governor's behalf. Morris refused. Cosby then threatened Morris, telling him that if he did not change his mind and order Van Dam to pay up immediately, he would be removed from the bench. Morris held fast. Cosby dismissed him. Morris swore revenge. The new governor's tenure was off to a contentious start.

Morris knew that revenge would not be easily achieved. In fact, under the law there was nothing he could do; the governor was within his rights to appoint and discharge justices of the court whenever he chose, without providing an explanation to anyone. So, as a few aggrieved parties had done before him and countless numbers have done since, Lewis Morris sought redemption in the press. He did not approach the *New York Gazette*, the colony's most influential paper, for it was also the official printer for the Crown in New York and would not risk its government contracts by taking issue with Cosby. Instead, Morris appealed to Zenger, formerly an apprentice at the *Gazette*, who had recently set up a shop of his own and begun to publish the *New-York Weekly Journal*. It was a paper that, in the hopes of a letter to the editor appearing in the first issue, would be "a Fort, impregnable by all Assaults of Vice, Folly, and Misfortunes, and a secure Rock against all the Casualties of Misery." In the Cosby case, at least, it would turn out to be just that.

Whatever his faults as a craftsman, Zenger was not a timid person. And, having been raised under the heel of an oppressive government in Germany's Upper Palatinate, he had no tolerance for similar rule by an American despot. Cosby, Zenger decided, was a threat to all that America seemed to stand for, and not just because of the way he had treated Morris. In his brief time in office, the governor had raised taxes on traders and merchants like Zenger; had refused to grant audiences, or even accept written communication, from those who disagreed with him on virtually any subject; had appointed his son to a government office for which he was not qualified and, because he was underage, not even eligible; and had several times made a "public display . . . of his debauchery, which the people were painfully aware they were financing."

Zenger told Morris he would be more than willing to volunteer his paper to the cause. Others, however, would turn out the articles; Zenger was far from being a gifted writer. A young attorney named James Alexander seems to have produced most of the *Weekly Journal*'s pieces against the governor, but with Cosby as the target, there was no shortage of volunteer marksmen to assist him. And with John Peter Zenger as printer, there was no shortage of desire to state the charges against Cosby forcefully and distribute them widely. He would get the most out of that old machinery of his; he would make his paper as legible and timely as could be.

The *Weekly Journal* set the stage for its campaign against the governor by publishing a two-part letter that did not even mention him by name. Instead, it declared that "[t]he Liberty of the Press is a Subject of the greatest Importance, and in which every Individual is as much concern'd as he is in any other Part of Liberty." Then Zenger proceeded to put that liberty to the test. In subsequent issues, the *Weekly Journal* admonished Cosby for all manner of offenses, among them cronyism in government and neglect of security—he had allowed French warships to sail unchallenged into New York Harbor, where they could spy on the city's defenses and perhaps, if provoked, even initiate an attack. There were also charges that the governor was lining his pockets with public funds in the New World no less than he had in Minorca. Cosby and his henchmen were not only crooks, said the *Weekly Journal*, but "monkeys" and "spaniels," animals in positions that would have been better served by human beings with consciences and a sense of civic responsibility.

The effect of all this, the paper went on, was that the citizens of New York were about to become slaves to a government that had no right to think of itself as their master.

Cosby was not a magnanimous sort in the best of circumstances. These, he let it be known, were among the worst. Here he was, a duly appointed representative of His Majesty, the King of England, and he was being excoriated in a public forum by a mere colonist, a laborer, a man who happened to run a printing press yet possessed no qualifications, no knowledge, and no "authority" to publish an opinion of any sort on anyone's actions, much less those of the Crown. It was not to be tolerated.

Cosby struck back at the *Weekly Journal* through the pages of the *New York Gazette*, which "directed a stream of vituperation at [Zenger] in the unbridled style of the era." Among the governor's contentions was that newspapers should remain silent about affairs of state. The *Weekly Journal* disagreed.

Some have said, IT IS NOT THE BUSINESS OF PRIVATE MEN TO MEDDLE WITH GOVERNMENT; a bold false and dishonest saying; and whoever says it either knows not what he says, or cares not, or slavishly speaks the Sense of others. It is a Cant now almost forgot in *England*, and which never prevailed but *when* LIBERTY *and the* CONSTITUTION *were attacked*, and never can prevail but upon the like Occasion.

Not only did the *Weekly Journal* refuse to be silent, it continued to speak out as boldly as its typefaces allowed. Although still refraining in most cases from calling Cosby by name, the paper never left any doubt about the subject of its excoriations. The governor had been hatching "SCHEMES OF GENERAL OPPRESSION AND PILLAGE, SCHEMES TO DEPRECIATE OR EVADE THE LAWs, RESTRAINTS UPON LIBERTY AND PROJECTS FOR ARBITRARY WILL." These were "INSTRUMENTS OF PUBLICK RUIN" and "have generally at once intailed misery upon their Country and their own race."

Cosby was not an easy man for a colonial newspaper to defend. The *New York Gazette*, with all those government printing contracts at stake and with a strong sense of loyalty to the Crown in virtually all of its edicts, regardless of their validity, gave it a try.

COSBY *the Mild, the happy, good and great,*
The strongest Guard of our little State;
Let Malecontents in crabbed Language write,
And the D—b H—s belch, tho' they cannot bite:
He unconcern'd will let the Wretches roar,
And govern Just, as others did before.

It was a children's-verse defense for a man of grown-up turpitude and folly.

❖

LETTERS TO THE EDITOR were more important to newspapers in colonial times than they are today. They took up more space, often an entire page or more out of the usual four, and they were as likely to furnish the paper's actual catalog of events as to offer a layman's commentary. They might be dropped off at the print shop by a reader, as Silence Dogood's ruminations were provided to the *New England Courant*, but they were just as likely to be ordered up by the publisher to suit his editorial desires.

It seems to have been just such a letter to the editor that brought matters to a head in the Zenger-Cosby controversy. In the autumn of 1734, the *Weekly Journal* published the opinion of a New Jersey resident who believed that there was "a Nullity of Laws" in New York. It was, to Cosby, a more serious charge than it perhaps sounds; he was, after all, the chief enforcer of laws in his colony, and by his own lights he had been enforcing them effectively. For a newspaper to charge otherwise was offensive. And for it to claim that as a result of a nullity of laws, "The Support of Government [will be] but temporary, and in a little Time will expire by its own Limitation" proved even more offensive. The *Weekly Journal* was predicting that Cosby's rule was so ineffective his subjects would soon rebel.

These were "Scandalous, Virulent and Seditious Reflections," the governor replied, and offered a reward of fifty pounds (more than $11,000 today) for the identity of the "Wicked Authors" responsible for them. He also ordered the publisher's arrest, accusing him of criminal libel and setting bail at 800 pounds (more than $180,000 at present). Zenger could not even come close to raising such a sum; he had no choice but to surrender to authorities, who promptly escorted him to a jail cell and, for the first week, permitted him no contact with the outside world. He could not receive visitors, could not write notes to James Alexander or anyone else.

As a result, the *Weekly Journal* missed an issue, and Zenger, believing he had let down his subscribers, despaired. The following week, however, his captors relented. They allowed the prisoner's wife to visit and to provide him with writing materials, placing no restrictions on his use of them. Zenger felt as if he had been reprieved and, further, given a sign to resume his verbal warfare against William Cosby. Through his wife, he issued instructions to Alexander to write further exposés of the governor. Zenger even turned out an article himself for the next issue.

To all my Subscribers and Benefactors who take my Weekly Journall, Gentlemen, Ladies and Others;

AS you last week were Disappointed of my *Journall*, I think it Incumbent upon me, to publish my Apoligy which is this. On the Lords Day, the Seventeenth of this Instant I was Arrested, taken and Imprisoned in the common Gaol of this City, by Virtue of a Warrant from the *Governor* . . . I was put under such Restraint that I had not the Liberty of Pen, Ink, or Paper, or to see, or speak with People, till upon my Complaint to the Honourable the Chief Justice, at my appearing before him upon my *Habias Corpus* on the *Wednesday* following. Who discountenanced that Proceeding, and therefore I have had since that time the Liberty of Speaking through the Hole of the Door, to my Wife and Servants by which I doubt not yo'l think me sufficiently Excused for not sending my last weeks *Journall*, and I hope for the future by the Liberty of Speaking to my servants Thro' the Hole of the Door of the Prison, to entertain you with My weekly *Journall* as formerly. *And am your obliged Humble Servant.*

Zenger continued to oversee publication of the *New-York Weekly Journal*, his editor's office now a jail cell, until his trial began nine months later.

❁

ON AUGUST 4, 1735, New York City Hall was overrun by people attracted not so much by the momentousness of the issue as by their disgust for the plaintiff. Some did not even know the charges Cosby had filed; they simply wanted to encourage a court to rule against him regardless of the reason, and to support a man willing to criticize him so often and so publicly. "In the height of summer," writes William Lowell Putnam, "one can only imagine that the physical heat of the scene was fully as great as the political."

Things did not start out well for Zenger. The judge was James DeLancey, who, worse than being just a Cosby lickspittle, was in fact the very man the governor had appointed to succeed Lewis Morris on the bench after Morris defied the governor in the Van Dam matter. Worse yet, in instructing the grand jury that had indicted Zenger some months earlier, DeLancey had accused the printer of "seditious Libels" which "with the utmost Virulency have endeavored to asperse his Excellency and vilify his Administration." The judge, in other words, was something less than an impartial arbiter.

Given these circumstances, Zenger's attorneys, not unreasonably, asked DeLancey to remove himself from the case. DeLancey refused. Furthermore, he told the counselors that their request was an insult to whatever integrity he believed he possessed, and he threw them out of the courtroom; according to one account, he even tried later to have the two men disbarred for their impertinence. The proceedings were barely under way and already poor John Peter Zenger, a man of conviction but not of means, was sitting alone at the defendant's table, confused and alarmed and certain about nothing except that whatever happened next would make matters even worse for him than they were at present.

He was wrong. After a few confusing days, fifty-nine-year-old Andrew Hamilton strode into James DeLancey's courtroom, pulled up a chair next to Zenger, and announced that he was taking over the defense. It is likely, if not certain, that Zenger had heard of Hamilton; although he lived in Philadelphia, he was known throughout New York—and, in fact, in most of the colonies—for his "legal and oratorical brilliance." He dressed fashionably, carried himself regally, and wore his full head of white hair upswept in such a manner that when it rose into view, some observers thought of a large, proud ship riding the waves into shore.

Hamilton was also a man with a famous friend, Benjamin Franklin, whom he had known for many years and in whose company he had once sailed to Europe. Franklin may, in fact, have secretly arranged for Hamilton to take over Zenger's defense, believing that the case was an important one, not just for the *New-York Weekly Journal* but for all of American journalism.

Hamilton opened his defense of Zenger by surprising not only his client and the judge but all within earshot. At the time, the law did not permit truth to be used as a defense for libel. In fact, as was said at the time, perverse though it seems, "The Greater the Truth, the Greater the Libel." A jury had but two questions to answer in a case of this sort: Was the material in question libelous; that is, did it maliciously and unjustly defame its subject? And had the material appeared, as charged, in a given publication?

Hamilton conceded both points. To those in attendance at the trial, it seemed that he had also conceded defeat. The judge certainly thought so; when Hamilton continued to speak, DeLancey interrupted him. There is nothing more to be determined here, he said to the jury; the defendant's counsel has admitted the validity of the plaintiff's position, "[a]nd that is a matter of law, no doubt, and which you may leave to the Court."

Hamilton paused; he may even have smiled. Then he brushed a hand dramatically through his white shock of hair and began immediately to add to his reputation for brilliance under fire.

Unable to argue the innocence of his client, Hamilton argued instead the error of the law. Truth had to be a defense against libel, he claimed. Truth had to be served regardless of the repercussions and regardless of whether the person who felt the repercussions was a governor or a smithy, a throne-sitter or a weaver. The statutes of the Crown had to be subservient to logic. "The question before the Court," Hamilton said, "and you, gentlemen of the Jury, is not of small or private concern; it is not the cause of a poor printer, nor of New York alone, which you are trying. No! it may, in its consequences, affect every freeman that lives under a British government on the main of America." To publish by authority, Hamilton well knew even if he did not say it before Judge DeLancey, was to publish the dictates of authority.

Zenger must be found not guilty, Hamilton insisted, because a free press in the New World must be found not guilty.

> Power may justly be compared to a great river which, while kept within its due bounds is both beautiful and useful; but when it overflows its banks, it is then too impetuous to be stemmed, it bears down on all before it and brings destruction and desolation wherever it comes. If this then is the nature of power, let us at least do our duty and like wise men use our utmost care to support liberty, the only bulwark against lawless power. . . .

It was liberty about which Hamilton really wanted to speak, liberty, which was to him

> the best cause . . . and I make no doubt but your upright conduct, this day, will not only entitle you to the love and esteem of your fellow-citizens, but every man, who prefers freedom to a life of slavery, will bless and honor you, as men who have baffled the attempt of tyranny; and, by an impartial verdict, have laid a noble foundation for securing to ourselves, our posterity, and our neighbors, that to which nature and the laws of our country have given us a right—the liberty—both of exposing and opposing arbitrary power in these parts of the world at least, by speaking and writing truth.

Judge DeLancey was not moved. He admitted Hamilton's eloquence, and may even have acknowledged it in that imperious manner of his, but he reminded the jury that virtually every word

Hamilton had uttered was irrelevant. He told its members yet again that the fate of John Peter Zenger was to be decided solely on the basis of whether the publisher had, in fact, allowed the pages of the *Weekly Journal* to impugn the character of the lawfully appointed governor of the royal colony of New York—and there was no denying, even by Hamilton, that he had.

But the jury was of a different mind. It listened carefully to the judge's instructions and, as soon as he finished, tramped out of the courtroom and ignored them, spending but a few minutes in seclusion, then returning to announce a decision that not only astonished observers of the period but has echoed through the ages. John Peter Zenger was not guilty. The fault, as Hamilton had insisted, belonged to the law.

"The reception of the verdict by the crowd was enormous," writes William Lowell Putnam. "Reflecting public approval of this rebuff to the unpopular governing elite, shouts of joy filled the hall." A few men whistled; a few threw their hats in the air; men and women alike clapped their hands. Judge DeLancey tried to restore order, even threatening the celebrants with prison. But it seems likely that his words were not even heard. They were certainly not heeded.

Zenger was released from jail the next morning, and he wasted no time in getting back to work, once again editing the *Weekly Journal* as it continued its reporting on the events of the day in New York, the hearings and ordinances, the robberies and fires, the comings and goings of ships, the openings and closings of shops, and, most notably for the time being, the results of its publisher's trial.

[T]he jury having taken the Information out with them, they returned in about Ten Minutes, and found me *Not Guilty*; upon which there were immediately three Hurra's of many Hundreds of People in the presence of the Court, before the Verdict was returned. The next Morning my Discharge was moved for and granted, and sufficient was subscribed by my fellow Citizens for payment of sundry Debts, for which I was also charged in Custody, and about Noon I had my Liberty from my long Imprisonment above eight Months.

Accounts of the verdict in the British press were more enthusiastic than Zenger's. According to a letter from a Londoner to Benjamin Franklin's *Pennsylvania Gazette*, published much later, reports of the publisher's fate were "so greedily read and so highly applauded. . . . Our political Writers of different Factions, who never agreed in any thing else, have mentioned the Trial in their public Writings with an Air of Rapture and Triumph. A *Goliath* in Learning and Politics gave his opinion of Mr. *Hamilton's* Argument in these terms, *If it is not Law it is better than Law, it Ought to be Law, and Will Always be Law wherever Justice prevails.*"

Hamilton left New York the day after the trial, returning to Philadelphia. Wrote the *Weekly Journal*, "he was saluted with the great Guns of several Ships in the Harbour, as a public Testimony of the glorious Defence he made in the Cause of Liberty in this Province." Later, New York's board of aldermen would send Hamilton a present, a gold box containing the keys to the city.

John Peter Zenger also continued to inform his readers about the malfeasance of William Cosby, who insisted again that he was being wronged in print just as he had been wronged in the courtroom by this commoner, this laborer, this mere drudge of the printing press and the band of perversely supportive jackals who somehow found their way onto the jury. But fewer people were paying attention now; although still the colonial governor, Cosby had become as much a joke to the people of New York as he had ever been a ruler. He died the following year, cursing Zenger to the end.

❋

THE JOHN PETER ZENGER TRIAL was a landmark in the history of American journalism, the first significant court decision in its behalf. Although another six decades would pass before the truth was formally acknowledged as a defense against libel, lawyer and author Seymour Wishman believes that Zenger was responsible for an important precedent. "The independence of the jury was established in America," Wishman writes, "when the role of the jury as conscience of the community was recognized." The role of the newspaper as conscience was also recognized. As a result, the Zenger verdict encouraged more colonists to go into the newspaper business, more editors to speak their minds openly, and more readers to put their trust in those editors. And it allowed future newspapers to expand the boundaries of free speech, to move into all sorts of territory that would have been unimaginable without Zenger's having crossed the frontier.

The verdict also was the first substantial piece of evidence that the colonies had recourse against those actions of the Crown it found unjust. In other words, the jury's decision was a political victory for Americans no less than a journalistic one, and this author believes that Hamilton knew it, and was aiming at such an outcome, all along. Consider his words again. Read them out of the context in which he uttered them.

The question before the Court . . . may, in its consequences, affect every freeman that lives under a British government on the main of America.

And:

[L]et us at least do our duty and like wise men use our utmost care to support liberty.

And:

[E]very man, who prefers freedom to a life of slavery, will bless and honor you, as men who have baffled the attempt of tyranny

. . . exposing and opposing arbitrary power in these parts of the world at least, by speaking and writing truth.

It was one of the first such arguments ever made in America— in so formal a setting, at least—and there would be many more in the years ahead. For Hamilton does not seem to be pleading here merely for freedom of the press; he seems, rather, to be pleading for freedom from the caprices of authoritarian rule. And in fact it was precisely the kind of grievances that the people of New York felt against William Cosby, and the struggles of the Crown to suppress criticism of them, that led to the first disputes between England and its American colonies—disputes that in turn led to even more disagreements of an even more substantial nature and then, in another forty years, to the blood and fury of war. After the Zenger trial, independence was in the air, however tentatively. Perhaps more important, it was also on the page, and it would remain there for the duration.

II

THE APPROACH OF WAR

✸

CHAPTER SEVEN

Severing the Snake

A FEW YEARS LATER, ever alert for new opportunities, Benjamin Franklin decided to publish the first magazine in the colonies. So did a competitor, William Bradford, editor of the *Pennsylvania Journal* and the owner of a coffeehouse where a number of Philadelphians came to sip their beverages as they read his paper. Both men wanted a new kind of news, more thoughtful and enduring and lengthier in presentation than what they were now supplying. Newspapers were introductions to the events of the day; magazines could provide details. Newspapers offered the facts of most recent vintage; magazines could provide background.

And, being businessmen as well as purveyors of current events, Franklin and Bradford were interested in a new source of revenue, a use to which to put their printing presses when they were not turning out weekly or biweekly papers.

Franklin and Bradford raced to print, and Bradford won. On February 13, 1741, he published the first issue of the *American Magazine, or A Monthly View of the Political State of the British Colonies.* Among other things, it would report on "Party-Disputes, carried on in other publick Prints, which may tend to clear up any controverted Points, or discover the Springs and Motives of Action." It would introduce "Accounts of remarkable Trials as well *Civil* as *Criminal*" and "Collections and Abstracts from other Papers." It was also meant to provide a service to people, many of whom did not live within range of a newspaper—or at least not the right kind of newspaper.

As several Colonies have no Printing-Press, and in others where there is but one, and even in those Places where there are more, it is complained (whether with Justice or not we do not undertake to determine) that the Printers are often under the Influence of parties, and cannot, with much Difficulty, be prevailed upon to publish any Thing against the Side of Question they are of themselves.

Three days after Bradford's *American Magazine* first appeared, Franklin answered with the *General Magazine and Historical Chronicle for all the British Plantations in America*, which aimed to be "as entertaining and useful as possible." Surprisingly, though, for a Franklin publication, it seemed to emphasize the latter at the expense of the former. In addition to essays from other journals and some verse that was not much better than the lines Franklin himself had written as an apprentice for the *New England Courant*, the magazine provided "*Brief Historical and Chronological* NOTES *of several Princes, States, Governments, &c.*," "*Proceedings in the Parliament of* Great-Britain *on the Affair of Paper Money in the* American Colonies," and an "*Account of the Export of Provisions from* Philadelphia, *Anno* 1740."

It sounds like a table of contents inspired by John Campbell, not Benjamin Franklin.

Among other such publications to appear between midcentury and the start of the Revolutionary War were the *Royal American Magazine* in Boston and the *Monthly Magazine for the British Colonies* in Philadelphia. They, too, were more ponderous than engaging. And they were not good business: too many pages, too much expense, too few readers and advertisers. It was from newspapers that most Americans continued to learn about the events of their world, and in the early 1740s a dozen of them were being published in the colonies:

- In Massachusetts, the *Boston News-Letter*, the *Boston Gazette*, the *Boston Evening-Post*, the *Boston Post-Boy*, and the *New England Weekly Journal*

- In Pennsylvania, the *American Weekly Mercury* and the *Pennsylvania Gazette* (both in Philadelphia)

- In New York, the New York *Weekly Journal* and the *New York Gazette*

- In Maryland, the *Maryland Gazette* (Annapolis)

- In South Carolina, the *South Carolina Gazette* (Charleston)

- In Virginia, the *Virginia Gazette* (Williamsburg)*

In 1754, the *Boston Gazette* had a circulation of about 600. So did the city's other journals. Figures were similar for the papers in the colonies nearby: 500 here, 400 there, 700 somewhere else on a particularly good day. Circulation would not pass 1,000 for any American newspaper until the postal service improved, as it was now beginning to do under former publisher and now Co–Deputy Postmaster Franklin, and until relations with Britain worsened, as they were now beginning to do under Georges II and III. Historian Arthur M. Schlesinger has calculated that in 1765, the year Parliament passed the Stamp Act and bonfires of protest spread through the colonies in response, "the *New-York Journal* had 1500 [subscribers]; in 1768 the *Boston Chronicle*, a Tory publication, 1500; in 1770 the *Pennsylvania Chronicle*, 2500."

By the time another four years had passed, several more publications were up and running. The one that Campbell had started

---

*The term "gazette," which originally referred to an official government publication, once appeared in the names of a majority of American newspapers but has since lost favor. Of the 100 largest daily papers in the United States in 2004, only three called themselves a gazette.

early in the century in his post office had merged with another: "the *Massachusetts Gazette and Boston News-Letter* and the *New-York Gazetteer* . . . possessed 1500 and 3600 [subscribers] respectively; and in 1775 the *Constitutional Gazette* in New York mustered over 2000, while the *Boston Gazette* and the *Massachusetts Spy* (before the outbreak of war forced them from Boston) boasted 2000 and 3500 each."

It was a boom time for American journalism, the first it had ever known, and the papers of the era were quick to praise themselves for their growth and increasing importance to the colonial public. The following appeared in the *New York Gazette, or, Weekly Post-Boy* in the spring of 1770:

'Tis truth (with deference to the college)
News-papers are the spring of knowledge,
The general source through the nation,
Of every modern conversation.
What would this mighty people do,
If there, alas! were nothing new?
A news-paper is like a feast,
Some dish there is for every guest;
Some large, some small, some strong, some tender,
For every stomach, stout or slender.

And, not to be outdone, from the *New-York Journal* three days later:

Our services you can't express,
The good we do you hardly guess;
There's not a want of human kind,
But we a remedy can find.

❀

MUCH OF THE NEWS in American papers of the eighteenth century was political, and much of the political news was foreign. In the 1740s, for example, the colonists followed the Wars of the Austrian Succession, even though, in addition to Austria, their repercussions were felt primarily in France, Spain, Bavaria, Saxony, Sardinia, Poland, and Prussia—not in North America. And they followed the ongoing struggles between England and France, not only in Europe but in India, where the two nations were vying for control of trade routes. They followed them not necessarily because they found them relevant, but because they were entertaining, tales of royal intrigue and foolhardy adventure that appealed for the same reasons as fictional tales of the same nature.

But some of the foreign news did have domestic repercussions, and it was these reports that engaged Americans most. In 1733, for instance, Parliament passed the Molasses Act, taxing not only molasses but also sugar imported from the parts of the West Indies that were not under British control. The Act meant to eliminate competition from the French and to create a monopoly in molasses and sugar for subjects of the Crown.

The colonists read intently about the new law. They just as intently ignored its requirements—so intently, in fact, that the legislation was eventually repealed. One of the most popular activities in America at the time, as it had been from the beginning and would long continue to be, was drinking rum; the colonists were not about to pay higher taxes for the beverage's principal ingredient.

Americans were no less interested in newspaper accounts of the French and Indian War, from 1754 to 1763. Some of the battles were fought in Europe, where they began in 1756 and were more commonly known as the Seven Years' War. But North America was the primary battleground, with the French and Indians fighting the British and their colonial brethren for control of the New World from the Allegheny Mountains to the Mississippi River, and for the lands around the Great Lakes and Lakes George and Champlain in what are today New York and Vermont. The French wanted to settle at least some of the territory. The Indians wanted to continue living in the rest of it, hunting and fishing and worshipping as they had been doing for centuries. The British wanted to expand their North American colonies. The clashes that developed as a result of these conflicting desires soon began to threaten the colonies' very existence.

Early on, the *Pennsylvania Gazette* reported that the French and Indians were on the move in the Ohio region: 400 Frenchmen were coming up the Ohio River, 600 Indians were preparing to join them, and "many more French are expected from Canada." The *Gazette* further stated that the Americans in their path feared they would be scalped or murdered, and it lamented "the present disunited State of the British Colonies, and the extreme Difficulty of bringing so many different Governments and Assemblies to agree on any speedy and effectual Measures for our common Defence and Security."

What is most notable about the issue of the *Gazette* in which this report appeared is not the article itself but what the paper published directly beneath it—a visual exhortation for the colonists to resist their French and Indian attackers. It was a woodcut of a snake, hacked into eight pieces, each of them bearing the initials of a colony: S.C., N.C., V., M., P., N.J., N.Y., N.E. (New England). "JOIN OR DIE," the caption read, and many colonists believed their options were precisely that stark. Benjamin Franklin no longer owned the *Gazette*; he had sold his share in 1748 and begun to involve himself in colonial politics. But some people believed the severed snake was his idea. Others thought he might even have drawn it himself; he was, after all, a man of boundless talent. It was the first editorial cartoon ever published in an American newspaper, and would in time acquire a different and even more provocative meaning. Franklin never admitted that it was his doing.

❊

IN THE SPRING OF 1765, the Stamp Act became law and a dividing line was crossed in American history. Before the Act, few colonists longed to be free of British rule, and fewer still conceded the possibility that such a desire would lead to violence; those who were dissatisfied with various measures of the Crown thought in terms of renegotiating the conditions of dependence, nothing more—certainly nothing as extreme as attempting to launch a nation of their own.

But to many the Stamp Act was a sign that the colonies would never be taken seriously or treated fairly by the nation that was home to most of them. Perhaps it was even a sign that they no longer had a home—not, at least, as they had thought of it before. Even those Americans who had been most optimistic about the intentions of the British government began to lose hope; as a result, it was the pessimists who took the lead in planning for the future. And it was the pessimists who began to dominate the press.

News that Parliament had approved the Stamp Act rode the waves slowly across the Atlantic. But once it landed in the colonies, it spread quickly; there were now twenty-four newspapers in America, twice as many as there had been two and a half decades earlier, and almost all of them were opposed to the new law. It was, in fact, the Stamp Act that first introduced Americans to the notion of "taxation without representation," a phrase that became a rallying cry and the first slogan of the upcoming mutiny.

The Act was a comprehensive one, imposing taxes on virtually every kind of colonial printed matter, from legal documents to playing cards, from diplomas to licenses to contracts, and even on some nonprinted matter, like dice, which were the companions of playing cards in some games. The colonists were to purchase the stamps from an official known as the Stamp Commissioner; they were then to affix them to all relevant items they possessed (although one wonders how a stamp could be stuck to a die and be expected to roll). An item covered by the Act but left unstamped would subject its owner to a fine or imprisonment.

To many Americans, though, newspapers seemed the Act's primary target. It "assessed a halfpenny on each copy of a newspaper printed on what was called 'half a sheet' and a penny on the next larger size. It then added 2s. [shillings] for each advertisement, an amount which by any standard was excessive, since the publisher himself received only from 3 to 5s. and still less for repeated insertions."

In other words, the tax was not just a subject for the American press to report; it was a burden on the press's very existence. It was a "fatal *Black-Act*," as one journalist of the era called it, even though newspapers in England had been paying a similar tax, without uproar, for more than half a century. And even though on at least two previous occasions, the British had taxed newspapers in Boston and New York, again without uproar. And even though, as historian Bernard Bailyn concedes, "the sums involved were in fact quite small."

True enough, all of it. But the Stamp Act was more sweeping than the previous measures had been, taxing a greater number of goods, and its timing was much worse. Some colonists had been accumulating grievances against the Crown since the *New England Courant* first began to detail them, if not even before. Others had not, and, having been caught off guard by what seemed the punitive nature of the Stamp Act, were even more offended. After all, the tax had been imposed less than two years after the end of the French and Indian War, which for the Americans had been a time of great hardship and sacrifice, and for which they were trying to pay by taxing themselves.

But the war had been an even greater expense in England, as had other wars going back to the previous century, and as were the continuing hostilities with France in both the New World and the Old. For this reason, members of Parliament saw the new levies as not only fair but essential, and, to the extent that they thought of the American reaction at all, they assumed it would be acquiescent. Surely Americans understood their responsibility to help the motherland with its bills. Surely they understood the need for an outpost of the empire to subordinate itself to the Crown. And just as surely, believed those who sat so distantly in Parliament, the Stamp Act would eliminate most, if not all, of the nearly eternal British deficit; and the Americans, still Englishmen at heart, could take a certain satisfaction from that. At the very least, members of Parliament wanted to prevent their fellow citizens of the British Isles from being subjected to a tax increase of their own. The legislation, it seemed to them, was the ideal solution to a deep-rooted problem.

Americans did not agree. For some, the initial reaction was "daze and indecision." Benjamin Franklin, now an agent for the colonies in England, spoke for many of his fellow citizens of the New World when he said that he "had not only a respect, but an affection, for Great Britain." For that reason, he felt sorrow more than anger at Parliament's action. "I think [the Stamp Act] will affect the Printers more than anybody," he said, "as a Sterling Halfpenny Stamp on every Half Sheet of a Newspaper, and Two Shillings Sterling on every Advertisement, will go near to knock up one Half of both." But he did not discuss his reservations with British officials, nor did he write them up for his old newspaper, the *Pennsylvania Gazette*. Publicly, Franklin urged restraint, asking Americans to abide by the Stamp Act, at least until he and his fellow colonial agents could help persuade Parliament that it had made a mistake.

America did not listen to him. According to a proclamation of the Massachusetts Assembly, "The Stamp Act wholly cancels the very conditions upon which our ancestors, with much toil and blood, and at their sole expense, settled this country and enlarged his majesty's dominions." John Adams, who would later serve in the assembly, believed that the Act did what no act of a governing body should ever do, sanction inequality, "taking from the poorer sort of people all their little subsistence, and conferring it on a set of stamp officers, distributors and their deputies." And George Washington, at the time engaged in battle against the French and Indians, warned that "[t]he Stamp Act engrosses the conversation of the speculative part of the colonies, who look upon this unconstitutional method of taxation as a direful attack upon their liberties and loudly exclaim against the violation."

Before long, the colonists began to express themselves in deed rather than word, and newspapers reported that there had been outbreaks of violence in a number of colonies—Pennsylvania, Connecticut, Maryland, and New Jersey among them. Stamp commissioners were being hanged in effigy and forced to resign and in some cases physically assaulted, and supplies of stamps and stamped papers were being burned, thrown into rivers, and cast to the winds.

In South Carolina, angry colonists broke into the homes of two commissioners and upended furniture, scattered clothing, and hurled rocks through windows. "A New York crowd," one historian writes, "led by two carpenters in the ship construction yards, wrecked some property and hanged the governor in effigy, using an elaborately prepared dummy that included Satan whispering in the chief executive's ear."

But the American press did not merely publicize the actions of others; it began to encourage those actions by setting forth its own opinions:

The *New Hampshire Gazette*: "*I must die*, or submit to that which *is worse* than Death, *be Stamp'd*, and lose my freedom."

The *Boston Gazette*: "AWAKE!—Awake, my Countrymen, and, by a regular & legal Opposition, defeat the Designs of those who enslave us and our Posterity."

The *New York Mercury*: "Alas! What have we done to merit such treatment from our Mother Country, and our Brethren? Have we deserved to be this degraded and dishonoured, and used by them, as the most inveterate Enemies? What strange infatuation has prevailed in their Councils: To distress, ruin and enslave us, when our rights and privileges are precisely the same, and our Interests inseparably united."

The *Boston Evening-Post*: "Saturday last was executed Henry

Halbert . . . for the murder of the son of Jacob Woolman.—*He will never pay any of the taxes unjustly laid on these once happy lands.*"

These were not editorials. There were no such things as editorials in the newspapers of the colonial period.

❁

SOME PAPERS CONTINUED TO PUBLISH without stamps, openly defying the British mandate. John Holt, of the *New York Gazette, or, Weekly Post-Boy,* said he had no choice; he could not order stamped paper from the Crown "without certain Destruction to his Person and Property from the General Resentment of his Countrymen."

Other papers found a loophole in the Stamp Act, for the time being at least: according to the new law, "[i]f a newspaper were published without title or masthead, it was technically no longer a newspaper and therefore not taxable." So a paper would not reveal its name as prominently as before, perhaps tucking it into the body of a story, perhaps dropping the name altogether, although its subscribers would still recognize it from the typeface and layout.

Other journals ignored the tax in more devious fashion, claiming on their front pages that there was "*No Stamped Paper to be had,*" and thus, however much they might regret defying the Crown, they were forced to go to press with the untaxable variety.

A few papers went out of business, at least for the nonce, and one of them did so in especially melodramatic fashion. On October 31, 1765, William Bradford set the columns in his *Philadelphia Journal* so that they resembled a tombstone; there were black borders, black margins, and two sets of skull and crossbones, one at the top of the front page and another in the lower right-hand corner. The front page read, in part:

EXPIRING: IN THE HOPES OF A RESURRECTION TO LIFE AGAIN

I am sorry to be obliged to acquaint my readers, that as the

Stamp Act is feared to be obligatory upon us after the Fifth of November ensuing (the fatal Tomorrow) the Publisher of this Paper unable to bear the Burden, has thought it expedient to stop a while, in order to deliberate whether any method can be found to elude the chains forged upon us, and escape the Insupportable Slavery; which it is hoped from the just representations now made against that Act; may be effected

William Bradford

The *Maryland Gazette* also went on Stamp Act–induced hiatus; when it began publishing again, its masthead announced that what readers held in their hands was but "[a]n Apparition of the late Maryland Gazette, which is not Dead but Sleepeth."

Newspapers that stopped printing for any length of time were forced to lay off workers, and the papers still on the market published stories about them, lamenting their plight and castigating the British for having brought it about. In the larger cities, the newly unemployed took to the streets. In some cases they simply marched in random paths cursing the legislation that had idled them; in others, they set upon the stamp commissioners, chasing them from their quarters, vandalizing them, and then setting fire to the stamps left behind.

Several papers even brought back the *Pennsylvania Gazette*'s severed snake. Initially employed to exhort the colonists to unite against the French and Indians, who were foes long acknowledged, it was now pressed into service to promote a unanimity of response against the British, who had, since the beginning of the colonial experiment, been friend, neighbor, family. The snake made the transition nicely. Had this been a more recent time, it would almost certainly have become a symbol for mass consumption, printed on T-shirts, stuck onto automobile bumpers, and perhaps, in the case of the especially zealous, tattooed onto forearms. "Unite or die" would have been written on placards and chanted by protesters in the streets.

Letters to the editor in a number of papers suggested a petition to colonial authorities to express dismay at the Stamp Act, and a few urged a boycott on British goods. According to some reports of the time, which do not seem to this author credible, the boycott was so successful, at least in the short term, that it reduced the amount of British imports by 50 percent.

Journals that were favorable to the Crown, both in the colonies and abroad, could not understand the fuss or the explosive forms it took or what they perceived to be the virtually treasonous impulses behind it. They took their cue from New York Lieutenant Governor Cadwallader Colden, who said that the opposition press showed "every falshood that malice could invent to serve their purpose of exciting the People to disobedience of the Laws & to Sedition. At first they only denied the authority of Parliament to lay internal Taxes in the Colonies, but at last they have denied the Legislative authority of the Parliament in the colonies. . . . " Pro-British publications also took their cue from the Royal Governor of New Jersey, who criticized "the many Seditious inflammatory Writings" appearing in so many American papers. Another official of the Crown cursed those writings because, he said, they "*excluded every thing that tended to cool the minds of the people.*"

Ultimately, however, the hot minds would not be denied. On May 16, 1766, Bostonians learned that, after a long and acrimonious debate, Parliament had repealed the Stamp Act a month and a half earlier. It was "GLORIOUS NEWS," the newspapers declared, some of them in the largest and blackest type they had ever employed. The decision was received, said the *Boston Post-Boy & Advertiser*, with "the inexpressible Joy of all." Some newspapers, rather than charging for the editions that printed the Stamp Act's obituary, gave them away for free, and people ran through the streets with them, ducking into shops and taverns and even churches, waving the papers over their heads, reciting lines from the stories as if they were an incantation of some sort, and passing the journals around from so many people to so many other people that, ultimately, the most visible signs of the day's emotions might not have been pumping fists or enormous grins but ink-stained hands.

According to an Englishman writing to the *Newport Mercury*, even King George III was delighted by the repeal. "His Majesty seemed much pleased, and in high spirits," the correspondent claimed, although it is hard to imagine the monarch flashing a grin about colonial insurrection, Parliamentary capitulation, and a loss of revenue for the Exchequer linked in one unforeseen chain of events.

The *Virginia Gazette*, however, looked back in a more sober mood, troubled at how close a call it had been. "There is no doubt but [British Prime Minister George] Grenville's management had nearly drawn England and her colonies into hostilities, had really shut up commerce between them, the life of both, and this for a trifle. A much superior wisdom, and a far better temper, saved us, and them, when we were, where his blindness and obstinacy pushed us, at the very edge of the precipice." The *Gazette* clearly feared that the colonies would stand at another precipice before long.

The Stamp Act would not have been rescinded so quickly had it not been for the fiery rhetoric of American newspapers, of that there is no doubt. A letter in the *New Hampshire Gazette* claimed that "[t]he press hath never done greater service since its first invention." Certainly the press had never demonstrated such power before, and it is reasonable to assume that even those who wrote and edited the papers were surprised by the attention people had paid to them and the extent to which they had been moved by the reporting either to action or to a different or stronger opinion. A newspaper might be more than just a means of informing the populace; it might, in certain circumstances, act as an irresistible force to contend with an immovable object.

❁

IT WOULD SOON RESIST ALL THE MORE. The year after the Stamp Act was repealed, Parliament, simultaneously demonstrating deficiencies in both hindsight and foresight, imposed a new set of taxes on the colonies, "once again placing itself directly behind the mule's hind legs," as Kenneth Davis puts it in his lighthearted volume, *Don't Know Much About History*. The taxes were named after Chancellor of the Exchequer Charles Townshend—a dubious honor—and the so-called Townshend Acts were a miscellany, once again slapping a levy on paper but adding to the list such unrelated items as glass, lead, paint, and tea.

The colonists, of course, would not have been receptive to the Acts under any circumstances. But they were even less so when they learned that the purpose of the Townshend Acts was to raise money for the salaries of royal officials in America, to whom many of their subjects objected both personally and in principle. Far from wanting to provide those officials with compensation, the Americans wanted them to go back to England and earn their keep some other way, in a manner not so injurious to colonial commerce or offensive to colonial sensibilities.

Again there were calls, both in the press and in the streets, for a boycott of British goods; again there were estimates that its success rate was 50 percent or higher. There were also calls for Americans to develop their own manufacturing capability so that they did not have to rely so heavily on British products. A few papers, at least on a few occasions, offered free advertising to local merchants and manufacturers, hoping they would take advantage of it to promote their products and encourage readers to purchase them rather than goods made abroad.

The Townshend Acts were repealed in 1770—all but one of them, that is, and a most unfortunate one, as things would turn out. But American newspapers were much more restrained in their celebrations than they had been with the repeal of the Stamp Act. They expressed their approval and were pleased that Parliament had come to its senses; Benjamin Franklin seemed especially relieved, although, commenting on the exception, he said that the "Duty on Tea . . . remains to continue the Dispute."

Not everything, however, was dire. Not every American newspaper suggested in every issue that the colonists and the British were growing irrevocably apart, and even those that did were more often than not restrained in their coverage. They continued to run their ads, to print government documents, to tell of the openings of new shops, the arrivals and departures of ships and coaches. They continued to report on marriage, including that of "Miss Grace Coit, of this Town, a young Lady embellish'd with every Qualification requisite to render a married life agreeable," and to report on death, including that of one Edward Ashby, "a very inoffensive man, in the hundred and ninth year of his Age," and of John Levine, whose spirit "ascended to the Skies."

For the most part, though, the colonial press was certain that there would be more trouble ahead between the Old World and the New, and could not help but wonder how soon it would appear and what forms it would take.

❁

THE MOST FAMOUS of journalistic responses to the Townshend Acts, and possibly the most famous of all prewar rebuttals to the Crown to emerge from a print shop, was eloquent, lengthy, and repetitious: a dozen articles called *Letters from an American Farmer in Pennsylvania to the Inhabitants of the British Colonies*, written by John Dickinson. They appeared in the *Pennsylvania Chronicle* from December 2, 1767, to February 15, 1768, and were not what they seemed—not, as historian Walter A. McDougall tells us, "letters in the sense of real correspondence, but a series of tracts. Dickinson was not a farmer, but an accomplished lawyer trained at Middle Temple in London. He did have a residence in Philadelphia, but he was born in Maryland and raised in Delaware."

Prior to that, he had lived a life of moneyed ease, having been tutored privately on his father's 16,000-acre plantation. When he went to London to study law at Middle Temple, the most prestigious institution of its kind, he became "one of the few political activists of his day to see the mother country at first hand."

As a result, Dickinson's analysis of British tax policies was reasoned, thorough, dispassionate, and decidedly negative. He did not want the colonies to separate from the motherland, but neither did he want the relationship between the two to continue under its present terms. In the second of his letters, he wrote:

> I have looked over every *statute* relating to these colonies from their first settlement to this time; and I find every one of them founded on this principle, till the STAMP ACT administration. *All before* are calculated to preserve or promote a mutually beneficial intercourse between the several constituent parts of the empire; and though many of them imposed duties on trade, yet those duties were always imposed *with design* to restrain the commerce of one part, that was injurious to another, and thus to promote the general welfare. The raising a revenue thereby was never intended.

The raising of a revenue by the Townshend Acts, Dickinson found, was "an innovation; and a most dangerous innovation." Thus the purpose of his letters, he said, was "to convince the people of these colonies, that they are at this moment exposed to the most imminent dangers; and to persuade them immediately, vigorously and unanimously, to exert themselves, in the most firm, but most peaceable manner for obtaining relief."

Such relief was necessary, Dickinson warned, because "[n]o free people ever existed, or ever can exist, without, keeping, to use a common but strong expression, 'the purse strings' in their own hands."

Dickinson concluded his final letter as follows:

> For my part, I am resolved strenuously to contend for the liberty

delivered down to me from my ancestors; but whether I shall do this effectually or not, depends on you, my countrymen.

How little soever one is able to write, yet, when the liberties of one's country are threatened, it is still more difficult to be silent.

A FARMER

John Dickinson's *Letters from a Pennsylvania Farmer* were, in a manner of speaking, "syndicated," meaning they were reprinted in other newspapers, which were as likely to swipe stories from domestic sources as they were from those abroad. Benjamin Franklin's Polly Baker hoax had been "syndicated" in this sense, as had the severed snake cartoon and a number of other pieces of journalism up to that point. But nothing had been reprinted as widely as the views of the so-called farmer on the relationship between taxation and freedom. One historian reports that they were published in twenty-one of the twenty-five American newspapers of the time, after which they "were gathered and issued in a pamphlet that outsold every other political tract published in America before 1776."

This development was not just evidence of growing disgust with the Crown's policies. It also demonstrated that American newspapers were becoming united and ever more aware of the power they could wield in opposing the policies. And those who read them were becoming united as well.

In Sidney Kobre's opinion, this was an achievement that has not received nearly the notice it deserves:

The colonists lived in isolated settlements in the previous century. In such communities, they had had no bond of sympathy or interest with neighbouring seaboard colonies, since little trade and few facilities for communication existed. Now the bonds of trade bound them together. They had also intermarried. Moreover, they sent their sons to college in other colonies. And the newspaper, which was the most regular means of printed communication, told news about people in other colonies, who were no longer strangers to each other.

It was Franklin, though, who most succinctly and accurately assessed the role of the media in the days leading up to war. It was he, astute as ever, who pointed out that the press not only can "strike while the iron is hot," but it can "heat it by continually striking."

And no newspaper made things hotter or struck more continually than the *Boston Gazette*, which will now be considered at length, as will the man who made it famous, the "patriarch of liberty," as he is now known to some, and perhaps the least ethical newsmen of the entire colonial era, if not the entire history of American journalism.

CHAPTER EIGHT

"The Weekly Dung Barge"

*T*HE *BOSTON GAZETTE* had been around since 1719. It was a reputable enough paper, but had only a few hundred subscribers, and they did not take it to heart. Some days its lead story was not a story at all, but a government document, printed exactly as it had been received from the authorities, the broad strokes of which were already known to most readers by word of mouth. Or it was the notice of a public meeting or the announcement of a new business in town; at Christmastime in 1753, it was the publication of a new law authorizing *"the killing of Wolves, Bears, Wild Cats and Catamounts within this Province."* Those who brought down the beasts were

> intitled to the following Premiums out of the publick Treasury, that is to say, For every such grown Wolf of one Year old, *Four Pounds*: For every Wolf's Whelp under one Year old and not taken out of the Belly of a Catamount, *forty Shillings*: For every grown Wild Cat, *ten Shillings*: For every Wild Cat's Whelp under a year old as aforesaid, *five Shillings.*

But less than two years later, with fewer feral creatures roaming the streets of Boston and with printers Benjamin Edes and John Gill having purchased the *Gazette* from its previous owners, it started, however gradually, to become "the most radical paper in the colony"—so radical, in fact, that in their planning for war before the fighting actually got under way, British officers placed the paper's name on a list of enemy institutions to be captured and, if possible, laid waste. The British wanted to torch the enemies' supply depots, overrun their military encampments, trample their farm fields—and to make the *Boston Gazette* no less a casualty of war. "[T]hose trumpeters of sedition, Edes and Gill," as some called them, were to be put out of business once and for all.

The *Gazette* was the only paper in colonial America so honored. To those who opposed its views, it was the most irresponsible of all American journals: it reported fabrications as facts; its predictions were unfounded; it was less a source of news than a vehicle through which Americans could "spit their venom" at royal officials. James Rivington, who published a pro-British newspaper in New York at the time, referred to the *Boston Gazette* as "The Weekly Dung Barge."

But if Edes and Gill were the trumpeters, it was Samuel Adams, that most hot-blooded of patriots, who composed the music and lyrics for rebellion; Sam Adams, whose aims, it has been said, "were to destroy British prestige, unshackle English bonds and make America free." He would end up doing just that.

❁

ADAMS WAS NOT BORN with a grudge against the British, but he developed one at an early age. He saw what the Crown had done to his father, and his resentment was mother's milk to him; he weaned himself on it, never forgetting, never forgiving, never missing an opportunity to seek vengeance.

Samuel Adams senior, a brewer and a churchman, referred to by some who knew him as the Deacon, was also one of the investors in a land bank, an institution that specialized in real estate transactions. It seems to have done so honestly and efficiently, providing its customers with a service that they found invaluable and providing the elder Adams and his fellow owners not only with a suitable income but with the satisfaction of knowing that they were partners in the commercial growth of Boston and the surrounding area.

Nonetheless, after being in business but a short time, the bank was shut down by an act of Parliament. Adams and his partners were livid, demanding an explanation. What they learned was complicated, but part of it was that some British banks wanted to offer that same invaluable service to the colonists, perhaps even charging higher interest rates and making more of a profit, and they had lobbied Parliament to get rid of their American competition. Parliament had acceded to their wishes with little debate.

Adams and the others went through every proper channel they could to get the bank reopened: beseeching Parliament, sending a message to the king, importuning his ministers in North America—all to no avail. Then, it was whispered, they tried a few channels of the improper variety: same result. The closing of the bank was a financial blow to all the investors, and a formative experience for young Sam Adams, although this is not to say that his feelings about the British were selfish in origin. As he grew older, he would find other reasons to object to British policy, reasons that he shared with scores of his countrymen, many of them more rational in their responses to the Crown than he. But like James Franklin before him, Adams seems to have been born to defy authority; Parliament's action against the family business was simply kindling to a combustive political temperament.

Despite the hardships brought about by the bank's closing, Deacon Adams found the money to send his son to Harvard, where, as an undergraduate, he wrote an essay on "Liberty" and, for his master's thesis, chose to consider "whether it be lawful to resist the Supreme Magistrate, if the Commonwealth be otherwise preserved." He decided it was. Sam earned his master of arts degree in three years; it took most people four or more in the eighteenth century.

Upon graduating in 1740, the young man began looking for a career. None was eager to present itself. His family suggested the ministry; Sam said he had no interest. His father proposed the law, in part perhaps to help protect the family against future usurpations by royal officials of its business. But Adams's mother thought a courtroom was not a respectable place for her boy, and Sam readily agreed.

It was next proposed that he become a businessman. This turned out to be the worst idea of all. Sam was apprenticed to a friend of his father, a wealthy trader named Thomas Cushing, who "had no trouble separating his trading practices from his liberal politics. Within a few months, however, he saw that Samuel Adams was not able to make that distinction." The apprenticeship ended. It began to seem that the young man would never make his way.

Running out of ideas, the Deacon lent his son 1,000 pounds, "an impressive sum for the times," and encouraged him to make his fortune with it. Or at least to strive for solvency. Instead, Sam went broke. He allowed a friend to borrow half the money and it was never repaid; the other half vanished in several other ill-considered transactions. A frustrated and discouraged Samuel Adams Sr. had no choice but to find a place for a frustrated and discouraged Samuel Adams Jr. in the family brewery, where he could keep a close eye on him and try to keep his decision making to a minimum.

Adams was not an untalented young man, merely distracted. He did not care about theology or law, trade or beer; he cared about the political issues of the day. In time he would devote himself to those issues, but not by seeking a government position; to hold public office, even in those times, required a certain amount of tact, and Adams neither had such a quality nor wished to cultivate it. Instead, he would write about the issues, for which tact was not a necessity or even an asset; after all, with relations between the British and the Americans becoming ever more acrimonious, should journalism not reflect, even stimulate, the acrimony?

Sam Adams would write about other subjects, too; he proved an ardent and articulate foe of the Anglican church and, when he put his mind to it, a thoughtful analyst of economics and commerce. But it was politics that engaged him most, and politics that would make his name.

It would not happen immediately, however. Adams's career as a political reporter started out no more auspiciously than had his others. In 1750, after his father died and he had been freed from the daily duties of the brewery, and after he had worked briefly as a tax collector, threatening his fellow colonists with "the steps of the law being taken" if they did not pay their fair share, Adams and some friends began publishing a journal called the *Independent Advertiser*. It was a radical publication, one that found almost constant fault with the Crown, questioned the actions of Parliament, and "assailed the royal governor so persistently that conservatives called [Adams and his mates] 'the Whippingpost Club.'"

But the *Independent Advertiser* lasted less than a year and did not leave much of a mark on either the rulers or the residents of Boston. As Adams biographer John C. Miller writes, though, it contained "the germ of the ideas for which Adams was to fight for the greater part of his life, ideas which were later to form the political testament of the Whig Party in the American Revolution."

At the time, Sam Adams was a well-built young man of average height, blue-eyed and fair of complexion, described by his cousin John Adams, the future president, as the possessor of "engaging Manners." He was modest in attire and unremarkable in appearance. And, it seemed, unremarkable on the page. He would grind out his articles for the *Independent Advertiser*, sometimes help set them in print and hang them up to dry, and wonder why others did not notice them, did not talk about them, did not fall under the spell of either his emotions or his reasoning. Perhaps the blade of his prose was not yet sharp enough. Perhaps he should give it more of an edge.

To do so, he followed the example of Benjamin Franklin, committing himself to a mastery of the language, a regimen of self-study, and, in the process, turning himself into almost as demanding a critic of his journalism as he was of British policy in North America. But his was not the light touch of Franklin, not the casual style or the humorous example; Adams came to believe that the more subtle he was, the greater the likelihood that the reader would miss his point. He would not take the chance.

After the *Independent Advertiser* folded, Adams joined the *Boston Gazette*, which boasted of "Containing the freshest Advices, Foreign and Domestic," a slogan that gave no clue about the mischief the paper would soon be causing. But Edes and Gill did more than just give Adams a job; they yielded control of the print shop to him, allowing him to publish whatever he wanted to publish and to hire whomever he wanted to hire. His "editorial staff" consisted of John Adams, Joseph Warren, Josiah Quincy, and James Otis. All were eloquent in their patriotism, all astute in their perceptions about the motherland and the colonies; it could not have been a more prestigious group.

But it contributed more to the *Gazette* in name than in deed. Warren and John Adams wrote for the paper infrequently, and then in measured, sometimes even stilted tones. As for Quincy, although no less ardent in his beliefs than Sam Adams, he also picked up his pen sparingly. Otis advised Sam more than he wrote himself. Edes and Gill were determined foes of the Crown and their loyalty to colonial freedom was unquestioned, but they seem to have been merchants as much as reporters or polemicists, concerned with the bottom line perhaps even more than the headline. The *Boston Gazette*, virtually from the moment he joined it, was Sam Adams's paper, a mouthpiece for his disgust at what he would later refer to as Britain's "iron Hand of Tyranny."

❁

IT WAS THE STAMP ACT that finally made the *Gazette* mandatory reading for Bostonians and gave Adams the career he had sought for so many years; it was a tax that angered this former tax collector so much he was able to turn his disgust into a vocation.

He began by rejecting his cousin's style. John had responded to the Stamp Act with a series of essays called "A Dissertation on the

Canon and the Feudal Law," which, as legal philosophy, was considered by some to have been a masterwork. As journalism, however, it was so circuitously written and moderate in tone that, reading it, one struggles to remember that it was inspired by a tax hike that the majority of Americans thought unjust.

Sam, on the other hand, had lit a fuse under the populace even before the Stamp Act was passed, while it was still under consideration in Parliament. He and James Otis jotted down the names of those colonial officials who, in their opinion, were likely to support the Act. They called their roll a "Black List" and published it in the paper, as John C. Miller writes, so "[t]hat the Boston mob might know its enemies." Note Miller's use of the word "mob"; he is correct in assuming that Adams and Otis had compiled their list for just the sort of people who were likely to react to it violently. The journalists were, in other words, less interested in appealing to a knowledgeable readership than to one that was excitable enough to mutiny.

Then, writing under pseudonyms like Philo Patriae and Paces, (Latin for "Love of Country" and "Peace," the former of which, at least as far as Adams was concerned, made the latter unlikely), Adams questioned the Stamp Act in such a way that there could be no doubting the answers he meant to elicit.

> Is it not the distinguishing character of an Englishman, that he is free? Is he not born with an inherent right of assisting in the making of those laws by which he is to be taxed and governed, and of judging of those when they are made—Is this not the very spirit of the British constitution? Are not these the essential Rights of a Briton? . . . Were the colonies represented in the parliament when the Stamp Act was made? . . . Is it possible for any man in England to have such a knowledge of our internal circumstances, ever varying in an infant state, as to be capable of representing us? If not, tis plain we cannot be represented there.

This essay appeared on page two of the *Boston Gazette* on July

15, 1765. Preceding it, on page one, Edes and Gill demonstrated that bottom-line orientation of theirs, trying to make a few bucks by selling copies of the very legislation that Sam Adams was so energetically denouncing.

Just Published, and to be Sold by
EDES & GILL,
In Queen-Street
An ACT

For granting and applying certain STAMP DUTIES, and other Duties, in the British Colonies & Plantations in America, toward further defraying the Expences of defending, protecting, and securing the fame; and for amending such Parts of the Several Acts of Parliament relating to the Trade and Revenues of the said Colonies and Plantations, as direct the Manner of Determining and recovering the Penalties and Forfeitures therein mentioned.

You cannot fully appreciate the *Boston Gazette*'s disdain for the Stamp Act, the paper's publishers seemed to be saying, unless you read the document for yourself in all its perfidious glory—and we will be pleased to lighten your purse by a reasonable sum toward that most noble of ends!

❄

IT IS NOT KNOWN what Sam Adams thought of the ad. He might have been offended; he might have been amused to think that his business partners had figured out a way to make a few bucks from legislation intended to bring a windfall to the British.

What is known is that at this stage of his career, Adams enraged the British more by the frequency of his criticisms than the malevolence of his language. He had not yet become the most abusive critic of the motherland's policies in North America, but he was from the outset the most constant; few were the issues of the *Boston Gazette* after the Stamp Act that did not refer to the greed of the Crown or the coldheartedness of its representatives in America or the utter corruption of their motives. Fewer still were the issues that considered the British side of the dispute, except to dismiss it as wrongheaded and venal. Speaking of Sam Adams, Massachusetts governor Francis Bernard said, "Every dip of his pen stung like a horned snake." There was no one in America stinging the British as Sam Adams was.

And he proved even more anti-British off the page than on it, carrying activism in journalism to a degree never imagined by Franklin—or anyone else, for that matter. On the page: He wrote that Andrew Oliver had been appointed Stamp Master by the Crown, meaning that he was to supervise collection of the new tax, and that he would be zealous, even heartless, in his performance of duty. Off the page: Adams encouraged his friends and followers to take action against Oliver, perhaps even organizing it himself. As a result, Oliver was burned in effigy in August 1765, and then, two nights later, the same mob that had hung the effigy tore its head off as they proceeded to Oliver's office and demolished it with axes before moving on to his residence, where they battered the walls and shattered windows and hurled curses with no less energy or sense of commitment. The rebels demanded that Oliver resign his position. Fearing for his life, he agreed.

A few days later, the homes of two other representatives of the Crown, William Story and Benjamin Hallowell, both vocal in their support of the Stamp Act, were also damaged. In the following weeks, a number of other men, either British officials or colonists who did not object to the Act, were assaulted—sometimes verbally, sometimes physically—in the streets.

When the *Boston Gazette* reported on such doings, as it made a habit of doing promptly, it was not to denounce them or even simply to relate the details; it was to approve, to cheer, to provide justification for the assailants and assign blame to the victims. After a demonstration against the Stamp Act that attracted a crowd of 200 or so, the *Gazette* reported the protesters as "an indignant band of thousands." It also reported that the band of thousands chanted "Liberty, property and no stamps!" According to Adams, they had improvised the slogan themselves. But the very same words had appeared in an article that he had written for the *Gazette* only a few days earlier, one of the many Sam Adams pieces that doubled as a war cry.

Perhaps the band of thousands had seen the slogan in the paper. Perhaps Adams had taught it to them before assigning them to the streets. Perhaps Adams, in denying that he had had anything to do with the chant, did not think he was lying so much as obfuscating for the greater good.

❀

BUT EVEN MORE THAN HE HAD ANDREW OLIVER, ADAMS fired up opposition to Thomas Hutchinson, Oliver's brother-in-law and a man who had long been an official of the Crown in Massachusetts. At the time, Hutchinson was serving under Governor Bernard as the colony's lieutenant governor and chief justice. He was highly regarded in Boston—even the *Boston Gazette* was impressed by him, at least for a time, finding Hutchinson "a tall, slender, fair-complexioned, fair-spoken, 'very good Gentleman,'" who had "captivated half the pretty Ladies in the colony and more than half the pretty Gentlemen."

Sam Adams soon fell into the minority. He blamed Hutchinson not just for rabid enforcement of the Stamp Act, but for influencing Parliament to pass the Act in the first place, which does not seem to have been true. No matter: Adams despised the man, and he wanted his readers to despise him too. In fact, he wanted them to react even more violently against Hutchinson than they had against Oliver, to reveal to him the full measure of American loathing for the Crown's disposition.

One night some of them did just that. They were old men, young men, and boys barely old enough to read, all of them jacked up on ninety-proof Sam Adams prose, and they assembled outside the lieutenant governor's mansion and attacked it as if the structure itself were their enemy. It was a "hellish crew," Hutchinson later said, and it "fell upon my house with the rage of devils." They "split down the door and entered," he went on, and he "was obliged to retire thro yards and garden to a house more remote where I remained until 4 o'clock."

The hellish crew remained on the premises almost as long, not only wrecking but looting; Hutchinson later told authorities that 900 pounds in cash was missing, as well as books and clothing, table settings and jewelry, and perhaps even more; he was in no condition, he declared, to make a dispassionate inventory. For some time, he had been writing a history of Massachusetts, which he seems to have almost finished; the rebels found the manuscript and threw it into the mud in the front yard, ruining it. Hutchinson never had the heart for a rewrite. "Nothing remained" of his house, he said, "but the bare walls and floors."

Outside, the attackers even cut down the trees.

Hutchinson was devastated by the assault, unable, at least initially, to express either his anger or his sorrow. He could not believe that people he regarded as fellow Britons could behave in such a manner; it was a loss of innocence for him as well as a loss of property. He said that he would pray for the souls of those who had treated him so viciously. He prayed as well that he would be spared such unwarranted vindictiveness in the future.

Even the *Gazette* seemed to concede that things had gone too far on this occasion. "Such horrid scenes of villainy as were perpetrated last Monday night it is certain were never seen before in this town," the paper wrote, "and it is hoped never will again." Those responsible for it, the *Gazette* went on, were "rude fellows," and they had been "heating themselves with liquor" before exhibiting their "hellish fury" on Hutchinson's abode. The *Gazette* even published the proclamation of a British official about the incident, referring to "a great Number of People unlawfully and riotously assembled," who had "committed . . . Outrages and Enormities to the great Terror of His Majesty's liege Subjects."

But was Sam Adams's paper really contrite? Did it really believe that the deeds of those who had followed its editorial guidance were responsible for "horrid scenes of villainy"? It seems doubtful. More likely, the *Gazette* was making a tactical, and altogether brief, retreat, waiting for the British to calm themselves about the outrages and enormities, and for Bostonians to catch their breath, at which point it would be safe for Adams to light a fuse under them yet again, to incite yet another uprising for yet another reason. It was a dangerous game Adams played; the ingredients he stirred were volatile ones.

In fact, one suspects that Adams was himself stirred up in ways that were deep, complex, and not readily apparent either to friend or foe. He would, for example, write about the Stamp Act in the pages of his newspaper, calling it "*detestable*," suggesting that it would lead to "the ruin of the most glorious Empire the sun ever shone upon," more than four years after it became law. It was a long time to hold a grudge, especially since the Act had been repealed for three of those years.

As was suggested at the time and seems no less valid a conjecture today, the Stamp Act triggered something in the Deacon's son that resulted in his making Hutchinson a symbol for the misfortune of his father; the legislation had been merely the latest in a series of indignities that had begun with the closing of the land bank, and Hutchinson was a loyal representative of the government responsible for both. In fact, Hutchinson had supported the measure that led to the bank's demise, but so had numerous others associated with the Crown, many of them far more enthusiastically than he.

Nonetheless, Hutchinson had come to personify all that was England to Sam Adams, and England had come to personify all that was evil. Perhaps by focusing his distemper on a single individual, Adams was able to give it a greater, more satisfying, and more productive intensity.

❂

BETWEEN SEPTEMBER 1768 and August 1769, the *Boston Gazette* published a series of articles, in most issues calling it "Journal of the Times" and in others "Journal of Events." It was, in the opinion of many, "some of the most effective propaganda [Adams] had ever manufactured," a collection of "piping hot atrocities" guaranteed to inflame all who sampled them. Adams described the behavior of British soldiers on the prowl in the New World, accusing them of beating children, forcing their attention on young ladies, stealing merchandise from shopkeepers, and violating the Sabbath by getting drunk and racing horses through the streets of Boston, endangering all who crossed their paths. "If Adams and his fellow journalists were to be believed," it has been remarked, "scarcely a day passed without a British soldier's assaulting a woman."

Adams and his mates *were* believed, and, not only that, they were applauded for ferreting out such odious and upsetting truths and relaying them to the citizens of Massachusetts. But, in fact, they were not truths at all. Small boys had not been attacked by British men in uniform. Neither the honor of American women nor the cash drawers of merchants nor the intent of the Sabbath had been violated, at least not in the manner described by the *Gazette*. Yet the articles were widely reprinted, first in New York, then in newspapers all over the colonies, not a single one of which seemed to care any more about accuracy than the *Gazette* did. A few of Adams's pieces even appeared abroad. They might well have been the best fiction written in the English language for the entire period between Laurence Sterne and Charles Dickens. They were certainly the most compelling.

❖

LATER, AS A RESULT OF AMERICAN OPPOSITION to the Townshend Acts, the British engaged in what has deftly been called "a typical Superpower response—they sent in troops." The exact number is not certain, but it seems to have been about 4,000, which means that there was now one British soldier patrolling the streets of Boston for every four colonists. It was a show of "arbitrary power," Sam Adams wrote, from which Americans, a people "as yet unsubdued by tyranny," could only conclude that the British would never treat them as equals, as the countrymen they still believed themselves to be.

Adams's readers agreed. They were already upset about the Townshend Acts, but for the Crown to have dispatched an army, an occupying force, to punish what they believed to be a justified disobedience to those Acts virtually guaranteed rebellion. The duties on paper, glass, lead, paint, and tea could, for many, be ignored. The presence of British soldiers in the streets and taverns of Boston could not; they became a daily, visible reminder of oppression. The Crown should have known it, but apparently did not; Sam Adams did, and intended to take full advantage.

He got his chance late in the winter of 1770—as it happened, on the very day that most of the Townshend Acts, all except the tax on tea, were abolished by Parliament. That night, one of the coldest and iciest of the year, a small crowd assembled on the street in front of the Custom House for no other purpose, it seemed, than to taunt the lone British soldier on patrol there. Perhaps the loudest and most persistent of the taunters was a wigmaker's apprentice named Edward Garrick.

The guard tried to ignore Garrick, not speaking to him, not even making eye contact; he kept walking back and forth in front of the Custom House in his regular, carefully measured steps, thinking his own thoughts. Another soldier, however, was not as successful in restraining himself; approaching from a nearby sentry box, Private Hugh White not only cursed at the young wigmaker but "swung his musket and struck Garrick a blow on the side of his head with its butt. Dazed and reeling, the young man ran to the doorway of a shop and began to yell for help. White followed and hit him again." Or so went one version of the incident.

Suddenly, church bells sounded in the distance. To this day, no one can say who rang them; no one was seen in the bell tower, and no one ever admitted to having been there. At this time of night, though, the sound was more likely a notice that fire had broken out somewhere than that worship was about to begin. Several hundred men and women responded to the bell, appearing in the street and beginning to march toward their brethren already gathered at the Custom House. But none of them carried buckets, and no flames were visible, and there were never any reports from the scene of anyone's smelling smoke. According to an observer, "It is very odd to come to put out a fire with sticks and bludgeons."

Private White saw the Americans advancing on him and called for help; soon he was reinforced by eight of his fellow British troops under the command of Captain Thomas Preston. But their sudden appearance, rather than daunting the colonists, seemed to be the only provocation they needed. "Shouting, cursing, the crowd pelted the despised redcoats with snowballs, chunks of ice, oyster shells, and stones."

A few minutes later, and perhaps inevitably, shots were fired; as far as anyone knows, only the British had guns. Five Americans eventually died, including Crispus Attucks, the escaped slave who is thought to have led the rebels. Six more were injured, and with no hospital in Boston at the time, they could be treated only in private homes, in a nearby tavern, or in the street where they had fallen.

The uproar was immediate, and it came from all quarters. Those who were there told those who were not, and those who were not told others who were not, who told others, each rendering of the tale making British behavior more vile, the conduct of the Americans more innocent. To Benjamin Franklin, learning of the deaths while still in London, the soldiers were "detestable murderers." Sam Adams agreed, and would later refer to them as "imprudent and fool-hardy" and worse. But they were also helpful, providing him with yet another opportunity to raise the temperature of his readers with a tale, by far the most unconscionable yet, and in some ways the most accurate, of British cruelty.

He began by giving the incident its name, telling the populace what to call the "bloody Butchery": it was henceforth to be known as the "Boston Massacre." Then he wrote in the *Gazette* that as a result of "this fatal maneuver, three men were laid dead on the spot, and two more struggling for life; but what shewed a degree of cruelty unknown to British troops, at least since the house of Hanover has directed their operations, was an attempt to fire upon or push with their bayonets the persons who undertook to remove" the bodies of the victims from the scene.

Did the soldiers really behave in this manner? Possibly. But we have Sam Adams's word for it, and no one else's. And we know that the Americans milling about the Custom House that night were hardly loyal subjects of George III; if they were not necessarily eager for a confrontation, they were at least ready and willing.

Edes and Gill accepted the Adams version without argument. Then they tried to make even more of a profit from the Boston Massacre than they had from the Stamp Act. First they took Captain Preston's money for an ad in which he hoped to clear his name. *"Permit me thro' the Channel of your paper,"* the captain wrote, *"to return my Thanks in the most publick Manner to the Inhabitants in general of this Town—who throwing aside all Party and Prejudice, have with the utmost Humanity and Freedom stept forth Advocates for Truth, in Defence of my injured Innocence, in the late unhappy Affair that happened on Monday Night last."*

The *Gazette*, however, did not believe in Preston's injured innocence, placing his ad in a black-bordered edition of the paper, a few inches down the column from a drawing of several coffins for which, in the *Gazette*'s view, Preston himself was at least partly responsible.

Then, two weeks later, Edes and Gill hired America's most famous silversmith, Paul Revere, to memorialize the Boston Massacre with an engraving, a piece of work that proved to be one of his most popular. They advertised the product, and the price they were charging, in the pages of their paper.

> To be sold by EDES and GILL,
> (Price Eight Pence Lawful Money)
> A PRINT containing a Representation
> of the late horrid Massacre in King Street.

The original engraving was done in black and white. According to Revere biographer Esther Forbes, the few copies extant today were at some point painted over by a watercolorist who was a Revere contemporary. "Special emphasis is laid on the scarlet of British uniforms and Yankee blood. Blackened by time and the soot of country kitchens (where many of them were hung), they still have today an elemental horror. The red of gore and 'lobster-backs' [a reference to those scarlet uniforms] glows in pristine fury and the darkening of the prints produces at last a night effect. Generations of children learned to hate England by gazing at these crude prints."

❈

AS FOR THE TORY PRESS, it had little to say about the Boston Massacre. Some papers, especially those outside Massachusetts, either ignored it or reduced it to a line or two at the end of a page, the journalistic equivalent of an aside. Others gave more detail but, fearing reprisal, were careful not to assign blame. "For some days bye-past," wrote the *Boston Chronicle*, "there have been several affrays between the inhabitants, and the soldiers quartered in this town." The affray at the Custom House, the *Chronicle* went on, was "a most unfortunate affair," resulting in the deaths of some colonists and the arrest of Captain Preston. But: "*We decline at present, giving a more particular account of this unhappy affair, as we hear the trial of the unfortunate prisoners is to come on next week.*"

In fact, the trial was a few months away, as was the next significant reference to the shootings in the *Boston Chronicle*; the paper preferred praising the Crown to questioning the conduct of its fighting men. Less than two weeks after the Massacre, in fact, the paper was proud to publish a copy of "*His Majesty's most gracious Speech*, To both Houses of Parliament." The subject of the speech was the "distemper among the horned cattle, [which] has broke out in this kingdom." It was a much safer topic for the *Chronicle* than the distemper of a different, more virulent, sort that had also broken out in the kingdom.

❖

BEFORE LONG, Adams was able to lash out yet again at Thomas Hutchinson, now the colony's acting governor. Somehow Adams got his hands on a few letters Hutchinson had written to a fellow servant of the Crown, in one of which he stated that "there must be an abridgement of what is called English liberty" in Massachusetts. It was a sentiment guaranteed to incense the citizenry if it became known. And, thanks to Adams, it did.*

But merely publicizing Hutchinson's correspondence was not enough for him. Adams printed the letters out of context, eliminating the more moderate views that the author expressed, of which there were many, and adding phrases of his own, slurs and slanders and fabrications, putting words into Hutchinson's mouth that he had never uttered and passing them off as the historical record.

*It might have been Benjamin Franklin who provided the letters to Adams. Franklin did not trust Hutchinson but was not as bitter toward him as Adams was and surely did not imagine that Adams would employ the letters as dishonestly as he did.

For instance: Hutchinson was quoted in the *Gazette* as having persuaded the Crown "that all is in *anarchy* here." He might, in fact, have felt that way. But there is no evidence that he ever said, or wrote, such a thing. For instance: The *Gazette* quoted Hutchinson as having written that only one thing "yet remains to compleat my wishes and *designs*," and that was the arrival of more British soldiers to maintain order in Boston. He never said that, either. Adams so falsified the interim governor's correspondence that those who read the expurgated versions in the *Gazette* believed he had been responsible not only for the Stamp Act, as Adams had previously charged and now repeated, but also the Townshend Acts and the Boston Massacre and an entire "plan of slavery" that the Crown had for so long intended to impose on the colonies. It was yet more Sam Adams fiction, of the very worst, and worst-intentioned, kind.

※

HUTCHINSON RAGED at the *Boston Gazette*, complaining to an official in London that "seven eighths of the people read none but this infamous paper." Furthermore, he said, the *Gazette* was read in other colonies, and was lying to people, manipulating them, transporting them beyond the reach of reason.

The *New York Gazette*, in Hutchinson's view, told the truth.

What was the Consequence [of the Boston Massacre]? The lower sort of People, whose Minds were poisoned to that End, instead of looking on the Soldiers as fellow Subjects, and Countrymen, they viewed them with the malignant Eye of Detestation, and Insult, as a mercenary Banditti, in the Hands of most benevolent Majesty, ready to perpetrate every Act of Devastation and Cruelty.

But Hutchinson knew that the New York paper was one of America's softer voices, a whisper compared with Sam Adams's roar; it was widely regarded as a royal mouthpiece, and its version of events was therefore dismissed by most colonists. It was the *Boston Gazette* whose version mattered, the *Gazette* whose version would continue to influence the tide of events. Hutchinson warned the Crown that Sam Adams "would push the continent into a rebellion tomorrow, if it was in his power."

It seemed, at times like this, that it was.

❀

THE SOLDIERS WHO HAD BEEN ARRESTED for the Boston Massacre went on trial in October 1770. To the surprise of many at the time as well as many who read about the trial today, the men were represented by John Adams, who was one of the most respected lawyers in Massachusetts. His co-counsel was fellow *Boston Gazette* contributor Josiah Quincy. And in fact, it might even have been Sam Adams who urged the two of them to take the case, believing that his purposes would be served by either outcome: if the soldiers were convicted, the Crown would not be able to claim it was the fault of inept counsel; if his cousin John won their freedom, the colonists would seem to the Crown remarkably just in their handling of the case, clearly the moral superiors of their assailants. And, even more important, an acquittal would make many colonists so furious that Sam Adams could rouse them to further acts of violence, which would in turn bring them that much closer to insisting on their independence.

As for John Adams, he seems sincerely to have believed that the British soldiers deserved the best defense possible, and that he was capable of providing it. He also seems to have had misgivings about the account of the Massacre in the *Boston Gazette*, even though his cousin had produced it. Perhaps it was not the whole truth; perhaps there was more to be learned and understood about that terrible night.

Adams was also troubled because he knew that his defense of the

British would cause Americans to question his loyalty, his character, his motives. He knew that the trial would be an ordeal for him no less than for his clients. But he also knew that shirking what he believed to be his duty would, in the long run, be a greater ordeal.

His strategy was a simple one. With the court's approval, he would try the captain and his men separately, insisting on the innocence of both, the former because there was no compelling evidence that he had given an order to fire, the latter because they had acted in a brief fury, a *furor brevis*, the result of their having felt imperiled by the mob of angry colonists that had first surrounded them and then begun to advance.

The jury was sympathetic. In fact, both juries were. In the first trial, Captain Preston was found not guilty. In the second, two privates in the British army were declared guilty of manslaughter and sentenced to jail but were instead burned on the hand, a mild torture, then set free. The other defendants were set free without application of flame. Even Thomas Hutchinson was pleased; he thought that John Adams had "closed extremely well & with great fidelity to his Clients," and, more condescendingly, that the men who heard the case made "[p]retty good distinctions for an American jury."

Sam Adams responded to the trials with the bitterness that he had almost certainly wanted to feel all along. He returned to the offices of the *Gazette* and, either alone or with the help of Edes and Gill's journeymen, began stuffing letters and punctuation marks into composing sticks and sentence after sentence into chases and, as Hutchinson would put it later, tried the soldiers all over again, simply changing the venue from courtroom to page. He asked how the defendants could have received such a light punishment for an act of savagery so extreme that it resulted in the dogs of Boston "greedily licking human Blood in King-Street." He dismissed his cousin's contention that the British had acted under duress.

The *furor brevis* which we have heard much of, the fury of the blood which the *benignity* of the law allows for upon sudden provocation, is suppos'd to be of *short* duration—the shooting a man dead upon the spot . . . an attempt to stab a second person immediately after, infers a total want of remorse at the shedding of human blood; and such a temper of mind afterwards discovers the rancorous malice before, especially if it be proved that the same man had declared that he would never miss an opportunity of firing upon people, and that he had long'd for an opportunity so to do: If this does not imply malice at first, I do not see but he might have gone on stabbing people in his *furor brevis,* till he had kill'd an hundred; and after all, it might have been adjudg'd, in indulgence to the human passions, *excusable* homicide.

In response to this article—and to virtually every other piece that the *Boston Gazette* had published about the Massacre—another of the city's papers, the *Massachusetts Gazette*, edited by Richard Draper, accused Sam Adams of bias. Adams could not believe the effrontery. He erupted into italics for his denial.

SOMEBODY, in Mr. Draper's paper of Thursday last, charges me with *Partiality* . . . on the subject of the late Trial—*I deny the Charge, and desire he would explain himself.* He also says, I freely charge *Partiality* on others: *I utterly deny that also; and call upon him to point out one Instance.* . . . He *insinuates* that I have cast the most *injurious* reflections upon Judges, Jury and Witness: *Again, I deny it.*

Adams had "no Adherents," he said a few lines later, "but in the cause of truth."

And he did not just report the truth, or his version of it, at the time of the trial; he kept reporting it, kept coming back to it, just as he had returned to the Stamp Act long after it had ceased to trouble his countrymen. For the next several years, the *Gazette* would observe the anniversary of the Boston Massacre in such a way as to stir continuing resentment rather than simply mark the passage of time. In 1771, the first anniversary, the paper wrapped a black border around itself and devoted its entire front page to "a solemn and perpetual Memorial of the Tyranny of the British Administration of Government in the Years 1768, 1769, & 1770: Of the fatal and destructive Consequences of quartering Armies, in Time of Peace, in populous Cities: Of the ridiculous Policy, and Infamous Absurdity, of supporting *Civil* Government by a *Military* Force."

But the colonists who confronted the British soldiers that night at the Custom House were a military force of their own. They might have heard bells that seemed to signal a fire and made their appearance shortly afterward, but it was revenge for which they had prepared themselves, an assault upon the Crown, not the stifling of flames. Some historians believe that Adams had a hand in planning the confrontation that led to the Boston Massacre; he had certainly suggested acts of rebellion in the *Gazette* around that time, and perhaps in conversations with like-minded patriots he was more specific, settling on a time and place and method. Others, like historian Robert Middlekauf, disagree, finding that the violence was "not . . . the result of a plot or plan on either side, but rather the consequences of deep hatreds and bad luck." There is, at this distant point in time, no way to know the truth.

But there is clear evidence of yet another Adams lie. He had written that the tax money raised in the colonies as a result of the Townshend Acts, which had led to the Massacre, was not only, as advertised, going to pay the salaries of Crown officials in America—although that would have been bad enough. Rather, wrote Adams in the *Gazette*, the money had already made its way into the pockets and purses of the "hirelings, pimps, parasites, panderers, prostitutes and whores" whom men like Hutchinson, members of an "abandoned and shameless ministry," so freely patronized.

Sam Adams had now moved beyond fiction to farce.

❈

ONE NIGHT LATE IN THE AUTUMN OF 1773, Adams and some friends, men who were known admiringly to their fellow colonists as the Sons of Liberty and derisively to the British as the Sons of Violence, sat in the *Gazette*'s back room and began to plan the Boston Tea Party. A few days later, also in the *Gazette*'s back room, they finalized their plans. On the night in question, in the same back room, they darkened their faces, disguised themselves as Mohawk Indians, and set out for the harbor. After the raid, it is possible that some of them returned to the *Gazette*'s back room for a cheerful postmortem. The Boston Tea Party was at least as much the newspaper's as it was the town's.

A few months earlier, the Crown had granted a monopoly on American tea shipments to the British East India Company, a trading firm created by the government more than a century and a half earlier, and which had now become so powerful that, in parts of the Eastern Hemisphere, it acted as a government in itself. But in recent years it had become overextended, much like a modern retailer opening too many outlets or a corporation taking on too many subsidiaries. As a result, it was no longer profitable and had long been imploring Parliament to allocate funds to save it from bankruptcy. The Tea Act of 1773, which created the monopoly, was supposed to do that.

Americans, of course, did not care about the financial woes of any agency of the Crown. They seemed equally indifferent when British officials assured them that because the Tea Act eliminated various middlemen, the price of the beverage would decrease. But their indifference turned to anger when they learned that it was not just the British East India Company that would profit from the Act but also certain colonists who had friends in Parliament and would now be the only merchants authorized to sell tea. Among them were the sons of Governor Hutchinson.

Tea was the ostensible reason for the Boston Tea Party. The real reason was virtually everything that the British had legislated, enacted, and even contemplated in the preceding decade or more that related to North America, where patience with even the Crown's most benign decisions was almost totally exhausted.

And so it was that on the night of December 16, 1773, the men from the *Gazette*'s back room joined more than a hundred of their fellow rebels at the Boston wharf, where three tea-laden ships had been sitting at anchor for close to a month. Most of the men remained on the wharf. But about thirty of them, "likely longshoremen who knew their way around the dark hold of a ship and who were accustomed to hard physical labor," climbed onto the vessels. They whooped, they hollered, they did a thoroughly unconvincing impersonation of Mohawks on the warpath. As their fellow colonists watched from shore, and as some British sailors watched from a nearby ship and a British admiral observed them from a house near the docks, the Americans opened more than 300 chests of tea and dumped them into the harbor—every last chest, every last leaf, from all three ships. The estimated value of the cargo: 15,000 pounds (about three-and-a-half million dollars now). The reaction of the admiral, sticking his head out of an upstairs window of the house: "Well, boys, you have had a fine, pleasant evening for your Indian caper—haven't you? But mind, you have got to pay the fiddler yet."

It took almost three hours for the ersatz Indians to ransack the ships, trashing the fittings and furnishings as well as the merchandise, and when they were done, writes A. J. Langguth in *Patriots: The Men Who Started the American Revolution*, "Boston's harbor looked less like a teapot and more like a vast dank beach. Shaped into dunes, the tea lay upon the water and clogged the sea lanes. Sailors had to row out to churn the sodden heaps and push them farther out to sea. As far away as Dorchester, tea was found spread like hay in long lines where the wind had carried it."

On the front page of its next issue, the *Boston Gazette* decided that discretion was the better part of bravado. Seeking to deflect attention from itself, the paper refrained from comment on the incident, instead reprinting a resolution passed by the neighboring town of Lexington, referring indirectly to the tea raid. "[W]ith gratitude to our brethren in Boston and other towns," it read, "we do express our satisfaction in the measures they have taken, and struggles they have made, upon this as well as many other occasions, for the liberties of their country and *America*."

The Tea Party was a surprise to the Crown. But many colonists knew it was coming. On the day of the raid, the *Massachusetts Spy*, one of the newer papers in Boston, seemed to be preparing the British for the plunder by chiding them for their paternalistic and monopolistic leanings, facetiously printing some "RULES *In which a* GREAT EMPIRE *may be reduced to a* SMALL ONE." The rules, addressed "to all ministers who have the management of extensive dominions, which from their very greatness are become troublesome to govern," began by telling the ministers "to consider, that a great empire, like a great cake, is mostly easily diminished at the edges. Turn your attention therefore first to your remotest provinces; that as you get rid of them, the next may follow in order." Another rule: "To make your taxes more odious, and more likely to procure resistance, send from the capital a board of officers to superintend the collection, composed of the most *indiscreet, ill-bred* and *insolent* you can find. Let these have large salaries out of the extorted revenue, and live in open grating luxury upon the sweat and blood of the industrious." And another rule: "Redress no grievance lest [the colonists] should be encouraged to demand the redress of some other grievance."

A week later, the *Spy* published an anonymous letter to Governor Hutchinson, following the Sam Adams example in assigning blame for the Boston Tea Party where none was appropriate. "At length, Sir," said the writer to the governor, "your politics have arrived at maturity, and a noble crop you have reaped."

"But outside New England," Arthur M. Schlesinger observes, "even in New York and Pennsylvania, the sentiment was chillingly reserved. The newspapers for the most part contented themselves with reprinting accounts of the Tea Party from the Boston press without comment. There were virtually no expressions of approval or support; rather, a stunned silence." Perhaps the rebels had gone too far this time, even for some of their own.

Among those who were stunned, although not into silence, were John Dickinson, the so-called Pennsylvania farmer, and Benjamin Franklin. Dickinson thought that the destruction of the tea was far more a criminal act than a political statement, and he denied charges that his writing had, however inadvertently, led to such an outcome. When some of his friends suggested that the Sons of Liberty be presented with a letter of commendation for the Boston Tea Party, Dickinson talked them out of it.

Franklin was even more disturbed by the behavior of his fellow Americans, blaming them for "carrying Matters to such Extremity, as, in a Dispute about Publick Rights, to destroy private Property." He was still posted in London, his charge to do whatever he could to improve relations between the Crown and the colonies: negotiating settlements, reducing tensions, forestalling as best he could the possibility of war. His job had just gotten a lot harder. The iron, at least for the time being, was too hot to handle.

❁

THE BRITISH WERE MORE UPSET by the Boston Tea Party than they had been by any act of American defiance yet, and in a gesture as self-defeating as an alcoholic's getting drunk to help himself through the rigors of rehab, they promptly converted their umbrage into even more legislation. Parliament passed a bill that called for the closing of the port of Boston until the waters were clean and the tea paid for in full. It passed another bill that repealed the Crown's charter for Massachusetts, thereby denying citizens of the colony the right to choose the members of their own town councils. It passed another bill that allowed crimes committed in the colony to be tried in England if the authorities so chose. It passed yet another bill that curtailed the westward expansion of

America by extending the borders of Quebec to the south and west. Ignoring the lessons of the Boston Massacre, it passed one more bill allowing the Crown to continue quartering troops in the colony, but now requiring the citizenry to provide food and shelter for them upon request—to act as hoteliers for their invaders. And it passed even more bills, an edict here, an edict there, a geyser of regulatory vituperation against the citizens of the colony that had so wantonly defiled Boston Harbor.

To Americans, not only in Massachusetts but elsewhere, these were the Intolerable Acts, sometimes known as the Coercive Acts —not policy but punishment, not rule but retribution. The *New York Journal* responded ominously; it was among several papers to warn its readers yet again that they must "UNITE OR DIE." The *South Carolina Gazette* responded passionately: "Rise just indignation!" it implored on its front page. "Rise patriotism! To the aid of our much injured country." The *Newport* [Rhode Island] *Mercury* responded irrelevantly: "How will you feel," it asked, "to see a ruffian's blade reaking from a daughter's heart, for nobly preserving her virtue?"

At the *Boston Gazette* it was business as usual, with Sam Adams warning the neighbors of Massachusetts that the British had designs on them, too. "*Our sister colonies behold in this metropolis a specimen of what they may expect after we are subdued*," he wrote, and explained the following week that the Intolerable Acts were part of "a plan of despotism and arbitrary power" that "has incessantly been pursued, during the present reign."

In its June 29, 1774, edition, the *Pennsylvania Journal* published a letter to Thomas Gage, the newly appointed governor of Massachusetts, stating, "Your Excellency has arrived at a juncture when the harmony between Great-Britain and the colonies is greatly interrupted." Then it interrupted that harmony all the more, printing a special supplement that explained in detail what Parliament was planning in the wake of the Intolerable Acts, which was to act in a manner even more intolerable:

It was going to deny British citizens the right "to settle and dwell [in America] for any *longer* time than the space of seven years."

It was going to require that American couples pay a fee for a marriage license, and that any marriage performed without a license "shall be void in law to every intent and purpose whatever."

It was further going to require "that on the birth of every male child, the sum of Fifteen Pounds, and on the birth of every female child, the sum of Ten Pounds sterling money shall be paid to the Governor of the Colony or Plantation in which such children shall be born." For a child born out of wedlock, there would be a fine of fifty pounds, "paid by the *Mother* of such bastard child."

Taxes were also to be imposed on flour and wheat, and the money "shall be applied towards RAISING A REVENUE the better to ENABLE his MAJESTY to BUILD FORTS and to GARRISON the same, and to support and maintain such a REGULAR and STANDING ARMY in the said PLANTATIONS as shell be sufficient to enforce the EXECUTION of all such Acts of the BRITISH PARLIAMENT, as are already passed, or may hereafter be passed, relative to the said AMERICAN COLONIES." In other words, the new tax would go toward the reimposition of the very conditions that had led to the Boston Massacre in the first place.

It was outrageous, alarming, this news of the motherland's coming salvos, a virtual declaration of war on the colonies by the British authorities who oversaw them.

It was also untrue. Parliament was considering no such levies as the *Pennsylvania Journal* reported, and never would, and the *Journal* almost certainly knew it all along.

❖

As for the relatively few newspapers in America that were loyal to the Crown, they were dismayed that so much duplicity had been set in type and run off the presses and accepted as gospel by so many colonists. The *Massachusetts Gazette*, referring euphemistically to the Boston Tea Party as a "meeting," found it "an affront to the common sense of mankind and to the dignity of the laws, to assert that such a meeting as was held in the town of *Boston* . . . was either lawful or regular: And further that the said meeting and the conduct and determination therein do not appear to us to be either necessary or laudable, or in any degree meriting the Gratitude of those who wish Well to America."

But as this passage indicates, loyalist newspapers were cautious about expressing their disapproval in what was looking more and more to them like enemy territory. James Rivington, of *Rivington's New-York Gazetteer*, thought to be one of the staunchest journalistic supporters of the motherland, simply said that he would not publish articles that demeaned either the king or Parliament because to do so would be to cross "the line of decorum."

❁

IN TIME, QUITE A LOT OF TIME, Adams would mellow—or would at least give that impression. His favorite activity in the years after the war seems to have been visiting his grandchildren, playing games with them, and sometimes preaching impromptu sermons on liberty, his old Harvard topic, and the lengths to which one was justified in going to achieve it. He might also have talked to them about the education of women, a subject that had become important to him in his later years. But the *Boston Gazette* was out of business by then, a relic of a different era, and Adams wrote no articles about it.

Most of his writing now consisted of letters to old friends, essays of reminiscence and advice. One of his correspondents was John Adams, whose fondness for him as a person transcended mere familial ties and whose respect for Sam as a patriot led John to think of his cousin as one of the great Americans. Sam was flattered. When he corresponded with John, he signed his messages, "Your Old and unvaried Friend." Yet when Thomas Jefferson defeated

John Adams for the presidency in 1800, Sam expressed his pleasure; he does not seem to have thought that his cousin had the heart for the job, the passionate commitment to justice, the true and eternal flame of radicalism that the nation still required of its leaders.

Jefferson, equally pleased at receiving Sam's support, was quick to praise him as "the helmsman of the American Revolution." When newspapers turned on Jefferson, as they did even before he took office, Adams lashed out at them, saying that Jefferson was being "calumniated for his liberal sentiments," that charges were being leveled against him in the press "without the least shadow of proof." He did not understand how a reporter could do such a thing.

What seems to have delighted old Sam Adams most was recalling his days at the *Boston Gazette*, the days of what he called the "great" or "glorious" cause, the days of journalism as brute force. Like the moralist that he was, Adams had reduced matters to their simplest terms: the colonists were virtuous, the British wicked; nuances were for those of far fainter heart than he, those afraid to take a stand in the public prints. As a younger man, Adams was never more comfortable than when he stood by a printing press with a grievance in his soul and a composing stick in his hand.

He published none of his articles under his own name, however. One biographer has counted at least twenty-five pseudonyms that Adams used in his career at the *Boston Gazette* and thinks there were probably more. He was, at various times, not only Philo Patriae and Paces, but Vindex the Avenger, Determinatus, Decant Arma Togae (which seems to be a reference to weapons being visible beneath one's apparel), Principiis Obsta (principal obstacle), and various other historical personages known for their love of freedom: Valerius Poplicola, Candidus, and Populus. He was also An American, A Tory, Alfred, A Son of Liberty, A Puritan, and A Religious Politician, among many.

Nor was Adams alone in claiming other identities. Alexander Hamilton might have ranked second in number of pen names, having written as Publius, Pacificus, Catallus, Americanus, Metellus,

Horatius, Philo Camillus, Tully, Monitor, Phocion, The Continentalist, and H.G., to name a few. Benjamin Franklin, in addition to being Silence Dogood and Polly Baker and Richard Saunders (Poor Richard of *Almanac* fame), was Anthony Afterwit, Martha Careful, Alice Addertongue, Celia Shortface, Harry Meanwell, Fanny Mournful, Obadiah Plainman, Busy Body, and Sidi Mehemt Ibrahim. John Adams was Novanglus, Sui Juris, U, Davila, and Humphrey Ploughjogger; James Madison signed himself Helvidius on an occasion or two; Robert R. Livingston went by Cato; and the list goes on. The more pseudonyms an author used, the more likely it was that readers would think of him as several authors, a company of them, an army; his views, therefore, would seem to be held by many, rather than simply one man with a prolific pen.

But there were other reasons for the deception. Writers liked the cachet of a pseudonym, the classical allusions, the implication of ancient learning that was thereby conferred, or the association with the figure whose name had been appropriated. Or they liked the witty sound of a pseudonym, which prepared the reader for the levity to follow.

More often than not, though, there was no levity. "The fashion of allowing anonymous attacks," writes Hamilton biographer Ron Chernow, "permitted extraordinary bile to seep into political discourse, and savage remarks that might not otherwise have surfaced appeared regularly in the press." Some writers of the period believed that pseudonyms, as a form of disguise, would enable them to avoid charges of libel or treason when the remarks were even more savage than usual and their victims sought legal remedy. In most cases, though, and certainly in the case of Adams, the author's identity was well known despite the evasion.*

---

*The use of pseudonyms or anonymity was a common practice in American journalism from its very beginning until three years into the Civil War, when Union General Joseph Hooker insisted that those who wrote about the fighting do so in their true identities. He was not trying to make newsmen angry; he was trying to make them accountable. Hooker hoped that if a man attached his name to his views, he would be more responsible in giving voice to them.

❀

SAM ADAMS DIED on October 2, 1803. He was eighty-one years old and, it had been reported, "suffered from nervous disorders." The event was seen as a calamity, and not just in Boston.

> The entire country joined in mourning for the Grand Incendiary. President Jefferson issued a statement paying tribute to him, and John Randolph delivered a long, stirring eulogy in the Congress. Adams's request for a quiet funeral was ignored, and he was given a burial in state, with an escort of troops. . . . The church bells of Boston tolled, shops were closed, and the guns on Fort Independence in the harbor were fired at sixty-second intervals.

The Boston *Independent Chronicle* framed its announcement of Adams's death in black, as if the page were a headstone, and referred to him as "the consistent and inflexible Patriot and Republican," "our *political parent*," "the undeviating friend of civil and religious liberty." In his diary, John Adams wrote that his cousin was "always for softness and delicacy and prudence where they will do but staunch and stiff and rigid and inflexible in the cause." And, some years later, Thomas Jefferson would refer to Sam as "truly a great man . . . whose deep conceptions, nervous style, and undaunted firmness made him truly our bulwark in debate."

Adams was more than just a journalist. After having written a series of essays for the *Gazette* in support of a Continental Congress, he was chosen as a delegate to both the First and Second Congresses. When the war was over and independence had been won, he served as lieutenant governor and then governor of Massachusetts—the same positions that Thomas Hutchinson had once held, except that Adams was not appointed by the Crown. He had long advocated a Bill of Rights, and when the Constitution was written, he became a leading voice for ratification. He behaved more honorably in each of these instances than he did in the print shop.

But it was as a newsman that Adams was first known and best known, and as a newsman that he most readily thought of himself. Once, when asked about his work at the *Boston Gazette* and the methods he employed, he said, "It would be the Glory of this Age, to find Men having no ruling Passion but for the Love of their Country, and ready to render her the most arduous and important Services with the Hope for no other Reward in this Life than the Esteem of their virtuous Fellow Citizens." As far as most of his countrymen were concerned, Adams had earned that esteem.

The view of a more objective posterity, however, cannot be so generous. History has vindicated Adams's political ends; it cannot justify his journalistic means. "Truth was his first victim," writes William H. Hallahan in *The Day the American Revolution Began.* "To radicalize the populace Adams had adopted a total disregard for it. In his writings he employed slanderous lies, unvarnished propaganda, and rabble-rousing rhetoric. He whipped the people of Massachusetts and many other colonies into an anti-British fury."

It was a fury that would become even more furious in the years ahead, and one that the pro-British press, in at least one case, would finally answer.

CHAPTER NINE

❊

The Tory Dung Barge

*T*HE TRUTH WOULD HAVE BEEN A VICTIM even without Sam Adams's example. The *New York Journal* (a different paper from John Peter Zenger's *Weekly Journal*), for example, was among several papers in the years just before the war to publish a series of reports called the "Journal of Occurrences," which, like Adams's "Journal of the Times" or "Journal of Events," was a catalog of supposed atrocities perpetrated by the British troops stationed in Boston. From December 1768:

> A Married Lady of this Town was the other Evening, when passing from one House to another, taken hold of by a Soldier; who otherwise behaved to her with great Rudeness; a Woman near Long Lane was stopped by several Soldiers, one of whom cried out seize her and carry her off; she was much surprised, but luckily got Shelter in a House near by; Another Woman was pursued by a Soldier into a House near the North End, who dared to enter the same, and behave with great Insolence: Several Inhabitants while quietly passing the Streets in the Evening, have been knocked down by Soldiers.

Was it true? Were three women and some other citizens of Boston being treated like this by the men of the Crown's army? "Clues to the reliability of these reports," observes Mitchell Stephens in *A History of News: From the Drum to the Satellite*, "can be found in the facts that victims went unnamed and that the Boston papers themselves waited months to reprint them."

In *The Compact History of the American Newspaper*, John Tebbel, another observer of journalistic malfeasance in colonial America, compares two lengthy accounts of the same incident, which took place four months before the war broke out. The first appeared in the *Boston Gazette*, although it is believed to have been written by publisher Edes rather than ace reporter Adams:

A little after ten o'clock this evening, two young men passing down Milk Street, near the entrance into Long Lane, they were accosted by an officer, not in the English, but as they supposed in another language, which they did not understand; they asked him what he meant; he replied he meant to tell them to go about their business. They had not gone far before the officer called to them to stop. They stopped till he came up to them, and angry words ensued. The young men, however, parted from him the second time, and went on their way towards their homes. The officer followed and overtook them near the head of the lane, and stopped them again, telling them he supposed they were stiff Americans; to which one of them said he gloried in the character. Here again words ensued, and the officer drew his sword, flourished it and struck one of the young men on the arm, who immediately seized him. At this junction, three or four of the town watch, who were upon the patrol, came up and separated them, advising them to go home. The two young men did so, but the officer refused, saying he was prisoner of the watch and would go with them; they told him he was not their prisoner, but might go where he pleased, and if he desired it, they would see him safe home: but he insisted upon it that he was their prisoner. The watchmen went down the lane towards their head-quarters in King Street, where they had been going before, and the officer accompanied them. In the way they met with several persons, whom they took to be servants of officers, who, supposing the officer to be in custody of the watch, attempted to rescue him, but he insisted upon being a prisoner, and said the watchmen were his friends, and he *would* go with them. They then went forward, and in Quaker Lane, which leads into King Street, they were met and assaulted by more than twenty officers of the army, who took several of their watch poles from them, and wounded some of them.

By the standards of the *Gazette*, this is a tame report, the language descriptive more than inflammatory, and there are no calls for reprisal. But did the incident happen as Edes wrote it? Not if one is to believe another version, this one provided by James Rivington in his *New-York Gazetteer*—and so different that it is barely recognizable as the same occurrence. Rivington was no longer reticent in his reactions to the anti-British press.

You have read in that fund of lies and sedition, Edes and Gill, of a "high-handed riot." There have been five field officers on a court of inquiry, to inspect into the conduct of the officers concerned on that occasion. It commenced by Lieutenant Myers, 38th Regiment, being, without the smallest cause, insulted by two townspeople, who not only called him a Tory, rascal, scoundrel, &c., but damned the king, governor, army, and every friend to government; the former he put up with, the latter resented, by knocking the person down. He was immediately surrounded by the watch; and though he immediately surrendered, and gave his sword to a Mr. Winslow, who came up at the time (a private gentleman), and informed them, and this gentleman, of the cause of the quarrel, they treated him with every indignity possible; not only allowed the two men to knock him down in the midst of them, but they themselves kicked and beat him all the way to the watch-house, a little short of a quarter of a mile. The noise about the watch-house brought together a few officers, whom Mr. Myers requested not to interfere, concealed from them the cruel treatment he had met with, and insisted on remaining in custody. The insolence of the watch to those gentlemen occasioned a fresh riot, when the interposition of a party from the main guard prevented any bad consequences. Immediately after, Myers was released, by order from the governor. Complaints were immediately lodged against the officers, and bail is to be given to-morrow for their appearance. I cannot quit this subject without observing that the high-flyers are much disappointed in the vent of this riot; not only at the little mischief done, but at the ready submission of every officer concerned, to the laws of the country.

The spirit of the people here seems to subside a little; and we have every reason to believe, that, in order to keep it up, the vagabonds of the town are employed to insult the troops, which they do daily, in hopes of bringing about another massacre.

What is apparent in reading both the *Gazette* and the *Gazetteer* is that, in all probability, neither paper told the complete truth because neither paper knew the complete truth. How could it? Who, after all, was the source? Where is the attribution? The papers do not mention a witness who could have described the incident accurately, and there was no official record of the confrontation that a newsman could have consulted after the fact. Was Edes there? Was Rivington? It is not likely. What probably happened was that, a day or two later, Edes talked either to a watchman or one of his cohorts and Rivington to the so-called prisoner or a cohort, and that each man accepted the version of events provided by his ideological compatriot, perhaps even embellishing it to further suit the demands of his particular bias.

It seems that Rivington wanted to be to the Crown—or to its sympathizers, known as Tories or loyalists or royalists—what Sam Adams and his mates at the *Gazette* were to the Whigs—referred to as rebels or patriots. Perhaps, for a time, he was. But he was something else as well, something very different from what he appeared, the most mysterious man to print a newspaper in colonial America. It is puzzling that he has lost his place in history. He regains it, briefly, in the following pages.

❀

THEY CALLED HIM JEMMY, and he was born into wealth, his family owning a large and successful British publishing house early in the eighteenth century. As a result, some of his friends were aristocrats, and he would socialize with them and talk like them and dress like them, hoping that people would believe that he was titled as well as rich. He also liked to gamble, especially on the horses, as a result of which he lost much of his fortune and even more of his self-respect. Embarrassed, and vowing never to be embarrassed for such a reason again, Rivington decided he would come to America and start a newspaper of his own, a paper that both he and the Crown could be proud of, and, if all went well, a paper that would reestablish him as a man of means.

Artistically, it proved an immediate success. *Rivington's New-York Gazetteer*, the first American newspaper to include its publisher's name in the title, was said to be "one of the handsomest in the colonies. It had ornamental borders and many wood cuts, and carried many advertisements."

Jemmy was a bit of an ornament himself, continuing to favor the garb of nobility, decking himself out now and then in "a rich purple velvet coat, full wig and cane, and ample frills" as he strode through his print shop and adjoining bookstore, instructing his employees, persuading his customers to buy his various publications and to subscribe no less enthusiastically to his views on colonial insurrection.

The *Gazetteer* started out presenting both sides in the conflict between colonies and Crown, but it soon became a voice almost exclusively for the latter, the loudest in all of New York. It pleaded with Americans to ignore the cries of the Whigs, not "to submit to their unreasonable, seditious and chimerical resolves, doing thereby the most cruel and unparalleled violence to their liberties, under the pretence of relieving them from imaginary grievances." The

Gazetteer encouraged readers who were opposed to the notion of American independence, urging them to hold their ground. A few months before the war began, it published a letter from some colonists in Connecticut who wanted "to assure the public, that we are open enemies to any change in the present happy constitution, and highly disapprove of all measures, in any degree calculated to promote confusion and disorder . . . adopted for the purpose of opposing British government. . . ."

To his foes, Rivington was a "dirty" man, "malicious," a "JUDAS," "either an ignorant pretender to what you do not understand or a base servile tool, ready to do the dirty work of any knave who will purchase you." And he was "a most wretched, jacobitish, hireling *incendiary*," according to Solomon Southwick, editor of the *Newport Mercury*, whom Rivington had earlier abused in the *Gazetteer* in a verse he called "Solomon Saphead."

If thou a writer must commence,
For Heav'ns sake give us common sense:
Not reason turn'd to ridicule,
To shew Mankind thou art a fool,
Degen'rate Wretch, what could excite
Thee ever to pretend to write?

Sometime later, frustrated with the views of a Whig paper in North Carolina, Rivington berated the paper as "a most infamous publication," one that was "most traiterously [sic] declaring the intire [sic] dissolution of the laws, government, and constitution of this country." The paper was "repugnant to the laws, and subversive of his Majesty's government." And as if all that were not enough, Rivington charged that the North Carolina journal supported the horrid cause of colonial independence, "the preposterous enormity of which cannot be adequately described and abhorred."

The *Gazetteer* was no less abhorred by those who stood opposed to its politics, or the enormity of its own preposterousness. It was the "Lying Gazette," some insisted, guilty of all manner of "Twistifications" and "false colourings" over the years, most egregious among them a report that Benjamin Franklin had been wounded in battle and was not expected to live—Franklin had never even taken part in a battle. Another story claimed that George Washington had been killed in a skirmish with Indians—on the occasion in question, Washington had not been fighting Indians and had not been wounded by anyone. When this fact was called to Rivington's attention, he reacted with a shrug and a hasty change of subject, returning to his press to claim that Washington, far from being the republican that he professed, was at heart a monarchist, wanting one day to be king of the colonies, yet another George on a throne with America at his feet.

Furthermore, as the *Gazetteer* portrayed him, Washington was pretentious and arrogant, underskilled and overrated, less intelligent and much more severe in disposition than most people thought. America was being "misled by dangerous and ill designing men," proclaimed George III in a document that Rivington was only too happy to reprint prominently in his paper, men who were committing "various disorderly acts" in the process of "traiterously [sic] preparing, ordering, and levying war against us." The chief misleader, the chief traitor, Rivington made clear, was George Washington. Those who followed him, the *Gazetteer* asserted, were "execrable mobs," guilty of "treasonable associations, unlawful combinations, seditious meetings, [and] tumultuous assemblies."

As things turned out, Rivington was but the warm-up act for the more virulent abuse Washington would receive from other publishers after the war.

❖

HE WAS A MASTER OF ACCUSATION, this Jemmy Rivington, and he could plant one in a story of any kind, sneak it in where no one expected it. He "injected partisan bias even into his society items," it has been noted, "remarking pointedly, for example, that 'not a single whig' was among the forty-seven guests at a wedding in White Plains." His goal, he wrote in one of his issues, was "that the people of this province at large may be acquainted with the enormities, violences, and disorders herein before recited, which manifestly tend to the destruction of their peace and welfare." Rivington intended "fully to forewarn the people of the dangers and calamities to which the men who have set themselves up for leaders in sedition and treason are courting them."

When he founded his *Gazetteer* in 1773, Rivington was dismayed that there were so few Tory publications in the colonies at so crucial a time. Almost immediately, his became the most influential, boasting a circulation of 3,600, "a number far beyond the most sanguine expectations of the Printer's warmest friends." And, perhaps, far beyond the bounds of reality. Regardless, the force of the *Gazetteer*'s opinions was felt not just in New York but well outside the precincts in which it was published.

Up and down the coast Tories turned hungrily to the *Gazetteer* as their political bible. Joseph Galloway in the Pennsylvania Assembly acclaimed Rivington an "honour to his Country," the Anglican cleric Jonathan Boucher in Maryland styled him America's only "impartial" publisher, and Governor Josiah Martin of North Carolina feelingly told the Ministry [a reference to the British government, headed by prime minister Lord North] that the New Yorker's courage was "really signal in the present times." In like spirit [Massachusetts] Governor Gage distributed 400 copies of each issue of the paper to the military personnel and Tory civilians in Boston.

Rivington also claimed a significant foreign circulation: the West Indies, France, Ireland, and, of course, England, where copies of the *New-York Gazetteer* were received as rare expressions of sanity, proof in some quarters that all was not lost in the New World.

Although the patriot newspapers were dubious about Rivington's claims, believing that the man was no more to be trusted about his number of readers and their geographic diversity than he was about the content of his stories, they took him seriously, and the *New York Journal* tried to bring him down in verse just as he had tried to bring down Solomon Southwick.

> In politics your very self,
> An ign'rant, yet a treach'rous elf
> The public now have found;
> For, trying metal as they shou'd,
> They, judging 'twixt the bad and good,
> Condemn you from your *sound*.

Members of the Whig party in New York passed a resolution suggesting "to every person who takes [Rivington's] paper, to immediately drop the same." A similar resolution was approved in New Jersey, and in both colonies there were discussions among patriot leaders about the possibility of boycotting the *Gazetteer*'s advertisers, and in fact at least a few, when threatened with violence, seem to have dropped out. Threats were also made against people seen reading the paper in public; they were shouted at, sometimes chased down the street, and on a few occasions even kicked and beaten. One might as well have attired himself in lobster-backed crimson as perused a copy of the *New-York Gazetteer* where patriots might see it.

Several communities went so far as to ban the *Gazetteer*, stopping those who delivered it at the town lines, searching the bags of postmen to make sure they were not hiding any stray copies. Circulation dropped; by this time it was certainly not 3,600. Profits dropped as well. Even more troubling to Rivington were the bands of angry patriots that had begun to assemble outside his print shop on occasion, hollering imprecations and demanding that he take the rebel side. Others hanged him in effigy; a dummy of Rivington was strung up in New Brunswick, New Jersey, for example, and although the publisher was not actually there, it nonetheless inspired him to print a woodcut of the event and to comment on the motives behind it in the *Gazetteer*'s next edition.

> The Printer is bold to affirm that his press has been open to publication from ALL PARTIES. . . . He has considered his press in the light of a public office, to which every many has a right to have recourse. But the moment he ventured to publish sentiments which were opposed to the dangerous views and designs of certain demagogues, he found himself held up as an enemy of his country.

In the summer of 1775, Rivington's real self was almost hanged. About two months after the colonists and the British finally went to war, a mob of patriots, believing the *Gazetteer*'s pro-Tory rants were now officially treasonous, "rode into the city [of New York] . . . and, armed to the teeth, entered Rivington's house, demolishing his plant and carrying off the types, which were converted into bullets." They wanted to carry off the publisher as well, but could not find him; he is thought to have been hiding nearby, possibly watching the destruction from a neighbor's house.

Rivington decided he could take no more. He threw some clothes into a satchel and dashed from his sanctuary, wherever it was, making his way to New York Harbor and climbing aboard a British naval vessel, an "ark of refuge," where he tried to figure out his next move. Should he try to publish his paper in another city, perhaps another colony? Should he remain in America but seek a different occupation? Should he remain aboard his ark, and ride it to safety? With a certain eagerness, not to mention a dry sense of humor, the *Pennsylvania Journal* awaited news of the ship's departure: "We hope the Non-exportation Agreement to Great-Britain will always except such traitors to the Liberties of America."

But Jemmy Rivington was not quite ready for export. After a

few days of exile, he petitioned the Second Continental Congress for a pardon, doing so in the third person, which was considered a more humble form of address than it is today. Rivington stated that "however wrong and mistaken he may have been in his opinions, he has always meant honestly and openly to do his duty." He asked for another chance. He wanted to remain an American newspaperman. And perhaps, at this crucial hour, he came to a decision about how far he would go to reach that goal.

Among those who supported Rivington was the patriot Gouverneur Morris, grandson of former New York Chief Justice Lewis Morris, the man who had enlisted John Peter Zenger to do verbal battle against the despised William Cosby. Morris, who would one day be the primary drafter of the Constitution, had already established a reputation for fairness and wisdom. But some years earlier, his reputation was not so secure; in fact, he had been suspected of siding with the British himself and thus was sympathetic to Rivington's plight. "Morris urged that the 'unfortunate printer' be treated charitably," according to biographer Richard Brookhiser. "'Magnanimity,' he wrote one patriot, 'will dictate . . . the true line of conduct.' 'Not one month ago,' he reminded another, patriotism 'was branded with infamy. Now each person strives to show the excess of his zeal by the madness of his actions.' He ended this letter with a credo: 'I plead the cause of humanity to a gentleman.'"

The plea was heard, the cause of humanity served. Jemmy Rivington got his pardon, although one of the requirements was that he sign a pledge of loyalty to the patriot cause. He did so without hesitation, and he was allowed to continue publishing his newspaper in the colonies.

But how? The printer no longer had a press, his types had been melted into missiles, his supplies of ink had been dumped onto the printshop floor, and his various frames had been reduced to kindling. Of course, he could always rebuild, but what was to prevent another gang of patriots from paying yet another visit to his premises and renewing his losses? The pardon, Rivington realized, was a gesture more than a victory; it did not seem likely that he would be able to find a new place of business, or new equipment with which to conduct it, in the Whig-dominated society that surrounded him.

Perhaps, he began to think, it might not be a bad idea to export himself after all, at least for a while.

❁

IT WAS ON APRIL 15, 1775, that the unthinkable, which had gradually become the possible and then rapidly the inevitable, finally happened. A group of American settlers and some soldiers of the Crown faced one another in an open field in Lexington, Massachusetts, and shots were fired. "Long months of pent-up resentment in the British troops exploded," writes William Hallahan, although the colonists had been accumulating resentment for an even longer period, and it would prove to be no less explosive.

A few hours later, the so-called "shot heard 'round the world" was repeated in the nearby town of Concord. The American colonies were officially seeking their independence from the nation responsible for their existence, and the motherland was determined to vanquish them so completely that they would never so much as think of freedom again, much less take up weapons in its pursuit. It was for both sides a war of principle, the most vicious kind.

At the time, according to one tally, there were twenty-five newspapers in America supporting the rebellion and thirteen opposing it. All thirty-eight of them, in their own ways, were about to report the most important story that would ever occupy their pages.

CHAPTER TEN

❖

The Shot Spread 'Cross the Page

*T*HE MOST RESPECTED JOURNALIST of the Revolutionary period, at least as far as historians are concerned, was Isaiah Thomas. He was no less partisan than Sam Adams, but considerably more ethical; he did not encourage violence, did not ignore facts, did not draw up diagrams for acts of public revolt. Thomas admired Adams, was as fervent a supporter of independence as he, and in fact claimed to have been inspired in his choice of career by the fire-and-brimstone thunderations of the *Boston Gazette*, which was a perfect match for his own political views and uncompromising patriotism. Otherwise, though, he had more in common with Benjamin Franklin, who had long since left the print shop for the corridors of power.

Like Franklin, Thomas started his career early. Franklin was twelve when he began toiling for his brother; Thomas, whose widowed mother had four other children to support, forced him into an apprenticeship when he was half as old. And, like Franklin, Thomas was prohibited by the terms of his indenture from engaging in all manner of activities irrelevant to a six-year-old, among them marriage, fornication, gambling, and consumption of alcoholic beverages.

Like Franklin, Thomas was a laborer at first, a boy doing the dirty work of a man's trade, although he was a boy so small that when he first entered the print shop, he had to stand on a stool eighteen inches high to set the type for master Zechariah Fowles's jobs. "I early became intimately acquainted with the whole transaction," he said many years afterward, "and deep impressions were then made upon my mind in favor of the liberty of the press."

Like Franklin, Thomas eventually tired of his master and refused to remain in his service any longer despite his affection for the work. When he was sixteen, although still legally bound to Fowles, he ran away, ending up in Nova Scotia and finding employment at the *Halifax Gazette*. It proved a fortuitous landing place, for despite his youth—or perhaps because of it, if the owner somehow believed that no one of such limited years could cause unlimited mischief—Thomas was allowed the same free rein that Edes and Gill had allowed Adams at Boston's *Gazette*. It was not, for the Canadian, a good decision.

Thomas made his position known from the first issue he produced: the British had shown themselves to be miscreants in virtually all of their edicts regarding the American colonies, and they were especially to blame for the insensitivity and excesses of the Stamp Act. Thomas varied his terms but repeated the charges in the next issue, and the next, and more. The paper's owner, whose name is lost to history, told his editor to pipe down. The editor refused. The owner had no choice but to fire the boy, and after considering and rejecting several courses of action, Thomas headed back to Boston.

Like Franklin, Thomas was lacking in formal education. But he borrowed books and read them well into the night with unbroken concentration, memorizing long passages of history, biography, religion, philosophy, and science. Says John Tebbel, Thomas "emerged from a lifetime of study as one of the finest scholars in America, the possessor of one of its best private libraries, a historian of note, and a founder and first president of the Antiquarian Society. Thomas got his education from setting type and reading galley proofs, and from living with books all his life."

Also like Franklin, Thomas did not marry as suitably as he might have. In fact, after he and Mary Dill had two children, Thomas told a Massachusetts court that he had just learned something horrifying about her: before they met, she had given birth to a "bastard sone [sic]" and, not only that, "had been prostituted to the purposes of more than one." Thomas asked for and was granted a divorce. Mary Dill sorrowfully consented. As far as Thomas was concerned, the woman was now a stranger to him; from this point on, even though he would marry again twice, it was his newspaper to which he was truly wed.

Thomas further calls Franklin to mind in that he became a newspaper publisher in his early twenties; he was barely twenty-one when he produced the first issue of the *Massachusetts Spy* in 1770. His partner was Zechariah Fowles, of all people, whose tutelage Thomas no longer needed but whose financing had proved to be indispensable. But only at the outset; before long, the *Spy* became so successful that the former apprentice was able to buy out his old master as well as to win the respect of his declared political opposite, Jemmy Rivington, who conceded that "few men, perhaps, were better qualified [than Thomas] . . . to publish a newspaper. No newspaper in the colonies was better printed, or was more copiously furnished with foreign intelligence."

Rivington's respect for Thomas was not tinged with approval. When the latter dug up the *Pennsylvania Gazette*'s old snake cartoon and attached the parts and printed it again, stretching it across most of his front page, directly under the masthead, as a means of urging the colonies to stand together against the Crown, Rivington could not help but hiss at him in print.

> YE Sons of Sedition, how comes it to pass,
> That America's typ'd by a SNAKE—in the grass?
> Don't you think 'tis a scandalous, saucy reflection,
> That merits the soundest, severest Correction,
> NEW-ENGLAND's the Head too;—NEW ENGLAND's
>   abused;
> For the *Head of the serpent* we know *should be* Bruised.

❁

AS A RULE, newspaper publishers of the time did not chase after interviews or hustle to the scenes of events with their juices flowing and pen fingers twitching. For the most part, they were denizens of the print shop, preferring that the news be spoken in their ears or slipped under their doors—that it be delivered to them, in other words, as spices were delivered to the grocer or bolts of cloth to the tailor.

Thomas, however, was different. If not exactly a man of action, he was at least a man who preferred to be closer to the action than most of his colleagues did. On April 18, 1775, he "sat in the belfry of the Old North Church . . . along with other Minutemen, and flashed the signals which sent Paul Revere on his ride." The next day, having journeyed to Lexington, he wrote of the mayhem before him, becoming in the process the first American war correspondent.

AMERICANS! Forever bear in mind the BATTLE of LEX-INGTON!—where British Troops, unmolested and unprovoked, wantonly and in a most cruel manner fired upon and killed a number of our countrymen, then robbed them of their provisions, ransacked, plundered and burnt their houses! Nor could the tears of defenceless women, some of whom were in the pains of childbirth, the cries of helpless babes, nor the prayers of old age, confined to beds of sickness, appease their thirst for blood!—or divert them from their DESIGN of MURDER and ROBBERY!

That was how Thomas's report in the May 3, 1775, issue of the *Massachusetts Spy* began. Then he shifted tone dramatically, going from firebrand to meticulous and relatively neutral observer, writing of troop movements, of verbal exchanges between militiamen and redcoats, of guns being drawn, of ground being gained and lost and regained. At which point he shifted tone again, returning to partisanship and possibly exaggeration. "We have the pleasure to say," he wrote near the end of the account, "that notwithstanding the big provocations given by the enemy, not one instance of cruelty, we have heard of, was committed by our Militia."

The following week, Thomas reminded the Crown that "[t]he *whigs* call no man *master* under heaven." The week after that, he blasted British lawmakers as "the most sanguinary and despotic court that ever disgraced a free country," then referred to King George III and his ministers as "the most profligate and abandoned administration," and dismissed the citizens of the British Isles as "a venal and corrupt majority." By this time his paper was calling itself the *Massachusetts Spy, Or, American Oracle of Liberty*, and above the name on the front page, he sounded an alarm to all readers: "Americans!—Liberty or Death!—Join or Die!" The snake, which he continued to present unsevered, must forever remain that way.

Fearing that the British had come to revile the *Spy* no less than they did the *Boston Gazette*, and therefore that troops would destroy his business if they happened upon it, Thomas moved from Boston to a less conspicuous building in nearby Watertown. And he came to fear for his life as well as his livelihood. "Twice he was threatened with assassination," writes biographer Alice Marble, and "once warned by a British officer, whom he had befriended, that his name was among those 'proscribed.'" Thomas had to be cautious now in his actions; he would not, however, be cautious with his words.

❁

OTHER PAPERS WERE SIMILARLY URGENT about the outbreak of war. The *New Hampshire Gazette* had "BLOODY NEWS" to report. The *Essex* [Massachusetts] *Gazette* proclaimed that the

"Cruelty" on the part of the British at Lexington and Concord was "not less brutal than what our venerable Ancestors received from the vilest Savages of the Wilderness." The *New-York Journal* opted for sarcasm rather than invective, remarking, "The kind intentions of our good mother—our tender, indulgent mother—are at last revealed to all the world."

The *Pennsylvania Gazette* took a different tone, publishing a letter, a plea from someone calling himself Memento "to stop the further effusion of the BLOOD of our COUNTRYMEN, and prevent us from being engaged in all the horrors" of armed conflict. But in the *Boston Gazette*, which had also moved to the outskirts of town for the time being, Sam Adams, his prose now more agitated than ever, implored those who supported the Crown to

> repent of your villainies, before it be too late, that you may avoid the just execrations of an injured people, who possibly may execute upon you the punishments you by your complicated crimes have merited, and you should suffer the more terrible punishments of another world. For the sake of Great Britain, do not resolve with your *deluded king* steadily to pursue such measures for the support of the constitutional rights of Great-Britain, *as will inevitably destroy them*, and such measures for her commercial interest, *as will infallibly annihilate it*, lest your old CHASTISERS should make use of that great Supporter of the rights of mankind, the Printing Press, which is now preparing for the further scourging of Tyranny and Tyrants, and hand your name down with infamy, 'till its hateful sound shall be banished from America.

Tory newspapers were equally spiteful, but because they lived in the shadows of retaliation, not nearly as often. Later in the year, for instance, the *New York Gazette and Weekly Mercury* reported that "[t]he shattered Remains of the Rebel Army, 'tis said, are got over into the Jersies. Humanity cannot but pity a Set of poor misguided

Men who are thus led on to Destruction, by despicable and desperate Leaders, against every idea of Reason and Duty, and without the least Prospect of Success."

In time, success would come for the patriots. The Tory press would do its best to ignore it.

❁

THE REVOLUTIONARY WAR was not an easy one to cover. For one thing, once the fighting started there was more news than ever but no more shipments of ink or type or spare parts for the presses coming into American ports. There were no more shipments of paper either, and, as for the quantities still available or smuggled into the colonies from a friend in the motherland or a trader in another European nation, there were higher priorities for it than journalism. Legislative bodies needed it for their records and proclamations, businessmen for their accounts; army officers were still issuing orders, clergymen still writing sermons. "*Rags taken in at the Printing Office*," wrote *The Freemen's Journal or New-Hampshire Gazette*, urging its readers to provide them, "For the Paper-Mill now erected at Exeter." But few such structures were being built during the war.

There was also a shortage of printers now; many of them were on the battlefield making news rather than in their shops publishing it. And, understandably, there was a shortage of men willing to risk their lives by sneaking past British battalions and dodging bullets to deliver papers to their subscribers. The numbers of subscribers had thinned as well; they too were making news rather than reading it. Furthermore, the hardships of war were such that some people could no longer afford to pay for their weekly dose of current events.

It is for these reasons that seventeen newspapers existing before the war failed to survive it. A similar number started publishing during the war but quickly went out of business.

But even the papers that were able to carry on, to find enough manpower and supplies to turn out their editions regularly, found themselves struggling. Information was hard to come by. There were no "embedded" journalists at the time and virtually no journalists of any sort close to the action. There were no daily briefings from the Pentagon or officials in the field, no official dispatches of any sort that the newspapers could publish or at least rely on for a few details.

As a result, one of their main sources of information was the letters and reports sent by George Washington, commander in chief of the Continental army, to members of Congress. Some of them were battle cries; Washington viewed the war as "a noble Cause we are engaged in, it is the Cause of virtue and mankind, every temporal advantage and comfort to us, and our posterity, depends upon the Vigour of our exertions." Most of Washington's wartime correspondence, though, seems to have been written by aides and was practical more than hortatory: updates on recent battles, requests for more men, money, and materiel, and, in at least one case, an order from Washington relayed from Brigadier General William Woodford through the pages of the *Virginia Gazette*:

> I have it in express command from his Excellency General WASHINGTON to order all officers belonging to the continental army in this State, whose furloughs have expired, or who were not limited to any particular time, to join their respective corps with as much expedition as possible. Many, weighty reasons influence the Commander in Chief to wish a punctual compliance with this order, the most striking one is, that the enemy are drawing their force to one point.

On occasion, a journalist would decide he wanted to do more than merely publish a letter from Washington or one of his subordinates. He wanted to talk to the general himself, ask him in person about an issue, implore him to expand on this point or clarify that one or answer a question about a matter he had not addressed at all.

Washington did not encourage such requests, but neither did he try to deceive. "There is no evidence," writes biographer James Thomas Flexner, "that Washington ever tried to influence the writers except by controlling the information they in the first place received. He on one occasion asked congress for 'a small traveling press to follow headquarters' and 'an ingenious man to accompany this press and be employed wholly in writing for it. . . . If the people had a channel of intelligence that from its usual authenticity they could look up to with confidence,' that would frustrate false rumors, undermine despondency and the propaganda of the enemy."

Other news on the fighting, however sketchy, came from the dispatches of Washington's generals to their various colonial governments and from letters that soldiers sent to their friends and families, which the recipients read eagerly, then passed along to their local newspapers—an informal information network, a kind of loose-limbed and not always reliable Associated Press. The *Pennsylvania Gazette* published a letter from an officer aboard the man-of-war *Somerset*, which had recently engaged the enemy at sea, and the officer swore that he and his mates were serious in their desire to repel the British, "that neither BLOOD nor TREASURE shall be spared to bring our brethren to what is called a sense of duty." Some time later, *The Freemen's Journal or New-Hampshire Gazette* shared with its readers the conviction of a young soldier that his commanding officer did not deserve the criticism he was receiving from some quarters. "His Excellency General WASHINGTON, is a Man," the letter began, "just, wise, and merciful: loving all good Men, and beloved by them, and beloved by his Soldiers remarkably: a stranger to envy, ill-will, and fear of Death: in dangers martial, magnanimous, persevering . . . equally dear to all the Friends of America, and dreadful to all her Enemies!"

One assumes the soldier felt the same way when his letter was finally published; the news was, after all, still moving slowly. The first shots of the war were reported in at least one Boston paper on April 19, the same day they were fired. But Philadelphia learned of them on April 25; New York and Baltimore on the 27th; Williams-burg, Virginia, on the 29th; Charleston, South Carolina, on May 9; and Savannah, Georgia, not until May 31, almost six weeks after the fighting had begun.

❁

SHORTLY AFTER RECEIVING HIS PARDON, Jemmy Rivington, whose paper had been among those highly critical of Washington, had returned to England in search of equipment and approbation. He wanted a new printing press; he wanted British officials to ex-press their appreciation for his support in the face of overwhelm-ing opposition in hostile territory. To his great satisfaction, and perhaps surprise, he got both, and more. Rivington was welcomed effusively by a number of officials both at court and in Parliament; he was thanked heartily and provided not only with a new press and several trays of type but also with an appointment as the Crown's official printer in New York—all of which led him to be effusive in his own expressions of gratitude.

But he took his time about returning to the colonies, afraid to avail himself of either his apparatus or his appointment until the summer of 1777, when the British captured New York and Riving-ton thought he could once again settle in the colonies and earn a living without peril. He arranged passage to New York, perhaps anonymously, arriving without fanfare and starting anew with both his newspaper and his bookshop.

It was in the autumn of that year, in his new capacity of "Printer to the King's Most Excellent Majesty," that Jemmy Rivington began producing a paper again, determined both to keep up the verbal bombardments on the patriots and to recoup some of the money that their pillaging had cost him. Like Edes and Gill before him, he seems, at least on occasion, to have been a merchant more than an ideologue. The following ad appeared in what was now called the *New York Royal Gazette* in November 1777:

JAMES RIVINGTON

Has brought from LONDON *a variety of articles purchased of the*
neatest and most excellent manufacturers in their several faculties:
GENTLEMEN's SHOES, neatly stitched and
Bound, of London manufacture.
Gentlemen's SILK STOCKINGS
of various prices and patterns, with or without embroidery
clocks and random figures, gauze, wove, spun,
knit, ribbed or plain, adapted to the form,
lusty, moderate, or emaciate.

Rivington also hawked a selection of other goods: snuff, fishing tackle, mathematical instruments, magnifiers, shoe buckles, sword belts, and money scales "for weighing gold, with spare pennyweights and grains." All items were available for purchase, at the fairest of prices, from the aforementioned Mr. Rivington at his place of business.

And then, a few months later, ever resourceful, ever seeking a return to the riches of his youth, or at least the modest income of the days before his print shop was vandalized, he came up with yet another money-making scheme, this time running an ad for

AN
HISTORICAL ACCOUNT
OF THE
WAR IN AMERICA
From the affair of LEXINGTON:
I. This work to be bound, and illustrated with plans,
shewing the marches of the army, &c.
II. The price to subscribers, TWO DOLLARS,
—The money retained in the hands
of the agent in England until the work is ready to be delivered
. . . six months after the war is over.

The fighting was still intense, the end of it not in sight, the out-come far from certain—and already a publisher was hawking the official record of the war's outcome. The book was never written, though, and if it had been it would not have had the ending that one of the *Royal Gazette*'s letter writers had so confidently predict-ed late in the winter of 1780:

Mr. RIVINGTON,

I am convinced the rebellion is nearly over many known and generally received reasons might be adduced to prove this, such as the depreciation of Congress dollars and the general misery and distress of those who were once men of property and now have in a refugee'd state nothing to depend upon but what they can procure by the sale of plate and old cloaths.

❀

FEW WERE THE PATRIOTS who availed themselves of Jemmy Rivington's various moneymaking schemes. As the *Gazette* contin-ued to portray such people as ingrates—their politics misguided and their papers indecent and their manners no better than those of the animals they raised on those farms of theirs—they were not about to help the publisher unload the merchandise from his brief hiatus in Britain and turn exile into a profit-making venture. So controversial had Rivington become, in fact, that Governor William Livingston of New Jersey would eventually write to Gou-verneur Morris to chastise him for his previous support of the printer and to say, "If Rivington is taken, I must have one of his ears; Governor Clinton [of New York] is entitled to the other; and General Washington, if he pleases, may take his head."

Washington, were he one to collect such trophies, might have chosen a hand, or perhaps both hands, those that set the type against him, attacking him so unyieldingly and, as the years went by and the war ground on, sometimes resorting to snideness rather than polemic. "Our old acquaintance Mr. Washington," the *Royal Gazette* wrote in 1780, as Washington led his troops toward a confrontation with the British in New York, "we learn is approaching us Polyphemus-like, with hasty and ample strides, his dire intents (supported by myriads of heroes and in his train a thirteen-inch mortar drawn by eight charming lively oxen) are given out to be another coup upon Powles Hook."

But in fact Washington would not have harmed Rivington, not under any circumstances, because the hands that operated the printing press so critical of the general were also hands that passed along secrets of the British navy to colonial leaders. For Jemmy Rivington—dandy, Tory, and longtime public foe of America's commander in chief—was a spy. How long he had been one no one knows. Nor can anyone say what made him turn or how passionate he was in his eventual commitment to the rebel cause. But as the publisher of New York's leading anti-patriot paper, he found himself trusted with details of many of the Crown's military maneuvers, and at some point he began passing them along to his supposed foes. He would write down the information on pieces of paper, slip the sheets into the books that he sold in his shop, and then pass the books along to colonial agents pretending to be customers.

It was a valuable service that Rivington provided; on one occasion, he helped to break a British code, a feat that, although it did not lead to victory, almost surely saved American lives during one of the war's earlier battles. On other occasions, his intelligence enabled the patriots to avoid ambush, rethink strategy, and protect encampments. Jemmy Rivington turned out to be quite a different man in deed than he was on the page.

Another Englishman who immigrated to America and who shared with Rivington a passion for journalism would provide a valuable service of his own to the rebel cause, and would do so in a much more direct and open manner.

CHAPTER ELEVEN

Uncommon Prose

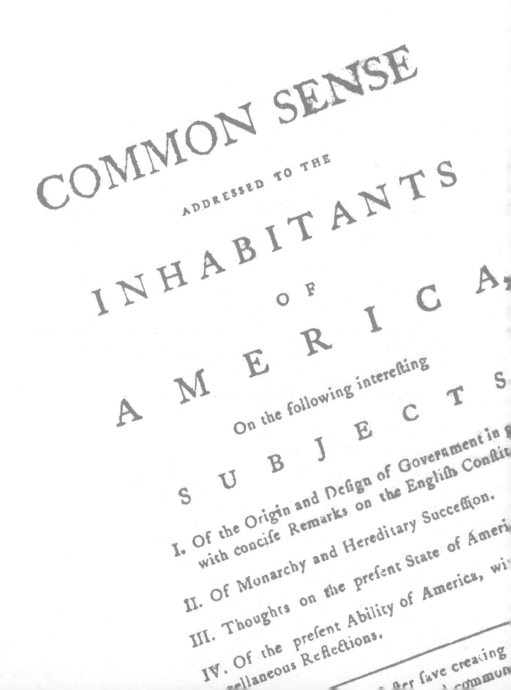

COMMON SENSE

ADDRESSED TO THE

INHABITANTS

OF

AMERICA,

On the following interesting

SUBJECTS.

I. Of the Origin and Design of Government in
with concise Remarks on the English Constit

II. Of Monarchy and Hereditary Succession.

III. Thoughts on the present State of Ameri

IV. Of the present Ability of America, wi
    ellaneous Reflections.

*C*OLONIAL PRINTERS did not just publish newspapers—not before the war, not during, not afterward. They continued to publish documents for agencies of government and various other materials, such as sermons, speeches, and contracts, for private clients. Sometimes they published old-fashioned broadsides: single sheets, single points of view, similar to the handbills passed out on street corners today that advertise cheap haircuts or designer suits for men at half price.

And they turned out pamphlets, Sunday supplements of a sort, commentaries on the news of the day, which, because they were separate business ventures from their newspapers, provided printers of the era with the additional income that Franklin and Bradford had hoped might one day come from magazines. They also provided deniability; a printer could disavow the contents of a pamphlet if he so desired, since those who wrote them were simply using the printer's facilities, not speaking for him as employees or associates. The facilities were, in a manner of speaking, a form of vanity press for the authors. And because the authors were not affiliated with the newspaper, they were often new voices in the community debate, new sources of information and perspective; their work, at least theoretically, would make the debate more varied and substantive.

Furthermore, pamphlets were considerably longer than newspaper articles, which allowed a more detailed examination of their subjects, background as well as foreground—if not necessarily several sides of an issue, at least a thorough presentation of the case for one side.

For these reasons, most printers in the eighteenth century were as eager to encourage the pamphlet trade as they were to publish their gazettes and courants and chronicles and journals. The trade quickly became a booming one, all the more so when, as was often the case, the tone of the writing was intemperate. As the *Pennsylvania Gazette* put it:

> Pamphlets have madden'd round the Town
> And drove poor Moderation down.

James Otis wrote several pamphlets, although with "Gothic irregularity and intemperance." Perhaps the best known was *The Rights of the British Colonies Asserted and Proved*, published by Edes and Gill in 1764, a year before the Stamp Act. Later events would prove the author to be more than a little naive. "We have every thing good and great to hope from our gracious Sovereign, his Ministry and his Parliament," Otis opined,

> and trust that when the services and sufferings of the British American colonies are fully known to the mother country, and the nature and importance of the plantation trade more perfectly understood at home, that the most effectual measures will be taken for perpetuating the British empire in all parts of the world. An empire built upon the principles of justice, moderation and equity, the only principles that can make a state flourishing, and enable it to elude the machinations of its secret and inveterate enemies.

The following year, dozens of pamphlets rolled off presses in response to the Stamp Act. Perhaps the most influential was the work of a Maryland attorney named Daniel Dulany, who, in *Considerations of the Propriety of Imposing Taxes in the British Colonies,* declared that propriety was altogether lacking; since Americans were not represented in Parliament, they should not be taxed by Parliament—it was as simple, and as obvious, as that. Later, James Bowdoin, who would one day be the governor of Maine, was one of several men responsible for a lengthy analysis of the Boston Massacre; it was distributed in all the colonies and probably informed more Americans about the violence at the Custom House than any other single source.

According to biographer Dumas Malone, Thomas Jefferson's *A Summary View of the Rights of British America*, from 1774, "gained wider currency than any other writing of his that was published during the Revolution except the Declaration, and it clearly anticipated that more famous and more polished document. It contributed to his contemporary reputation, and until this day it has commanded the deeply respectful attention of historians."

In the spring of 1776, a year after the war had begun, North Carolina congressman William Hooper wrote to fellow congressman John Adams asking for his ideas on proper governance. Adams wrote back, happy to supply them. A sample:

> The wretched condition of this country [England], however, for ten or fifteen years past, has frequently reminded me of their principles and reasonings. They will convince any candid mind, that there is no good government but what is republican. That the only valuable part of the British constitution is so, because the very definition of a republic is "an empire of laws, and not of men." That, as a republic is the best of governments, so that particular arrangement of the powers of society, or, in other words, that form of government which is best contrived to secure an impartial and exact execution of the laws, is the best of republics.

When Hooper told others about Adams's response, they requested copies. Soon the letter would be printed as a pamphlet, first in Philadelphia, then in Boston, then elsewhere. Called *Thoughts on*

Government: Applicable to the Present State of the American Colonies, it was modest in title but mighty in effect; at least two states would model their constitutions on the pamphlet, agreeing with Adams that the British system was no longer the model for effective rule.

And then there was the pamphlet that would prove to be the most influential of them all, one that, for a time, would be read as widely as the Bible in North America and would sell a hundred times more copies in a single year than John Dickinson's *Letters from a Farmer in Pennsylvania* did in eight. Its author, an unknown when he picked up his pen, would become a major figure of the colonial era, and his work is almost as widely known today as it was then.

❋

Thomas Paine's life did not begin promisingly. He was born in 1737 in a small town about seventy miles north of London, the son of a corset maker and a woman whose parents had hoped she would marry someone of higher station. At sixteen he had grown into his adult body: taller than average for the time, well-built, and broad-shouldered. "His eye," said a friend, "of which the painter could not convey the exquisite meaning, was full, brilliant, and singularly piercing; it had in it the 'muse of fire.'"

But he could not yet see a future for himself. With his formal education and a term of employment in his father's shop behind him, the teenager ran away to sea. He should have known better; the ship on which he sailed was called the *Terrible* and the captain's name was William Death, the names proving to be omens as forbidding as they seemed. The experience was one that Paine would never forget, try though he might. He would stay on land as much as possible for the rest of his life.

Returning to England and having no idea what to do with himself, the young man took one job after another, showing little interest in any of them and making little money. In his spare time he sought more education—reading philosophy, studying science and geography, and debating the day's most controversial issues, such as the rights of both women and prison inmates, with anyone who would engage him.

Later he become a customs official, otherwise known as an exciseman. But he was less than diligent at the job, in part because it did not pay very well, and in part because he had so many other things on his mind at the time. Compounding the problems was his inability to manage his earnings wisely.

In 1772, thirty-five and broke, Paine began dealing in smuggled tobacco on the side. Once again he left his excise duties unattended, and on April 8, 1774, he was fired. To avoid debtors' prison, he had to auction off all his worldly goods. Meanwhile, his own fellow excisemen accused him of embezzling upward of £30 for his own use from a fund established to manage their petition to Parliament. Even Paine's own mother disowned him as a disgrace. For a man of real capacity, with a scientific intelligence (he later designed a remarkable iron bridge) as well as literary aptitude and ability, it had been a dismal life.

It would not remain one. In October 1774, Paine went to sea again, but only for a few weeks, this time sailing for America and what he hoped would be a new start. He traveled light. "Besides two letters of recommendation from Benjamin Franklin, whose acquaintance he had made in London," writes Scott Liell, who has studied Paine's life and work, "he came to Philadelphia carrying little in the way of money, reputation or prospects. What he did possess—to a degree that even Franklin might have blushed at— was a passionate attachment to liberty in all its forms and an abiding hatred of tyranny, especially in the English form."

Less than a year and a half later, after struggling to make both money and friends in the New World, Paine found a printer for a pamphlet he had written but not yet titled. The printer was Robert Bell, and the deal was this: Bell would publish a thousand copies of the pamphlet, as a result of which his total supply of paper would be exhausted. Paine would pay all costs, about £30. If more copies were required, the printer would come up with more paper and Paine with more money. And someone would have to come up with a title for the work.

Paine's first thought was *Plain Truth*, "perhaps," as has been suggested, "in homage of Dr. Franklin who had written an earlier pamphlet of the same name." But the more Paine thought about it, the less he liked it; he might have admired Franklin, but he wanted a title of his own. He finally decided on *Common Sense*.

The war was nine months old at the time, and at least a few of Paine's new countrymen were already disillusioned. The British army seemed too mighty to them, the colonial militia too disorganized and unprepared. The grievances of the past had perhaps been exaggerated, a number of Americans thought, and whether they had been or not, were insufficient provocation for the bloodshed of the present. Furthermore, the Crown was a force with history on its side; the colonists were afraid they might not even be a force at all. These were not the views of the majority, but they seemed to be gaining momentum: "patriotic fervor," as Joseph J. Ellis has commented, "began to erode just as the war became politically official and militarily threatening."

Thomas Paine set out to rally his fellow Americans.

He began *Common Sense* by claiming that he meant to offer, in addition to the title attribute, "nothing more than simple facts, [and] plain arguments." He was being modest. In prose both passionate and dignified, Paine pulled off that most difficult of literary feats, that rarest of essays, a scholarly polemic.

He told Americans who had begun to think of reconciliation with the motherland to think again.

Men of passive tempers look somewhat lightly over the offences of Britain, and, still hoping for the best, are apt to call out, *"Come, come, we shall be friends again, for all this."* But examine the passions and feelings of mankind, bring the doctrine of Reconciliation to the touchstone of nature, and then tell me, whether you can hereafter love, honour and faithfully serve the power that hath carried fire and sword into your land. If you cannot do all these, then are you only deceiving yourselves, and by your delay bringing ruin upon posterity.

There was, in fact, not "a single advantage that this continent can reap, by being connected with Great Britain." And Paine proceeded to make the case in every possible way in his forty-six-page pamphlet: politically and economically and geographically, legally and militarily, practically and theoretically. Sometimes his sentiments soared, at other times they proceeded in small, carefully measured steps. He had mastered all forms of argument, all styles of expression. He was, after all, "another of the self-educated polymaths the 18th century produced in such large numbers."

Finally, Paine urged Americans to free themselves from England once and for all.

Were a manifesto to be published, and dispatched to foreign courts, setting forth the miseries we have endured, and the peaceable methods we have ineffectually used for redress; declaring, at the same time, that not being able, any longer, to live happily or safely under the cruel disposition of the British court, we had been driven to the necessity of breaking off all connections with her; at the same time, assuring all such courts of our peaceable disposition towards them, and of our desire of entering into trade with them: Such a memorial would produce more good effects to this Continent, than if a ship were freighted with petitions to Britain.

Under our present denomination of British subjects, we can neither be received nor heard abroad: The custom of all courts is against us, and will be so, until, by an independence, we take rank with other nations.

These proceedings may at first appear strange and difficult; but, like all other steps which we have already passed over, will in a little time become familiar and agreeable; and, until an independence is declared, the Continent will feel itself like a man who continues putting off some unpleasant business from day to day, yet knows it must be done, hates to set about it, wishes it over, and is continually haunted with the thoughts of its necessity.

A few weeks before *Common Sense* was published, American troops had tried to seize Quebec and failed. There had been other failures as well, and George Washington could not help but fear even more in the future. He wondered how much support he had from the governments of the various colonies. He wondered about the will of his men, so poorly had they been trained, such unforeseen privations were they suffering. He also wondered about the effect of two "flaming arguments," as he called them, that British troops had recently made against the Americans—the fires they had set that ravaged two American ports.

And then one night, in a state close to despondency, Washington was given a copy of Thomas Paine's pamphlet and sat down to read. He was not only impressed but inspired. "A few more of such flaming arguments," he said, "as were exhibited at Falmouth and Norfolk, added to the sound doctrine and unanswerable reasoning contained in the pamphlet '*Common Sense*,' will not leave numbers at a loss to decide upon the propriety of separation."

Washington told his aides about the pamphlet. They read it for themselves and were no less inspired than their leader by Paine's arguments and his means of expressing them. Immediately a new ritual was established for the colonial militia in their struggles against the British. The commander in chief ordered his officers henceforth to gather their men around them in the evening and recite portions of *Common Sense* to them as if they were members of a congregation and the word of Paine were the word of the Almighty. "Conservatively," estimates John Ferling, "between January and July [1776] probably a quarter million colonists read it or heard it, roughly every other free adult living in Anglo-America."

The *New York Gazette and Weekly Mercury*, a Tory publication, could not understand such a reception. "Is this *common sense* or common nonsense?" it asked. Other Tory publications either ignored Paine's writing or dismissed it in similarly curt phrases. But the reaction of the patriot press was unanimously favorable, even adulatory. "Into an atmosphere of uncertainty and doubt," Scott Liell tells us, "*Common Sense* had come like the revelation of an absolute truth. As Samuel Adams would say, the people acted as if they had been 'awakened' by *Common Sense*—they now felt that they knew what must be done in the face of the gathering crisis."

And, as a young correspondent wrote to Nathan Hale, an American spy who would not live to see the war's end:

> Whether we ought in point of advantage to declare ourselves an independent state and fight as independents or still continue to resist as subjects is a question which has of late very much engross'd in these parts the conversation of every rank more especially since the appearance of a little pamphlet called *Common Sense*. . . . Have you seen it? Upon my word 'tis Well done—'tis what would be common sense were not most men so blinded by their prejudices that their sense of things is not what it ought to be—I confess a perusal of it has much reformed my notions upon several points & I own myself a staunch independent and ground my principles on almost innumerable arguments.

Years later, Paine would call to mind his feelings at the time that he was drafting *Common Sense*, and his hopes for the pamphlet once it was published:

> I saw, or at least thought I saw, a vast scene opening itself to the world in the affairs of America; and it appeared to me that unless the Americans changed the plan they were then pursuing

with respect to the government of England, and declare themselves independent, they would not only involve themselves in a multiplicity of new difficulties, but shut out the prospect that was then offering itself to mankind through their means. It was from these motives that I published *Common Sense*, which is the first work I ever did publish; and so far as I can judge of myself, I believe I never should have been known in the world as an author on any subject whatsoever had it not been for the affairs of America.

Paine thought of *Common Sense* as a gift to the nation he now called home. But the gift turned out to be far more than mere words on a page; it became, rather, a kind of endowment, for, as historian Benson Bobrick writes, he "had signed over the copyright of *Common Sense* to the Congress. At two shillings each, it went through edition after edition, until half a million copies had been sold. Penniless when he arrived from England, Thomas Paine had donated a fortune to the American cause."

Later, Paine would come to question that cause, or at least the way George Washington, as president of the United States, was interpreting it and, more to the point, the way he was treating Paine himself. But for now, in the early months of the war, the author could not have been more pleased by the effect his pamphlet was having on Americans at virtually every site of battle and every legislative chamber in the colonies. *Common Sense* was a troop of reinforcements for the morale of an army that seemed at times hopelessly overmatched.

❖

CHAPTER TWELVE

A Sword of a Different Kind

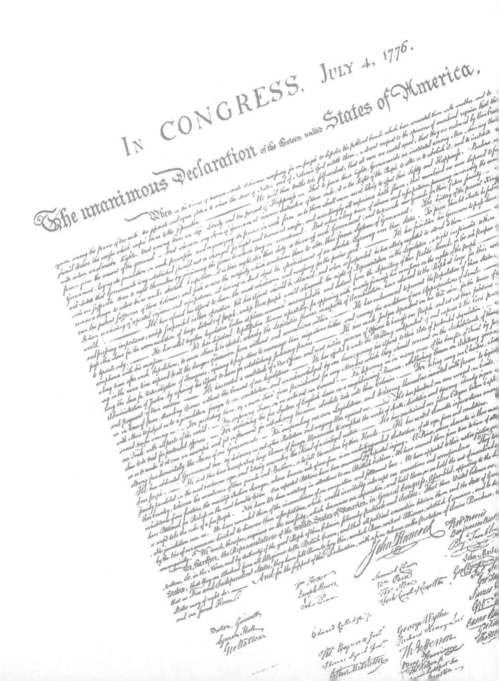

*B*UT THE MOST IMPORTANT LITERARY EFFORT of the war years was not *Common Sense* or any other pamphlet. It was not a letter posted from friend to friend or a letter to the editor of a newspaper or an article for a paper or a series of articles. It was, rather, the document that had sanctioned the fighting in the first place—and most Americans knew nothing about it until they saw it in the newspaper.

The first to learn were readers of the *Pennsylvania Evening Post*, which, on July 6, 1776, announced the signing of the Declaration of Independence.

On July 10, the *Massachusetts Spy* published a note from someone in Maryland who did not yet know that the paperwork for freedom had been adopted but was obviously hopeful. "The grand, the alarming, though necessary crisis," the writer said, "is at length arrived, for a public declaration of independence. Are there any of you so deficient in principles of virtue as not to approve of it?"

In the next few days, several papers reported that copies had reached the troops, especially in the New York area, and were being read aloud to them.

Public readings to civilians also became common—on street corners, in churches and taverns and town halls, as a prelude to meetings of town councils. Late in July, the *Massachusetts Spy* reported on one such reading in Boston, when

a number of patriotic gentlemen, animated with a love of their country, and to show their approbation of the measures lately taken by the Grand Council of America, assembled on the green, near the liberty pole, where, after having displayed the colours of the thirteen confederate colonies of America, the bells were set ringing and the drums a beating: After which, the Declaration of Independence of the United States was read to a large and respectable Body . . . who testified their approbation by repeated huzzas, firing of musketry and cannon, bonfires and other demonstrations of joy: When the arms of that tyrant in Britain, George the III of execrable memory, which in former times decorated, but of late disgraced the Court House in this town, were committed to the flames and consumed. To ashes; after which, a select company of the sons of freedom, repaired to the tavern lately known by the sign of the King's Arms, which odious signature of despotism was taken down by order of the people, which was cheerfully complied with by the innkeeper, where the following toasts were drank; and the evening spent with joy, on the commencement of the happy era.

Before long, papers would publish the Declaration of Independence in its entirety, with a paragraph of hosannas at the beginning and another of gratitude bringing up the rear. But, initially at least, the *Boston Gazette* printed the Declaration without comment. So did the *Virginia Gazette*. So did the *Pennsylvania Journal*. So did the *New York Journal*. So did the *Newport Mercury*. In fact, the majority of colonial papers at the time presented the Declaration without offering opinions of any sort, apparently believing that most Americans had already made their own private declarations and that the public version, the one that history would so revere, spoke for itself, having been written so clearly and eloquently by Jefferson and others that nothing more needed to be said. Which means that, in a sense, people thought of the Declaration of Independence as a formality, perhaps in some cases even a redundancy, the word catching up at long last to the deed. It is probably for this reason that John Adams, after signing the document, wrote a letter to his wife in which he did not even mention it until the seventh paragraph.

❁

AMERICAN JOURNALISM during the Revolutionary war was not what it had been before. No longer needing to preach rebellion, newspapers became more objective, or at least less provocative; no longer needing to laud the ideals of liberty and damn the British for their refusal to grant it to the colonies, newspapers settled for a more businesslike tone. Perhaps they believed that their readers would best be served in the struggles ahead by being told precisely how the struggles were going and, in at least one case, to lament the colonies' fate in almost Job-like terms.

Fall, 1776: George Washington had, in the view of many, failed in his first command; the British had forced him to evacuate Manhattan Island and to lead his troops northward to safety in White Plains. The *Massachusetts Spy* believed that Washington shared the blame with an unholy populace.

> We have thought God was for us, and had given many and signal instances of his power and mercy in our favor, and had greatly frowned upon and disappointed our enemies; and verily it has been so. But have we repented and given him the glory? Verily no. His hand seems to be turned and stretched out against us—and strong is his hand.

Spring, 1777: The fighting was two years old, and no decisive battles had yet been waged. British troops had just destroyed an important American storage depot at Danbury, Connecticut. A few miles away, in Ridgefield, General Benedict Arnold, not yet a traitor, was about to defeat a minor enemy force. For the most part, though, the Crown and the colonies still seemed to be devising strategies and jockeying for position rather than making real progress toward victory. From the *Boston Gazette* came a report about a battle in Fish-Kill, New York, in which the patriots did not fare well.

> By the Morris-Town post we are informed, that early last Sabbath day morning, a large body of the enemy attacked about 400 of our troops at Bound Brock, and that after a smart engagement, they got possession of the village.
>
> A Gentleman just now arrived from headquarters, says, that we left 2 men killed, and 20 taken prisoners, also two field pieces; and that the enemy are gone off again. The same gentleman says, three British men of war are gone up the river Delaware.

Late winter, 1778: There was confidence in the air, an occasional whiff of it at least, as the colonies had recently signed two separate treaties with the French for assistance in the war. Occasionally, a paper could not restrain itself. A few months after General Horatio Gates defeated the British under General John Burgoyne in an important battle at Saratoga, New York, *The Freeman's Journal or New-Hampshire Gazette* decided that a mere report was not enough; it would, rather, rhapsodize.

> HAIL! Glorious chief, whom distiny [sic] has chose
> To bound the limits of thy country's woes;
> Whom all, with pleas'd astonishment surveys,
> Shall the adventurous muse presume to praise . . .
> . . .
> Thee then I sing—ye gracious nine [the muses] inspire
> Unnumber'd beauties to attend my lyre;
> Be silent all—its laurel-d triumph rears
> The name of Gates, which tyrants trembling, hears.

But this kind of thing, both the poetry and the effusiveness of the praise, was the exception in war reporting.

Spring, 1778: General George Rogers Clark headed west and captured a British outpost on the Mississippi River near the present-day site of East St. Louis, Illinois. Meanwhile, the news of Burgoyne's defeat had been carried to France, where, according to the *Boston Gazette*, it was "received with as much joy as if a victory by their own troops had been announced. Our Plenipotentiaries took this opportunity again to attract the attention of the Court of France to the object of their negociation."

Late spring, 1778: That object was to enlist even more French support for the American war effort, and in no small part because of Gates's performance at Saratoga, which convinced the French of American military competence, the object was successful. *The Freemen's Journal* reported on British reaction to the news that France was no longer in league with Indians against the colonists but was now their ally against the Crown.

His Majesty having been informed, by order of the French King, that a Treaty of Amity and Commerce, has been signed Between the court of France & certain persons employed by his Majesty's revolted subjects in North-America, has judged it necessary to direct, that a copy of the declaration delivered by the French ambassador to Lord Viscount Weymouth, be laid before the House of Lords; and at the same time to acquaint them, that his Majesty has tho't proper, in consequence of this offensive communication on the part of the court of France, to send orders to his ambassador to withdraw from that court.

Spring, 1779: The British were making some progress in Virginia, burning sections of Portsmouth and Norfolk. But with that and a few other exceptions, the war was going well for the colonists in the South, and the *Boston Gazette* was unable to resist a few words of optimism.

General Ash's division will be crossed Savannah this evening, and General Williamson's follows to-morrow, with the wagons &c. to proceed in the rear of the enemy, who from authentic accounts are retreated below Bryar-creek. We shall soon have a force as will oblige the enemy to quit the State of Georgia.

Summer, 1780: But optimism was not always warranted, and when it was inappropriate, it did not make its way onto the composing stick. The *Pennsylvania Gazette*, for example, informed its readers that all was not well at a river crossing near Philadelphia.

While the enemy were making demonstrations to their left, their right column advanced on Major Lee. The bridge was disputed with great obstinancy, and the enemy must have received very considerable injury, but by fording the river, and gaining the point of the hill, they obliged the Major with his party to give up the pass. At this instant of time, their left column began the attack on Col. Angell; the action was fevered and lasted about forty minutes.

As a result, the British "forced our troops to retire over the second bridge."

❁

IN THE FALL OF 1781, the war took its most dramatic and decisive turn, one that had been gloomily expected by the British press. Shortly before the defeat of British troops under Lord Cornwallis at Yorktown, Virginia, the London *Courant* predicted that a "crimson coloured curtain" would soon drop, bringing to an end the "dreadful TRAGEDY we have been acting in America."

When the curtain fell, the *Boston Gazette* published one of the few genuine headlines of the period, the type not only large but exultant: "CORNWALLIS TAKEN" it blared for all to see, and the article went on to describe the victory, which effectively ended the war, as a "glorious Conquest." Fully half of the American soldiers at Yorktown, writes historian Stacy Schiff, were in fact French.

The *Pennsylvania Journal* was, at least to modern ears, more droll than hearty in its account of Yorktown. "I have the honour to inform Congress," wrote one of Washington's aides in a letter that became the *Journal*'s war dispatch, "that a reduction of the British army, under the command of Lord Cornwallis, is most happily effected." But before the letter was published, in the early morning hours of October 2, 1781, many Philadelphians heard news of Yorktown from someone else, not the *Pennsylvania Journal* or any other newspaper but a "running patterer," one of the city's night watchmen, described as a German immigrant who "shattered the breathless hush of night by belting out the . . . tidings in every street in the capital: 'Basht dree o'clock, und Gorn-wal-lis isht da-ken.'"

Most American newspapers, though, told of Cornwallis's defeat with little self-congratulation and less emotion. They reported it as they had reported so much of the rest of the war, in relatively brief stories that often appeared on page two or three or even four, as the front pages continued to feature letters to the editor about matters other than war, or the minutes of legislative proceedings, or the proclamations of various governmental bodies or, more than anything else, ads: shoes and stockings were ever for sale, soaps and sweet oils still begging to be purchased, anvils and nails ready as always to assist the artisan.

Journalists, it appears to us now, simply could not decide what to make of events as momentous as a war for independence against the nation that most Americans called home. Had they gotten used to the notion that the purpose of a press was to dwell on matters quotidian more than monumental? Did they believe that their readers would seek information about the war no matter what page it was on and how dryly it was rendered, and decide what to make of it without undue assistance? If so, there was no need for a publisher to disturb his usual patterns of story placement. Or was it that Americans were an essentially modest people who could not help but be modest in their ordering of events?

Whatever the reason, it is surprising to read the colonial papers today and come across such earth-changing events rendered, more often than not, in such understated fashion, and to see that advertising intruded on occurrences no less then than it does today.

And when those papers finally had an end of the war to report, an official end, they did so with relief more than bravado. Again, many of them refrained from comment, simply publishing the preliminary articles of peace agreed to in Paris, which pointed out, according to the *Newport* (Rhode Island) *Mercury*, that both sides were "animated with an equal desire to put an end to the calamities of war." When the articles became final, the *Pennsylvania Journal* hoped that the Treaty of Paris would allow the colonies and the motherland "to forget all past misunderstandings and differences that have unhappily interrupted the good correspondence and friendship which they mutually wish to restore, and to establish such a beneficial and satisfactory intercourse between the two countries, upon the ground of reciprocal advantages and mutual convenience, as may promote and secure to both perpetual peace and harmony."

In London, the *Gentlemen's Magazine* was similarly wistful, stating that if the Crown had granted American independence without a war, the former colonies "would have been our ally and friend, and many thousands of lives and millions of money, would have been saved to both nations."

❖

PERHAPS THE IMPORTANCE OF THE PRESS to the outcome of the war can be exaggerated, but not easily and not by much. It was newspapers that kept the colonies informed of the progress of the fighting in a way that letters and patterers could not have done, and in the process united the colonies in a way that was beyond the ability of the jerry-built wartime government.

Certainly the war would not have begun as soon as it did without the encouragement of the press. As *New York Journal* editor John Holt said on one occasion to Sam Adams, "It was by means of News papers that we receiv'd & spread the Notice of the tyrannical Designs formed against America, and kindled a Spirit that has been sufficient to repel them."

And, almost certainly, the war would not have ended with an American victory in a period of seven years from first shot to signed treaty had not the newspapers—and some pamphlets—constantly reminded the colonists of the cause they shared, thereby inspiring the valor of soldiers and the patience and support of civilians.

The British knew it, too. The *Boston Gazette* was the only paper on their hit list before the war began, but as battles raged and patriot prose became ever more the tie that bound the colonies into a makeshift nation, the British set upon print shops as they did stray battalions of colonial militia. Sometimes, rather than wrecking the supplies and equipment, they stole them and delivered them to Tory publishers for more sympathetic use. Virtually all colonies suffered losses, although a private secretary to one of the British admirals rued the fact that so many patriot printers managed to stay in business regardless. "Among other Engines, which have raised the present Commotion next to the indecent Harangues of the Preachers," he complained, "none has had a more extensive or stronger Influence than the Newspapers of the respective Colonies."

In 1789, an American physician named David Ramsay wrote one of the first histories of the Revolutionary War. It was richly detailed and even more richly biased; referring to patriot Colonel John Laurens, for instance, Ramsay pointed out that "Nature had adorned him with a large proportion of her choicest gifts. . . . A dauntless bravery was the least of his virtues, and an excess of it his greatest foible."

But for all the favoritism he showed, Ramsay keenly understood the role that newspapers had played in the outcome of the war, and he put it nicely: "In establishing American independence," he wrote, "the pen and the press had a merit equal to that of the sword."

The pen and the press would continue to be wielded, perhaps even more viciously than before, although for entirely different reasons, in the years ahead.

III

The Tumult of Peace

CHAPTER THIRTEEN

The Passionate Decade

THE FEDERALIST

A COMMENTARY ON THE CONSTI-
TUTION OF THE UNITED STATES

BEING A

COLLECTION OF ESSAYS

WRITTEN BY

ALEXANDER HAMILTON,
MADISON AND JOHN

In Support of the Constitution Agre
September 17, 1787, by the Federal C

WITH AN INTRODUCTI

YLORD B
Yal

N O SOONER DID AMERICANS stop fighting the British than they started fighting one another. After newspapers ceased to report on military exploits and denunciations of the Crown they began to fill their columns with the cannonades of politics. Having briefly put aside their old ways of lying and dissembling, exaggerating and trivializing, distorting and abusing and insulting, journalists turned to them again with a new and even more pointed vehemence as they began to consider the most important question of the time, possibly the most important question Americans have ever had to ask themselves: Now that we have won the right to govern ourselves, how, precisely, do we go about it?

The question was not a new one. It had first been raised, although in a different context, at the Albany Congress of 1754, where delegates from seven colonies joined representatives from the six nations of the Iroquois and tried to answer the most important question of that particular age: What is the best way for us to protect ourselves from attack by the French and Indians, who, each for their own reasons, had joined forces against the New World colonists?

One possibility was to persuade the Iroquois to shift their allegiance from the French to the British; they seemed more likely candidates for a change of heart than did most of the other North American tribes. Another possibility was to listen to the delegate from Pennsylvania, who had been thinking long and hard about the matter and who had a track record of thoughts turning out successfully. Benjamin Franklin arrived in Albany "far-sighted as always," in Walter A. McDougall's view, "with an extraordinary plan for a colonial federation led by a President-general and Grand Council empowered to raise money and troops for the common defense. After some tinkering, the delegates at Albany accepted the plan."

Then they sent the plan to their respective colonial legislatures, where it was unanimously, and in most cases quickly, rejected. For the colonies to form a union, they feared, would be for them to surrender autonomy, and they could not bring themselves to do that, to allow others to make decisions for them, even if the decision makers were fellow Americans who had been chosen by a free and open vote. The Albany delegates seemed to fear a slippery slope—a president-general today, a monarchy tomorrow; a grand council now, a loss of freedom later. And they feared, as always, unjust taxation. They wanted guarantees that none of this would happen in the future, guarantees beyond the mere promises of Franklin and his supporters; without them, said the *South Carolina Gazette*, one of many newspapers skeptical of the congress up North, "we shall gradually consume ourselves in vain, and waste our Strength."

Franklin was disappointed. He thought that in rejecting his plan, his countrymen had cast a vote for chaos. They did not trust government and they did not trust size, and they had allowed these separate misgivings to coalesce into a single fear of size *in* government, leading them, in Franklin's view, to make the wrong choice, both for themselves and for the future.

Looking back on the Albany Congress as an old man, Franklin still believed that if his plan had been approved, the British would not have had to tax the colonies as they did for defense against the French and Indians, and the Revolutionary War would have been postponed, or perhaps never fought at all. He might have been right.

Two decades later, at the First Continental Congress in the fall of 1774, Americans made another attempt at organizing themselves for the greater good. This was the Galloway Plan of Union, offered by Joseph Galloway, the speaker of the Pennsylvania Assembly. The Galloway plan was modeled on Franklin's proposal at Albany. It called for a new American government whose assembly would consist of a single house in which the colonies, not the Crown, would choose the representatives, and each colony would be equally represented. The Crown would appoint a president-general as overseer. The assembly would stand alongside the House of Commons and the House of Lords as the third branch of British government, the American branch.

It seemed to many the best of all possible compromises. It would avoid both total submission to the Crown, which to most colonists was untenable, and a war for independence, which to most colonists at the time seemed both unwise and unwinnable.

Unlike Franklin's vision at Albany, The Galloway Plan almost became reality; in fact, more delegates to the Continental Congress favored it than opposed it. The final vote, however, was by colony, not individual, and an American branch of Parliament was narrowly turned down. The reasons were many and complex, and historians differ on their number and relative importance. But prominent among them, and perhaps underlying them all, was the colonists' continuing mistrust of large governing bodies. Both the delegates and the men they represented were people for whom self-reliance was the first commandment of secular life. They were not fond of debates about the proper means of relying on others, no matter how compelling the reasons or how necessary the reliance in times of hardship or emergency. The Galloway Plan was ultimately Franklin's plan with a few different terms, a few new phrases—an old pariah in a new set of clothes. It could not help but meet the same fate.

This time, though, the naysayers should have known better; before the war with England was over, most of them would.

❖

From the first battles at Lexington and Concord in 1775 until the spring of 1781, the colonies were governed by Congress, which printed a currency, carried on diplomatic missions abroad, and managed the military—but did none of it efficiently. Then, for the next six months or so, until Cornwallis's defeat at Yorktown, the colonies held themselves together, however tenuously, with the Articles of Confederation, which, despite the best efforts of those who drafted them, did not confederate very well.

The Articles allowed for a president, but because they gave him no power, no one actually held the office; they continued to provide for a Congress, comprising representatives from each of the states, but because they did not allow it to raise money through taxation, it was not as powerful as it needed to be at a time of crisis. Nor did the Articles allow the states to regulate trade with one another or enforce a uniformity of laws; they were, in practice, more of a gentlemen's agreement than a strict set of guidelines, and the gentlemen who devised them, the delegates to the same Continental Congress that passed the Declaration of Independence, did not in all cases behave as gentlemen. The Articles were outdated and impractical from the moment of their birth. They were also the perfect reflection of the will of those who had voted down Franklin in Albany and Galloway in Philadelphia; it might not have been chaos that these people supported, but neither was it efficacious rule.

By trying to wage war against Britain under the Articles' provisions, however, and before that with even less structure, Americans were dooming themselves, if not to defeat, at least to a struggle much greater than it needed to be. As historian John Ferling has written:

> With the national government powerless to find revenue, the war was nearly lost. The army could not be supplied, and soon it was virtually immobilized. Morale buckled among civilians, who were nearly driven to want by runaway prices. . . .

With [Commander in Chief George] Washington warning
that the American Revolution and the new nation were "verging
. . . fast to destruction," Congress in 1781 appealed to the states to
permit the national government to levy an impost—a revenue
tariff—on trade. That would have secured the funds to supply
and pay the army, but the move failed. Unanimous consent was
required. Rhode Island voted it down.

This would have been taxation *with* representation, and still a
state had opposed it! Washington was livid. He could not understand the decision, nor could he avoid taking it personally; it was,
after all, his desires that had been rejected, his experiences with
underfed, underclothed, and underpaid soldiers that were being ignored. He wondered to his aides precisely what he had been fighting for and whether victory was possible with so little in the way of
support.

When the war finally ended, Americans reacted with relief and
joy and a certain amount of apprehension. Now what? they asked
themselves at home and in their churches and taverns. Now what?
the newspapers echoed. The Articles of Confederation—was *that*
what? They were still in force, still supposed to keep the country
chugging along, but even their strongest supporters admitted that
the Articles were a rickety structure, capable of falling apart at any
time, and if the United States was to survive and prosper, it needed
something more reasoned, farsighted, and enduring. Yet four years
would pass from the official end of the Revolutionary War until
the gathering of the delegates at the Constitutional Convention in
Philadelphia in the spring of 1787. When it finally happened,
George Washington was chosen to preside; Alexander Hamilton,
whom Washington trusted without hesitation, stood beside him to
advise.

At the time, though, it was not called the Constitutional Convention. No one envisioned, or at least publicly admitted, the possibility of a new blueprint for union. The assembly was known

then as the Federal Convention of 1787, and its ostensible purpose was to rewrite the Articles of Confederation: a tweak here, a tweak there—it seemed to the more cautious delegates to be all that most Americans would tolerate, and thus it was all they intended to do.

But other delegates had something more drastic in mind—a brand new document, a brand new start; there was, in other words, a certain duplicity to the convention's mission even before the opening gavel fell. This is one of the reasons that it met behind locked doors and shuttered windows, no matter the specific topic of the day's debate, no matter the stultifying effects of heat and humidity. It is also one of the reasons that the gentlemen of the press were kept on the other side of those doors and windows throughout the proceedings, given not so much as a hint of what was going on inside.

And they did not utter so much as a whimper in protest. Whereas today's news organizations would have demanded access and, if denied, filed lawsuits and hired spies and perhaps even dropped them down the chimneys to get at the convention's business—and, failing all those attempts at entry, at least have unleashed their pundits to speculate shamelessly on the proceedings beyond their ken—yesterday's accepted their exclusion gracefully. Even so hot-blooded an organ as the *Boston Gazette* commented, "Though we readily admit the propriety of excluding an indiscriminate attendance upon the discussions of this *deliberative* council, it is hoped that the privacy of their transactions will be an additional motive for dispatch, as the anxiety of the people must be necessarily encreased, by every appearance of mystery in conducting this important business."

One of the convention's delegates was the remarkable Benjamin Rush, who signed the Declaration of Independence, served a term in Congress, and co-founded both the Philadelphia Bible Society and Dickinson College. He was perhaps the leading abolitionist of his time, and later in life would finance a school for children of African descent. He also advocated schools for women and wrote a pamphlet called *Thoughts upon Female Education*. In addition, Rush composed the first anti-alcohol treatise in America, which proved to be the foundation for later temperance movements; he wrote the first anti-tobacco treatise in America, which led to nothing in the short run but would one day be vindicated in virtually all of its particulars by medical science.

And it was Rush, more than anyone else of the time, who befriended the immigrant Thomas Paine and helped him find a publisher for *Common Sense*. It might even have been Rush who provided the title. He did not deserve to be reviled in the press, which he would be, by one newspaper above all others, to an unconscionable degree, in another decade.

Rush was also America's leading physician of the era and an enlightened reformer in the treatment of the mentally ill, although he would turn out to be even more perceptive about politics than he was about medicine. "The American war is over," he said in the mid-1780s, "but this is far from being the case with the American Revolution. On the contrary, nothing but the first act of the great drama is closed. It remains yet to establish and perfect our new forms of government; and to prepare the principles, morals, and manners of our citizens, for these forms of government, after they are established and brought to perfection."

But what, exactly, were those forms to be? Was there such a thing as a compromise between chaos and monarchy? If so, what was it? How could the individual be permitted to flourish without interference at the same time that he was sheltered by the various rights and protections that only a government could offer? And what kind of government would do the offering? One that was strong and central and could guarantee those rights and protections? Perhaps, but might such a government also be so rigid in its definition of the rights and protections that it ended up denying freedom as much as safeguarding it?

Some people believed that a weaker source of authority would be preferable, one that acted as a kind of overseer to the states but allowed each to remain sovereign, to answer for the most part to its own chief executive and legislature and, ultimately, the people who had voted them into office. But what if that government was *too* weak? What if it could not support the states adequately and people were left with too few rights, not enough protections? And what would a state do when, as was the case in the recent war for independence, it had to join with other states for the common good? How would the states be brought together when the need arose? And who would then assume control of the assembly of states and its subsequent actions? How, in other words, would a weak central government function adequately when strength was required?

Four months after opening, the Federal Convention of 1787 produced the Constitution of the United States, a document that addressed some of these issues while providing "artful ambiguities" in other cases. Most newspapers supported it, in principle if not in all details. "Should the citizens of America ratify the proceedings of the Convention," wrote the *Boston Gazette*, finally having learned what those proceedings were, "the happy event will form an epocha more peculiar in its nature, more felicitating in its consequence, and more interesting to the philosophic mind, than ever the political history of man has displayed."

Washington and Hamilton agreed. Hamilton was particularly fond of the "artful ambiguities" because he could interpret them as license for an even stronger union than some of his fellow delegates had envisioned. Once this became apparent to his foes in the press, Hamilton turned into the biggest newsmaker, and news instigator, of the entire postwar era.

❈

SPECIFICALLY, HAMILTON BELIEVED that the United States could not develop a healthy economy without a strong government to fund and regulate it; could not expand and then keep its new states and territories safe from attack by Indians or foreign foes without a strong government; could not maintain a consistent rule of law or protect its citizens from outbreaks of local tyranny or ineptitude; could not protect the men and women in its smallest states from the caprices of those in the largest; and could not trade successfully with other nations. What would have been the point of having fought so long and arduously for freedom, Hamilton in effect asked, if the nation that came into being as a result of those struggles were governed not by the will of the victors, but by the turmoil of inactivity?

These were among the topics addressed in *The Federalist Papers*, a series of eighty-five essays written in the form of letters to the New York *Independent Journal*, most of them in 1787 and 1788, and then reprinted, at least in part, in almost every other paper in America. Hamilton wrote fifty-one of them, future president James Madison twenty-nine, and John Jay, who would be the first Chief Justice of the U.S. Supreme Court and later governor of New York, five. They argued, to put it simply, that the Constitution should be adopted as written, and that it had been written in such a way as to ensure that a national government should take precedence over the states; power centralized, *The Federalist Papers* insisted, can accomplish more good than power diffused. They also insisted that there were enough safeguards written into the Constitution to prevent abuses of that power. *The Federalist Papers* were journalism at its most erudite, most detailed, most voluminous.

And most lasting. The letters are still quoted today, read in history and politics courses, and pored over by scholars, some of whom believe that the Constitution probably would not have been adopted without them and certainly would not have been interpreted as it was. Others downplay the importance of the *Papers*, insisting that they were written in too academic a fashion to inspire a consensus and, even more to the point, that even before they were published, "most of the people who counted had already made up their minds."

The most famous of the letters was the tenth, written in typically bulky prose by Madison. In it, he set out to still the fears of those who believed that a band of unscrupulous citizens could more easily seize control of a single government entity than they could thirteen or more, and thus subvert it to selfish ends.

[I]t is to be remarked that however small the Republic may be, the Representatives must be raised to a certain number, in order to guard against the cabals of a few; and that however large it may be, they must be limited to a certain number, in order to guard against the confusion of a multitude. Hence the number of Representatives in the two cases, not being in proportion to that of the Constituents, and being proportionally greatest in the smallest Republic, it follows, that if the proportion of fit characters, be not less, in the large than in the small Republic, the former will present a greater option, and consequently a greater probability of a fit choice.

Thomas Jefferson was not persuaded. In time, Madison himself would begin to waver on federalism, or at least on the Alexander Hamilton brand of federalism, and become perhaps Jefferson's strongest ally in the struggle for less centralized authority. But for now, Jefferson could only read Madison's sentiments and shake his head ruefully. *The Federalist Papers* were a collection of "heresies," Jefferson declared, their goal not to enlighten Americans about what kind of union would serve them best but to deceive them into as demeaning a servitude as they had ever known under the British.

In place of that noble love of liberty, & republican government which carried us triumphantly thro' the war, an Anglican monarchical, & aristocratical party has sprung up, whose avowed object is to draw over us the substance, as they have already done the forms of British government.

Federalists, as Jefferson explained in a letter to his friend Philip Mazzei, were "timid men who prefer the calm of despotism to the boisterous sea of liberty, British merchants & Americans trading on British capitals, speculators & holders in the banks & public funds, a contrivance invented for the purposes of corruption, & for assimilating us in all things to the rotten as well as the sound parts of the British model." Jefferson was not like that, and did not want America to be like that. He would dedicate himself wholeheartedly to being an *anti*-federalist, a political being that soon became known as a republican.

❁

It was a complicated matter, this dispute between what seemed to be mutually exclusive theories of government. A Philadelphia newspaper called the *Aurora*, which will figure mightily in this narrative a few chapters hence, decided to simplify it, publishing a primer of sorts, summing up the two contrasting views. In keeping with the spirit of the times, it would not do so objectively.

ATTENTION!
CITIZENS OF PHILADELPHIA
TAKE YOUR CHOICE

FEDERAL	REPUBLICAN
THINGS AS THEY HAVE BEEN.	THINGS AS THEY WILL BE.
1. The principles and patriots of *the Revolution* condemned and stigmatized.	1. The Principles of the *Revolution* restored: its Patriots honored and beloved.
2. *Republicanism*, a badge for persecution, and federalism a mark for monarchy.	2. *Republicanism* proved to mean something, and Federalism found to mean nothing.
3. The *Nation* in arms without a foe, and the nation divided without cause.	3. The *Nation* at peace with the world, and United in itself.

4. *Federalists* gradnating [sic] a scale of "*hatred and animosity*," for the benefit of the people; and aiming "a *few bold strokes*" at political opposition, for the benefit of themselves.

5. The reign of terror created by false alarms, to promote domestic feud and foreign war.

6. Systems of rapine, fraud, and plunder by public defaulters, under countenance of public servants.

7. Priests & Judges incorporated with the Government, for political purposes, and equally polluting the holy altars of religion, and the seats of Justice.

8. Increase of Public Debt. Additional Taxes, Further Loans, New Excises, Higher public salaries, and Wasteful Expenditures of the public money.

9. Quixotish embassies to the Turks, the Russians, Prussians, and Portuguese, for the Quixotish purposes of holding the balance of Europe.

10. A Sedition Law to protect corrupt magistrates and public defaulters.

11. An established church, a religious test, and an order of Priesthood.

4. *Republicans* allaying the fever of domestic feuds, and subduing opposition by the force of reason and rectitude.

5. Unity, peace, and concord produced by republican measures and equal laws.

6. Public plunderers & defaulters called to strict account, and public servants compelled to do their duty.

7. Good government without the aid of priestcraft, or religious politics, and Justice administered without political intolerance.

8. Decrease of public debt. Reduced taxes. No Loans. No Excises. Reduced public salaries, and a system of economy and care of the public money.

9. The republican maxim of our Washington, "Not to intermeddle with European politics."

10. The liberty of the press, and free enquiry into public character, our constitutional charter.

11. Religious liberty, the rights of conscience, no priesthood, truth and Jefferson.

What is most notable about the preceding is that it was published October 14, 1800, more than a decade and a half after the Treaty of Paris was signed and long after the Constitution had been written and ratified by the states. Washington had already served two terms as president and John Adams one term, and Jefferson would soon take his turn. The House and the Senate had met on many an occasion, passing some of the laws they considered, rejecting others; they had set up committees, agreed on procedures, and established precedents. The government, in other words, had assumed at least a preliminary shape, and a relatively productive one as well, which is to say that the arguments over the viability, and in fact the very definition, of federalism should by now have taken a more sophisticated and specific form than they did in the *Aurora*.

That they did not demonstrates the continuing and remarkable contrast between the accomplishments of eighteenth-century Americans and the vulgarity of their journalism, of the continuing triumph, on page after page after page, of fervor over civility, prejudice over fairness, simplemindedness over accuracy. It would become even more apparent in the battles between federalism and republicanism than it had been in the earlier struggles with the British.

This kind of journalism also demonstrates the frenetic quality of the century's concluding years. It was a time when Indians continued to attack American outposts in the West, although now without the French at their side, and an increasing number of settlers fought back with increasing brutality; a time when the West kept getting pushed back, farther and farther west, with new states and territories being added to the union, and new towns and villages being added to the states and territories, and new roads being built to connect all of them to one another and to the eastern seaboard. It was a time when the invention of the first steam-powered cotton-processing machines in Rhode Island and the cotton gin in the South helped to bring the Industrial Revolution, and its attendant social and economic revolutions, across the Atlantic; a time when canals were being built and were opening up new patterns of trade and travel and communication, and mobs were rioting in the streets over the unheard-of practice of dissecting human cadavers in medical schools, which seemed one of the strangest and most powerful challenges ever made to religious orthodoxy. It was a time when farmers in western Pennsylvania were rebelling over taxes on whiskey, and when epidemics of yellow fever were killing thousands in New York and Philadelphia and elsewhere, and when the French Revolution, with its high-minded ideals and its bloody renderings of justice, seemed to be inciting as much comment in America as it was in France.

In the view of John Ferling, the 1790s were "one of America's most passionate decades." The nation's journalism could not help but reflect the heat.

❖

IN 1790, there were 100 newspapers in the United States, some appearing weekly or less, some biweekly or more, a few turning up at almost random intervals. By 1800, the number of papers had doubled. At the midway point of the decade, it has been estimated, about 14 percent of the American press was republican. Three years later, the proportion was up to 28 percent, and by the turn of the century republican journals are thought to have made up as much as three-fifths of all American newspapers.

Was there such a thing as a neutral publication? Was there a paper that presented the arguments for and against federalism with equal devotion, or at least tried to? Alexander Martin, the editor of the *Baltimore American and Daily Advertiser*, did not think so and in fact said that finding such a paper was no more likely than finding a clergyman preaching "*Christianity* in the morning and *Paganism* in the evening." Others agreed. Still others believed that a nonpartisan paper, if it existed, would be a disservice to all who read it, too noncommittal for the exigencies of the times. "A despicable impartiality I disclaim," wrote the editor of a newspaper in Danbury, Connecticut, speaking for many of his brethren. "I have a heart and I have a country."

Other than pugnacious, what were the papers of the postwar period like? Much like those of prewar times. "A typical issue," writes Ron Chernow, "had four long sheets, crammed with essays and small advertisements but no drawings or illustrations. These papers tended to be short on facts—there was little 'spot news' reporting—and long on opinion. . . . Often scurrilous and inaccurate, they had few qualms about hinting that a certain nameless official was embezzling money or colluding with a foreign power."

The first page of most papers was still reserved for ads, which, although small, were plentiful. And now that the war was over and manufacturing and foreign trade had resumed at previous levels, the ads promoted an increasing number and variety of products: green coffee, fresh teas, fresh drugs, Jamaica rum, books, property and houses, new brands of hosiery, openings of new plays and new theaters, household furniture, and, in an especially odd example from the leading federalist paper of the period, containers whose contents had been consumed: "The highest price in Cash, will be given for EMPTY BOTTLES. A preference will be given to Claret Bottles."

But for all the similarities, there was also something different about American newspapers in the 1790s, something edgier, more menacing, although it might be apparent more in retrospect than it was at the time.

The two conflicting views of American government led, albeit indirectly, to the two-party political system that is at once the core and the bane of American politics today. First, though, they led to a press that was no longer united against the British, as had been the case so recently, but divided against itself: James Franklin's brand of rowdyism more than Benjamin Franklin's discipline and reserve. The federalist editors would read the republican papers and take every article as a challenge; the republican editors would read the federalist papers and take every charge as a personal insult. And when they were done reading, they would head for their type trays and ink beaters and chases and presses and avenge themselves in their next issues, back-and-forthing, tit-for-tatting, attacking and counterattacking, determined at all costs to have the last, if not the most sensible, word.

The two sides had one thing in common. They knew that their cause would not succeed if their publications didn't, that the newspaper page was as important a battleground for them as Yorktown and Saratoga had been for the colonists during the war. Sometimes they encouraged existing papers to support their points of view. Sometimes they threatened opposing papers with boycotts if they did not modify their views. Sometimes they started publications of their own.

> Political leaders furnished funds to launch newspapers. Parties also subsidized established editors to keep them operating when their income was insufficient. Party leaders also gave publishers jobs as postmasters or government printers. Some politicians in office appointed editors to other governmental positions. . . . Frequently, friendly newspapers received legal government advertising from officials or members of the legislature. On all levels, government officials and party leaders gave exclusive news to papers representing the party's views. Businessmen who had advertisements to insert in a weekly or daily gave their patronage to their party newspapers.

These papers remind us, if we need the reminding, that the Founding Fathers were not, as we sometimes like to think, a single entity, a group of men bound together by genius, good will, and identically defined concepts of love of country; in fact, they were not a group at all, but individuals in the most cantankerous sense, often at odds with one another, often contemptuous of one another.

The nation they bequeathed to posterity was more the result of the compromises they made grudgingly than the points to which they acceded with grace. On Mount Rushmore, Jefferson peers contentedly over Washington's shoulder; in real life, the two men were seldom that close, and Jefferson did not always regard the first president with so placid an expression.

At various times, and with varying degrees of intensity and openness, the period's other sets of combatants were as follows: Adams versus Franklin, Jefferson versus Franklin, Gouverneur Morris versus Jefferson, Adams versus Washington, Madison versus Washington, Madison versus Hamilton. And then there were the tag teams, the compositions of which would change from time to time—Madison and Jefferson versus Jay, Hamilton and Jay versus Jefferson, Monroe and Jefferson and a few others versus Hamilton.

The two preeminent foes of the period, though, the two men who most symbolized their respective positions on federalism and thus the extreme polarity of American politics at the time, were Jefferson and Hamilton, respectively the secretary of state and secretary of the treasury under Washington as the passionate decade began.

Jefferson, some believed, wanted to hand the country over to the farmers, while Hamilton supposedly wanted to hand it over to the financiers.

Jefferson, it has been said more recently, favored a seventeenth-century economy, while Hamilton embraced notions that would not come to full flower until the twentieth.

Jefferson wanted the states to pay their own Revolutionary War debts as a means of retaining their autonomy, while Hamilton wanted the federal government to assume them, a gift horse, some Americans feared, that would make the states ever more subservient to their benefactors.

Jefferson wanted the government to institutionalize the planter society of the South, or at least certain aspects of it, while Hamilton lobbied for urbanity and industrial growth.

Jefferson supported the French Revolution even when the extremists known as the Jacobins turned it into the Reign of Terror, in part because it reminded him of the American revolution, in part because the French had aided the colonists' efforts during the war, and in part because he had served as the American minister to France from 1784 to 1789 and found it the most congenial of places. Hamilton, on the other hand, grew ever more repulsed by the behavior of the Parisian mobs, ever more respectful of the orderly proceedings of the British king and Parliament.

The arguments between the two men were bitter, devious, and unremitting, a source of constant vexation to the chief executive in whose cabinet they served. According to Joseph J. Ellis, who has written biographies of both Washington and Jefferson:

> Jefferson accused Hamilton of plotting to commandeer the government after Washington's departure, establishing his banker friends as the new American aristocracy and himself as king, emperor, or dictator, depending on Hamilton's whim. For his part, Hamilton charged Jefferson with working behind the scenes to undermine the Hamiltonian fiscal program and subvert Washington's policy of neutrality by aligning the United States with France, all part of a well-orchestrated Virginia conspiracy to capture the federal government for its slave-owning supporters.

A federalist was said to be Hamiltonian in his outlook, a republican Jeffersonian; the two antagonists gave their names as well as their certitudes and energies to their opposing visions of the American future. They could also have given their names to the era's two principal varieties of strident, squawking journalism. In some cases directly, in others indirectly, they were the men most responsible. And before too many years had passed, in an almost grotesque example of poetic justice, they would also be the two most unfortunate victims of that journalism.

❁

SOMETHING ELSE WAS DIFFERENT about the press in those days.

For one thing, it began to promote, or at least acquiesce to, new kinds of deceit. As Oliver E. Allen writes in a history of New York, "[Aaron] Burr and his henchmen developed techniques that would become staples of American politics: they reported to the newspapers, for example, that their candidate had spoken eloquently to a series of well-attended gatherings at which his remarks had been lustily cheered—whereas in actuality the meetings had been attended only by the candidate and two friends or had not taken place at all."

And the violence that had sometimes been a part of the prewar era, when the Whigs set upon and in some cases demolished the print shops of the Tories, returned in the days of nominal peace. But it seemed a more informal thing now, less premeditated, suggesting that those responsible for the violence felt even more justified in it, or at least less concerned with the consequences, than they might have been a decade earlier.

In 1789, to give but one example, a random assortment of New Yorkers was parading through the streets celebrating the news that the Constitution had been ratified. They were cheering and chanting; some had been drinking, and all were in boisterous spirits of some sort or another. At one point they rounded a corner and came upon the office of the *Independent Gazette, or, the New-York Journal Revived*, a republican paper that had opposed ratification, although for the most part in civil, carefully rationed language.

No matter. The marchers knew of the *Gazette*'s position and invaded its quarters as if it were a cache of weapons that had previously been fired in their direction. They mangled the press, the trays, the frames; they trashed the paper's supply of back issues; they reduced tables and desks and chairs to splinters, leaving the building unfit to be occupied by any kind of business. When they finished, the *Gazette* was no longer capable of publishing so much as a paragraph.

The parade, however, continued, as the revelers left their pillaging behind them and resumed their marching, picking up the beat, one imagines, right where they had left off.

The atmosphere was toxic, and not just in New York. Americans were discouraged by the future, by the prospect that their government would not live up to their hopes, and they were discouraged by the present, by the acrimonious nature of the times, by a divisiveness that seemed to validate their pessimism about the years ahead. Jefferson would complain that the "pleasures of society" had given way to the bitter discourse of politics and that, as a result, men "who have been intimate all their lives, cross the streets to avoid meeting, and turn their heads another way, lest they should be obliged to touch their hats."

George Washington regarded the times, and the role of newspapers in setting the tone, no less ruefully.

❂

CHAPTER FOURTEEN

The Not-So-Unlikely Target

23.

Speech of the President of the United States To both Houses of Congress — 30th of April 1789 —

Fellow Citizens of the Senate and of the House of Representatives —

Among the vicissitudes of Life, no event could have filled me with gre[at] than that of which the notification was tr[ansmitted by] your order and received on the 14th da[y] month —

On the one hand I was summon'd whose Voice I can never hear but with vene[ration] from a Retreat which I had chosen wit[h] : lection, and in my flattering hopes w the asylum of my declining y

H E WAS THE PERFECT MAN FOR THE JOB, so much so that he was the only person considered at the time and no one else can even be imagined now. He had the perfect background, the perfect bearing, and was even regarded, at least by a few of his contemporaries, as "America's secular saint." Says historian Garry Wills, "For some writers, it was natural to compare him with later heroes of the Bible, since they had cast Christopher Columbus in the role of Moses. That still left an opportunity for Washington to play David, or Elijah, or Noah, or Joshua, or Hezekiah, or Josiah . . . [or] the new Zerubbabel returning God's people from exile."

He was tall, handsome, athletic; when he walked into a room, all eyes turned to him and the conversation hushed, awaiting whatever signals he would give. He did not give them freely; some found him a bit aloof. But in one way, at least, it was easy to communicate with him. Late in the eighteenth century, the people who received mail were the ones who paid for it, not those who sent it; but if you wanted to write to Washington, not only during his days as president but afterward as well, the post office did not charge him for the privilege of reading your sentiments, and if he decided to respond, you would not be charged on the other end. George Washington transcended conventional categories; allowances were made for him that seemed altogether fitting.

He was a virtuous man whose appeal, in part, was that he did not carry his virtues too far. He was ambitious, although not to the extent of Hamilton; he was cultured, although not to the extent of

Jefferson; and he did not make a show of his rectitude the way John Adams sometimes did. As a young man, he had not just led his men into battle in the French and Indian War, he even designed their uniforms. They were to be made of "fine Broad Cloath," Washington stipulated, "The Coat Blue, faced and cuffed with Scarlet, and Trimmed with Silver: The Waistcoat Scarlet, with a plain Silver Lace, if to be had—the Breeches to be Blue, and every one to provide himself with a silver-laced Hat, of a Fashionable size."

When, at the end of the Revolutionary War, Washington resigned his post as commander in chief, voluntarily giving up power to return to a simpler life at Mount Vernon, his Virginia estate, the king of England, who would never even have considered such a thing and whose forces the American had just vanquished, was struck by "a Conduct so novel"; Washington, George III could not help but conclude, was "the greatest man in the world."

Which made him not just the perfect man to be president of the United States, but the perfect man to be the *first* president.

Washington and his image were not unflawed, however. As a military strategist, he was inconsistent; he lost more battles over the course of his fighting days than he won. As a military leader, Garry Wills says, he was sometimes "afraid to use power as actively as he could have, to take greater risks for greater results, out of excessive regard for his personal equanimity and fame." And because of that excessive regard, he was often intolerant of those who questioned his equanimity or doubted that his fame was valid. His reputation was as important to him as any of the positions he held, any of the successes he achieved, any of the objects he owned; he thought of reputation "as a thing that might be destroyed or sullied—some valuable cargo carried in the hold of the self."

It is in some ways a healthy attitude; prizing one's reputation as Washington did makes one less likely to act in a manner that will defile it; his regard for the opinion of others is, so to speak, his conscience. But he can carry this regard too far, become too sensitive to criticism, too fearful of incurring the disdain of others even when his motives are honorable and his actions proper.

And for Washington, disdain was plentiful. Yes, he was the most venerated man of his time; yes, he was not just the leader of his country but a virtual synonym for it; and yes, he was America's primary means of support as it began taking baby steps from colonial status to productive nationhood. But it was this very eminence that made him so irresistible to the opposition press; Hamilton might have been the more extreme federalist, but Washington was the more estimable figure, and therefore the more attractive target. His demise, more than Hamilton's, would be federalism's demise, and republican newspapers were determined to do all they could to bring it about.

❖

HAMILTON, WE MAY SAY, was a federalist by theory. Much of what he intended for the United States had no precedent in either the Old World or the New; it was simply what he believed, based on the application of a unique intelligence to the unique problems and needs of his country at so formative and critical a time.

Jefferson, we may say, was a republican by theory, although he would surely disagree, citing his experiences in Virginia both before the war and afterward, believing in a republican nation because he had lived in and helped to create a colony and then a state that was, at least to a degree, republican itself. But it remained theory, and some said fantasy, for him to assume that the United States could one day become Virginia on a large scale.

Washington, however, was a practical federalist—more moderate than Hamilton, to be sure, but no less committed to the necessity of a strong government. He had, after all, suffered the ineptitude of a weak government during the war and had pleaded with the Constitutional Convention not to allow such a thing to happen again. As president, he was still pleading, although now to legislators. And, as he did, he was remembering. Joseph J. Ellis writes poignantly of the winter of 1780 in Morristown, New Jersey, and of soldiers serving under Washington who

> had not been paid for a year and had not eaten in four days. Half the men had no shoes, but were intending to walk home because they had long since eaten their horses. Down in New Jersey, where the countryside had been picked clean after four years of foraging, Washington was forced to order a general confiscation of cattle and grain from the local farmers, noting that the choice was between stealing or starving: "We must assume the odious character of plunderers instead of the protectors of the people."

Fully a third of the men who survived that winter with Washington, who did not desert him and walk home shoeless, were too sick to fight, too sick on some occasions to pitch their tents or stand guard duty or even heat a cup of coffee in the fire. A different kind of government, Washington believed, one with the full support of the people behind it and a full complement of resources upon which to draw, would have made all the difference. "Certain I am," he wrote in the horrible winter of 1780, "that unless Congress speaks in a more decisive tone; unless they are vested with powers by the several States competent to the great purposes of War, or assume them as a matter or right . . . that our Cause is lost. We can no longer drudge on in the old way. I see one head gradually changing into thirteen."

If, as the head of the government of the United States, its first officially-sanctioned leader, Washington was to be the victim of journalistic abuse because of beliefs like his, which were the result of experiences like his, which were in turn the result of a devotion to his new nation's cause, so be it.

❁

AT TIMES THE ABUSE CAME IN TORRENTS, with the republican press referring to him variously as "a gambler, a cheapskate, a horsebeater, a dictator, and a most horrid swearer and blasphemer." He was labeled "treacherous," "mischievous," and "inefficient." He was said to favor "stately journeying through the American continent in search of personal incense" and to enjoy "ostentatious professions of piety." He was, appearances notwithstanding, a "frail mortal"; no less was he "a spoiled child, despotic," "a tyrannical monster." It is a collection of terms that does not come readily to mind these days when the subject is George Washington.

His opponents warned him that "posterity will in vain search for the monuments of wisdom in your administration." *His* monuments, it was suggested, were more superficial than that, expressions of vanity rather than erudition: "put off your suit of buckram," he was advised, "and condescend to that state of humility, in which you might hear the real sentiments of your fellow citizens."

Even Thomas Paine, who had once admired Washington and been moved by his earlier praise of *Common Sense*, and who had so strongly advocated the independent America that Washington, more than anyone else, had brought into being, would in time sour on him. It seems that Paine had sent Washington copies of a later pamphlet, *The Rights of Man*, and the president, for reasons unknown, had either not responded at all or had done so less enthusiastically than Paine had desired. And later Paine had gone to France, where, having alienated the leaders of that country's Revolution for being insufficiently sympathetic to their violent ways, he was thrown into prison and threatened with worse. He expected Washington to demand his immediate release and to warn the French against further insult. There was no response this time either, although Washington, if indeed he knew of Paine's fate, would probably have decided he was powerless to alter it.

Paine felt he had been betrayed. The man who had once been his idol now became his most bitter foe. Washington had turned into "the patron of fraud, . . . " Paine declared, "treacherous in private friendship ... and a hypocrite in public life." People would ask themselves, Paine said, "whether you are an apostate or an imposter, whether you have abandoned good principles, or whether you ever had any?" Paine raised these questions in an open letter to Washington, published in several newspapers, in which he went on to admit that he had begun to pray for Washington's death, and the sooner the better.

Compared with these, the criticisms of old Jemmy Rivington were almost a form of boosterism. And more criticism, no less meanly intended or hurtful, was ahead.

✼

IN ALL LIKELIHOOD, Washington had seen it coming. A private man suspects the press because it pries into the lives of its subjects. A public man suspects the press because it misrepresents his actions and motives. A public man with a deeply private vein, like Washington, is the most mistrustful of all. In fact, he was disappointed in newspapers long before newspapers even hinted at disappointment in him. As far back as 1777, when the war was not going well for the Americans, he blamed some of his problems on irresponsible reporting, even in papers sympathetic to the patriot cause, and did so for the same reasons that a modern general might express. "It is much to be wished," he said, "that our Printers were more discreet in many of the Publications. We see almost in every Paper, Proclamations or accounts transmitted by the Enemy, of an injurious nature. If some hint or caution could be given them on the Subject, it might be of material Service."

After the war, in his days as a private citizen, Washington complained to his friend Lafayette that "Newspaper Accounts are too sterile, vague & contradictory, on which to form any opinion, or to claim even the smallest attention." To another friend he wrote: "I have Such a number of Gazettes crouded upon me, (many without orders) that they are not only Expensive, but realy useless; as my other avocations, will not afford me time to Read them oftentimes; & when I do attempt it, find them more troublesome, than Profitable."

The first indication that the American press was in turn growing disenchanted with Washington came shortly before he assumed the presidency. Some papers printed rumors that he had cheated his Virginia neighbor, Lord Fairfax, and swindled him out of some land. In fact, the two families were friends of long standing; Lord Fairfax had been a patron of sorts to Washington as a young man, and Fairfax's cousin gave Washington his first job as a surveyor. The rumors of fraud were untrue, and even the few papers that printed them could not keep them alive for more than an issue or two. But Washington was not relieved; to him, the stories were an omen, as was the fact that none of the papers that printed them had offered a retraction when they were proved to be without merit.

As Washington's first inauguration approached, the federalist newspapers were praising him almost uncontrollably, each article a snippet of hagiography. Washington was not comfortable with that kind of treatment either. One paper in particular, the *Gazette of the United States*, pointed out that the "spontaneous effusions of gratitude to the illustrious WASHINGTON, exhibited by all ranks of people, in a thousand various indications of the sublime principle, are the highest reward that virtue enjoys." In the adjoining column, the *Gazette* turned to verse for further effusion.

> HAIL, thou auspicious day!
> Far let America
> Thy praise resound:
> Joy to our native land!
> Let ev'ry heart expand,
> For WASHINGTON's at hand,
> With glory crown'd:
> . . .
> Illustrious Warrior hail!

Oft' did thy sword prevail
Oe'r hosts of foes;
Come and fresh laurels claim,
Still dearer make thy name,
Long as immortal Fame
Her trumpet blows!

. . .

Far be the din of arms,
Henceforth the olive's charms
Shall war preclude:
These shores a HEAD shall own,
Unsully'd by a throne,
Our much lov'd WASHINGTON,
The great, the good.

One cannot imagine, say, the *Washington Times* going quite that far on the eve of a Republican's ascension to the White House today.

❁

THE ANTI-FEDERALIST PAPERS were not so amorous as Washington prepared to assume the presidency, but they seemed to have called a truce. They did not, for the time being, impugn his character or question his motives for accepting the presidency. And, perhaps at great effort, they refrained from agreement when, in his inaugural address, Washington confessed that he was "unpracticed in the duties of civil administration" and, worse, had "inherit[ed] inferior endowments from nature."

But Washington was not misled. He thought of the press in those days in military terms, as an army lying low for a time, trying to lull the enemy into a lesser state of vigilance as it prepares for what will be its most brutal offensive yet. He feared that soon "the extravagant (and I may say undue) praises which they are heaping upon me at this moment" would eventually become something else altogether: "equally extravagant (that I will fondly hope unmerited) censures."

When the censures came, Washington ignored them—in public, at least; he was, after all, "the most notorious model of self-control in all of American history, the original marble man." Privately, though, in the company of friends or in correspondence to them, he unburdened himself, answering his critics in terms both plaintive and choleric. The attacks on him in the republican press were "outrages on common decency," he wrote to fellow Virginian Henry Lee. They were "arrows of malevolence" that struck him but would never bring him down. He was tired, he said, tired to his marrow of being "buffited in the public prints by a set of infamous scribblers."

❀

HE WOULD REMAIN TIRED. A few years later, Washington complained to Jefferson, who was at the time a private citizen, that newspapers were printing the "grossest and most insidious misrepresentations" of his deeds and thoughts. And, in the process, they were resorting to "indecent terms as could scarcely be applied to a Nero, a notorious defaulter, or even to a common pickpocket." Jefferson agreed, and claimed to sympathize. "Nothing can now be believed which is seen in a newspaper," he said to Washington. "Truth itself becomes suspicious by being put into that polluted vehicle." What Jefferson did not say, what he would never admit despite a great deal of supposition and, in time, evidence to the contrary, was that, while serving in Washington's administration, he had been secretly and shamefully polluting the vehicles himself, doing so for his own ends, which were seldom the same as the president's.

Washington even had the press on his mind when he was leaving office and its vitriol had already begun to flow away from him and in the direction of his successor, John Adams. In the first draft of his farewell address in 1796, Washington complained that some of the Gazettes . . . have teemed with all the invective that disappointment, ignorance of facts, and malicious falsehood could invent, to misrepresent my politics and affections; to wound my reputation and feelings; and to weaken, if not entirely destroy the confidence you had been pleased to repose in me; it might be expected at the parting scene of my public life that I should take some notice of such virulent abuse. But, as heretofore, I shall pass them over in utter silence never having myself, nor by any other with my participation or knowledge, written or published a scrap in answer to any of them.

Washington read his words over a time or two, and perhaps having decided that expressing such sentiments was not really the best example of "utter silence" on the matter, that he was in fact writing considerably *more* than a scrap in answer, excised the paragraph in his final draft. His farewell address, by the way, was never read before Congress or any other public assembly; rather, it was written for and published in the *American Daily Advertiser*, in Philadelphia, after which it was reprinted by virtually every other paper in America. It was a rare example, and perhaps the only one, of Washington exercising control of his words in the press.

❖

ONE SEARCHES IN VAIN for some actual Washingtonian praise of a newspaper—for a few kind words, an expression of support either in specifics or in principle. Well, not entirely in vain. Washington did on one occasion admit that there was a section of the newspaper he enjoyed, that actually provided him with a service. "Having learnt from an Advertisement in the New York Daily Advertiser," he wrote to one of his cabinet officers shortly before his inauguration, "that there were superfine American Broad Cloths to be sold at No. 44 Water Street; I have ventured to trouble you with the Commission of purchasing enough to make me a suit of cloaths."

But at some point in his presidency, Washington decided that there was a certain impracticality to his contempt for the press, that he would be better served to make use of journalists than to stew in constant resentment of them. And so, as James Thomas Flexner puts it, he "invented" the news leak. He does not seem to have engaged in the practice himself, but there is no doubt that he encouraged it in others, directing his staff to invite newsmen to their offices or a nearby tavern and treat them to a beverage, perhaps a meal, and some privileged communication. They were to tell reporters the secrets of government. They were to give them scoops for their publications only. They were to promise that there was even more highly placed information waiting for them where these nuggets had come from; all the reporters had to do was print them precisely as the government instructed. They were to pat the reporters on the back and praise them for the sagacity of their political perceptions and the cut of their waistcoats. They were, as we say today, to spin.

It was, of course, a ruse. The information being leaked was information meant to be leaked, tailored to Washington's specifications, facts and figures and suppositions designed expressly to promote the administration's ends, the journalists being duped into service as errand boys. "Orders or advertisements which are intended to be put into the public Gazettes," Washington once wrote to a cabinet officer, "ought to be well weighed and digested before they are inserted, as they will not only appear in all parts of Europe, but may be handed to the enemy. To publish beyond the limits of the army, or the vicinity of it, the dastardly behavior of one's own Troops, is not a very pleasant thing."

But like many another invention, the news leak could not be controlled once it was brought into existence and knowledge of it became widespread. Soon members of Washington's inner circle were leaking what should not have been leaked; worse, they were leaking not only in support of administration policies but in support of their own agendas, which were, on occasion, opposed to the administration's. This official wanted to promote a measure in which he could make a financial investment; that one wanted to stop a project that seemed to him wasteful or counterproductive. "Aides to Treasury Secretary Alexander Hamilton," writes journalist Hedrick Smith, "leaked to allies of Thomas Jefferson that Hamilton was trying to make the United States a lackey of Britain."

To Jefferson, who was at the same time being accused of trying to make the United States a lackey of France, it was as serious a charge as could be made.

❖

PERHAPS THE MOST SURPRISING THING about Washington's attitude toward the newspapers of the passionate decade was that he said almost nothing about the *Gazette of the United States*, which had so rapturously reported his inaugural festivities; the paper might have embarrassed him with its flattery, but at least it did not infuriate him with its carping. Once, in fact, Washington even criticized the *Gazette*, when he found out that its editor planned to defend him by shifting the blame for some matter or another from the president to Benjamin Franklin. Washington thought it a disreputable thing to do. "We have some infamous Papers calculated for disturbing if not absolutely intended to disturb, the peace of the community," he wrote to a friend.

John Fenno was probably surprised to learn of Washington's disapproval, for his *Gazette of the United States* should have been one of the greatest sources of comfort to George Washington that ever a printing press provided.

CHAPTER FIFTEEN

❁

The Gazette . . .

OR A TIME AS A YOUNG MAN, John Fenno attended Holbrook's Writing School in Boston, but he never really got the hang of it, never wrote anything memorable or even anything he was especially proud of. He was not inept so much as uninspired; during the Revolutionary War, he kept the orderly book for General Artemas Ward and seems to have dashed off some letters for other American generals, excerpts of which might have been printed in a newspaper or two. But that was as close as Fenno ever came to earning a living with his pen. As a publisher, however, one who devoted his press to the glories of federalism and the whims of Alexander Hamilton, he left an indelible imprint on his time.

And that, in fact, is almost all that is known of John Fenno. Was he tall or short, voluble or withdrawn, pious or profane? No one can say. He was born in Boston in 1751, was a teacher for a while after the war, perhaps at another writing school, and then worked in the import business, at which he was slightly successful, then less successful, then bankrupt. Other than that, says George Henry Payne, he is a historical John Doe, a "a man without a biographer."

But Fenno's newspaper, the *Gazette of the United States*, was the first influential federal journal in the country. It gave Washington almost unqualified support, gave Hamilton a forum he could not have done without, and gave Jefferson all the reason he needed to lie awake at night and grind his molars into a fine powder. In fact, the *Gazette* made the hostility between Hamilton and Jefferson all the more vicious by making it all the more public, in the process making it all the more accessible not just to those who read about it at the time but also to historians of the future, who as a result understand much more about the early battles over American government than they would have otherwise. Perhaps John Fenno deserves a biography after all.

If so, it would have even more interesting questions to raise than those asked above. How did Fenno, who seems to have been the most inconspicuous of young men, manage to arrange a letter of introduction to Hamilton's friend Rufus King, the orator, diplomat, and delegate to the Constitutional Convention? Why was King so taken with Fenno that he introduced him in turn to Hamilton? Why was Hamilton so taken that he chose Fenno to publish the federalists' house organ, a position that required not only skill as a printer but commitment as an ideologue? And how did the two men manage to work so well together for almost a decade despite Hamilton's demands and Fenno's eccentricities—and, on one occasion, the latter's apparent and inexplicable apostasy? Why did not financial disagreements, if nothing else, drive them apart?

In the absence of answers to these questions, we must content ourselves with the few available facts. The *Gazette of the United States* was born on April 15, 1789, a month before the Constitutional Convention, which is to say that it was already in place when the battle for the soul—or at least the shape—of the United States began in earnest. "At this important Crisis," Fenno wrote on page one of that first issue,

> the ideas that fill the mind, are pregnant with Events of the greatest magnitude—to strengthen and complete the UNION of the States—to extend and protect their COMMERCE, under *equal* Treaties yet to be formed—to explore and arrange the NATIONAL FUNDS—to restore and establish the PUBLICK CREDIT—and ALL under the auspices of an untried System of Government, will require the ENERGIES of the Patriots and Sages of our Country—*Hence the propriety of encreasing the Mediums of Knowledge and Information.*

Although Fenno went on to say, "The Editor of this Publication is determined to leave no avenue of Information unexplored," what he had really determined was to leave no means of persuasion untried. He would cajole his readers, deceive them when necessary, rile them when advisable; he would praise public officials and other newspaper editors who agreed with his positions and drub those who did not, assailing their intelligence, their character, their patriotism; and he would publish the records of legislative proceedings that advanced the federalist agenda while either ignoring or deriding or sometimes even falsifying documents to the contrary. No wonder the republican press would defame him at every opportunity, bemoaning the very existence of "such a contemptible creature as Johnny Fenno."

Fenno took his mission seriously. "*He that is not for us, is against us*" would eventually become the *Gazette's* motto—a long way from "All the News That's Fit to Print." He was also serious in his criticisms of other newspapers, and not just because some of them disagreed or otherwise found fault with the *Gazette*. Most of the competition, he thought, was poorly written; it did not engage either the mind or the emotions. He believed that "more than nine-tenths of the scanty literature of America is made up of newspaper reading," and he found the prospect upsetting. Fenno might not have been able to produce literature himself, but he was determined that his paper would publish it, or something close to it, and often; the *Gazette of the United States* started out as a biweekly but before long became one of America's first dailies.

Some of the literature it published, if it can truly be called that, was anonymous, including a poetic attack on Jefferson's poetic notion that the American farmer was inherently high-principled and the tradesman inherently venal.

Virtue was ne'er confined to dwell,
In cloisters drear or hermit's cell—
She seeks as her supreme delight,
The heart that wishes to do right;

And scorns the vicious mind to own,
In shady groves, or smoky town—
For grant that ignorance confines
The farmer's views in narrow lines,
Afford them power, knowledge choice,
And idleness will nurse each vice—
With all the gaudy scenes of things,
Which envy round the villages sings.

But the primary contributor to the *Gazette of the United States*, in more ways than one, was Hamilton, perhaps the most prolific of all journalists among the Founding Fathers, at least after Franklin gave up the pen—so much so, in fact, that even Jefferson had to admit that his adversary was "an host within himself." Hamilton might have been a cabinet officer when the *Gazette of the United States* began publishing, but he was a journalist when the Washington administration, and the Treasury Department in particular, came under attack from republicans, or, as Hamilton thought of them, the forces of ignorance and subversion.

Unlike Fenno, Hamilton was a man whose literary abilities matched his zeal. In 1793, writing as Pacificus, Hamilton did not merely support Washington's policy of neutrality as tensions were increasing between England and France; he castigated the republicans for their desire to side with the French and in the process to romanticize Jacobin brutality. The republicans "have been urged in a spirit of acrimony and invective," Hamilton announced, and they were hopeful, more than anything else, of "weakening the confidence of the people in the author [Washington] of the measure [the Neutrality Proclamation], in order to remove or lessen a powerful obstacle to the success of an opposition to the government, which however it may change its form, according to circumstances, seems still to be adhered to and pursued with persevering industry."

Hamilton's series of essays on the Neutrality Proclamation take up seven issues of the *Gazette of the United States*. He was not only a prolific writer, but, as he had demonstrated in *The Federalist Pa-*

pers, a thorough one, able to state his various cases with meticulous precision and from so many different perspectives that one imagines a printing press groaning under the weight of his arguments and readers buckling under the burden of his extraordinary detail.

Sometimes Hamilton stuck to issues. Other times he got personal, naming names, and one name far more often and far more bitterly than any other. In a 1796 issue of the *Gazette*, under the pen name Phocion, Hamilton expressed his alarm at the "pretensions of Thomas Jefferson to the Presidency." Jefferson was in that category of men who are "most dangerous," against whom the populace must be constantly "on our guard." Hamilton suggested that Jefferson was a "demagogue," that he wore the "*garb of patriotism*," but only as a disguise; that he spoke the "*language of liberty*," but only to deceive others about his real intentions.

In a preceding issue, under another pseudonym, Hamilton had offered "a few comments on T. Jefferson's very ridiculous and elaborate attempt to prove that the *negroes are an inferior race of animals*." Hamilton hoped that the comments "will place in just light the *philosophical* merits of the author."

Jefferson had never encountered a foe like Hamilton, so highly placed yet so hostile, so erudite yet so unwilling to concede the validity or even the charms of Jefferson's own erudition. And Hamilton had never had an ally like the *Gazette of the United States*. Under his direction, it lay in wait for Jefferson like a skulker in a hedgerow, ready to pounce whenever he spoke, to distort whenever he tried to set the record straight. The *Gazette* was, Jefferson said, "a paper of pure Toryism, disseminating the doctrines of monarchy, aristocracy, and the exclusion of the influence of the people." He knew it was Hamilton's paper, that it existed solely to reduce to ashes the republican beliefs he so devoutly cherished. What he did not know, at least for the time being, was what to do about it.

❖

WHAT EDES AND GILL were to Samuel Adams, John Fenno was

to Alexander Hamilton. But there was a difference. The *Boston Gazette* had been publishing for many years before Adams came along; it was a going concern that he joined, one whose place in the community had already been established and whose biases had evolved over time and changes of management to favor the goal of independence from Britain; Adams's job was to make the biases into a form of scripture.

Fenno, on the other hand, had been hired by Hamilton specifically to give bias a home. The newspaper was Fenno's idea; as his letter of introduction to King put it, he wanted to publish a paper "for the purpose of demonstrating favorable sentiments of the federal constitution and its administration." But it was Hamilton who made it possible, Hamilton who raised the money to get the *Gazette* started, Hamilton who saw how Fenno's desires could serve his own, and federalism's, ends.

They were an excellent match. Although uncertain of Fenno at first, Hamilton quickly came to respect his diligence and knowledge, perhaps even to exaggerate them. Fenno respected Hamilton's brand of federalism and the ease with which he committed its various definitions to paper; in fact, with but a single exception, Fenno would turn out to be "adoring in his treatment of Hamilton" in the *Gazette*. Fenno took orders from him happily; sometimes he even took dictation.

Hamilton, meanwhile, placed the government at Fenno's disposal, or at least as much of it as he could. He saw to it that all of the Treasury Department's advertising went to the *Gazette of the United States* and encouraged friends and firms that did business with various governmental agencies to put their own ads in the paper, the implication being that Hamilton would consider such transactions a favor and that favors were more often than not returned. The way things are done today is also the way they were done yesterday.

In addition, Hamilton arranged for Fenno to get as many of Treasury's printing contracts as possible, for pamphlets and posters, formal resolutions and public notices. In fact, as Ron Chernow points out, Fenno "was even listed in the 1791 Philadelphia directory as an officer of the U.S. government." Such a relationship between journalism and government could not exist today, not openly at least, and would be scandalous if revealed.

Despite all this, the *Gazette of the United States* was yet one more American newspaper of the eighteenth century that did not prosper. Perhaps it was too partisan to engage the casual reader, perhaps too contentious for federalists of moderate persuasion. Whatever the reason, Fenno was forced to ask Hamilton for more assistance, this time in the form of a job in addition to that of editor; he thought a position in banking might be suitable. Hamilton said no, telling Fenno that he had provided all the employment and emoluments that he could—any more and the *Gazette* truly *would* be a scandalous operation, one that President Washington would have condemned even though it supported his administration. Fenno seems to have accepted the rebuke gracefully.

But sometime later, when he pleaded for a loan of $2,000, swearing that the *Gazette* could not go on without it, that it might not even be able to print its next edition, Hamilton came to the rescue, providing half the sum himself while his friend Rufus King provided the other half. When King questioned the expense, Hamilton assured him that Fenno would not have asked for the money had it not been necessary. It was, on Hamilton's part, an unquestioning display of trust.

And Fenno deserved it. He was Hamilton's employee, but he was federalism's servant, and on one occasion, he went to extraordinary lengths, even in these times of scorched-earth journalistic practice, to do what he believed would promote his master's interests.

❀

THE WAR IN ENGLAND had been over for several years now, but disagreements remained, as neither side was abiding fully, or sometimes at all, by the terms of the Treaty of Paris. The Americans, for instance, were not allowing British subjects to collect the debts owed them before the fighting had begun. They were not treating fairly the loyalists who had fled to England during the war and were now returning. For their part, the British were claiming the right to search American vessels for deserters from the British navy. In addition, they were insisting that the troops they had stationed on America's northwest frontier had a right to remain there to protect British interests. According to the treaty, none of these practices was allowed.

Something had to be done, and both sides knew it: either a new pact had to be agreed upon or the provisions of the old one had to be clarified and tightened. And, oh yes, obeyed. To represent America in negotiations with the Crown, President Washington chose John Jay, and in 1794 Jay sailed to London as a special minister, his charge to make the peace between the two nations more peaceful at last, but without alienating the French any more than necessary. It was the most delicate of undertakings.

In public, Washington was hopeful that Jay would succeed. To aides, however, he confessed his fear that the British were less interested in negotiating than they were in strengthening their various positions, which is to say, in weakening the Treaty of Paris even further. Jay's mission, Washington believed, was a crucial one, but he was not optimistic. Nor should he have been. Although Jay was greeted courteously in London, he found himself almost immediately frustrated; the British listened to his proposals but agreed to few and always with reservations. For four months this went on, with Jay engaging in almost daily meetings and ending up with far less to show for it than he had hoped and trying as best he could to rationalize his disappointment.

The result of his efforts was the so-called Jay Treaty, and early in the summer of 1795 it became the subject of what is considered the first scoop in the history of American journalism. Someone calling himself "A Citizen," most likely, although not definitely, Virginia senator Stevens T. Mason, wrote to the Philadelphia *Aurora*, saying that he had

> been daily hoping to see in the public prints a copy of the late treaty with Britain; but as such a publication has not been made, I transmit the enclosed heads of that instrument collected from memory after an attentive perusal. There necessarily must be deficiencies in an account of this kind which depends entirely on memory, and for the same reason there may be inaccuracies, but I trust the latter are few.

"A Citizen" went on to reveal the preamble to the treaty and to devote a hefty, detail-laden paragraph to each of its articles—his memory was a well-honed instrument, his inaccuracies few indeed.

The Jay Treaty turned out to be a series of compromises that, in the way of such things, pleased neither side completely. But it seemed to upset the Americans more than the British. Some did not like the fact that although the Crown had agreed to remove its soldiers from northern postings, they would not be withdrawn immediately. Others did not like the restrictions placed by the treaty on U.S. trade with the West Indies. Still others did not like the treaty's provisions for a joint American-British commission to resolve the issue of debt payment, a commission whose decisions would be final; Americans wanted to make their own decisions on this subject, as on all others.

The treaty was seen, at least by its numerous opponents, as a sellout, a genuflection to the throne by a nation that had fought a war to deny a throne's validity, a defeat for the former colonies almost as decisive as Yorktown had been for the British. Republican papers bludgeoned Jay for his efforts, which, as far as they were concerned, had been ill-conceived from the start; they would have preferred that he negotiate an alliance with the French *against* England. Jay became a victim of the journalist James Thomson Callender, a republican at the time, who referred to "Jay's desertion" of American interests and "Jay's capitulation" to the merchants and politicians of Britain. Callender's future victims would not be treated in nearly so restrained a manner.

Some federalist papers were also critical of Jay's efforts; they would have preferred that he made fewer concessions, although they seemed to credit him with doing all he could under the circumstances. And among men and women of various political persuasions who heard about those concessions, there were several who began to think of Jay as something of a traitor; at one point, Jay "claimed he could have walked the entire eastern seaboard at night and had his way illuminated by protesters burning him in effigy."

As for the president, who had initially been disappointed in the treaty but had come to believe that neither Jay nor anyone else could have gotten more from the British, he was dismissed by the republican press as behaving like "the omnipotent director of a seraglio" and accused of having "thundered contempt upon the people with as much confidence as if he had sat upon the throne of Industan."

The treaty was sent to Congress that summer. The Senate ratified it with relative ease; the House, however, spent several sessions debating the necessary appropriations, a debate so long and nasty and rancorous that the split between federalists and republicans was, in a manner of speaking, formalized; in other words, by the time the House was finished arguing about how much money to spend on the Jay Treaty and how best to provide it, the two-party system, which few people of either political persuasion claimed to like, was assured of becoming a permanent part of American government.

Nonetheless, the treaty was approved later in the summer, and went into effect immediately.

But all was not yet well. Opposition remained, both in print and elsewhere, and perhaps no one was more troubled by it than Hamilton, who, like Washington, thought that Jay had done as well as he could have in the negotiations and that the result was a better relationship with the British than had existed before. Hamilton snapped his fingers, and the *Gazette of the United States* leaped to attention.

Over the course of the next several weeks, Hamilton and others wrote a series of articles praising the treaty and blasting its foes, and from Fenno, straining at the bit to do some writing of his own for a change, came an admonition to those foes. Hold your tongues, he demanded; speak not a word of blame or doubt—not because your point of view is erroneous but because your very premise, that you are entitled to a point of view in the first place, that you may somehow speak with impunity against the decisions of the Washington administration, "is a most dangerous one— tending to subvert all governance, and introduce anarchy and confusion."

Seldom has a journalist made such a statement. In a nation founded on dissent—or at least one variety of it, colonial opposition to the policies of the motherland—here was a newspaper dissenting *against* dissent. It was one thing for a federalist paper to belittle the views of its republican competition, or vice versa, and quite another for it to insist that conflicting views not be uttered at all. The *Gazette of the United States* would never take such a position again, on any issue.

❖

Hamilton did not comment on Fenno's radical show of support, at least not on the record. If he was surprised, it would not have been the first time and it would not be the last. A few years before the Jay Treaty, for instance, Fenno had published a letter from a certain Aristides that began as follows:

MR. FENNO,

In your Gazettes of the 4th and 11th of last month, there appeared two publications under the signature of "AN AMERI-

CAN," replete with the most virulent abuse of Mr. Jefferson; and containing charges against him, founded in the basest calumny and falshood. The intemperance of this writer, and his utter disregard of truth and candor, will be readily perceived by an impartial public....

Subscribers to the paper must have flipped back to the mast-head; was this *really* the *Gazette of the United States* they were reading? Was this in fact the newspaper edited by John Fenno giving space to someone defending Thomas Jefferson and casting aspersions on Alexander Hamilton? For it was indeed Hamilton to whom the anonymous Aristides referred, Hamilton who was, in truth, "AN AMERICAN," the man who had been responsible for the "two publications." Aristides never mentions Hamilton by name in his missive, but later he writes that "a certain head of a department is the real author or instigator of this unprovoked and unmanly attack on Mr. Jefferson," and "no man can envy the depravity of heart he possesses."

Hamilton's "unmanly attack"? His "depravity of heart"? What was going on here?

Unfortunately, there is no ready answer. John Fenno edited the *Gazette* for more than nine years, and the preceding is, according to this author's research, the only example to be found in all that time of the paper's turning against its leader; in fact, it may be the only example from the entire era of any avowedly factional newspaper sniping at its own viewpoint, however briefly.

Had Fenno developed a sudden, and short-lived, craving for fairness? Did he believe that publishing a letter like this would give the *appearance* of fairness, which would make the *Gazette* seem a more objective publication and thus increase the likelihood that its future attacks on republicanism would be taken more seriously? Had the Aristides letter been slipped into the paper without Fenno's knowledge, possibly when he was ill or inebriated or otherwise engaged? Or might it be that he and Hamilton had had a rift of some sort—perhaps over financing—and Fenno decided to teach his patron a lesson? We will never know; the letter remains an anomaly, and if Hamilton ever complained about it or Fenno ever offered an explanation, the exchange is lost to history.

But although this was the only time Fenno lashed out at Hamilton, it was not the only time he seems to have displayed a certain whimsical nature, a fondness for the unpredictable, the kind of trait that would have endeared a biographer to him. Despite needing money, Fenno would occasionally cut back on the number of ads in the *Gazette*, seeming to believe that readers were put off by them: one day's paper would be full of ballyhoo for products and services, merchants and traders, and the next as barren as a Treasury Department edict about exchange rates.

And Fenno was occasionally known to publish a letter on the most trivial of matters, perhaps having decided that his readers needed occasional relief from the paper's more serious, nation-forging preoccupations. One of them, addressed to a Mr. Hull, popped up in the paper one day as unexpectedly as a spring snowstorm.

> SIR,
>
> I am informed that you keep a Billiard Table in town, and that you do no other business than to attend it. You are able to cut down twenty trees 3 feet over, in a day:—labour bears a great price; and it would be much more to your honour to go into the woods and clear a fallow of ten acres, than to support yourself as you do.

And then there were times when Fenno enlivened his paper with something even less expected, less relevant, as if he were wondering how closely people actually read the *Gazette* and had decided to plant an item to test their attentiveness. A month after chastising Mr. Hull for his billiard table, Fenno decided to share with his readers a little number called "The Potatoe, a rhapsody," which praised, in terms unequivocal if not exactly comprehensible,

Roots of pure fruit, all flavory from the ground,
Diffusing plenty 'mong the sons of men!

For the most part, though, the *Gazette of the United States* es-
chewed paeans to vegetation and toed the party line as strictly as it
could. It proposed federalists for sainthood, consigned republicans
to the fieriest precincts of perdition. It was a political paper, the
first American journal to be a virtual branch of government, and it
took pride in administering lash after lash across the backs of those
who found it misguided and deceitful and incompetent.

Thomas Jefferson finally decided he could take it no longer.

CHAPTER SIXTEEN

. . . *versus the* Gazette

*I*T WAS TIME, the secretary of state now believed, to fight newsprint with newsprint. "Were I to undertake to answer the calumnies of the newspapers," he would later write, "it would be more than all my own time, and that of twenty aids [sic] could effect." For now, though, he thought he had no choice but to try.

In October 1791, Jefferson and some like-minded republicans endowed a paper of their own, the *National Gazette*, to be published twice a week, to cost $3 a year for a subscription. Its editor would be Philip Freneau, a college classmate of James Madison at Princeton and, as far as Madison was concerned, "a man of genius and a friend of the Constitution [who] was without a rival in the whole catalogue of American printers." But he was a friend of Jefferson's interpretation of the Constitution, which is to say that although he believed in a central government, he thought it should be limited in both size and scope and that the states should make most of their own decisions. And he thought there should be a newspaper as forceful on this side of the question as there was on the other.

Unlike Fenno, Freneau had been a figure of some renown before his career as a newspaperman, so much so, in fact, that he remains one to the present day. A gifted writer, perhaps the most respected of his time, Philip Freneau was "the Poet of the American Revolution," and his work still appears in anthologies, although perhaps as much because of its period flavor as its inherent quality. In fact, looking at a picture of Freneau, one can see, or imagine, that he was born to the calling; there seems a certain delicacy of features, a certain sharpness of eye.

Here is Freneau paying tribute to an aeronaut as he soars above the Earth in a balloon:

Yes—wait, and let the heav'ns decide;—
Your wishes may be gratified,
And you shall go, as swift as thought,
Where nature has more finely wrought,
Her crystal spheres, her heavens serene;
A more sublime, enchanting scene
Than thought depicts or poets feign.

In what is probably his most famous poem, *The Indian Burying Ground*, Freneau sympathizes with the men and women who had settled America first and were then driven from their homes by his fellow Europeans.

In spite of all the learned have said,
I still my old opinion keep;
The posture that we give the dead,
Points out the soul's eternal sleep.
Not so the ancients of these lands—
The Indian, when from life released,
Again is seated with his friends,
And shares again the joyous feast.

And in the following lines, Freneau celebrates nature in one of her smaller manifestations.

Fair flower, that dost so comely grown,
Hid in this silent, dull retreat,
Untouched thy honied blossoms blow,
Unseen thy little branches greet:

No roving foot shall crush thee here,
No busy hand provoke a tear.

He does not sound like the kind of fellow whom Jefferson would enlist to spit in the face of the federalists.

❁

BUT PHILIP FRENEAU HAD ANOTHER SIDE TO HIM, less gentle if equally metrical. He "was a good hater," writes Moses Coit Tyler in his two-volume literary history of the times; "his was the wrathful muse; his chosen warfare was grim, unsparing, deadly." And decidedly anti-federalist.

Yet Freneau's verse was sometimes satirical in tone, a rapier instead of a cudgel, such as when he wrote about a printer for whom he had lost all respect long before John Fenno came along. The poem is called "Rivington's Last Will and Testament," and Freneau writes it in what he imagines to be Jemmy's own distinctive voice.

"To the king, my dear master, I give a full sett,
In volumes bound up, of the Royal Gazette,
In which he will find the vast records contain'd
Of provinces conquer'd, and victories gain'd.

"As to Arnold, the traitor, and Satan his brother,
I beg they will also accept of another;
And this shall be bound in morocco red leather,
Provided they'll read it, like brothers, together.
. . .
"I know there are some, that would fain be thought wise
Who say my Gazette is a record of lies;
In answer to this I shall only reply—
All the choice that I had was, to starve or to lie.

Perhaps Freneau was the right man to take on the federalists after all.

❀

INITIALLY, THOUGH, he was not interested in the job. He was living in New Jersey when Jefferson came calling, and planning to publish a small weekly newspaper of his own while continuing with his poetry. He had long preferred verse to prose, and perhaps, despite his strong republican leanings, nature to politics. But he also preferred income to penury, and, then as now, it was hard to make a living in America as a hinterlands newsman and part-time bard.

So Madison, a congressman from Virginia at the time, kept after him, promising Freneau that if he would edit the *National Gazette*, Madison would write for him, and, true to his word, his first offering was a series of eighteen articles, a pamphlet's worth and then some. Published anonymously, the pieces criticized the Washington administration in virtually all of its endeavors. Those who supported the president, Madison implied, and thus opposed Jeffersonian views, were "stupid, suspicious, licentious. . . . [They] look at the surface only, where errors float, instead of fathoming the depths where truth lies hid." Not only that, they were people "destitute . . . of every quality of a good citizen, or rather of a good *subject.*" To them, Madison said, "You have neither the light of faith nor the spirit of obedience. I denounce you to the government as an accomplice of atheism and anarchy."

Madison had done a nice job in overcoming the lofty tones of *The Federalist Papers.*

Jefferson also kept after Freneau. He would not write articles for the *Gazette*, he said, but would allow the occasional letter of his to be printed and would perhaps write a letter from time to time with publication in mind.

And he would do more. He would hire Freneau at the State Department as a translator; assure him of government printing contracts on the side; and provide the *Gazette* with inside information whenever he could. He made good on his word in the most surreptitious of manners. "With his pass key," writes Jefferson biographer Willard Sterne Randall, "Freneau entered Jefferson's office at night, copied out reports left in plain sight for him, then ran them in his newspaper, sometimes before President Washington ever saw them." In other words, Jefferson would leak the news that he wanted leaked.

Save for the key and the midnight sneaking, it was virtually the same relationship that Hamilton had with Fenno—with one glaring exception. Jefferson arranged for Freneau to receive a salary of $250 a year; Hamilton had seen to it that Fenno was much more lavishly compensated, reportedly arranging to pay him ten times that amount, which, according to the *National Gazette*, "cannot otherwise than have some sort of influence on the Editor of the Gazette of the United States, especially when his avaricious principles are brought into view."

Fenno, however, believed his principles were noble, not avaricious, and the great journalistic feud of the age was under way.

The *Gazette of the United States*, July 25, 1792: "The editor of the *National Gazette* receives a salary from the government," readers are informed in a back-page letter, which then asks how such a publication can be trusted. "Whether this salary is paid him for *translations*; or for *publications*, the design of which is to vilify those to whom the voice of the people has committed the administration of our public affairs—to oppose the measures of government, and, by false insinuations, to disturb the public peace."

The *National Gazette*, July 25, 1792: Freneau demonstrates that he is able to serve Jefferson without giving up his poetic leanings after all. In the following, Pomposo is Hamilton; his dull printer, of course, Fenno.

Since the day we attempted the *Nation's Gazette*
Pomposo's dull printer does nothing but fret;
    Now preaching,

Now screeching,
Then nibbling,
And scribbling,
Remarking,
And barking,
Repining,
And whining,
And still in a pet,
From morning till night, with the *Nation's Gazette.*

The *Gazette of the United States,* July 28, 1792: "It appears evident from circumstances," says a letter from someone signing himself Detector, "and the general complexion of the publications in the *National Gazette,* that it is only the tool of a faction, and the prostituted vehicle of party spleen and opposition to the great principles of order, virtue, and religion."

The *National Gazette,* July 28, 1792: Freneau returns to prose, dismissing Fenno as a "vile sycophant" of the administration.

The *Gazette of the United States,* August 2, 1792: Fenno replies that "[t]he National Gazette is—the vehicle of party spleen and opposition to the great principles of order, virtue, and religion."

The *National Gazette,* August 4, 1792: Freneau, in verse again, praises his paper's "spirit . . . of democratic proof" and refers to that devil Fenno's "canker'd hoof."

The *Gazette of the United States,* August 4, 1792: Fenno publishes a letter from Hamilton saying that Jefferson is guilty of "an experiment somewhat new in the history of political maneuvers in this country: a newspaper instituted by a public Officer, and the Editor of it regularly pensioned with the public money in the disposal of that officer: an example favouring not a little of that spirit, which in the enumeration of European abuses is the continual theme of declamatory censure: an example which could not have been set by the head of any other department without having long since rung throughout the United States."

But was Hamilton not guilty of the same thing? Was he not in fact as much a hypocrite as Jefferson, pursuing his own political ends at the expense of taxpayers, many of whom disagreed with those ends? He thought not. *The Gazette of the United States* was using government money to support government positions, Hamilton explained, and he believed that to be a perfectly legitimate expense. The *National Gazette*, he wrote, was doing something entirely different, thoroughly disreputable; again on August 4, 1792, Hamilton asked, "Is it possible that Mr. Jefferson . . . can be the patron of a paper, the evident object of which is to decry the government and its measures?"

Hamilton's paper, on the other hand, was not decrying the government. It was, rather, promoting the Washington administrations's every position, its every goal, and insisting on its rectitude and being as accurate as it could be in reporting it. Hamilton wondered why others could not see the logic of his distinctions and might instead think him duplicitous or subversive. As late as 1796, Hamilton was still writing in the *Gazette of the United States* about Jefferson's having "conferred a *sinecure* office in [the State] department . . . on Mr. Freneau to induce him to remove to Philadelphia, and set up a newspaper at the seat of government called the *National Gazette.*"

Was it Jefferson, then, who played the hypocrite? Had the secretary of state been making it a practice to speak one way and act another, while refusing to acknowledge the contradictions, even to himself? Well, yes. He certainly had, but hypocrisy was the lesser of Jefferson's evils in this contest of dueling political journals, for while he admitted to friends and foes alike that Freneau was an acquaintance and someone who supported his viewpoints on most issues, he said that he knew Freneau only casually, that the two of them seldom talked. And he went further: Jefferson swore that he had nothing whatsoever to do with either the financing or the content of the *National Gazette*. But too many people knew otherwise; Jefferson's reputation would not survive the lie untarnished.

HAMILTON AND JEFFERSON seemed never to tire of their mutual enmity, and their press secretaries, Fenno and Freneau, were equally energetic in bringing matters to the public's attention, applying the proper amounts of praise and scorn as befit their respective positions. It was, after all, the reason that the two printers had been set up in business in the first place.

Late in the winter of 1792, the *National Gazette* referred to the "sad effects" of Hamilton's financial policies and their "numerous evils," which were "pregnant with every mischief." The "baneful" system that Hamilton had devised was "as unjust in its operation on individuals, as it has been ruinous in its effects on the public: for whether we consider the losses sustained by the farmer and the soldier, who advanced their persons and property in defence of their country: and the immense profits made on those losses by greedy speculators: or take a more extensive view, and contemplate the great national evils it has involved us in, we are equally led to deprecate its injustice and impolicy."

Among other things, Hamilton had proposed that the United States establish a mint, and that Washington's face appear on its first batches of coins. *The Gazette of the United States* supported the proposal. The *National Gazette*, believing it to be yet further evidence that Washington wanted to be King George, did not.

> Can wits or serious sages say,
> Why Congress should refuse that Head
> A place upon their coin this day,
> O'er which the world hath laurels spread?
>
> Yes; Liberty, celestial Maid,
> By whom *its* right to crown was given,
> The eager hands of Congress staid;
> And claim'd that place, as sent by heav'n.
>
> Shall WASHINGTON my fav'rite Child,
> Be rank'd 'mongst haughty kings, the cry'd;

Of manners pure, affections mild,
For wild ambition be decry'd.

Or shall each vile successor share
That honor which you think *his* due?
Or granting this were right, who dare
This path of monarchies pursue?

Because a sycophantic race
Worshipp'd in every form their kings,
And on their coins to their disgrace,
Plac'd them, if wise, or silly things.

It seems to have been about this time that Hamilton went to Washington and accused Jefferson of being an "intriguer." Jefferson said the same about Hamilton. Hamilton told Washington that Jefferson's notion of foreign policy was "a womanish attachment to France and a womanish resentment against Great Britain." Jefferson replied that Hamilton's policies, especially his fiscal policies, were causing Americans "to occupy themselves and their capital in a species of gambling"; it was, Jefferson said, "destructive of morality."

But the backstabbing between the secretaries of treasury and state was also destructive in that it chipped away at the chief executive's sanity, or at least his contentment. In the summer of 1792, as Fenno and Freneau kept blasting away at each other in the press, Washington met with Hamilton and Jefferson, although whether together or separately is not certain. He told them that the public nature of their disagreements was not only hurting the administration but adding to the divisions in the country and, further, making it look to foreign powers as if the United States, because divided, might be vulnerable either to attack or economic pressures. Worse, Washington must have thought, their disagreements were a reflection on him, a stain on the reputation he prized so highly. He had previously believed that "mutual forebearances, and temporizing yieldings on all sides" would permit Hamilton and Jefferson to work together more harmoniously; after all, the problems were merely "a fraternal spat between two of his surrogate sons." But he now knew it was more than that. There were fundamental differences between the two men, and Washington could do nothing about them.

What he could do was ask Hamilton to restrain himself for the good of the nation. Hamilton said he would try, and perhaps even meant it. And Washington could ask Jefferson to restrain Freneau. Jefferson dissembled. "As to the merits or demerits of his [Freneau's] paper," he would later explain, "they certainly concern me not. He & Fenno are rivals for the public favor. The one courts them by flattering, the other by censure, & and I believe it will be admitted that the one has been as servile, as the other severe." Jefferson still would not admit his connection to the *National Gazette*, and Washington, at this point, does not seem to have realized that his own State Department was, at least in part, subsidizing the journalistic bombardments against him.

❖

THE PRESIDENT'S CAUTION did no good. The two cabinet members kept up their fire; the two newspapers did the same. At one point, the *National Gazette* took the extraordinary step of reprinting, in its entirety, an article from the *Gazette of the United States* so that Freneau could rebut it in the greatest detail possible. The Fenno article had been "critical of Mr. Jefferson's conduct in the particulars which have been suggested," so the Freneau response suggested some particulars of its own, and they led to entirely different conclusions. Said the *National Gazette* in its final paragraph: "So far, then, as any imputation has been raised, against a distinguished and patriot citizen [Jefferson], I have furnished the reply, and I presume, shewn not only his innocence of any impropriety of the allegations suggested, but likewise that impunity of the motives which dictated the attack."

For Washington himself Freneau had a message, equally reproachful but more personal. In the summer of 1793, with the president too favorably disposed toward the British to suit republican sensibilities and the *National Gazette* overflowing with sarcasm in search of an outlet, the paper advised him that his countrymen's sympathies were with the French and that he would do well to take them into account.

> I am aware, sir, that some court satellites may have deceived you with respect to the sentiment of your fellow citizens. The first magistrate of a country, whether he be called king or president, seldom knows the real state of a nation, particularly if he be so buoyed up by official importance to think it beneath his dignity to mix occasionally with the people. Let me caution you, sir, to beware that you do not view the state of the public mind at this crucial moment through a fallacious medium. Let not the little buzz of the aristocratic few and their contemptible minions of speculators, tories and British emissaries be mistaken for the exalted and generous voice of the American people.

This might have been the article that occasioned the outburst Jefferson revealed sometime afterward. Washington, he told an acquaintance,

> . . . adverted to a piece in Freneau's paper of yesterday, he said he despised all their attacks on him personally, but there has never been an act of the government . . . which that paper had not abused. . . . He was evidently sore & warm, and I took his intention to be that I should interpose in some way with Freneau, perhaps withdraw his appointment of translating clerk in my office. But I will not do it. His paper has saved our constitution, which was galloping fast into monarchy, & has been checked by no means so powerfully as by that paper.

When another screed in the *National Gazette* infuriated Washington even more, Jefferson wrote, "The President was much inflamed," and then said that Washington claimed "he had rather be on his farm than to be made *emperor of the world* and yet they were charging him with wanting to be king. That that *rascal Freneau* sent him 3 of his papers every day, as if he thought he would become the distributor of his papers, that he could see in this nothing but an impudent design to insult him."

More insults were coming. Early the next year, Washington celebrated his sixty-first birthday with a ball that was far too grand for Freneau's simpler tastes, too lavish and pomp-riddled, and, even worse, a bad precedent for future residents of America's presidential quarters.

Who will deny, that the celebrating of birth days is not a striking feature of royalty? We hear of no such thing during the republic of Rome. . . .

If this evil was of no greater extent, than merely debasing those who are in the practice of it, I should not feel much concern. But when I consider it a forerunner of other monarchical vices, and holding up an improper example in this country, and an example of *precedent*, I cannot but execrate the measure.

In fact, every time Washington observed a birthday during his years as president, the opposition press tore into the ceremony as if it were as offensive to American sensibilities as the Stamp Act. In one case, a paper likened the observance to a "'Political Christmas'! what is the idea of this expression, but ranking WASHINGTON with JESUS CHRIST?" A few years earlier, the same paper had resorted to its favorite, all-purpose, anti-Washingtonian adjective. Soldiers who marched in a birthday parade in 1795, it was said, "assist in establishing *monarchical* fashions."

Washington could not understand journalism like this, could not tolerate it, especially when, at the same time, the *National Gazette* was finding the behavior of the secretary of state to be all the things the president's was not. "The *unity* of your conduct," said an article Freneau published on one occasion about Jefferson, in tones so fulsome that the editor might have been seeking a raise; "your dignified and republican simplicity; your enmity to fastidious distance and reserve; your respect for the people, are subjects of affection and commendation, and ought to be of imitation to every man who is the friend of equality."

Your State Department budget at work, Mister President.

❀

ALMOST TWO YEARS after making its debut, the *National Gazette* did something no one would have thought possible. It published an article that brought a smile, and perhaps even congratulatory steins of rum, ale, or hard cider, to the lips of federalists. Actually, it was just a paragraph, the last paragraph in the bottom right corner of the last page, and it did not quite tell the truth. The date was October 26, 1793.

> With the present number (208) concludes the second volume, and second year's publication of the *National Gazette*. Having just imported, on his own account, a considerable quantity of new and elegant printing types from Europe, it's the Editor's intention to resume the publication of this paper in a short time and previously to the meeting of Congress on the second day of December next.

It might have been the editor's hope to publish again in a short time, but it would not happen, and Freneau almost certainly knew it. Others knew it, too; the *Gazette* was really saying farewell, not so long. A yellow fever epidemic in Philadelphia had claimed many of its readers, and perhaps one or two of Freneau's journeymen printers. Subscribers were falling behind in their payments and some not paying at all. But most damaging to the paper's prospects, Jefferson had resigned as secretary of state, which was the ultimate loss of support, financial and otherwise, for Freneau. The *National Gazette* simply could not go on.

The republicans would find another paper to promote their positions, many other papers actually, but one would rise to the fore, a rabble-rousing publication that already existed and, with the demise of the *National Gazette*, would begin foaming at the mouth about federalism even more profusely to take up the slack. It was the paper that had blasted the notion of "Political Christmas," that had accused the federalists of ranking Washington with Jesus Christ. In a few years, its editor, a little-known man with a famous name, would become the first American newspaperman since James Franklin to be arrested, although in circumstances far more ominous.

As for Freneau, he would return to his poetry, perhaps with a sense of relief, a feeling of gratitude for the coming of calmer times. In the years ahead, he would write an occasional newspaper article praising the French or condemning the British, advocating a republican presidency or fretting about John Adams's incumbency, but for the most part he would concentrate on birds taking flight and storms at sea, on disappearing wilderness and disappearing Indians, on "a Honey-Bee Drinking from a Glass of Wine." He does not seem to have written, either in verse or prose, about his experiences as a newspaperman in the service of Jeffersonian ideals.

That he was bitter, however, there is no doubt. That he felt unfairly treated by Fenno and other federalist newsmen is also certain. That he felt inadequately appreciated by Jefferson, at least on occasion, is likely. He may be forgiven if, at some point shortly after the *Gazette*'s final issue, he fell into a chair in a dark, empty room, fell even deeper into a melancholy reverie, and recited aloud, to himself and whatever gods were listening, the last four lines of a poem he had written some years before but seemed especially poignant now.

"The sun's in the west,
And I am opprest
With fellows attempting to blacken my muse,
Who hardly have genius to blacken my shoes."

CHAPTER SEVENTEEN

❈

Dark Whispers on the Page

THE

HISTORY

OF THE

UNITED STATES

FOR 1796;

INCLUDING A VARIETY OF

INTERESTING PARTICULA

RELATIVE TO THE

FEDERAL GOVERNM

PREVIOUS TO THAT PERI

I N THE SUMMER OF 1791, Alexander Hamilton made a mistake. It was a mistake that a lot of men had made before him and a lot of men have made since, men of high standing and low, statesmen and farmers, federalists and republicans. It was a mistake that had nothing to do with politics, with the goals of the Washington administration or the perceived fallacies of Jefferson and his followers. In Hamilton's case the mistake's name was Maria Reynolds, and she turned out to be not just a single mistake, but a whole series of them, one lapse of judgment after another, that would eventually be expensive, embarrassing, and, ultimately and most painfully for Hamilton, well publicized.

It had been a busy time in his life. In addition to his usual duties at Treasury and his usual struggles with those who were frightened by his blueprint for the American future, Hamilton was working on something called the *Report on Manufactures* that summer, a much anticipated document and one that would prove to be of lasting significance, a master plan for American industrial and commercial growth in which, as would later be observed, the secretary "prophesied much of post–Civil War America."

The project was a consuming one. After a day spent compiling information and analyzing statistics, trying to extract the most accurate meanings from them, and then setting forth his conclusions as lucidly and persuasively as he could, Hamilton was tired, sometimes nervous and overwhelmed; he needed to relax, escape, forget.

One night, as he sat alone at home with his wife upstairs preparing their children for bed, he heard a knock at the door. As he later explained: "a woman called at my house in the city of Philadelphia and asked to speak with me in private. I attended her into a room apart from the family." He offered her a seat, and Maria Reynolds no sooner took it than she began to speak to him with "a seeming air of affliction," complaining about her husband, a ruffian and philanderer named James. She told Hamilton that James had long been abusing her, showing her neither respect nor kindness, and certainly not connubial affection. Now, she said, he had gone even further; he had deserted her, packing up his belongings and moving in with another woman, a tramp of some sort whose name she claimed not even to know. Maria had come to Hamilton "to apply to my humanity for assistance."

Hamilton listened to the whole story. A man of average height, his childhood freckles still lightly visible, Hamilton did not think himself handsome, even with his "wavy chestnut brown hair, a classical nose, and deep-set violet eyes." But women were easily attracted to him, and Maria seemed to be among the easiest. He told her that "her situation was a very interesting one—that I was disposed to offer her assistance," but he could not do so at the moment; his wife would be summoning him any moment to say goodnight to the children. Maria said she understood and rose to take her leave; Hamilton walked her to the door. He would call on her later that night, he promised, and would bring with him "a small supply of money." She thanked him and hurried into the darkness.

Already much is unclear. Why had Maria Reynolds come to Hamilton with her tale of woe? She apparently told him that she was from New York and, since he had lived there as well, she felt drawn to him. But as the capital of the United States, Philadelphia was full of New Yorkers in those days; why would she choose to cry on the shoulder of a stranger who also happened to be the secretary of the treasury? Why had Maria sought him out at home rather than at his office, where she would be certain to avoid his wife and could disguise her visit as a business call? Why did Hamilton sit through her recital of woes? He was, after all, one of the most eminent men in the nation, not the proprietor of an almshouse or a man of the cloth with an especially ready ear. And why had Hamilton agreed to visit her the very same night with financial relief? Had she made a threat of some sort? Or, more likely, was it a hint, even a promise?

Hamilton recounts what happened next, after his children were asleep and he had made an excuse to his wife, telling her that he had an errand to run and promising that he would be back as soon as possible but she should not wait up.

> I put a bank bill in my pocket and went to the house. I inquired for Mrs. Reynolds and was shown upstairs, at the head of which she met me and conducted me into a bedroom. I took the bill out of my pocket and gave it to her. Some conversation ensued from which it was quickly apparent that other than pecuniary consolation would be acceptable.

And so Alexander Hamilton started consoling, as so many powerful men have consoled so many willing women over the eons, in a manner other than pecuniarily. He did so not only that night, but all through the summer of 1791 and into the fall and winter and through almost all of the following year, with his wife inadvertently getting her husband's misadventure off to a convenient start by taking herself and the children to Albany to visit her parents. She did so for her health and comfort, as she was pregnant with the couple's fifth child at the time, and the summers in Philadelphia were hot and humid and ripe with the prospect of yellow fever. And she did so because of her husband's busy schedule; she did not think that she and the children would see much of him, no matter where she was, and certainly would not have his full attention until the *Report on Manufactures* was finished in a few months.

But Hamilton did not work on the report every minute that summer, and when he took a break, it was often in the company of the supposedly forlorn Maria Reynolds, who had started out in life as Mary and whose name, as Ron Chernow points out, was probably pronounced Ma-*rye*-ah. First he took breaks in her bed, and then, once his family had departed from Philadelphia, he brought her to his own quarters. Hamilton was not in love with Maria, and never deluded himself, or her, into thinking he might one day be; it was his wife, Betsy, whom he loved and with whom he would live for the rest of his life, and it was his memory that Betsy would venerate, with unflinching tenderness, for the half century that she survived him. But, for a few months at least, Hamilton would be even more consumed by Maria Reynolds than he was by the future of American manufacturing.

❀

MORE THAN ONCE IN THE SUMMER OF '91, Betsy wrote her husband that she was planning to return home; she said she missed him, the children missed their father, she had had quite enough of Albany despite her fondness for her parents. And more than once, the lust-addled Hamilton pleaded with her to be patient. He expressed his "extreme anxiety for the restoration of your health." It would be "a great sacrifice" for him not to see her immediately, he claimed, but for her sake, and for the sake of the children, who were now beyond the reach of disease, he was willing to make it.

It is hard to imagine Alexander Hamilton behaving like this. Nothing in his past indicated that he would one day turn his back on those who meant the most to him and so eagerly lap up the illicit, or that he would tell such lies, engage in such ruses, to keep his licentious secrets. He might have had an eye for the ladies, as was later observed, but it was not like him to do more than look, or to do so *much* more than look. His needs were obviously great at this troublesome time in his life, as were Maria's attractions.

The latter were not just physical. Hamilton seems to have been ensnared as well by Maria's tales of mistreatment by her husband;

she kept him coming back by appealing to his sympathies as well as to his manhood. One night, complaining even more than usual about James, she told her lover "that [Reynolds] had frequently enjoined and insisted that she should insinuate herself on certain high and influential characters—endeavor to make assignations with them and actually prostitute herself to gull money from them." Which is, of course, precisely what she was doing with Hamilton. Apparently, if inexplicably, this made him sympathize with her all the more.

And perhaps, at least for a time, Hamilton was flattered by what seemed to be her neediness, her desperate if not almost mindless craving for him. There is always something irresistible to a man about a woman's loss of control in his presence, and Maria's ardor showed no signs of either abating or becoming more rational; the affair lasted not only beyond the return of Hamilton's family from Albany, but well beyond the point at which Hamilton wanted to put an end to it.

But whenever he tried to tell her that he would see her no more, that their entanglement was a mistake for both of them, that they should now go their separate ways and, truth be told, should never have taken up with each other to begin with, she would lose even more control, begging him, writing him letters that always managed to bring him back. Clearly, though, it was her longing for him, not her mastery of language, that so appealed, as the following pathetically demonstrates.

> Ben sick all moast Ever since I saw you . . . I have kept my Bed those tow dayes and now rise from my pillow wich your Neglect has filled with the shorpest thorns . . . I only do it to Ease a heart wich is ready Burst with Greef. I can neither Eat or sleep. I have Been on the point of doing the most horrid acts . . . I feel as if I Should not Contennue long and all the wish I have Is to se you once more . . . for God sake be not so voed of all humanity as to deni me this Last request but if you will not Call some time this

night I no its late but any tim[e] between this and twelve A Clock I shall be up.

Not long after receiving this letter, Hamilton would finally begin to pull away. But for the time being, he was still plucking the thorns from her pillow, if not on this particular night, then on all too many other ones, both before and after.

❀

DURING THE COURSE OF THE AFFAIR, Hamilton met Maria's husband, who at some point had moved back home, and the plot inevitably thickened. Maria told James that Hamilton was but a friend and told Hamilton that her husband's renewed presence in her life meant nothing to her; she was apparently hoping that neither man would upset the equilibrium of her relationship with the other. But now that each of the adulterers had a spouse in the house, their meetings had to be even more clandestine and carefully scheduled than before, and required more deception to consummate.

Which is to say that there was even more pressure on Hamilton, and more incentive for him to break things off. He began urging Maria to return to her husband, to forgive him his past misdeeds, to allow him to make amends. It is unlikely that Hamilton believed the Reynolds' union was worth saving, but by this time he did not care. He simply wanted to be done with her, to reclaim his life, his wife, and his self-respect.

But it was not just Maria he wanted to be rid of. Hamilton soon realized that James might prove to be an even bigger problem for him than his mate. From his first look at the man, Hamilton had been uneasy. Reynolds appeared coarse to him, unsavory; he was clearly not the type of person with whom the secretary of the treasury was used to consorting or with whom he would willingly have conversed had they met at a social function; in fact, the odds of their even attending the same function were negligible. It is also possible that Hamilton recognized Reynolds, that he knew him to be the same person who, a few years earlier, had figured out a scheme to cheat Revolutionary War widows out of the back pay they were owed for their late husbands' service. Even if he did not associate Reynolds with the fraud, he certainly took him to be the kind of man capable of such a thing. On those few occasions when Hamilton found himself in James Reynolds's company, he should have felt a noose begin to tighten.

It tightened all the more when, at one of their meetings, Reynolds told him that he knew of some shady dealings at the Treasury Department.

Hamilton continued the conversation warily, asking what he meant.

Speculators, came the reply, government employees who had gotten involved in a series of complicated and highly unethical financial dealings that had profited them greatly but could cause the secretary a lot of trouble if they became known. Hamilton should not worry, however, Reynolds said; he would be glad to identify both the men and the deeds, allowing the secretary to right his ship before any newspapers could learn of the speculations.

Hamilton, now even more wary, expressed his gratitude.

Oh, and by the way, Reynolds was wondering whether he might have a job at Treasury, a clerkship of some sort: reasonable compensation, responsible duties, not too much work.

Hamilton turned him down, asked no more about the alleged fraud in his department, and ended the conversation.

A short time later he received a note from Maria containing, as he had almost surely begun to fear by now, the first threat of blackmail. She wrote that if he did not accede to her husband's wishes for employment, Reynolds would tell Hamilton's wife about their affair. Not long afterward, Reynolds himself wrote to the secretary, admitting that he knew the real nature of Hamilton's relationship with Maria and setting the stage for the several requests for money that would follow:

Sir

I am very sorry to find out that I have been so Cruelly treated by a person that I took to be my best friend instead of my greatest Enimy. You have deprived me of every thing that's near and dear to me . . . [My wife] Called on you for the lone of some money, which you toald her you would call on her the Next Evening, which accordingly you did, and there sir you took advantage a poor Broken harted woman. Instead of being a Friend, you have acted the part of the Cruelist man in existence. you have made a whole family miserable. She ses there is no other man that she Care for in this world, now Sir you have bin the Cause of Cooling her affections for me.

He suffered from "wounded honor," Reynolds claimed; he wanted money to assist in the healing.

Hamilton biographer Richard Brookhiser is sympathetic to his subject in almost all of his undertakings. But not at the expense of candor: "A plain statement of the facts," Brookhiser writes, "is that Mrs. Reynolds was a whore, her husband was a pimp, and both were blackmailers; Hamilton was a john and a gull."

The john paid, and more than once. Reynolds first asked for $1,000, and Hamilton handed it over in two installments. There were other payments, these of $100, although it is not clear how many. In addition, Hamilton provided a "loan" of $300 for an investment that Reynolds believed could not fail. Apparently it did.

But Hamilton seems to have thought of his hush money as an investment too, and a sound one at that. He believed it would actually hush, that James Reynolds would be satisfied with the amounts and his wife willing to forgo her extramarital exertions; in other words, he believed that the shifty duo would keep their part of the bargain and leave him alone at last.

And, against all logic, they seem to have done just that. The affair ended. The demands for money ended. The child with whom Betsy had been pregnant at the time the affair started was more than a year old by now, and Hamilton, still basking in the praise he had received for his *Report on Manufactures*, had put the most uncharacteristic episode of his life behind him. Or so he wanted, with an almost frantic naïveté, to believe.

※

SHORTLY AFTER THE AFFAIR ENDED, James Monroe, who would be president of the United States after Madison and was now a senator from Virginia, found out that Hamilton had given money to James Reynolds. But he did not know why. He did not know when. He did not know how much. Monroe discussed the matter with two other lawmakers, Representatives Frederick Muhlenberg of Pennsylvania and Abraham Venable of Virginia, and the three of them decided to confront Hamilton. They appeared at the secretary's office one day in the middle of December 1792 and got straight to the point. It seemed as if Reynolds had been blackmailing Hamilton; was that, in fact, what had happened? Was the secretary guilty of financial skullduggery in the performance of his duties? If so, what kind? "Faced with Hamilton's wrath," writes Ron Chernow, "the three legislators reassured him that they were not making any accusations but felt honor bound to discuss the matter with him before reporting to Washington."

Hamilton calmed himself and told his guests he understood. If they would come to his house that night, he said, he would be happy to answer their questions.

The answers were, of course, yes and no. Reynolds had been blackmailing him, Hamilton told the men several hours later, but the corruption had been in his heart, not in the business of the Treasury Department. The secretary confessed his liaison with Maria Reynolds without attempting to justify it, and even showed Monroe, Muhlenberg, and Venable some letters that Maria and James had written him that seemed to support his version of events, that the extortion was the result of his philandering. The men asked for the letters. Hamilton handed them over without reservation. The lawmakers assured him that they would guard the letters carefully, and Hamilton apparently believed them.

He swore again that he had taken no liberties with the Treasury Department's budget, and, as no such charge had ever been made against Hamilton before and no one, not even his most fervent of republican detractors, had ever had reason to suspect him of wrongdoing of any sort, the men were inclined to accept him at his word. Nonetheless, Hamilton apologized for his behavior. He had acted irresponsibly, inexcusably, and he seemed shaken to admit it. He would not behave in such a manner again—that he could promise his visitors without qualification.

Venable apologized in return. He said he was sorry that he and his companions had misunderstood the secretary's actions and that their visit had caused him "trouble and embarrassment." Hamilton expressed his gratitude, and the three men shook hands with him, exchanged good wishes, and took their leave.

The meeting was over. The consequences had not even begun. That night's gathering, attended not only by Monroe, Muhlenberg, Venable, and Hamilton but also by Oliver Wolcott Jr., a friend of the secretary who would in a few years succeed him as head of the Treasury Department and who was apparently in his company that night to provide moral support, was the first link in the chain of events that would lead the Reynolds affair from the bedrooms of the participants to the front pages of American newspapers.

Hamilton should have known it. He should have known that the promise the three men made to keep the matter secret would one day be broken, if for no other reason than that Monroe was a close friend of Hamilton's most uncompromising and untiring adversary. In fact, at the time of that night's meeting, Monroe was in the midst of writing a series of articles for the *American Daily Advertiser* called "Vindication of Mr. Jefferson." In one of the pieces, Monroe insisted that despite some recent charges to the contrary, the secretary of state had been guilty of "no political impropriety." He was a man with "the most delicate sentiment of honor" when it came to carrying out his governmental duties. To suggest otherwise was "one of the most illiberal and contemptible efforts, to injure the character of a respectable citizen, that has occurred." And, of course, it was Hamilton more than anyone else who was responsible for those illiberal and contemptible efforts.

Once Monroe knew of the affair, it was certain that Jefferson would know. Once Jefferson knew, it was certain that eventually the republican press would find out and take upon itself the duty of informing others. What is surprising, at least to twenty-first-century sensibilities, is not that the details of the relationship finally saw print but that it took more than four years for them to appear.

By eighteenth-century standards, though, such reticence was to be expected. Jefferson, Monroe, and the others who knew of Hamilton's dalliance believed in the separation of public and private no less than they did the separation of church and state. They might despise Hamilton for his politics, but that meant that they were obligated to criticize him for his politics and for his politics only; personal shortcomings might be revealing of character and might in some cases be even more damning than malfeasance in government, but they were not a proper matter for a gentleman to raise. A code of chivalry existed in eighteenth-century America no less than it did in medieval England.

It may also be that Jefferson, whose relationship with the slave Sally Hemings was already the subject of furtive conversations in parlors and alcoves in Virginia, realized his own vulnerability in a matter like this and insisted all the more on gentlemanly conduct.

James Thomson Callender, however, was *not* a gentleman.

❁

AT LEAST JAMES FRANKLIN had an abiding interest in church and state and, for a time, however shortsightedly and wrongheadedly, the proper medical response to smallpox. At least Sam Adams had a powerful commitment to the cause of independence. At least Fenno and Freneau, themselves powerfully committed, remained true to their respective visions of the American future for the length of their careers as newspapermen, and in Freneau's case, for the rest of his days afterward.

Callender, on the other hand, seems to have been a pen for hire, the passionate decade's great journalistic mercenary and perhaps the possessor of its sharpest tongue. This is not to say that his republicanism was insincere, that he was untrue to himself when he criticized men and motives of federalist leaning—which he did often and sometimes with vicious abandon. Not at the start, at least. But Callender was more self-interested than politically devout, more an opportunist than an ideologue; he would turn on the republicans the moment he felt ill-used or even underappreciated by them. His loyalties were for sale and subject to wild fluctuations when the payments were not made as expected.

James Thomson Callender, born in Scotland in 1758, never had much to say about his early years. He seems to have been well educated, seems to have been drawn to politics at a young age, and was without question a writer of some skill. At thirty-five, he produced a pamphlet called *The Political Progress of Britain: Or, An Impartial History of Abuses in the Government of the British Empire*. In it he returned the abuses, accusing the British of being warmongers and then pointing out they were guilty of even more: "in the scale of just calculation," he wrote, "the most valuable commodity next to human blood is money. Having made a gross estimate of the waste of the former, let us endeavour to compute the consumption of the latter." And off he went, computing away to the almost total detriment of the Crown and its supporters.

The pamphlet was considered so incendiary by Scottish authorities that they indicted him for sedition. Faced with a choice of jail in Edinburgh or freedom in the United States, Callender headed straight for the docks and booked his passage. He arrived at his new home midway through the passionate decade, officially considered a fugitive from justice in Great Britain; as far as American republicans were concerned, it was an impeccable credential.

Biographer Michael Durey, sounding up-to-date in his terminology, believes that "Callender had a repressed and probably lonely childhood." As a result, in his adult years he became an alcoholic, or something close to it, as well as "a complex and contradictory character. He was self-righteous, strongly puritanical with regard to personal morals, insufferably proud, with a deep and abiding mistrust of human nature." The latter was evident in a number of ways, perhaps most succinctly in a couplet he once wrote:

Such is the in-born baseness of mankind,
A grateful heart We seldom hope to find.

One man who surely would have displayed an ungrateful heart toward James Thomson Callender was Samuel Johnson, the preeminent English man of letters of the eighteenth century, master of both wit and lexicography, astute satirist, engaging essayist, unmatched artist of conversation, supreme critic of Shakespeare, perceptive biographer, and himself the subject of the world's most famous biography. Callender's *Deformities of Dr. Samuel Johnson*, published in 1782, preceded *The Political Progress of Britain* by more than a decade but gave a better indication of the nature of the work Callender would do in the 1790s. In this earlier volume, he wrote of Johnson's "arrogant pedantry, his officious malice, his detailed assiduity to undermine his superiors, and overbear his equals." And he wrote of Johnson's "covetous and shameless prolixity; his corruptions of our language; his very limited literature; his entire want of general learning; his antipathy to rival merit; his paralytick [sic] reasoning; his solemn trifling pedantry; his narrow views of human life; his adherence to contradictions; his defiance of decency; and his contempt of truth."

Yet he also accused Johnson of having made an "invidious and revengeful remark" on a fellow author, one that "would have disgraced any other man." Funny he should say that—as Callender would in time make a career of such remarks himself. None but Johnson, Callender wrote with no apparent awareness of duplicity, "has discovered more contempt for other men's reputations."

He would be no less scathing, no less insolent and two-faced, when he moved to the United States and turned his attention to prominent federalists. In fact, it was he who wrote what has been referred to as "one of the most famous diatribes ever written" about the first president.

If ever a nation was debauched by a man, the American nation has been debauched by WASHINGTON. If ever a nation has suffered from the improper influence of a man, the American nation has been deceived by WASHINGTON. Let his conduct then be an example to future ages. Let it serve to be a warning that no man may be an idol, and that a people may confide in themselves rather than in an individual. Let the history of the federal government instruct mankind, that the marque of patriotism may be worn to conceal the foulest designs against the liberties of the people.

Callender would treat the first secretary of the treasury no more kindly. That "strongly puritanical" nature of his would be appalled by Hamilton's conduct with the Reynoldses. That opportunistic side of his would be delighted that he had a chance to ingratiate himself even more with Jefferson and his fellow republicans by vilifying Hamilton for his conduct. That mercenary side of his would regard such vilification as a good career move, and, in the short term, it was precisely that.

Hamilton would later come to believe that Monroe had told Callender about his affair with Reynolds. He would confront Monroe personally, accusing him of having given Callender the letters from James and Maria, feeling "very much agitated"; Monroe, agitated himself, denied his involvement, telling Hamilton that he no longer had the letters, he had given them to a friend for safekeeping shortly afterward. That is "totally false," Hamilton erupted and, as an observer of their exchange reports, the two men threatened to erupt even more.

> Colo. Monroe rising first and saying do you say I represented falsely, you are a scoundrel. Colo. H. said I will meet you like a gentleman[.] Colo. M. said I am ready get your pistols, both said we shall[,] for it will not be settled in any other way.

In fact, the dispute was not settled at all. The two men were separated before they could come to blows or agree on a duel or even challenge each other verbally anymore. But Hamilton remained convinced that Monroe had betrayed him and Monroe that Hamilton was an ignorant and irresponsible hothead, at least in this case.

The truth seems to be that Monroe *did* betray Hamilton, although indirectly, and that Jefferson and Muhlenberg and Venable were fellow betrayers, although they were subtle and unhurried about it. For several years after learning of Hamilton's infidelity, the four men and a few of their closest allies kept the matter to themselves. But they began to grow weary of their circumspection, especially as they grew ever more frustrated with Hamilton's notions of government and his unremitting animus toward Jefferson. They began to think that, for the good of the republican cause, which in their view was synonymous with the good of the nation, they should act less the gentlemen and more the practical politicians.

Besides, Monroe had recently been nominated as ambassador to France, and federalist newspapers, sworn to defeat him, were trashing his character and snickering at his qualifications in almost every issue. He was not experienced enough, not able enough, too much the Francophile and Anglophobe; he would promise the French too much and fail to take into account the legitimate interests of the British.

The republicans wanted revenge for accusations like these. What better way to achieve it than to sic their newspapers once again on Hamilton, to smear the reigning overlord of federalist journalism by publicizing details about the most compromising of matters.

What happened, in all likelihood, was that a man named John Beckley, the Clerk of the House of Representatives and a strong political ally of Jefferson, arranged a meeting with Callender and slipped him the Reynolds letters. Callender would have read them with a heady mixture of disgust and pleasure, like a cleric too long celibate contemplating a work of pornography. He had heard "dark whispers" about the affair—the phrase is Hamilton's; now Callender held the proof of it in his hands, and when he dropped the letters on his desk he must have rubbed those hands together in glee. When he finished, he picked up his pen and added to a series of pamphlets he had already begun to produce.

The History of the United States for 1796 was a bland enough title and, for the most part, a bland, if partisan treatment of its subjects: various decisions by Congress on matters of domestic import, the current state of relations between the United States and France, some raids that the British had been making on American ships despite the Jay Treaty. But even though it had happened before 1796, Callender also included the titillating particulars of the liaison between the secretary of the treasury, whom he portrayed as long-fanged and lecherous, and James Reynolds's wife, whom he portrayed as an innocent young lass who found herself tapping at Hamilton's door one fateful night, seeking merely companionship and solace. Writing furiously, in both senses of the word, Callender put to paper the details of the affair for the first time. End of blandness.

"We now come to a part of the work," Callender wrote, leading into the juicy part of his history, teasing his readers as Maria must so many times have teased Hamilton, "more delicate, perhaps, than any other," a part of the work that would enable Americans to

see this great master of morality, though himself the father of a family, confessing that he had an illicit correspondence with another man's wife. If any thing be less reputable, it is, that the gentlemen to whom he made that acknowledgement [Monroe, Venable, and Muhlenberg] held it as an imposition, and found various reasons for believing that Mrs. Reynolds was, in reality, guiltless. An attentive critic will be led to enquire what has become of her husband, and why the indignant innocence of Mr. Hamilton, did not promote the completion of public justice against a person, who had treated his name with such gross disrespect?

It seems circumspect language to us today; for the time it was quite explicit.

Callender went on: he believed that Hamilton's sexual improprieties were a secondary matter, a cover story concocted by the secretary and James Reynolds to deflect attention from Hamilton's true sins, which were fiscal rather than moral. "So much correspondence could not refer exclusively to wenching," Callender concluded. "Hence it must have implicated some connection still more dishonourable, in Mr. Hamilton's eyes, than that of incontinency." It was theft to which Callender alluded, claiming that Reynolds and Hamilton were crooks who had been, in effect, looting the Treasury Department through their manipulation of the sale of stock certificates, and that their scheme had been so bold in execution, so venal in intent, and so breathtaking in scope that it ended up costing the American citizenry $50 *million*!

The result of all these measures hath been a public debt of eighty millions, instead of thirty; a republican government harnassed [sic] in a monarchical faction; a continent overwhelmed with paper money, with jobs, and bankruptcies, of a nature and species of infamy unknown in Europe; the price doubled on every article of living; a commerce insulted and within sight of ruin; a public treasury without money, and without credit; and last and worst, a squadron of legislative conspirators, in the fifth Congress, who, by every insidious artifice, and every unblushing effort, pant and toil to bury their country in a British alliance and a French war.

Never before had charges like this been made against a man of Alexander Hamilton's stature. Never before had he been scrutinized by a man who so ardently believed in journalism as blood sport. Hamilton was startled by Callender's audacity, his ruthlessness, the self-assurance with which he told both his truths and his lies. Those who read his pamphlets, which were promptly collected and published as a book, were even more startled. Had Alexander Hamilton, of all people, *really* stolen the people's money? Would they ever be able to get it back? Was this fraudulent behavior an indictment of federalism as much as it was of its leading proponent? Did Washington have anything to do with it? And what about poor Mrs. Hamilton—what must it be like for her to have a husband who was both an adulterer *and* an embezzler?

Hamilton, of course, took up his own pen. No longer secretary of the treasury when the scandal erupted but an attorney with a successful private practice, he was able to put off his clients long enough to produce a pamphlet of his own, calling it *Observations on Certain Documents Contained in No. V & VI of "The History of the United States for the Year 1796," In Which the Charge of Speculation Against Alexander Hamilton, Late Secretary of the Treasury, Is Fully Refuted. Written By Himself.* It is known to us today, less cumbersomely, as "the Reynolds pamphlet."

"I dare appeal to my immediate fellow citizens of whatever political party," he wrote, "for the truth of the assertion, that no man ever carried into public life a more unblemished pecuniary reputation." That being the case, Hamilton continued,

> however natural it was to expect criticism and opposition, as to the political principles which I might manifest or be supposed to entertain, as to the wisdom or expediency of the plans, which I might propose, or as to the skill, care or diligence with which the business of my department might be executed, it was not natural to expect nor did I expect that my fidelity or integrity in a pecuniary sense, would ever be called in question.

"My real crime," Hamilton went on, "is an amorous connection with [James Reynolds's] wife for a considerable time with his privity and connivance, if not originally brought on by a combination between the husband and wife with the design to extort money from me."

His confession, he said, "is not made without a blush." He apologized to those who had lost faith in him, and, more than anyone else, to his wife: "I can never cease to condemn myself for the pang, which it may inflict in a bosom eminently intitled [sic] to all my gratitude, fidelity and love." And he hoped that "[t]he public too will . . . excuse the confession. The necessity of it to my defence against a more heinous charge could alone have extorted from me so painful an indecorum."

Hamilton's pamphlet satisfied some of the populace but left others still questioning his probity. Callender found it such an inept performance that he wrote to Jefferson about it, cackling. "If you have not seen it," he said, "no anticipation can equal the infamy of this piece." Other republican journalists agreed, declaring that a scoundrel in the bedroom is likely to be a scoundrel in other venues as well, and that Hamilton could no longer be regarded as a serious spokesman for any political viewpoint, even one as deeply flawed as federalism. To the *New York Journal*, Hamilton was "Tom S**t," and deserved to be called no better.

The *Gazette of the United States* surprised no one by springing to Hamilton's defense. Its method: attack his attacker.

> In the name of justice and honor, how long are we to tolerate this scum of party filth and beggarly corruption, worked into a form somewhat like a man, to go thus with impunity? Do not the times approach when it must and ought to be dangerous for this wretch, and any other, thus to vilify our country and government, thus to treat with indignity and contempt the whole American people, to teach our enemies to despise us and cast forth unremitting calumny and venom on our constitutional authorities?

Callender, John Fenno's publication continued, had been responsible for "sufficient slander on our country to entitle him to the benefit of the gallows."

He had also been responsible for a new kind of journalism: the celebrity sex scandal, an account of the tawdry behavior of a well-known individual presented in such a manner that the culprit was maligned at the same time that the reader was titillated. The first such article to appear in an American newspaper, as opposed to Callender's pamphlets, was written by a man calling himself Justice. Historians are not sure of his identity. That it was Callender, choosing to dish his dirt in a slightly different forum, is certainly possible.

"The volunteer acknowledgement of [Hamilton's] own *depravity*," Justice claimed, "will certainly teach a virtuous public the proper degree of credence to be given to his veracity." He continued in the same vein:

> Throughout the whole of his "Observations," Mr. Hamilton endeavours to impress the public with an idea of his *own purity*, and of the rancorous enmity of his opposers. He has drawn an hideous portrait; and, with one hand, he points at it as theirs,

while, with the other, over the magnitude of his own crimes, he artfully throws a veil. It is our duty, then, to drag him from his covert, and to shew him to the world in a proper point of view, shrouded in his own crimes. To accomplish this, let us examine what proof he offers of the "*uprightness of his principles.*" He tells us he was not guilty of speculation, but acknowledges himself an *adulterer*. Does this then prove him *upright*?

This taunt appeared in the newspaper that had now taken over, so to speak, for Philip Freneau's *National Gazette*, a publication whose editor seemed little concerned with birds soaring through the firmament and honeybees sipping wine.

CHAPTER EIGHTEEN

"The Arising Vapour"

General Aurora Advertiser

SURGO UT PROSIM.

PUBLISHED (DAILY) BY BENJAMIN FRANKLIN BACHE, No. 112, MARKET, BETWEEN THIRD AND FOURTH STREETS, PHILAD

THURSDAY, FEBRUARY 22, 1798.

Notice.

JUST PUBLISHED, AND FOR SALE at the OFFICE of the AURORA [Price one-eighth of a dollar.] An expostulatory letter, TO GEN. WASHINGTON (Late President of the United States) On the subject of his continuing a proprietor of slaves. Written by a citizen of Liverpool.

For Sale

JUST PUBLISHED, Price THREE EIGHTHS of a DOLLAR, And for Sale at FOLWELL'S Printing Office, No. 33, Carter's Alley, A short History of the Yellow Fever. That broke out in the City of Philadelphia, in July, 1797;

Fits Cured.

For the Relief & Cure OF COUGHS, ASTHMAS, and CONSUMPTIONS. CHURCH's COUGH DROPS,

Dr. James Church,

MORE THAN THREE AND A HALF DECADES after he sold the *Pennsylvania Gazette*, and while serving the United States as a minister to France, Benjamin Franklin introduced his grandson to the craft of printing. Franklin gave the boy his first few lessons on a press that he had installed in his home in the outskirts of Paris, teaching him how to treat the paper, set the type, and create the page. Benjamin Franklin Bache, known as Benny, seemed as enthusiastic as his grandfather had been at a similar age; Franklin watched him with enthusiasm of his own.

Shortly afterward, Franklin arranged for Benny to be taught by François Didot, France's most distinguished printer. Didot not only designed type but also made important improvements in measuring and naming the various sizes. He was a demanding tutor, and he seems to have been impressed by the devotion of his young charge.

Back in the United States in 1787, Benny graduated from the University of Pennsylvania, which Franklin had founded, and, to his grandfather's delight, chose printing as his life's work. Franklin helped him set up shop, making recommendations about everything from what kinds of materials Benny should publish to what styles of typefaces would make the most suitable impressions. Appreciative at first, Benny soon began to find his grandfather a bit overbearing, too much of a micromanager. It was not so bad, though; Benny might even have thought it preferable to the neglect he had so often felt when he was younger and his grandfather could not seem to find time for him.

Three years later, on April 17, 1790, worn down by trial and tribulation, age and accomplishment, Benjamin Franklin lay in bed with a fever and severe pains in his chest and lungs. He was unable to talk. At one point that night, he opened his eyes and reached out for his grandson's hand. Benny approached him and offered it tearfully. The two were still holding hands when Franklin died shortly after eleven. He was eight-four years old. He never knew what kind of printer Benjamin Franklin Bache would turn out to be.

❁

WELL BEFORE TRAINING on his grandfather's press near Paris, Benny had been a source of concern to his parents, so "turbulent and fractious" that he was once expelled from school. In later times, there would be those who wanted to expel him from the print shop. To some, he was "a base and unnatural miscreant," an "impudent dog," a man who "outraged every principle of decency, of morality, of religion and of nature" and, furthermore, regarded the world through a visage that was "hollow-cheeked [and] dead-eyed." Benjamin Franklin's grandson would prove to be even more controversial than Franklin's brother James.

Bache's paper, the *Aurora*, unyieldingly republican in its politics, was "filth," said a critic of the time. It excoriated Washington so much that the president could not help but comment on the "malignant industry and persevering falsehoods" with which "I am assailed in order to weaken, if not destroy, the confidence of the Public." John Adams fared no better. So often did the *Aurora* disparage him that Adams's wife, Abigail, would accuse Bache of possessing the "malice & falshood [sic] of Satan." She was not the type to compare a human being to the prince of darkness without provocation.

A competing journal, the *Massachusetts Mercury*, would refer to the *Aurora* as "this fountain head and source of calumny that the various political streams have issued which have defiled our towns and cities." Other federalist newspapers of the time would not refer to Bache's publication at all, unwilling, it seems, even to concede the existence of so malicious an organ.

It is, of course, too one-sided a view. Jefferson, as might be expected, was fond of Bache, finding him a man "of abilities and of principles the most friendly to liberty & our present form of government." Historian John Tebbel, milder in his praise, is willing to concede that the *Aurora* "was not entirely a bad paper. It did give a full account of the proceedings in Congress, at a painstaking length which the other papers did not emulate." And William Duane, who would eventually succeed Bache as the *Aurora*'s editor, claimed that the paper provided "the most formidable check upon ambition and false policy, which this nation has possessed for five years past."

Perhaps Duane exaggerates Bache's accomplishments. He does not exaggerate his intentions, however; Bache meant the *Aurora* to be all the things that he believed the Washington and Adams administrations were not. The former, Bache claimed, was riddled by ambition, which often led to decisions that benefited the government more than the people. Bache set out formidably to check them both. He thought of the *Aurora* as a kind of government-in-exile; it was loud and unceasing and as convinced of its own virtues as it was of the vices of its opponents.

In more recent years, Richard N. Rosenfeld has written glowingly about the *Aurora* in a study subtitled *The Suppressed History of Our Nation's Beginnings and the Heroic Newspaper That Tried to Report It*. Actually, the *Aurora* did report it, on numerous occasions; the reader of the present volume may decide for himself how heroically.

❁

NOT UNTIL THE LAST YEARS of his grandfather's life was Bache as close to him as he wanted to be, or as close as we might imagine, given the avuncular qualities that history has assigned to Benjamin Franklin. The old man clearly loved his daughter's child, but he showed it in a manner more distant than doting. Franklin arranged for Benny's education, dispatching him to a number of European boarding schools, one more demanding than the next; it amounted to boot camp for the brain, rigorous and in some ways beneficial.

But Franklin saw little of Benny during these years; he was much more comfortable with another grandson, Temple, the child of his own illegitimate son, who for a time served as his secretary. Franklin and Benny stayed in touch primarily through the mail, with the old man sending his grandson a steady stream of "didactic little essays." One of them urged the boy to succeed in school because those who do "live comfortably in good houses," whereas those who neglect their studies "are poor and dirty and ragged and ignorant and vicious and live in miserable cabins and garrets." It was Franklin in his Poor Richard mode; it is likely that he never had a less receptive audience for his maxims than this boy of his own blood two generations removed.

For his part, Benny may have wanted Franklin's approval more than his friendship, at least as he got older and gave up on the notion that their friendship would be as close and warmly expressed as he once seemed to have hoped. After he went into business as a printer at the age of nineteen, he would take pride in joining with his grandfather to found the Franklin Society, the first attempt at a union to protect printers' rights.

But William Vans Murray, a friend of John Adams who nonetheless looked kindly on Benny, believed that Franklin, however inadvertently, was more of a problem for the young man than a source of inspiration. The boy "had a philosopher for a grandfather," Murray opined, "for that idea was the food of much of his extravagance of mind, and placed him in a state of pretence where he was obliged to act a part for which he had not talents." In other words, thought Murray, Benny had large shoes to fill and, finding himself unable to do so, became ever more desperate in, and resentful of, the attempts he was forced to make.

But there was more on his mind than the old man's legacy and his attempts to be worthy of it. When he grew up, Bache became so zealous and widely known a republican that Jefferson is said to have approached him to discuss publishing a newspaper before contacting Freneau about the *National Gazette*. If that is so, Bache's reason for turning him down is a mystery. Later, Jefferson would subscribe to the *Aurora*, happily submitting his $8 a year, a small price to pay for all that glorious federalist bashing.

Like Jefferson, Bache was a devout supporter of the French Revolution, perhaps more than any other American journalist of the time and so much so that he was accused by one newspaper of accepting "French pay" and by another of being a "notorious hireling." Bache ignored the Revolution's violent excesses and praised its stated purposes in language so fervent and uncompromising that he alienated virtually everyone in the United States who thought that the French Revolution's means made a mockery of its ends.

Naturally, Bache was livid about the Jay Treaty. He found its provisions offensive and condescending, an almost total repudiation of what his countrymen had so valiantly won on the battlefield. But, even more, Bache fussed and fumed at the very idea that his countrymen should have negotiated with the British in the first place. As the *Aurora* wrote in April 1794:

> It is time Americans had done with humbly petitioning the British Court to do them justice. If we mean to negotiate with that arrogant nation, whose policy is plunder and whose law is power, we must first have a tie upon her interest by a sequestration of her debts here and then we shall be able to demand with effect a redress of our wrongs. By a continuance of a pusillanimous conduct we shall but encourage her insolence, decision alone can save us at this critical juncture from the horrors of war.

More than any other single issue during the passionate decade, it was the Jay Treaty that got the *Aurora*'s ink beaters beating, set its typefaces on edge. And, on one remarkable occasion, it inspired the paper's editor to take to the road. In the summer of 1795, Bache printed several hundred copies of the treaty at his own expense, stuffed them into trunks, and lugged the trunks to New York and Hartford and Boston and points in between, passing the documents out free of charge at public gatherings and afterward taking to the podium to read the treaty and roar as mightily as he could against it. Look at this, he would say to the crowds assembled before him. Can you believe that Americans will allow this, that we will put up with it, that we will permit our nation to be treated in such a manner? Can you believe that the men we have elected to represent us are now treating us as shamefully as the British once did? Benjamin Franklin Bache put his money, and his time, where his convictions were.

Meanwhile, back in Philadelphia, the *Aurora*, temporarily under the supervision of William Duane, hammered home the same points: the treaty was "principally calculated to promote the interests of G. Britain"; it "may be regarded as peculiarly hostile to the French Republic"; and it "would be dangerous as a precedent for other nations, with whom we may wish to make commercial compacts."

Later that summer John Hancock echoed these sentiments, writing a letter to the *Aurora* in which he declared the Jay Treaty "like a volcano," in that it "contains within its bosom the materials of destruction." The following day, Bache set a letter of his own in *Aurora* type, addressed to the president, in which he claimed that "the benevolence of the good man laments, and the spirit of the proud man abhors" the treaty, which was a sad example of "departed virtue."

The following year, during the debate on appropriations for the treaty in the House of Representatives, the *Aurora* let it be known that it did not think so much as a penny should be authorized for Jay's folly, nor that a budget should even be under discussion. It referred to those doing the discussing in the following terms:

The House of Representatives of the United States, that is a majority of it, and a respectable majority, nearly two to one, are called

Blockheads,

Invaders of power,

Usurpers,

Arbitrary,

Dishonest,

Anti-patriotic, and to wind up, it is insinuated, that they are bribed by foreign gold.

But more than Congress, more even than Jay, Benjamin Franklin Bache blamed George Washington for the treaty. He was, after all, the man who had sought an accord with the British to begin with and then accepted the one that Jay had so feebly arranged; thus it was he who "rewarded the people of the United States for their confidence and affection by violating their constitution, by making a treaty with a nation that is their abhorrence, and by treating their applications to him against the treaty with the most pointed contempt. Louis XVI, in the meridian of his power & his splendor never treated his subjects with as much insult. . . . "

Bache had been ranting against the president long before the Jay Treaty, however. In fact, his tirades had begun even before he had a newspaper to disseminate them. So upset had he been by the choice of Washington as the new nation's chief executive that he wrote a pamphlet on the subject and published it at his own expense. In it he declared Washington's election a calamity, one that would prove even more calamitous for the nation in the years ahead. It included, among other things, a brief explanation of its subject's success.

Tall and imposing in his person, silent and reserved in his manners, opulent in his fortune, and attached by a high post to a successful cause, Mr. Washington . . . found indeed no rival to his reputation in his own particular army; for he had condemned his own army to such complete inaction or had allowed so little opportunity to those who commanded under him to become signalized (unless by misfortunes occasioned chiefly by his own bad arrangements) that he had become the sole remarkable person in it.

Then, with Washington in office and Bache having assumed command of the *Aurora*, the pace of his reproaches picked up. The president was too imperious in his manner, Bache believed, too unfeeling of the populace's problems, too devious in his dealings with legislators. And why, the paper wanted to know, had those same legislators agreed to pay him so much money, far more than he or any other man was worth for the largely honorary position, as Bache saw it, of president of the United States? Even so, the editor claimed, Washington had overdrawn his salary by more than $1,000 before the end of his first term, and by early in the second term the figure would be more than $5,000. "Will not the world be led to conclude," the *Aurora* asked, "that the mask of political hypocrisy has been alike worn by a CAESAR, a CROMWELL, and a WASHINGTON?"

Two days before this tirade appeared, the *Aurora* had published a pseudonymous letter to the president that is one of the era's masterpieces of journalistic savagery.

You seem to have entered life with a mind unadorned by extraordinary features or uncommon capacity. Equal to the common duties of private life, it emitted none of those sparks of genius, however irregular and inconstant, which mark the dawn of future eminence.—Fortuitous circumstances yielded you in early life a small measure of military éclat, which arose chiefly from the barren talents of your predecessors in the Indian warfare. For some time after this you reposed in unambitious ease till the chances of a Revolution called you to the supreme command of the American army. An inoffensive neutrality had heretofore characterized your actions, and it was probably, because you were in principle neither a Briton nor an American, a whig nor a tory, that you slid into this important station.

It was enough to make even the vice president cringe. The *Aurora* "mauls" Washington, John Adams believed, a few years before it started mauling Adams himself. In fact, sometimes it seemed to exist primarily for that purpose, not caring about accuracy or even the illusion of it. In 1795, the *Aurora* published a series of letters that Washington supposedly wrote during the winter of 1777–1778, when he and his men were holed up at Valley Forge, freezing and starving and fearing that the war had turned against them and would not turn back. It was the most difficult and discouraging of times, yet Washington never lost his resolve, never gave voice to a lack of faith. The *Aurora's* letters, though, "portrayed Washington as a lukewarm patriot at best, a loyal subject of George III at worst, and at least a skeptic concerning independence."

It would have been a stunning revelation if true. But it was not. Washington never wrote the letters. They were complete fabrications, and although they were probably not fabricated by Benjamin Franklin Bache, he did not question their source; as the modern expression has it, the letters were "too good to check." Bache was only too happy to obtain them and reprint them and glory in the impression they gave of a man indifferent to the welfare of the nation he led. It is no wonder that the *Aurora* drove Washington to unholy extremes, once even causing him to utter an expletive, a rare occurrence for him, at least in the presence of others. According to Jefferson, an article that appeared in a January 1797 issue caused a "damn" to escape from the president's lips.

But lies and insults were not enough for Bache. Like Sam Adams before him, he wanted action. More than two years before Washington gave up the presidency, the *Aurora* tried to force him out. "*Retire immediately*," demanded a correspondent calling himself Scipio;

> let no flatterer persuade you to rest one hour longer at the helm of state. You are utterly incapable to steer the political ship into the harbour of safety.—If you have any love for your country, leave its affairs to the wisdom of your fellow citizens; do not

flatter yourself with the idea that you know their interests better than other men; there are thousands amongst them who equal you in capacity, and who excel you in knowledge.

When Washington finally did announce his resignation after two terms, the *Aurora* was so pleased, so relieved, and possibly even so startled that it fell into a swoon of sorts, donning a mask of cordiality that it had never displayed before toward Washington, or in fact toward any other federalist, and actually speaking highly of the president, or at least not as lowly as usual—and the report makes for remarkable reading. One wonders if Bache had simply decided not to press his luck, fearing that another screed at this point would make Washington change his mind and accept a third term for no other reason than to spite the *Aurora*. How else to explain sentiments like this: "The valuable legacy of good advice, which [Washington] has bequeathed on his departure from public life, the result of long experience, and expressed in the language of firmness and paternal affection, should, as we have no doubt it will, be engraven deeply on the minds of his fellow-citizens, and transmitted with their sanctioning approbation to their posterity."

It was a touching paragraph, a glowing valedictory, the *Aurora* at its warmest and cuddliest, its most hypocritically atypical. Then back to business as usual. When Washington's resignation became official, Bache published a pamphlet by William Duane that denounced Washington in the most comprehensive of fashions, assigning him responsibility for "all the misfortunes of our country." And on March 4, 1797, when John Adams was sworn in as Washington's successor, the *Aurora* opined as follows:

When a retrospect is taken of the Washingtonian administration of eight years, it is the subject of the greatest astonishment that a single individual should have cankered the principles of Republicanism in an enlightened people, just emerged from the gulf of despotism, and should have carried his designs against the public liberty so far as to put in jeopardy its very existence.

Such, however, are the facts, and with them staring us in the face, this day ought to be a jubilee in the United States.

It was, in the words of James Tagg, who has thoroughly studied Bache and his journalism, "the final stage of the *Aurora's* defamation campaign" against the first president, a campaign marked by viciousness and fallaciousness in roughly equal measure; and it was, in the opinion of Washington's friend Benjamin Rush, a most successful campaign. "It is even said," Rush stated at the time, "that [Bache's] paper inducted [Washington] to retire from the president's chair of the United States."

Not so. Rush gives the *Aurora* too much credit. Or blame. But the end of the paper's defamation campaign against the first president was not the end of its defamation. There was, after all, a second president.

❖

IRONICALLY, what seems to have infuriated Bache most about Adams was a peace offering he made to the French, an overture about which the president's fellow federalists were wary, while Bache and his fellow republicans, at least in the initial stages, offered support.

In 1797 the French were at war with England and at odds with the United States, whom they had aided in their own war against the British a little more than a decade earlier but who now seemed to be siding with their former oppressors under the terms of the Jay Treaty. The French were upset with the Americans for other reasons, too. One is that their wartime aid to the patriots had proved more expensive than they originally thought it would be; according to an estimate that Franklin biographer Stacy Schiff considers "conservative," the French donated the equivalent of $13 billion to the cause of American liberty. Another reason is that when President Washington had a chance to pay them back a few years earlier, simply by joining the French in taking up arms against the British, as the Americans had done so willingly in their own behalf a few years before that, Washington refused. Instead, he had issued his Neutrality Proclamation. To the French, there was nothing neutral about it; it was a slap in the Gallic face. Had *they* been neutral when the colonists came calling for help? The Americans were ingrates, they believed, and not without cause.

In response, the French broke off diplomatic relations with the United States. They seized U.S. vessels in the Atlantic and the Mediterranean, pretending to search for contraband but in reality looting and vandalizing them. And they threatened worse unless the Americans mended their diplomatic ways.

Despite reservations, Adams made an attempt to do just that. He had not been as outspoken in his opposition to the French Revolution as some other federalists, but neither had he supported it; for his tastes, it was too much democracy—*liberté, égalité,* and *fraternité* run amok. In fact, a few years earlier Adams had written in the *Gazette of the United States* that a nation should be ruled by a class of leaders rather than by the active participation of the masses in a voting booth: "an illustrious descent attracts the notice of mankind," as he put it. He went on to say, "Noble blood, whether the nobility be hereditary or elective, and indeed more in republican governments, than in monarchies, least of all in despotisms, is held in estimation for the same reason. It is a name and a race that a nation has been interested in, and is in the habit of respecting." To reject the notion of noble blood, Adams believed, was to promote the kind of violence that was the insignia of the French Revolution.

Nonetheless, the president dispatched John Marshall and Elbridge Gerry to Paris, where they would join the American minister, Charles Cotesworth Pinckney, in appealing to the government of France to settle their dispute.

It was a star-studded negotiating team. But it was a failed negotiation, one that could not be called a real negotiation at all. French foreign minister Charles Maurice Talleyrand refused even to meet with the Americans; instead, he sent three of his aides to head them off and present them with a set of demands that left Marshall, Gerry, and Pinckney aghast. The Frenchmen demanded a bribe of $250,000 from the Americans as well as a loan of $12 million. They further demanded a public apology for America's pro-British policies since the Jay Treaty—and once all of these conditions were met there was still no guarantee that Talleyrand would grant an audience to his visitors, let alone accede to U.S. proposals to repair the frayed relationship between the countries. The three men who demanded the tribute were called X, Y, and Z in the newspapers, and the incident, still an insult to Americans who know their history, is known as the XYZ Affair.

For federalists, though, it turned out to be a coup, as it seemed to justify their suspicions of French motives and their disdain for the brutal ways of the Jacobins in the Revolution; the French were still brutal, the federalists now charged, if perhaps in different ways: witness their deciding to answer diplomacy with bribery. Later, a Boston paper, the *Columbian Centinel*, would promote the federalist view of XYZ in what it claimed was an unusual manner. "*We have no partiality for* Acrostics—*They are but the toys of the Muses*," the paper said, "*and very seldom partake of any glimmer of Genius. The following, however, are politically good, if they cannot be poetically elegant.*"

TWO ACROSTICS

A CHARACTER

A DEADLY Foe to every rule of right,
J ovial in *Mischief*—'Tis his soul's delight.
A ctions unworthy [of] manhood are his boast;
C *aira!* Huzza! And *France* is all his toast.
O pinions stiff as *Atlas!* Black as hell
B ind up his faith, in one infernal spell.
I ntrigues accelerate his vile ambition:
N ature disdains him; claim him, then, *Perdition.*

THE REVERSE

A CTIVE, intelligent, urbane and just,
F aithful and worthy of each sacred trust;
E njoying every blessing, earth affords,
D elighting to adore the *Lord of Lords*!
E lated with no base ambitious views,
R eason his chart—he rectitude pursues;
A verse to Jacobins—those dregs of hell;
L aughs at their follies, and loud-roaring yell.
I nveterate foe to Faction's hated name;
S ociety his pride! His Cockade; fame;
T he "*rights of man,*" his motto, and his aim.

Some Americans were so offended by the XYZ Affair that they demanded an embargo on French goods. Others, though not many, even wondered about punishing French citizens on American soil. Still others believed that America should go to war to avenge itself against so grievous an insult. At the very least, they should make their displeasure known at the highest levels of government.

Benjamin Franklin Bache thought they were all crazy. Having endorsed the initial peacemaking overture from Adams, he now set out to defend, even more energetically, Talleyrand's behavior in its wake. The *Aurora* asked Americans to remember that the French, in the darkest days of the colonies' war of independence, "saved us from perdition." Have we forgotten the portentous year when

one half the United States was overrun by our enemy, when we were almost without an army, and that army without money to subsist it? . . . If we have not [forgotten], must we not be astonished that there are men among us who would hurry us into war with that very power whose succour alone saved us from perdition? And for what is such a state of danger to be hazarded? Truly, to compel France to receive our ambassadors!!

To republicans, the XYZ Affair was the most serious of blows, making their allegiance to France seem at best misplaced, at worst nearly treasonous. Bache's prose seemed positively scrawny against impressions so powerful. "The prejudices, which have been excited against *France*," wrote the *Aurora* in the winter of 1798, "have greatly deceived the American public. It is believed that the French deserve to be viewed in a light very different from what was lately pretended to be just."

As for the federalist press, it jumped on the *Aurora* as it had never jumped on a republican journal before, with the *Gazette of the United States* denouncing Bache for his hiring practices as well as his Francophilia. "The chance of truth in the Aurora was always bad, but its editor has recently taken into employ some assistants which afford it no chance at all."

It is James Thomson Callender to whom Fenno refers, the renegade reporter who had now taken up temporary residence at the *Aurora* and begun to defend the French as avidly as he had sought the destruction of Hamilton not long before. Callender would write voluminously on the XYZ Affair in the next two years, eventually concluding with what was for him something close to understatement: "It may be debated whether it was proper for this country to make such an advance of money. But there could be no harm in the proposal from Talleyrand. The triumvirate [Marshall, Gerry, and Pinckney] could not expect that he was, at the first brush, to give them every thing in their own way." And, a few pages later, an attack on the very motive of the mission: "By sending these ambassadors to Paris, Mr. Adams and his British faction designed to do nothing but mischief. This is, and it always has been, the universal opinion of the republican party; and it seems very hard if *one* man may not print what an hundred thousand profess themselves to believe."

The *Gazette of the United States* did not hesitate in replying to Callender's positions on XYZ. In what is perhaps the most splenetic example of them all, Fenno complained of

. . . the vile calumnies and falshoods [sic] that are fabricated in such abundance by the *vagrant Callender*—That a miserable, ragged vagabond, who has been whipped and kicked out of one of our capital cities, and applied for relief as a pauper in another, whose very appearance gives a disgustful idea of the collected dregs of corruptible meanness and filthy beggary, who would not be picked out of a ditch even by a *good Samaritan* . . . should dare to set himself up as the censor of the American people, the supreme judge of talents and patriotism, and abuse in the vilest terms the highest officers in our government and the bell men in our country is enough to drive an American mad.

Another federalist paper, also castigating Bache for his employment of Callender, became positively apocalyptical.

This AMERICANS, is the most awful warning you ever had. It is here proved, that the man [Bache], who, for six long years has been incessantly employed in accusing and villifying [sic] your government, and in justifying the French in all their abominable injuries and insults, is absolutely in close correspondence with the insolent and savage despots by whom those injuries and insults have been committed, and who now demand of you an enormous TRIBUTE or threaten you, in case of disobedience, with the fate of VENICE; that is, first with subjugation, and then with being *swapped away like cattle*, to that prince or mate, who will give them the most in exchange for you!

Americans were getting along much better with the French at the time of the XYZ Affair than Bache and Callender were with the federalists.

❁

THE *AURORA* HAD NOW REACHED the peak of its powers, and a

picture of Bache from the time, the only one known to exist today, seems to show his pride. He wears the same kind of wire-rimmed glasses that Franklin did, perhaps even the bifocals that Franklin invented; behind them, his eyes are knowing and resolute. His hair is thinning and cut shorter than was common at the time. He is well dressed, stiff-chinned; he seems the very model of the success- ful businessman. He was known now as "Lightning Rod, Jr.," and he appears pleased with the reference to his grandfather.

In 1798, the *Aurora* employed seven journeymen printers and four apprentices. It published six issues a week and the occasional supplement. Its circulation never surpassed 1,700—by contrast, the aforementioned *Columbian Centinel* had more than twice as many subscribers—but the *Aurora's* influence far exceeded its numbers; those who read it were loyal and committed and eager to spread the paper's word, while those who did not read it were all too aware of its deprecations and the discontent they sowed.

A few years earlier, the *Aurora* had scooped the competition with news of the Jay Treaty; in the wake of the XYZ Affair it came up with another scoop, somehow acquiring and then publishing a letter from Talleyrand to President Adams expressing regret for the recent unpleasantness; Adams's aides were still translating the mis- sive when the *Aurora* printed it in English. And there were other scoops, among them a scandal at the State Department involving passport fees; after Bache printed the details, two of the depart- ment's clerks were fired. Even some of its most rabid competitors could not help admiring the *Aurora's* enterprise and dedication— and, in these cases at least, its accuracy.

And something else separated the *Aurora* from its competitors. A careful reading of the paper suggests that its content was not de- termined just by its editor's position on this law or that one, on one public declaration or another, but by something grander; it was a philosophy that ruled the *Aurora*, not mere politics. "Few issues of the *General Advertiser* and *Aurora*," writes James Tagg, "failed to mention how artificial distinctions, privilege, inequality, hereditary monarchy, titled nobility, and aristocracy kept man ignorant, prejudiced, superstitious, enslaved, and incapable of improvement."

In other words, it was not just the Jay Treaty to which the *Aurora* objected, not just the American response to the XYZ Affair, not just the machinations of Washington or Adams; it was, perhaps even more, the pernicious effects of Alexander Hamilton on everything he touched. As far as Bache was concerned, the wide variety of Hamilton's interests and influence was proof that he threatened both individual citizens and the society as a whole with a wide variety of perils.

The *Aurora* never tired of reminding its readers of Hamilton's former fondness for Maria Reynolds (of which he had made "*adulterous confessions*," the paper pointed out) or his current fondness for Great Britain (he showed, after all, "wonted malice, against Jacobinism"). But Bache had begun aiming the *Aurora*'s guns at Hamilton as early as 1794, when farmers in western Pennsylvania were rebelling against the secretary of the treasury's tax on grains for whiskey and the secretary himself was riding with the army that attempted to enforce it. The *Aurora* said that "by many it is shrewdly suspected [Hamilton's] conduct is a first step towards a deep laid scheme, not for the promotion of the country's prosperity, but the advancement of his private interests." What those interests were, Bache did not say; it was enough for him simply to impugn Hamilton's motives.

When Hamilton left the Treasury Department early in 1795, the *Aurora* was thrilled to see him go, and appalled that the *Gazette of the United States*, citing one allegedly good deed after another performed by the secretary while in office, had mourned his departure.

The *Gazette* panegyrick on the late Secretary of the Treasury, is too much for the swallow of even the meanest toad-carrier of the administration. . . . It is well that he should rest from his labours, but, America will long regret, that his works live after him. . . . Has our Chief Magistrate done nothing? Have our

Representatives done nothing? Have the natural advantages of the country done nothing? And the glorious Constitution,—that nothing? No! no! no! The Secretary was the life, the soul, the mind of our political body: the spirit has flown—then we are a lifeless mass: dust, ashes, clay!!!

Such ripostes were not rare. The *Gazette of the United States* and the *Aurora* were constantly at each other's throats in those days, clashing on virtually every issue, every elected official, every action of government—clashes, James Tagg writes, that "were usually as unenlightening as they were frequent." He further states: "Having begun at a low level of accusation, Fenno and Bache seldom elevated the debate."

For instance, Bache: The *Gazette of the United States* was published for the "swinish multitude."

Fenno: Bache's readers were an "incendiary faction."

Bache: Fenno's readers were even worse; they were

Men bred in the schools of Britain and educated in the vile acts of sycophantic adulation; Speculators not worth one stiver [a Dutch coin] previous to the funding system though now worth their tens of thousands, and lastly, men who, though born in America rambled all over Europe under pretence of education, until the die was cast and American independence acknowledged by Britain; when over they came piping hot patriots, full of fight; claimed their estates and got into Congress as a reward for not opposing their good friends the British; voted for the funding system to pay themselves for all those great services, and now, like a beggar on horseback, would willingly ride the people to the Devil.

Bache, when he changed the name of his newspaper to the *Aurora* after it had previously been known as the *General Advertiser and Political, Commercial and Literary Journal*: Now, more than ever, he claimed, the paper "shall diffuse light within the sphere of its influence,—dispel the shades of ignorance, and gloom of error and thus tend to strengthen the fair fabric of freedom on its surest foundation, publicity and information."

Fenno, when he read Bache's claim and noted that the *Aurora's* new masthead featured a rising sun: Its early morning rays were "emblematic of the vapour which continually arose in that paper."

In the summer of 1795, Bache and Fenno took a break from their hostilities on the page and assailed each other in person. The occasion was a public debate about the Jay Treaty, in which the two men sniped away at each other for an hour or two before an audience of several thousand people in Philadelphia's State House Yard. One imagines a scene as rowdy and contentious as a bear-baiting, the debaters cursing each other, the onlookers shouting out their sympathies and pumping their arms. But one can do no more than imagine; no detailed records exist of the day, and neither man seems to have reported the confrontation in his paper.

Eventually, the Bache-Fenno rivalry would grow too acrimonious to be contained by mere words, whether spoken or printed. On three different nights in the spring of 1798, objects were thrown through the windows of Bache's home. On none of the occasions does anyone seem to have been injured. Or caught. Damage was minimal and Bache undeterred, and blame was almost unanimously assigned to those under the influence of the *Gazette of the United States.*

That summer, a mob headed for the *Aurora* print shop under cover of darkness and threw even more objects through the windows than they had at his house: rocks and bottles and pieces of wood and metal, anything they could pick up or carry with them. The projectiles not only smashed the glass but also damaged the presses and some of the furniture.

A few weeks later, Fenno's son, John Ward Fenno, to whom Bache had once referred in print as "the dirty tool of a dirty faction," happened to encounter his accuser on a Philadelphia street.

Fenno was accompanied by a man whose name we do not know; Bache had been strolling with his friend John Beckley, who had passed the Hamilton-Reynolds letters to Callender.

As the two companions stood by, young Fenno began yelling at Bache. Bache yelled back. Fenno then punched him in the face and, as one account has it, followed up by biting his finger. He knocked Bache backward, after which he grabbed him and tried to throw him to the ground. Apparently, he could not; Bache says that he responded with "a sound rap or two across the head and face," perhaps with a cane, which forced Fenno to retreat. The scuffle did not last long, probably no more than a minute or two, and neither man was seriously hurt. But according to Bache, John Ward Fenno's friend was so embarrassed by the incident that he later called at the offices of the *Aurora* to seek out Bache and apologize.

The incident was not unique. "Beating up editors was already commonplace in the young United States," writes historian Fawn Brodie, "and the practice had not been notably penalized." In one case, yet again involving the poor chief of the *Aurora*, it was even rewarded. When a man named Clement Humphrey began pummeling Bache because the paper had accused his father of condoning bribery in the construction of the frigate *United States*, Humphrey was promptly pulled away from him. The authorities calmed him down, reprimanded him, and fined him for assault. Then he was given a diplomatic mission in Europe by President Adams.

Some years before his grandson had taken over the *Aurora* and become the arsenic in the tea water of American federalists, even Benjamin Franklin had endorsed corporal punishment for odious journalism—"ironically," it has been said, "but with underlying earnestness." Franklin's proposal was "to leave the liberty of the press untouched, to be exercised in its full extent, force, and vigor; but to permit the *liberty of the cudgel* to go with it *pari passu.*"

As far as anyone knows, Dr. Benjamin Rush never wanted to apply his fists to the body of a newspaperman. If he did, there is no question that he would have chosen the one known as the Porcupine.

❁

CHAPTER NINETEEN

Cobbett's Quills

*W*ILLIAM COBBETT, pinkish of complexion, a "self-tutored English farm boy," one of those large men who, depending on their mood, seem either menacing or excessively collegial, landed in America in 1792, and it would be hard to say who was happier about it: Cobbett himself, the federalists whose means and ends he would soon so avidly promote in his new land, or the men in uniform whom he had taken to court in the old.

Cobbett had enlisted in the British army at the age of twenty, seeming an exemplary young man; his skills were above average, his obedience to his superiors unquestioning, his dedication to self-improvement apparent to all. In fact, in his spare time, while his mates might be drinking or whoring or napping, Cobbett was "sitting on the edge of his bed with a board on his lap as a writing table," teaching himself grammar. He rose to the rank of sergeant major; he seemed to have a bright future protecting the interests of the British empire. It would not happen.

Cobbett learned more about corruption in the service than he did about matters military or linguistic, learning in addition that he had no patience for corruption in any of its forms and that those who practiced and profited from it had no patience for him. He was stationed in Nova Scotia at the time, and became friends with his company's quartermaster. Soon Cobbett discovered that the man was a crook, a clever one, who had been keeping for himself much of the money that the soldiers were paying out of their own pockets for uniforms and equipment. The quartermaster was proud of the scam and readily discussed it with Cobbett. But Cobbett was appalled. He thought about trying to reason the quartermaster back to rectitude; he thought about threatening him with exposure. Then he decided that the wiser course was a more draconian one; he would collect evidence against the quartermaster and, when he had enough, file charges with military authorities in London.

But Cobbett was in for a surprise. It seems that the quartermaster's actions were but the tip of an iceberg. Other quartermasters in other outposts were cheating the military in the same way. Other officers in his own unit were also engaged in thievery—sometimes of related sorts, sometimes of other varieties. Officials much higher in the military's chain of command were complicit and were taking their own cuts; it is possible, in fact, that some of the very men who heard Cobbett's charges in the courtroom were guilty of condoning them. Without knowing it, Cobbett had uncovered "a whole system of army graft," powerful and pervasive, its participants willing to go to any length to make sure that its activities were neither punished nor publicized. Cobbett's charges were ignored, and charges were invented and filed against him. It would not be long, he feared, before he was arrested, tried, found guilty, and imprisoned.

So he had to write fast. In a pamphlet he called *The Soldier's Friend; or, Considerations on the Late Pretended Augmentation of the Subsistence of the Private Soldiers*, he told his fellow fighting men of "your rapacious Officers," explaining that they

> have not been content with their men dressing according to their rank and ability; they have obliged them to purchase articles of dress unheard of in former Armies, all of them far too expensive, and most of them totally useless. It may seem difficult to account for a conduct like this; why should Officers take a delight in extorting the poor wretches' pay from them with no other view than that of merely fooling it away.

Cobbett published the pamphlet, then got out of the country. He arrived in America with few possessions, fewer prospects, and a nickname. He was called "The Contentious Man," as he seemed willing not only to strike out at injustice when he believed himself or his fellow citizens to be its victims, but on occasion to make up examples of injustice for the simple pleasure of striking out, of finding someone or something with whom to argue. In the United States, he would acknowledge his prickliness by choosing another nickname, calling himself Peter Porcupine, and by putting that prickliness on display several times a week in *Porcupine's Gazette*, a paper that, in league with John Fenno's *Gazette of the United States*, gave the federalists as powerful a one-two punch in the press as either side had yet enjoyed in the struggle to determine the proper means of employing the U.S. Constitution.

It was clear from the outset what kind of paper Cobbett would publish and where its sympathies, and its interpretations of the truth, would lie.

> My *politics*, such as they are, are known to every one; and few, I believe, doubt of their continuing the same.
>
> Professions of *impartiality* I shall make none. They are always useless, and are besides perfect nonsense, when used by a newsmonger: for, he that does not relate news as he finds it, is something worse than partial; and as to other articles that help to compose a paper, he that does not exercise his own judgment, either in admitting or rejecting what is sent him, is a poor passive tool, and not an editor.

Porcupine's Gazette would be "a rallying point for the friends of government," Cobbett went on to say, a place where they "may speak their minds without reserve."

It was as much a challenge to the republican press as it was a statement of purpose. Yet no sooner had Cobbett issued it than he said he did not want to get into a "war of words" with an ill-tempered scandal sheet like the *Aurora*. That was fine with Bache, who said the same thing about *Porcupine's Gazette*; he would not allow himself to be drawn into "a newspaper controversy," he claimed, because he "too sensibly feels his inferiority in the arts of scurrility and defamation." Whereupon Bache and Cobbett took up precisely where Bache and Fenno had left off.

To Cobbett, the *Aurora* was "a vehicle of lies and sedition."

To Bache, *Porcupine's Gazette* was a waste of ink and paper. "Methinks I hear the reader exclaim, 'What! have we not Gazettes enough already?' Yes, and far too many: but those that we have are, in general, conducted in such a manner that their great number, instead of rendering mine unnecessary, is the only cause that calls for its establishment."

To Cobbett, Bache directed the salutation "my sweet sleepy-eyed sir" and asked, "[W]hat end you could propose to yourself in publishing not only what you knew to be a falsehood, but what you must, if you are not quite an ideot [sic], perceive every one else would look upon as such?"

For Cobbett, Bache felt "nothing but contempt."

For Bache, Cobbett felt the same, and then some:

> I assert that you are a liar and an infamous scoundrel. . . . Do you dread the effects of my paper? . . . I am getting up in the world, and you are going down. [F]or this reason it is that you hate me and that I despise you, and that you will preserve your hatred and I my contempt till fortune gives her wheel another turn or till death snatches one or the other of us from the scene.

One wonders how the two men would have carried on had they not previously announced their intentions not to engage each other in print.

❁

THE TWO OF THEM were still sniping more than a year after they began, with Cobbett declaring that "all the world knows and says

[Bache] is a liar; a fallen wretch; a vessel formed for reprobation; and therefore we should always treat him as we would a TURK, a JEW, a JACOBIN or a DOG."

When not responding to Cobbett's slurs, Bache continued to glorify the French. The Revolution was for the most part over now, but the rise of Napoleon Bonaparte in its wake seemed to please him no less than previous events in that nation. Bonaparte's European conquests were "a brilliant series of victories," the *Aurora* stated, and it continued to plead for the United States to develop closer ties with France at the same time that it loosened the bonds with England. "The United States are connected with England by conformity of manners, of language, and by commercial relations; by how many other ties ought they not to be connected with France?"

Few, answered the Porcupine; perhaps none. "No man is bound to pay the least respect to the feelings of Bache," Cobbett wrote, referring in this case to his adversary's unreasonable attachment to all things French. "He has outraged every principle of decency, or morality, or religion and of nature. I should have no objection to the boys spitting on him, as he goes along the street, if it were not, that I think they would confer on him too much honour."

Cobbett was proving to be an acquired taste that not all could acquire. Even in the federalist camp there were critics; spitting was, to some, as antisocial an act as dueling. Few among them would attack the editor publicly, but few would offer unqualified support either. George Washington, by this time a private citizen and much less in the crosshairs of journalistic weaponry than he used to be, could muster no more enthusiasm for *Porcupine's Gazette* than to say that it was "not a bad thing." And Fisher Ames, one of the lesser known of the founders but a man of persuasive erudition, wrote to his friend Alexander Hamilton that Cobbett was a powerful force for the federalist message. But he "might do more good," Ames believed, "if directed by men of sense and experience."

Jefferson, of course, abhorred Cobbett. "It is hardly necessary to caution you to let nothing of mine get before the public," he once wrote to an ally, because "a single sentence got hold of by the 'Porcupines,' will suffice to abuse and persecute me in their papers for months." The *New York Gazette*, a republican paper of undeviating faith, called Cobbett "the equal of the most atrocious felon ever executed at [the notorious British prison] Tyburn." And to the *Columbian Centinel* Cobbett was, as his nickname implied, something other than human. The federalists "should keep and feed a suitable beast" to attack the republican cause, the paper conceded, "and the 'fretful porcupine' was selected for this business."

There was still no such thing as an editorial in an American newspaper.

❧

WHEN THOMAS PAINE turned on George Washington, *Porcupine's Gazette* turned on Paine, berating him as "*the Apostle of the Devil, and the nuisance of the world*," a "profligate madman, who is now likely to provoke the indignation of all mankind." Paine "once lodged in Market Street, in this city," Cobbett wrote, beginning to sound profligate in his own madness, "where, I believe he never paid the good man of the house for his board, but certainly debauched his daughter."

The Porcupine, it seemed, would thrust his quills into virtually anyone, but they went more deeply into Benjamin Rush than into most of his other victims and stayed longer, to the ultimate sorrow of both men. Cobbett versus Rush—more than half a century after the original confrontation, it was James Franklin versus Cotton Mather all over again, the newspaperman versus the man with certain convictions about the practice of medicine. There were differences, however: this time the disease in question was yellow fever, not smallpox, and this time the journalist was correct, although so ragingly unfair about it that, as a result, he would lose both his fortune and his business, and perhaps even a portion of his sanity.

That Benjamin Rush, though a doctor, did not know how to treat yellow fever is unarguable. But neither did anyone else at the time: not until almost a century later would medical science realize that mosquitoes carried the disease; not until 1927 would it determine that the disease was caused by a virus; and not until 1937 would a vaccine be developed to prevent it. It does not speak harshly of an eighteenth-century physician to say that he knew neither the cause nor cure of the malady and that the attempts he made on his patients' behalf usually failed.*

Most commonly, those attempts involved bleeding; doctors of the time had concluded that to rid the victim's system of its blood would also expunge the diseases that the blood carried. And it seemed, at least in a few cases, to work. "The ultimate proof of [Rush's] theory," writes Daniel Boorstin wryly, "was that any patient who was bled long enough would eventually relax."

To William Cobbett it was preposterous. He knew no more than anyone else about yellow fever, but Rush was an irresistible target for him—a political foe as well as a physician, a republican as well as a bleeder—and this made him a fitting subject not just for *Porcupine's Gazette* but, before that, for the *Gazette of the United States*, in which John Fenno had "pounded away at the man he practically accused of being an out-of-control vampire who was daily sending to their graves seven out of eight of his patients and, in the bargain, causing the streets of Philadelphia to run with blood." Rush had responded by threatening a lawsuit. Cobbett decided to give him cause for a second.

---

*It was not just yellow fever that puzzled the medical community of Rush's time. Virtually all diseases were a mystery, and all cures a matter of guesswork, which was often counterproductive. It was an era when doctors believed that toothaches might be cured by first sticking a needle into a centipede and then inserting it into the patient's gums. They believed that wens and tumors were best addressed by digging up a corpse and cutting off a hand and applying it to the infected skin, where it should remain in place "till the Patient feel the *Damp* sensibly strike into him." Doctors also believed that several cups of chimney soot mixed with water, sugar, and cream were just the thing for typhoid fever. And they believed that a few bites of fried mouse pie would put an end to bed-wetting once and for all, although it seems to this author that the victim would be so frightened by the mere sight of the victual that even a modest amount of bladder control would be well beyond his ability.

He began with an article in *Porcupine's Gazette* called "Rush and His Patients," in which he claimed that the former was running out of the latter and needed to replenish his supply: "Wanted, by a physician, an entire new set of patients, his old ones having given him the slip; also a slower method of dispatching them than that of phlebotomy [opening a vein], the celerity of which does not give time for *making out a bill*."

Later in the piece, Cobbett referred to a story in another paper reporting that Rush might soon be offered a teaching position in New York; the paper favored the appointment, believing that Rush "is a man born to be useful to society." Cobbett agreed; Rush *was* useful: "And so is a *musquito* [sic], a *horse-leech*, a *pole cat*, a *weasel*: for these are all *bleeders*, and understand their business full as well as Doctor Rush does his."

A few weeks later, perhaps having exhausted his capacity for vituperation in prose, Cobbett took a breath and went after Rush with a couplet:

The times are ominous indeed
When quack to quack cries purge and bleed.

Rush fought back as best he could. He asked friends to write letters to Cobbett on his behalf, and they seem to have done so without hesitation, praising his knowledge, his dedication, even his bedside manner, which, in the words of Rush biographer Alyn Brodsky, "he bestowed with impartiality upon his most destitute patients as well as his most affluent." Rush's friends also wrote to other, more sympathetic papers, pleading the doctor's case, questioning the motives and veracity of *Porcupine's Gazette*. When Cobbett continued to ridicule him, Rush said he would sue, but since he had not yet made good on his promise to take Fenno to court, Cobbett assumed that he, too, was safe. As a result, he decided to publish the following article, supposedly an account of Dr. Rush's behavior during the Philadelphia yellow fever epidemic four years earlier.

So much was the Doctor about this period possessed with the notion that he was the only man of common sense existing, that he not only refused to consult with any but his former pupils, who submitted to obey his dictates, and rudely intruded his advice upon other people's patients. He also appointed two illiterate negro men, and sent them into all the alleys and by places in the city, with orders to bleed, and give his sweating purges, as he empirically called them, to all they could find sick, without regard to age, sex, or constitution; and bloody and dirty work they made among the poor miserable creatures that fell in their way. That his mind was elevated to a state of enthusiasm bordering on frenzy, I had frequent opportunity of observing; and I have heard from popular report, that in passing through Kensington one day, with his black man on the seat of his chaise along-side of him, he cried out with vociferation, "Bleed and purge all Kensington! Drive on, boy!"

It was all that Rush could bear, all that he was willing to read of himself in the malodorous pages of *Porcupine's Gazette*. He decided to go ahead with his suit; something, after all, had to be done about Cobbett's "genius for savage journalistic satire."

But nothing would be done quickly. It took two years for the case to come to trial and, in the interim, many who knew and cared for Rush advised him to drop it, telling him "to ignore Porcupine on the presumption that he, like the [yellow fever] epidemic, would run its course." The doctor, however, would not be dissuaded. His competence had been too thoroughly and publicly questioned, his life's work made to seem too unworthy. And he felt no less strongly that freedom of the press, which he ardently supported, should not be interpreted, as Cobbett was doing, as a license to revile without cause.

Still, Rush was doubtful about the outcome of his suit; at times he feared he had no chance of winning, as abuses by the press had long been so common that the courts were famously reluctant to penalize them. Nor were they eager to find against those victims of abuse who took out their frustrations by assaulting editors. The whole field of journalism seemed to exist in the wild, ungoverned by rules, unmanageable by men of good will. Rush fretted; he was all too aware of the toll that Cobbett was taking on him.

As it turned out, though, he was unduly pessimistic. It might have taken two years for the trial to begin, but once under way it proceeded speedily, ending in a few days, with the jury taking a mere two hours to deliberate before returning to the courtroom to announce not only that it had found Rush innocent but that Cobbett must pay the plaintiff $5,000 for his trouble. The editor's gasp might have been heard through the windows, out on the street. "Including the cost of defending the suit," writes Alyn Brodsky, "Cobbett's attacks on Rush had cost him $8,000—a truly considerable sum for the times."

And one that Cobbett did not possess and could not possibly acquire. A few days after the verdict, he swallowed a large portion of the pride remaining to him and asked Rush to settle for a reduced amount. Rush agreed; it was vindication he wanted, not profit. Still, the only way Cobbett could retire his debt, if not his animus toward the man responsible, was to borrow from friends and auction off his property and personal effects, which he did with the heaviest of hearts.

Rush took the money and donated it to charity.

❁

THE VICTOR WAS PLEASED with the jury's decision, but he quickly discovered, as so many victims of unfeeling journalism have discovered in the years since, that vindication in the courtroom is no match for the taint of accusation on the page. Some of the people who had trusted Rush before Cobbett's charges had long since begun to wonder about him; he could sense their doubt, hear their whispers. He knew that he did not cure as many people as he wanted to cure, that there was still so much to learn, not only for himself but for all men of medicine. According to his own writings, one of his patients "told me when dying that among other sins she had to repent of one was too much confidence in my remedies." Rush ruefully agreed.

But he also knew that he did the best he could with every person in his care, every malady; after the trial, he was more aware than ever that it was not enough. He was given, at various times in his life, to periods of depression, misgivings about not having chosen the law or some other vocation. This was perhaps the worst of them. Benjamin Rush had become, and to some extent would remain, a different man.

Among those to notice and comment on the changes, although from a vantage point of many years later, was L. H. Butterfield, who, midway through the twentieth century, would compile and edit Rush's letters. He also read Rush's autobiography and noted that there was a "self-justifying tone" to it, as there was in much of Rush's posttrial correspondence. This "must be partly attributed," Butterfield believes,

> to the wounds inflicted by the barbed quills of Peter Porcupine. The protracted feud with Cobbett hastened Rush's retreat from public life and humanitarian causes toward the sequestration of his later years. He was more tranquil, but he was also more disillusioned. His unbounded optimism had given way to resignation tinged with embitterment. Full knowledge of the Rush-Cobbett feud is necessary to understand that embitterment.

❋

As for Cobbett, he was embittered for his own reasons. In the final issue of *Porcupine's Gazette* in the winter of 1800, he revisited his dispute with Rush at some length; it was still a curse to him, a chronic low-grade fever, remarkably persistent, sometimes edging over into high-grade. He continued to rail about the money he had to pay to "the sleek-headed saint-looking Rush," and he believed that only by a perversion of the very concept of justice could he have been ordered to hand over so outrageous an amount to so despicable a human being.

> That this man, who had promulgated his opinions and extolled his practice in paragraphs, letters, pamphlets & books without number, & who had, in these various publications, ridiculed, decried & abused both the practice and the persons of his opponents; that this man should have the audacity to appeal to the law for a protection from the hostility of the press, astonished every body; and, though it was clearly perceived, that he never would have made the appeal but with the certitude of being able to bring the cause before a judge notoriously inimical to the defendants, yet no one imagined, that he would ever dare to pursue the matter to a trial.

A month later, Cobbett began publishing a magazine called *The Rush Light*; it lasted five issues, which is to say five issues more than it should have. The magazine was devoted to character assassination in all of its manifestations. Cobbett wrote that Rush had employed the services of corrupt lawyers to win his suit and had become an even more contemptible human being in its aftermath. Cobbett claimed that Rush changed religions constantly and without apparent conviction, that he accepted government money under dubious circumstances, and that he was ever the opportunist, ever looking for some quick way to make a buck or inflate his reputation, not concerning himself with legalities or even common decency. And, of course, Cobbett insisted, Rush was an incompetent physician, an ignorant politician, on and on.

There is a desperate quality to these accusations, to their randomness. Cobbett was striking out in any way he could to wound this man who had become such a *bête noire* to him, yet whom he had probably never met before the trial.

Some years later, Cobbett returned to England. Until his death in 1835, he worked on various reform movements, drifting through a number of occupations, in none of which he could make his mark. He never published a newspaper again, never returned to America, never spoke or wrote publicly about any of the various and vile defects of Benjamin Rush. But there is no reason to believe that he ever forgot them or that he ever regained his faith in a free press as he understood the term.

CHAPTER TWENTY

❖

Sedition

FIFTH CONGRESS OF THE UNITED STATES:

At the Second Session,

Begun and held at the city of Philadelphia, in the state of Pennsylvania, on Monday, the thirteenth of November, one thousand seven hundred and ninety-seven.

An ACT *in addition to the act, entitled "An Act for the punishment of certain crimes against the United States."*

Be it enacted by the Senate and House of Representatives of the United States of America, in Congress a

*T*HERE WERE TIMES in the old days when the Adams cousins would talk about journalism even more than politics. Not that the two topics were easy to separate back then or that they are easy to separate now; there was, after all, no sports section in newspapers of the late eighteenth century, no living section or style section, no comics, movie listings, or entertainment reviews, no stock market listings. Politics was the raw material of journalism at the time and journalism the means of conveyance for politics.

But John and Sam Adams would sit together once in a while in the back room of the *Boston Gazette*, with Sam jamming type into a composing stick while John, as he put it himself, was "Cooking up Paragraphs, Articles, Occurrences, &c.—working the political Engine." Perhaps John would show Sam an article he had just written in that civilized tone of his—as if he were trying to persuade the reader but not go so far as to plead with him or exhort him or, heaven forbid, tempt him to unreasoned action. Perhaps he showed Sam his article on liberty, the subject that Sam had written about in college, and that John thought

cannot be preserved without a general knowledge among the people who have a right from the frame of their nature to knowledge, as their great Creator who does nothing in vain, has given them understandings and a desire to know. But besides this they have a right, an undisputable, unalienable, indefeasible divine right to the most dreaded and envied kind of knowledge, I mean of the characters and conduct of their rulers.

Or perhaps John would show Sam something else, an article of a different sort, for a different paper, under a different name. As Humphrey Ploughjogger, John Adams would make the most remarkable transformation of any man of his time from person to page. He would not make it often, but when he did the pedant would become a rube, the statesman a farmer—and few were the people who could discern Humphrey's true identity. "I arnt book larnt enuff," he told the readers of the *Boston Evening-Post* in one of his essays, "to rite so polytly, as the gentlefolks, that rite in the Newspaper, about Pollyticks." And, in another essay: "It is a pleasant Thing to see ones Works inprint.—When I see the news, with my letter int about Hemp, I do say it made me feel as glad, as a glass full of West India rum, sweetened with loaf Sugar, would."

In still another article, Humphrey expressed his misgivings about Original Sin: "I cant hardly believe, that heathens and infants are all lost, for Adams first transgreshon, yet them doctrines are great misteries." Humphrey was fond of classical language, if hardly a master of it himself: "I love to see, now and then, some latin, in the books I reed. I amost think I understand it sumtimes." And Humphrey was critical of the behavior of "finery gentlefolks" in the capital of England, "Lunnun."

Adams as Ploughjogger—one cannot imagine a more unlikely alter ego; it was as if the most sober man in town sometimes slipped a lampshade over his head at a party and broke into a jig.

But when he wrote as himself or under a more conventional pseudonym, John Adams was far more dignified a journalist than Sam. He does not, however, seem to have felt any less strongly about the issues of the day and the people's right to know of them; in fact, it was John who at one point suggested a motto for the *Boston Gazette*: "*A Free Press maintains the Majesty of the People.*" Sam liked it. So did Edes and Gill. The paper adopted the slogan for a while, and John Adams was pleased with his contribution.

But by the time he got to be president, he did not trust newspapers any more than his predecessor had. It might have had something to do with his earlier experiences; knowing how high passions ran in the old *Gazette* print shop, he knew that they could be roused just as easily for a cause he opposed as for one in which he believed. He had, after all, watched Sam raise those passions so many times in readers, and could not help noting how easy it was for a fact to be mislaid, a figure to be distorted, an event to be misinterpreted or even invented so that the journalist could be true to his bias. And that, he believed, was what mattered most to those who controlled the printing presses—not accuracy, not objectivity, and certainly not the feelings of the poor soul whom the reporter had set out to flay.

Nor did newspapers seem predisposed toward John Adams. The more extreme of the federalist journals found him too moderate; the more extreme of the republican journals found him too dictatorial; papers less radical in their persuasions simply found that he was not as impressive a man, in either background or bearing, as Washington. He did not command a room, was not the sort who could inspire either an army or a legislative body. The New York *Time Piece* called him "a person without patriotism, without philosophy, a mock monarch."

The *Aurora*, on the other hand, initially believing that Adams would be less of a monarch than Washington, supported his candidacy, calling him a "man of incorruptible integrity" and expressing confidence that he would be "equal to the duties of his station." A few issues later it found him *un*equal, doing another of those rapid about-faces, like the one it had done on the occasion of Washington's departure from office. Benjamin Franklin Bache's journal now described Adams, who had long been soft and portly despite his attempts to walk as much as he could by way of exercise, as "old, bald, blind, querulous, toothless, crippled." The *Aurora* giveth, the *Aurora* taketh away.

Adams had believed that Bache was antisocial in his writings and virtually treasonous in his impulses even before this unflattering description appeared, and he thought he understood at least part of the reason. Some years earlier, Adams had served with

Bache's grandfather as a minister in France and had developed a rabid disrespect for the elder Franklin; Adams thought him lazy in his performance of duty, maddeningly imprecise when he did perform it, and too easily distracted from the cause of American independence by the attractions of Parisian society. Franklin knew how Adams felt; his colleague had made no secret of it. Perhaps, Adams now supposed, the old man's grandson was taking his revenge.

But Adams did not think highly of any republican editors of the time; they were to him a group that practiced what Adams called "terrorism" more than journalism. He had been "disgraced and degraded" by them for all too long and would not stand for it anymore. He would not have them abuse him as they had George Washington. He would not allow his good works to be made to appear otherwise. Hence he would not object when Congress, in 1798, decided to pass the notorious Sedition Act. Perhaps he thought back to the old days, to his motto for the *Boston Gazette*, and revised it, believing now that a free press did not maintain the majesty of the people when it reviled the majesty of their freely chosen leader.

❀

HISTORY USUALLY REFERS TO IT with its partner, telling of the Alien and Sedition Acts and considering them among the more un-American pieces of legislation in American history. The Alien Acts gave the president the ability to deport or imprison a foreigner if he was thought to be a threat of some sort to the United States. It also required that persons who came from other lands reside in the United States for fourteen years, rather than the previous five, before applying for citizenship.

The Sedition Act reads in part as follows:

That if any person shall write, print, utter or publish . . . or shall knowingly assist or aid in writing, printing, uttering, or publishing any false scandalous and malicious writing or writings against the government of the United States, or either house of Congress of the United States, or the President of the United States, with intent to defame the said government, or to bring them . . . into contempt or disrepute; or to excite against them . . . the hatred of the good people of the United States, or to stir up sedition within the United States, or to excite any unlawful combinations therein, for opposing or resisting any law of the United States . . . then such person, being thereof convicted before any court of the United States having jurisdiction thereof, shall be punished by a fine not exceeding two thousand dollars, and by imprisonment not exceeding two years.

It was less a piece of legislation than an act of vengeance by federalist lawmakers who decided to strike back at the republican newspapers that they felt had been demonizing their intentions and slandering their character for far too long. It was no longer necessary to punch an editor in the face; now one could have him arrested and imprisoned and fined and perhaps in the process driven into bankruptcy and put out of business once and for all, with the full weight of the federal government descending like an avalanche upon his print shop.

A few years earlier, such a measure could not have been passed; a few years later, with republicans in the ascendancy, it would not even have been considered. But with the XYZ Affair still a vivid memory and federalists still flexing their muscles because of it, the time for the Sedition Act was right.

It was also right because as John Adams assumed the presidency, 75 percent of the papers in the United States were controlled by federalists, meaning that they either would support the Act wholeheartedly or, if somewhat tempered in their federalism, would at least mute their criticism. As for the other 25 percent, their opposition could be shrugged off as typical partisan ranting against people who had now decided to place limits on partisan ranting.

The Sedition Act was first voted on in the Senate, which passed it, after less debate than it deserved, on the Fourth of July, 1798. Benjamin Franklin Bache was both appalled and delighted by the irony. In the next edition of the *Aurora*, he printed the Declaration of Independence in its entirety, not bothering to explain why, knowing that, as far as his faithful readers were concerned, he did not have to. He also knew that federalists would understand, that they would not like it, and that before long they would be coming for him.

The House considered the measure on July 5. Speaking most ardently on its behalf was Representative John Allen of Connecticut, a man who, according to James Thomson Callender, believed that "the federal constitution is not worth a *damn*, and that he would be glad to *give it a kick*." Said Allen about the Sedition Act: "If ever there was a nation which required a law of this kind, it is this. Let gentlemen look at certain papers printed in this city and elsewhere, and ask themselves whether an unwarrantable and dangerous combination does not exist to overturn and ruin the Government by publishing the most shameless falsehoods against the Representatives of the people of all denominations."

According to Allen, no paper was more guilty of publishing shameless falsehoods than the *Aurora*. Determined to make the case to his fellow legislators, or at least to those of federalist persuasion, Allen began to read aloud from several articles that had recently appeared in the paper. One that particularly incensed him concerned the Sedition Act itself, which, claimed Benjamin Franklin Bache, was "so diametrically opposed to the very letter of [the Constitution]. We are so accustomed to see violations of the spirit of this instrument as to think them mere matter of course; but such a gross attempt was never before made." If Federalist lawmakers continued on their present course, the *Aurora* said, "To laugh at the cut of a coat of a member of Congress will soon be treasonous; as I find it will be to give a Frenchman a dinner or a bed, as soon as this bill passes."

The more Allen read to his audience of congressmen, the more he ranted. How could a newspaper print such wanton misrepresentations, promote such salacious actions, take issue so brazenly with the truth as federalists knew it? How could a civilized nation allow journalism of so nefarious a sort to exist? It could not, Allen thundered, for the good of the present administration and of all administrations to come. This Benjamin Franklin Bache, Allen went on,

> declares what is unconstitutional, and then invites the people to "resistance." This is an awful, horrible example of the "liberty of opinion and freedom of the press." Can gentlemen hear these things and lie quietly on their pillows? Are we bound hand and foot that we must be witnesses of these deadly thrusts at our liberty? Are we to be the unresisting spectators of these exertions to destroy all that we hold dear? Are these approaches to revolution . . . to be observed with the eye of meek submission?

Apparently not. The House passed the Sedition Act as effortlessly as had the Senate, and President Adams signed it into law on July 14.

It was perhaps inevitable, something Americans had to try, something they had to get out of their system in the process of deciding what kinds of checks and balances should exist, if any, between journalism and government, between free speech and licentious accusation. Certainly the Puritan elders of Massachusetts would have been pleased to have had the Sedition Act in their arsenal in 1721 when James Franklin's *New England Courant* made a mockery not only of their position on inoculation but of virtually all that they believed in. Certainly the Act would have made it easier to drive Franklin out of business.

George Washington also seemed pleased with the legislation, if not as a permanent feature of American government, at least as an extraordinary measure for an extraordinary time. Washington believed that freedom of the press could be granted only to a press that behaved responsibly; otherwise, a nation was not only allowing its own best interests to be subverted but encouraging such subversion, rewarding iniquity at the expense of fairness. Most federalists, in fact, supported the Sedition Act to one degree or another, whether they held public office or tended shop or raised crops on their farms. The noted lexicographer Noah Webster, best known for producing the first American dictionary but before that the editor of the *American Minerva*, a newspaper that proclaimed itself "the Friend of Government," spoke for many of his fellow federalists when he insisted that it was "time to stop newspaper editors from libeling those with whom they disagreed."

When the press goes too far, reaction against it goes too far as well.

❀

As for Alexander Hamilton, he does not seem to have objected to the Act in principle, but he worried that in their zeal to restrain the republican press, the federalists would abuse the law's authority. "Let us not be cruel or violent," he cautioned members of his party before they began voting on the Act. "Let us not establish a tyranny." But his voice was not heeded, and he was troubled by the measure's final, unforgiving language.

There were, however, two provisions of the Sedition Act from which Hamilton, and others of more moderate inclination, could take heart. First, it had a built-in expiration date—March 3, 1801, less than three years away from its passage and one day before the next president of the United States would take office. There was always the possibility that the presidential electors would make a mistake and Adams's successor would be something other than a federalist—if so, he most certainly should not be granted the power to muzzle the opposition press.

Second, as had the Zenger case so many years before, the Sedition Act allowed the truth as a defense. A critic of the government could be as malicious as he pleased, as audacious and unconscionable, as pro-British or pro-French or pro-Egyptian, for that matter—but if what he said was true, he would not be prosecuted, would not be fined, would not be jailed. It sounded reasonable. In fact, however, it was not quite the safety valve it seemed. As those who drafted the Sedition Act well knew, it would be difficult if not impossible to establish the accuracy of one man's view of another man's character or ideas. How does one prove the truth of an opinion?

Jefferson was mightily opposed. He thought the Sedition Act an abomination, "an experiment on the American mind to see how far it will bear an avowed violation of the constitution. If this goes down, we shall immediately see attempted another act of Congress, declaring that the President shall continue in office during life, reserving to another occasion the transfer of the succession to his heirs, and the establishment of the Senate for life."

Naturally, Benjamin Franklin Bache could not have agreed more. In August, the *Aurora* featured a letter, signed Brutus, fulminating at "the late lawless proceedings" that had led to the Act as well as "the sanguinary and abominable publications which daily issue from the press of Porcupine" and others that promote the "diabolic designs" of the federalist legislators. In fact, Bache goes so far in his response to the Sedition Act as to seem to call for the populace to take up arms.

> To prevent the effects of their wicked machinations, the Republicans should not lose a moment in concerting a plan for their mutual defence—a proper system will tend as well to preserve the public peace, as to discountenance the base arts which are daily practiced, not only to destroy the freedom of speech, but that of voting in the members of Congress.

By expressing such sentiments, of course, Benjamin Franklin

Bache only made his opponents want to arrest him more quickly and keep him behind bars even longer after the trial.

❂

THE FEDERALISTS took to the Sedition Act like young animals to the freedom of a forest. They arrested twenty-five of their countrymen and indicted fifteen. One was Jedediah Peck, a member of the New York Assembly from Oswego County, who had been collecting signatures on a petition demanding that the Alien and Sedition Acts be repealed. But the arrest turned him into a hero, not a criminal; he was cheered by people who saw him being escorted to prison, and when they were done cheering, they started protesting, demanding an end not only to unjust legislation but to the terms of the federalists in government who had supported it. Eventually the case against Peck was dropped; he was reelected to the New York Assembly in a landslide.

Also indicted was Charles Holt, the editor of a newspaper in Connecticut, who had never cared much for Alexander Hamilton. In 1799, with the former secretary of the treasury about to assume a military command, Holt was even more disapproving. "Are our young officers and soldiers to learn virtue from General Hamilton?" the editor wrote. "Or, like their generals are they to be found in the bed of adultery?"

A third victim of the Sedition Act was Thomas Cooper, whose Pennsylvania paper, the *Sunbury and Northumberland Gazette*, was, despite its remote location and small number of subscribers, a crown of thorns for the president. "A meaner, more artful or a more malicious libel has not appeared," said Adams after reading one of Cooper's many diatribes against him. "As far as it alludes to me, I despise it; but I have no doubt it is a libel against the whole government, and as such ought to be prosecuted."

In fact, so stridently did Cooper attack Adams that the editor, perhaps feeling a pang or two of conscience, began to publish rebuttals. One of them, from a reader identifying himself only as "a native American," referred to Cooper as a caster of "ungraceful aspersions against a government which has afforded him an asylum and protection."

Adams was not impressed with this show of fairness. When, some time later, Cooper published a broadside charging the president, in biographer John Grant's paraphrase, with "all-around incompetence and dereliction, including the blunder of having caused a rise in the prevailing rate of interest by wrecking the public credit," Adams authorized Cooper's arrest. He was tried and found guilty of violating the Sedition Act. He served six months in jail. Fine: $400.

Of the fifteen people indicted under the Act, eleven went to trial. Ten were convicted. Seven of the ten, each a republican of one stripe or another, were journalists. As for the dozens and dozens of men chosen to sit on the juries, they were, almost without exception, federalists. It is remarkable, given such a stacking of the deck, that one of the eleven men tried under the new law was acquitted.

Benjamin Franklin Bache's many opponents vowed that he would not be similarly exonerated. To at least some of them, the *Aurora* was justification all by itself for the Sedition Act, for any one of a hundred or more articles it had published over the years. But the provisions of the Act stipulated that a specific complaint be filed about a specific offense—which is to say a specific article—before an arrest could be made. Representative Timothy Pickering, one of the most choleric of the paper's federalist foes, was only too happy to oblige.

Pickering called to the attention of his fellow congressmen the July 24, 1798, issue of the *Aurora*, which reported critically on the leaders of the two houses of the British Parliament, in large part because, in Bache's view, they were insufficiently conciliatory toward the French. To Pickering, this was thinly-veiled criticism of the Adams administration, which republicans also found lacking in admiration of France.

The two men were William Pitt and Lord George Grenville,

and the *Aurora* wrote of them, not altogether lucidly: "The acknowledged character of the two ministerial leaders, one in each house of Parliament for everything that is self-opinionated, arrogant, audacious, defamatory, and despicable renders in them a sincere application for peace to men, whom they have incessantly holden up to universal detestation as the most horrible monsters, all but an *actual impossibility.*"

Pickering believed that Bache meant his description of Pitt and Grenville also to apply to the heads of American government and that, as a result, the July 24 edition of the *Aurora* was "imbued with rather more impudence than is common to that paper" and thus gave just cause for reprisal under the terms of the Sedition Act. When he asked President Adams whether he agreed, Adams replied without equivocation.

> Is there anything evil in the regions of actuality or possibility that the *Aurora* has not suggested of me? You may depend upon it, I disdain to attempt a vindication of myself against any of the lies of the *Aurora*, as much as any man concerned with the administration of the affairs of the United States. If Mr. Rawle [the government attorney, who would have to file the charges] does not think this paper libelous, he is not fit for his office; and if he does not prosecute, he will not do his duty.

When Jefferson heard that Bache had been arrested, he was indignant. He met with Madison, and the two of them, declaring a private state of emergency, immediately began contacting their friends and urging them to subscribe to the *Aurora*, both to help spread the paper's anti-federalist message and, even more important at the moment, to raise money that Bache could apply toward his defense. Speaking about both the *Aurora* and another journal that the federalists had just targeted, the *United States Recorder*, Jefferson warned his mates that "if these papers fall, Republicanism will be entirely browbeaten."

Jefferson and Madison did more. They asked republicans who

already subscribed to the *Aurora* to make further donations as well as to write letters in support of Bache to sympathetic papers. They asked others to publish broadsides and pamphlets defending not only the *Aurora*'s editor as a person but the ideas for which he stood and the right that he had been guaranteed under the Constitution to express them, no matter how repellant they seemed to federalists. It was not merely Benjamin Franklin Bache who was about to stand trial, republicans believed; thanks to the Sedition Act, it was the principles of the entire nation.

❁

BUT BACHE NEVER APPEARED in a courtroom. He never heard the charges read against him, never watched a jury of federalists retire to decide his fate. As it turned out, Benjamin Franklin's grandson would fall victim not to a dreaded law but to an even more dreaded opponent, an outbreak of yellow fever. When stricken, writes James Tagg, Bache "was under arrest, his business was bankrupt, and his political views were seemingly under attack from all quarters. To make matters worse, his wife was pregnant with their fourth child."

He fought the disease as best he could. He would not allow himself to be bled; rather, he followed the advice of a French doctor who prescribed frequent, almost constant, baths, assuring him that the more time he spent immersed in a tub, the greater the chances of a recovery. For the last several weeks of his life, he spent few moments either clothed or dry, and those who visited him remarked on puddles of water all over the floors of his rooms.

But even with his health and business failing, Bache kept publishing his newspaper; it was important to him not to abandon his principles even as the spark of life was abandoning him. When, in the summer of 1798, he wrote that the *Aurora* had so far "escaped the affliction" of yellow fever, he was not bearing false witness so much as trying to ease the minds of those who read and supported him faithfully and had now begun to worry about him. And when he continued in the same issue of the paper, saying, "[S]hould the untoward fortune of our city also extend to us, our friends will make a due allowance for what may be inevitable, a temporary suspension of our labors." Bache knew that when the suspension came, it would not be temporary.

Three days later, he was dead. His wife published a notice of her husband's passing, calling him "a man inflexible in virtue, unappalled by power or persecution—and who in dying knew no anxieties but what were excited by his apprehensions for his country —and for his young family." Republican newspapers in other states mourned him in similar terms. He was a hero to some, an example to all. He might have gone too far on occasion, but always in the right direction. And apparently at great expense: when William Duane succeeded Bache as editor of the *Aurora*, he claimed that despite the paper's success, it was somewhere between $14,700 and $20,000 in debt.

To federalist journals Bache was no less unanimously a villain, a rogue, the printing press's great defiler. "The Jacobins are all whining at the exit of the vile Benjamin Franklin Bache," wrote *Russell's Gazette*; "so they would do if one of their gang was hung for stealing. The memory of this scoundrel cannot be too highly execrated."

The next paragraph, however, tried.

> "Ben Bache is dead—and eke to hell
>   Had gone, as prophets tell us,
> But that he *sinn'd*, and had *lied* so well,
>   It made the Devil jealous!"

❈

MEDICAL SCIENCE KNEW SO LITTLE about yellow fever in those days, and the illness took so many victims. Freneau had given up his paper in part because his subscribers were dying; the *Auro-*

ra's editor was now gone; and less than a week later, *Porcupine's Gazette* would tell of yet another passing from the disease, although much more reverently than *Russell's Gazette* had reported on Bache. "Died, last evening, Mr. JOHN FENNO, Editor and Proprietor of the Gazette of the United States." His departure, said William Cobbett's sympathetic account, will be "long and sincerely . . . regretted by his relations, and by the many friends his virtues have made."

❁

Bache's death was not the end of the government's case against the *Aurora*. In fact, there were federalists who disliked William Duane even more than they did his employer, for Duane not only shared Bache's worldview, but seems to have written more of the articles that enraged the federalists than did the deceased, more of the articles promoting the French and denigrating the British and damning the ignorance and conspiratorial nature of those who opposed republicanism.

And it was Duane who would later be memorably pilloried in verse in a federalist paper called *The Wasp*:

> William Duane—illustrious in the art of lying—
> "Some in the modern doctrines spy
> "A new commandment—*Thou shalt lie.*
> "And if there is, as who can tell,
> "There's no one, sure, he keeps so well."

And Duane wrote at least as much as Bache did in the *Aurora*'s pages about the intolerable excesses of both the Alien and Sedition Acts—which was bad enough, as far as proponents of the Acts were concerned. But Duane reinforced his words with deeds; like Jedediah Peck, he circulated a petition for repeal. As a result, Duane and the two friends who had joined him in the venture were arrested for violating the Sedition Act; their trial was scheduled to begin promptly.

Again, it was Timothy Pickering who took the lead for the federalists, charging that Duane was a curse to society more than a chronicler of it, and referring to the man's past to make his argument. It seemed that during the Revolutionary War, Duane had for a time been an exile, having left the United States for the British East Indies, where, Pickering asserted, "he committed or was charged with some crime, and returned to Great Britain from whence, within three or four years past, he came to this country to stir up sedition and work other mischief." And having treated with the British when they were America's enemy, Pickering went on, Duane was now in league with federalism's enemy, the French.

It was "matchless effrontery," said President Adams about Duane's conduct both during the war and at the *Aurora*, and he ordered the prosecution to get started. Unfortunately, it seemed as if it would never end. There were so many witnesses, so much questioning and then conferring among counsel and then more questioning, and there were such complications about both the law and the *Aurora's* motives.

The case dragged on for weeks and then months, and finally, to both the relief and frustration of all, and without a decision of any kind having been reached, it had to be dropped. Prosecutors feared that the Sedition Act would expire before Duane could be found guilty, and federalists feared—correctly, as it turned out—that the trial was bringing more scrutiny to the Alien and Sedition Acts than those twin pillars of legislative ineptitude could stand. There seemed no choice but to set the defendant free.

But Duane could celebrate only briefly before being forced to defend himself again. The more zealous of the federalists continued to hound him, both in and out of the courtroom, and Pickering, the most zealous of all, would see to it that Duane was eventually called before the U.S. Senate on charges of printing articles in the *Aurora* that were "false, defamatory, scandalous and malicious." The lawmakers found him guilty, scolded him, then released him, whereupon he returned to the print shop, seething more than ever, and, thus inspired, published the next several editions of the *Aurora* with renewed anti-federalist spite.

❀

The Sedition Act took a toll on Adams no less than it did those who were its direct victims. The president might have been avid in enforcing the Act, but he also felt guilty about his avidity; he might have believed that freedom of the press had to be limited, but he was troubled by the fact that he was the one forced to decide what the limitations were. He knew that he was using the Act for his own partisan ends, but such was his pique at those who criticized him in print that he could not do anything to stop himself. Nor, most of the time, did he think he should.

As has been noted about many other presidents of the United States, Adams seemed to age extraordinarily in office, after a time even beginning to resemble that unkind description of him in the *Aurora*. He was at least old*er*, bald*er*, blind*er*, and certainly more querulous than he had been before assuming the nation's highest office. He was not toothless, however, although he may have lost a few teeth to neglect in the past few years, and he was not crippled, although there were times when he found it a struggle to push himself out of a chair and even more of one to maintain a brisk pace as he walked.

And just as it had been speculated, although inaccurately, that George Washington gave up the presidency because of the offensives against him by the *Aurora*, so was it speculated that John Adams gave up the presidency because of the offensives he waged against the same paper. Referring to the Alien and Sedition Acts and the increasing criticism leveled at those responsible for them, press historian George Henry Payne says that "the passage of and enforcement of those laws led to John Adams's retirement to private life and contributed more than any other event to the passing of the Federalist party."

Payne exaggerates mightily. Adams was troubled by the Acts and the increasingly negative reactions to them by federalists and republicans alike, but they did not force him from office. Nor, as Payne well knows, did he retire; Adams ran for a second term as president and was defeated by his vice president, Thomas Jefferson. It might have been the nastiest and most abusive political campaign in the history of American journalism.

❁

IT WAS ALSO, as historian Susan Dunn has pointed out, the first presidential campaign truly to be contested—at least in a sense. Washington was the near-unanimous choice in the first two; in the third, Dunn writes, "power had been easily transferred from one Federalist to another, from outgoing president George Washington to his vice president, John Adams. But now, would Federalists willingly and peacefully hand power over to their political enemies, to these Republicans, men whom they not only loathed but also considered dangerous to the republic, to private property, to economic growth and a strong federal government, to everything they cherished and respected?"

The answer, at least as far as federalist newspapers were concerned, was no. And to try to make sure they would not have to report on the transfer of power to those whom they so despised, they began devoting their pages to the most dire of predictions. "Should the infidel Jefferson be elected to the Presidency," wrote the *Hudson Bee*, quoting another federalist paper, the *New England Palladium*, "the *seal of death* is that moment set on our holy religion, our churches will be prostrated, and some infamous prostitute, under the title of the Goddess of Reason, will preside in the Sanctuaries now devoted to the Most High."

From the *Connecticut Courant*: "Do you believe in the strangest of all paradoxes, that a spendthrift, a libertine, or an Atheist, characters which none of you would trust with the most trifling concern in your own private affairs, is qualified to make your laws and to govern you, and your posterity; to be entrusted with the treasure, the strength, and the destiny of the nation?"

From the *Gazette of the United States*: Jefferson had "embark[ed] upon the tempestuous ocean of public life . . . without a reference to the integrity of the means by which their ends are to be accomplished"; he had been "aiming at the . . . malignancy of a free people"; he "is an enemy to American manufactures, *absolutely and forever*"; and, furthermore, "he considers all the merchants of the *United States*, so many *curses* instead of *blessings*."

And from the same paper a few weeks before the election:

THE GRAND QUESTION STATED
At the present solemn and momentous epoch, the
only question to be asked by every American, laying his
hand on his heart, is "shall I continue in allegiance to
GOD—AND A RELIGIOUS
PRESIDENT;
Or impiously declare for
JEFFERSON—AND NO GOD!!!

In Boston, the *Columbian Centinel* started a new feature, an almost unending series of columns called "The Jeffersoniad," which examined in detail "the crooked character and principles of the Jacobin PRETENDER to the Presidency." In the sixteenth of them, the paper listed a dozen of Jefferson's character flaws, including his "insatiable ambition," "contempt for commerce and commercial men," "gross tergiversation and inconsistency," "departure from his *old principles*," "rooted antipathy to the Federal Constitution and his fixed determination to overthrow it," and his "deadly opposition to *Great Britain*, and his violent and ridiculous attachment to *France*."

❀

THE REPUBLICAN COUNTERATTACK was surprisingly feeble. Some papers praised Jefferson, in colorless language for the most part, for his perceptiveness and eloquence and experience. Other papers attacked Adams, but without much fire; one said that the incumbent wanted to start an American aristocracy by marrying one of his sons to a daughter of George III, but people had heard similar charges before and few of either political leaning could be bothered to believe this particular one. Apparently, at least some of the anti-federalist newspapers were confident of a Jefferson victory. As for others, it may be that after twelve years of reporting on the unconscionable manner in which their opponents had been running the government, they had simply exhausted their supplies of opprobrium.

❀

IN THE SUMMER OF 1800, with the campaign already having reached a nadir of aspersion and duplicity, some federalist publications tried to dig the hole a little deeper, publishing rumors that Jefferson had died. They did not know how, did not know where, did not know why; they could not say whether the death was the result of an accident or an illness or of a divine providence exhibiting strongly Hamiltonian tendencies. There was, in other words, not the slightest shred of meat on the rumor's bones. Nonetheless, the *Gazette of the United States*, after due deliberation, concluded that "the report of Mr. Jefferson's death appears to be entitled to some credit."

A week later, with Jefferson ensconced as he had been all along at Monticello, and people now beginning to doubt the tales of his demise, someone wrote to the *Connecticut Courant* and put matters into his own perverse perspective. Jefferson was probably alive after all, the paper's correspondent decided, but the hearsay to the contrary had been well intentioned: "some *compassionate* being," the fellow decided, was simply trying to raise people's hopes, to give them some good news during this woeful presidential campaign, and therefore had "very humanely killed Mr. Jefferson."

❁

ALTHOUGH JEFFERSON WON more electoral votes than Adams in 1800, he did not win more than Aaron Burr, and it was up to the House of Representatives to break the tie between them. Alexander Hamilton decided to help, and did so, of all things, in Jefferson's behalf, telling his friend Oliver Wolcott Jr. that Jefferson "is by far not so dangerous a man and he has pretensions to character." Burr, Hamilton continued, had none; he was "far more cunning than wise, far more dexterous than able. In my opinion he is inferior in real ability to Jefferson." It seems a remarkable turnabout for Hamilton, but one most accurately taken at face value: Hamilton had not softened on Jefferson so much as he found Burr even more repugnant, more dangerous to the American future.

After thirty-six ballots and innumerable threats and pleas, promises and expostulations, a number of them issuing from Hamilton and his supporters, the House decided on Jefferson. The republican press exploded in delight. Finally, one of their own in the nation's most powerful office. Finally, a man they could trust to right the course of American government, to set it on its true path, the one the Constitution had all along intended. Finally, the opportunity to break out a whole new set of adjectives in writing about the presidency.

The *Gazette of the United States* bit its tongue; all that was heard from John Fenno's son, who had succeeded his father as editor, was an admission that Jefferson's election was "a circumstance much regretted by the Editor of this Gazette and all real Americans." The *Columbian Centinel* sorrowed more. It began a long period of mourning by running an epitaph for what it believed to be justice and reason in government. The announcement was brief, heartfelt, and bordered in black:

YESTERDAY EXPIRED
Deeply regretted by MILLIONS of grateful Americans
And by *all* GOOD men,
The FEDERAL ADMINISTRATION
. . .
Its death was occasioned by the
Secret Arts, and Open Violence,
Of Foreign and Domestic Demagogues:
Notwithstanding its whole Life
Was devoted to the Performance of every Duty
To promote
The UNION, CREDIT, PEACE, PROSPER-
ITY, HONOR, and
FELICITY OF ITS COUNTRY.

Two weeks later, Thomas Jefferson moved into the President's House in the new city of Washington, District of Columbia, across the Potomac River from Virginia. He was accompanied by his French steward, a housekeeper, and three servants, one of whom might have been an attractive woman, about thirty years of age, a quadroon, which is to say a person with three white grandparents and one black, a woman who had served Jefferson for many years and held a respected position in his household hierarchy. Her name was Sally Hemings, and her son Tom was later said by James Thomson Callender not only to bear the same first name as Jefferson but to possess features that "bear a striking although sable resemblance to those of the president himself."

CHAPTER TWENTY-ONE

❈

Master and Mistress

*T*HE PAST TWO YEARS had not been kind to Callender, either personally or professionally. In 1798 his wife died, and according to a later article in the Richmond *Examiner*, Callender was largely to blame. He had, said the paper, treated her with "barbarity and brutality," leaving her "to wallow in filth, ignorance and misery, while he was indulging in intoxication," and, finally, allowing her "to perish in her own filth until maggots were engendered beneath her and along her spine!"

It is a brutal assessment, scatology more than journalism, the indictment as scathing as anything Callender had ever written about others. But one cannot help suspecting it contained a kernel of truth; a drunkard, which Callender had been for many years, is seldom the most affectionate of husbands, and a fanatic, into which category he also fell, is not always attentive to loved ones or aware of the effects of his neglect.

Yet Callender was devastated by his wife's death; to the extent that he had a hand in it, he was probably helpless to behave otherwise. And so he plunged even deeper into the bottle, wanting to forget. He also wanted to acquit himself of the *Examiner's* charges. And he wanted peace of mind and income, and he believed that the latter would make the former at least a possibility. He could see no other course but to leave his four young children with a friend, promising to send money for their upkeep, and set out in search of new commissions.

His old ones had made him the republicans' favorite hit man, especially his exposé of the Hamilton-Reynolds affair. That Hamilton had outlasted the scandal and maintained his standing in government, legal circles, and the society as a whole had more to do with the strength of his character and his support in the federalist press than with any tepidity in Callender's prose. Hamilton's survival, in other words, could not be blamed on the journalist who had tried so hard to bring him down.

Callender further solidified his reputation among republicans with a more recent publication, issued "in his customarily toxic style," called *The Prospect Before Us*. The purpose of this pamphlet, he declared at the outset, was to "exhibit the multiple corruptions of the Federal Government, and more especially the misconduct of the President, Mr. Adams."

According to Callender, "Mr. Adams has laboured, and with melancholy success, to break up the bonds of social affection, and, under the ruins of confidence and friendship, to extinguish the only Beam of happiness that glimmers through the dark and despicable farce of life." A serious if hysterical charge, but there were others. In his handling of the XYZ Affair, said Callender, Adams "designed to do nothing but mischief." At least one of his presidential addresses "was distinguished by vague and virulent invective against the republic." More broadly, "Mr. Adams has mistaken and misrepresented every thing." And perhaps even more broadly, the man did not deserve to be president in the first place, having defeated Thomas Jefferson for the office in 1796 through fraudulent means.

In Pennsylvania, [Adams] gained a vote, by the trick of a postmaster, who stopt the mail from Greene county, till the poll was closed at Philadelphia. In Maryland, he gained a second, by the folly of one Plater, who balloted both for him and Mr. Jefferson, from an anxiety that Mr. Adams should be *Vice* president. In Maryland, he gained a third suffrage, in the western district of that state by a majority of four voices, by the wonted negligence of one side, and the wonted knavery of the other.

It was an accusation no one had seriously considered before, and that no historian has ever validated.

Callender sent Jefferson a copy of *The Prospect Before Us* prior to publication. Jefferson read it, and must forever be faulted for his reaction. He should have been appalled, should have urged Callender to blunt his accusations, dignify his language, refrain altogether from claiming election fraud. Instead, meaning to encourage not only what Callender had written but what he would write in the future, Jefferson responded favorably. "Such papers cannot fail to produce the best effect," he told the journalist. "They inform the thinking part of the nation."

When Adams's wife, Abigail, read the pamphlet later, its "abuse and scandal" left her breathless. She believed that Callender was even more satanic than Benjamin Franklin Bache and that he should be marched up the steps of the nearest gallows and hanged for such a denunciation of her husband. "And once she found out that Jefferson had been subsidizing him," writes Jefferson biographer Fawn Brodie, "her cordial and affectionate friendship [with him], already greatly strained, froze into glacial silence."

Adams was not Callender's only prey in *The Prospect Before Us*. Digging back into the past, he criticized Washington for having "exceeded his lawful powers" and having attained "another topmast of absurdity" in his issuance of the Neutrality Proclamation, which had so offended the French. Other federalists were similarly scorned, in particular Hamilton, for offenses both old and new, especially all the money that he and James Reynolds had supposedly pilfered from the Treasury—"Thousands, and twenties of thousands of dollars are gone, God knows where!" Callender even tossed in a few good words for Bache, writing that federalists could not forgive him for "wishing to preserve the peace of the country, for exposing the follies and crimes of the British and presidential faction."

More than *The History of the United States for 1796*, which did not cut so wide a swath through the opposition's personalities and practices, more in fact than any other article or volume Callender had produced to date, *The Prospect Before Us* established the author as the boldest and most vengeful of republican spokesmen.

There was only one problem. The president of the United States at the time Callender wrote the pamphlet was not a republican. The House and Senate were not controlled by republicans. Neither were most state legislatures. Neither was the federal judiciary. It was the federalists who dominated not only the various branches of government when *The Prospect Before Us* was published but also the press, providing its most widely circulated papers and its most strident, and often persuasive, voices. Hence it was inevitable that as some among the republicans egged Callender on, the federalists were demanding that he be clubbed over the head with the Sedition Act and taken into custody by authorities. He appeared before a judge a few days after the pamphlet was published.

His trial was widely dismissed as a "mockery," and in fact it was a comedy skit of a proceeding; one imagines every sensible man in the courtroom, if indeed there were any, struggling to keep a straight face as the principals played out their parts. Consider: the jury was composed entirely of federalists, and most of them, it seems, were zealous in their views. Consider: the judge, Samuel Chase, "probably the most violent partisan who ever sat upon a bench," flaunted his bias when he "interrupted Callender's three defense lawyers so often and with such palpable contempt that they angrily withdrew from the case." And consider: Callender's brand of journalism was offensive not just to federalists but to fair-minded, levelheaded republicans as well. The latter might not have supported the Sedition Act, but as long as it existed, they could not deny the appropriateness of applying it to such a man as Callender; they cheered the judicial farce as unabashedly as the federalists, who presumably did not think it a farce at all.

The trial lasted all of a day, the jury's deliberations so brief that the members barely had time for a sip of cider as they cast their votes. Guilty, they announced promptly and proudly. Chase sentenced Callender to nine months in jail and a fine of $200. The sentence would begin immediately.

Callender was allowed paper, pen, and ink behind bars, and he employed them as rashly as he had when free, releasing new streams of malevolence against the foes of Jefferson, who were now, more than ever, foes of his as well. One imagines him so incensed with the verdict that he did not so much write on the paper as slash his words across it, wielding the pen as if it were a knife digging into federalism's flesh.

Friends would come to visit and would end up delivering Callender's latest missives to republican newspapers. But few of them published Callender's jailhouse rantings. Most editors were fearful of their seditiousness and therefore of exposing themselves to prosecution for providing Callender a forum. In fact, try though he did, the only real contribution Callender was able to make to Jefferson's presidential bid during his imprisonment was inadvertent. "When the minutes of Callender's trial were published and circulated as a campaign document in the election [of 1800]," writes Fawn Brodie, "the trial became a national sensation and did much to help Jefferson's election."

Callender was still in prison when he learned of Jefferson's victory and was jubilant at the news. "And so the day's our own," he wrote for the Richmond *Examiner*. "Hurraw! How shall I triumph over the miscreants! How, as Othello says, shall they be damned beyond all depth! What a burst of rapture one feels in the embraces of Victory! She is certainly the most charming of all Goddesses, Venus and the graces not excepted." He might have been even more jubilant had he known that at a tavern in Albemarle County, Virginia, one of Jefferson's supporters had insisted that all raise their glasses in the journalist's honor, a toast to "James Thomson Callender, who looks down on his persecutors with their merited contempt."

As it turned out, he would have nothing to celebrate at all. A few republicans here and there might have been drinking in his honor, but the incoming president, the most important republican of all, was not. Jefferson had heard tales of Callender's own drinking as well as his violent temper; the latter, so evident on the page, could not help but show itself elsewhere. Jefferson was wary of Callender's instability, and perhaps his deviousness. Furthermore, he seems now to have regretted his endorsement of *The Prospect Before Us*, finding it, upon reflection, too abusive, although little reflection should have been necessary for such a conclusion.

Jefferson certainly would not have approved of the second volume of the pamphlet, which Callender wrote at least in part while in jail, and in which he referred to Adams's behavior in the President's House as "absurd," his most trusted colleagues as a "flock of harpies," and to Adams's writing style as a "jumble of impertinence and contradiction, [which] displays the genuine standard of the president's intellect. Few other men were capable of cramming so great a quantity of nonsense within so small a compass of words."

But however much he wanted to, Jefferson could not turn his back on Callender. He was as fearful of him as Hamilton had been of James Reynolds some years earlier, and for a similar reason. Jefferson owed Callender, and was coming to believe that if he did not pay his debt, Callender would dip that pen of his into the federalist inkwell and make Jefferson himself the victim of his slashes against the page. It was, thought the incoming president, the most delicate of situations; he dealt, after all, with the most indelicate of men.

Callender was released from jail two days before Jefferson's inauguration. Shortly afterward, in one of his first acts as president, he granted Callender a full pardon, expecting him to be grateful, just as Hamilton had earlier expected Reynolds to be grateful when he received his first installment of hush money. The two Founding Fathers were, in these cases, equally naive.

Callender had already served his time; the pardon could do nothing more than clear his name, and even that was a dubious proposition; Callender had long suspected that his name would never be clear, not in any realistic sense. And when Jefferson also saw to it that Callender received a onetime payment of $50—a token of appreciation for services rendered? A bribe to placate him in the future?—the journalist went from being unimpressed to feeling positively insulted. He had still not been able to pay the $200 fine for his violation of the Sedition Act, and he was falling ever further behind in the money that was due to Thomas Leiper, the man who had been tending his children. And Jefferson, to whom he had rendered services of inestimable value, to whom he had dedicated his heart, soul, and vocabulary, whose election as president meant as much to the journalist as it did to the victor— was giving him a mere $50?

Callender wanted more. Just as Reynolds had asked Hamilton for a job in the Treasury Department, Callender told Jefferson that he was interested in a position of his own, specifically that of postmaster of Richmond. He deserved the job, he informed the president, and would settle for nothing less, and, by way of tempering his demand with enticement, he let Jefferson know that he would use his spare time, of which a postmaster could arrange large quantities, to continue writing for the republican cause.

Jefferson turned him down. It was one of the worst decisions of his presidency and, for Callender, the end of his days as a republican.

According to one Federalist account, probably apocryphal, Callender lingered outside the presidential mansion for several days after the inauguration hoping for a personal interview. When he spotted Jefferson at an upstairs window, he shouted out his threat: "Sir, you know that by lying I made you President, and I'll be d——d if I do not unmake you by telling the truth." Jefferson denounced Callender as "a lying renegade from Republicanism," then had Monroe, still governor of Virginia at the time, release statements denying that Jefferson had ever befriended or salaried Callender or had anything to do with his earlier diatribes against Adams.

If this account is false in its particulars, it is true in a more general sense, as it reflects the hurt that Callender felt at being denied his sinecure and the vehemence with which he swore he would avenge himself. Hell hath no fury like a toady scorned, and Callender would now vent that fury on the president as powerfully as he ever did on the president's foes.

❀

A NEW FEDERALIST NEWSPAPER in Richmond called the *Recorder* gave him the opportunity. The owner hired Callender to be his editor, delighted to have a former republican at the helm; no one, after all, is more committed to a religion than a recent convert, and the owner expected Callender to be a fanatic. Callender did not disappoint. He began his campaign of retribution by charging that although Jefferson had paid him poorly upon his release from jail, he had paid him well in previous times, subsidizing him for his revelation of Hamilton's affair and his various attacks on President Adams, including the first volume of *The Prospect Before Us.*

That is precisely what Jefferson had done. Either directly or indirectly, he had been Callender's patron for several years. He could not admit it, of course, not to the public, whom he might be able to fool, nor even to a friend who knew the truth that the president was now denying. "I am really mortified at the base ingratitude of Callender," Jefferson wrote to James Monroe, insisting that he had given him money in the past out of "mere motives of charity." Now, he said, he was afraid those motives would be misunderstood. Monroe, a friend indeed, seems to have gone along with Jefferson's deception.

The republican press defended its man, attacking Callender for his "apostasy, ingratitude, cowardice, lies, venality and constitutional malignity." It told lies of its own, a whole assortment of them, and it spiced them up with some selections from the catalog of unflattering truths about Callender. No toasts were being raised to him in republican taverns now.

And they would never be offered again. Callender made sure of it. In an absolute delirium of anger, distraught by his continuing financial woes and what he perceived to be his onetime benefactor's contribution to them by his betrayal, Callender became the first journalist to print the rumors about Jefferson that had long been uttered in the neighborhoods around Monticello. They had been heard as well in the surrounding towns and villages, both in the precincts where the white people lived and worked and in the black slave enclaves. They were now being spoken in the town of Washington as well, although only rarely and always with a question mark at the end. They were whispers, like the "dark whispers" about Hamilton, and when Callender finally decided to shout them, he added a truly vengeful, personal note at the end.

It is well known that the man, *whom it delighteth the people to honor*, keeps, and for many years past has kept, as his concubine, one of his slaves. Her name is SALLY. The name of her eldest son is TOM. His features are said to bear a striking resemblance to those of the president himself. The boy is ten or twelve years of age. His mother went to France in the same vessel with Mr. Jefferson and his two daughters. The delicacy of this arrangement must strike every person of common sensibility. What a sublime pattern for an American ambassador to place before the eyes of two young ladies! ...

By this wench Sally, our President has had several children. There is not an individual in the neighborhood of Charlottesville who does not believe the story, and not a few who *know it*. ... Behold the favorite! The first born of republicanism! The pinnacle of all that is good and great! In the open consummation of an act which tends to subvert the policy, the happiness, and even the existence of this country!

'Tis supposed that, at the time, when Mr. Jefferson wrote so smartly concerning Negroes, when he endeavoured so much to *belittle* the African race, he had no idea that the chief magistrate of the United States was to be the ringleader in shewing that his opinion was erroneous; or, that he should chuse an African stock whereupon he was to engraft his own descendants. . . .

If the friends of Mr. Jefferson are convinced of his innocence, they will make an appeal. . . . If they rest in silence, or if they content themselves with resting upon a *general denial*, they cannot hope for credit. The allegation is of a nature too *black* to be suffered to remain in suspense. We should be glad to hear of its refutation. We give it the world under the firmest belief that such a refutation *never can be made*. The AFRICAN VENUS is said to officiate as housekeeper at Monticello. When Mr. Jefferson has read this article, he will find leisure to estimate how much has been lost or gained by so many unprovoked attacks upon J.T. Callender.

The man responsible for the first sex scandal in American journalism had now topped himself with the second.

❀

IT WAS A STORY positively seismic not only in its implications but in the reactions it brought forth. Benjamin Harris's charge that the king of France "used to lie with" his son's daughter?—a trifle. Sam Adams's assertions that Governor Hutchinson had been the force behind the Stamp Act and virtually all of the indignities visited by the Crown on its North American colonies?—mere rhetoric, politics as usual. Even Callender's own revelation about Hamilton and Maria Reynolds paled in comparison with sex scandal number two; Reynolds was, after all, a white woman. (Although it should be pointed out that, as a quadroon, Sally Hemings was virtually, if not legally, a white woman herself—certainly not an African Venus. Had it not been for her lowly position, she could easily have passed.)

Other federalist newspapers reprinted Callender's tale. Some reacted with outrage that the president of the United States had been carrying on in such a manner. Others treated the news with a mocking, sniggering derision. Still others professed sorrow or puzzlement at Jefferson's behavior, a sense that they had been deceived. The *Boston Gazette*, no longer the fire-breathing journal that Edes and Gill and Sam Adams had created, and in fact no longer home to any of the three, offered a new set of lyrics to "Yankee Doodle" as they might have been written by Jefferson himself.

> *Of all the damsels on the green*
> *On mountain, or in valley*
> *A lass so luscious ne'er was seen,*
> *As Monticello Sally,*
> *Yankee Doodle, who's the noodle?*
> *What wife were half so handy?*
> *To breed a flock of slaves for stock,*
> *A blackamoor's a dandy.*

As for Callender, he did not content himself with the initial article. He wrote several other pieces for the *Recorder*, raising new questions, asking the old ones in more demeaning ways, doing what he could to keep the story alive and the disgust with Jefferson simmering. By the time a month had passed, he was criticizing Jefferson not just for the affair itself but for refusing to admit it. "When a person is desirous of denying truth," he stated, "*confusion is the only and inevitable resource.*" And Callender was predicting that one day Jefferson would be exhibited to the world "in his original nakedness and turpitude."

To be fair to the *Recorder*, it had now begun to publish refutations to Callender, or at least to question his accuracy. "Will the *damnable lie of Callender*," wrote one reader, "concerning a Negro slave in the house of the president of the United States, gain the least credit?" Other readers wanted the *Recorder* to offer proof of the Jefferson-Hemings liaison or drop the matter entirely.

Republican papers, on the other hand, did not know what to

make of all this. How could a man as noble in word as Jefferson have practiced the arts of seduction on a slave woman, a man as noble in deed have engaged in miscegenation? Not only did the Washington, D.C., *National Intelligencer* refuse to believe the charge, it refused to print it or even name the man who made it. Its editor "has determined not to disgrace the columns of a Paper that entertains a respect for decency and truth, by republishing the infamous calumnies and vulgarities of a man who has forfeited every pretension to character. . . . Without incurring any responsibility for the future, the Editor has prescribed to himself for the present the duty of suffering these base aspersions to perish unnoticed in their own infamy."

Other republican journals struck back by publishing letters from Jefferson's friends, of whom the most adamant in this case seems to have been Meriwether Jones, the publisher of *The Examiner*, the Richmond paper for which Callender had toiled before turning on the president. "Mr. Jefferson has been a Bachelor for more than twenty years," wrote Jones in his journal. "[N]ot a spot tarnished his widowed character until this frightful sea calf in his wild frenzy, thought proper to throw his phlegm at him. Are you not afraid, Callender, that some avenging fire will consume your body as well as your soul? Stand aghast thou brute, thy deserts will yet o'ertake thee."

Several weeks later, Jones had become so repulsed by Callender that he seems to have wished him death by drowning. "Oh! could a dose of James river, like Lethe, have blessed you with forgetfulness," he wrote again in the *Examiner*, "for once you would have neglected your whiskey."

The truth of Jefferson's relationship with Sally Hemings would not be known in his lifetime; the rumors, however, in Joseph J. Ellis's phrase, would be "a tin can tied to [his] reputation that has continued to rattle through the ages and the pages of the history books," all the way up to the end of the twentieth century, when DNA testing would reveal that our nation's third president had almost certainly fathered several children with a Hemings, and that Sally was the only likely candidate. James Thomson Callender's maliciously intended journalism, bloodthirsty and retaliatory, was in this case factual as well.

❀

THE SEDITION ACT had expired, as intended, the day before Jefferson took office in 1801, but the principle continued to tantalize: journalists should not be able to go too far; legislative bodies should be able to penalize them if they did. The power of the press should not be employed as a weapon; the government was entitled to disarm it when necessary. After all, the government had the right to punish all manner of offenses, from crimes against the person, such as theft and murder, to crimes against the state, such as treason and failure to pay taxes. Why should it not also be able to strike a blow against coarseness and mendacity as they were expressed by journalists, especially when the victims of such behavior were government officials themselves?

Among those who agreed was Jefferson, once an unblinking advocate of the press. "The basis of our government being the opinion of the people," he famously said, "the very first object should be to keep that right; and were it left to me to decide whether we should have a government without newspapers, or newspapers without a government, I should not hesitate a moment to prefer the latter."

But by the time he began residing in the President's House, Jefferson had had enough free speech to last him the rest of his life. He had also, perhaps, begun to indulge in a little goose-and-gander reasoning: if the federalists had been able to prosecute journalists for the supposed malevolence of their work, should not republicans have a turn of their own, a chance to avenge themselves or at least to set the record straight according to their most cherished precepts? Might two wrongs not, in this case, even justice's scales?

Jefferson thought they might, and no sooner had he announced a pardon for all those convicted under the Sedition Act, which he referred to as an "unauthorized" congressional action, than he approved the filing of charges against Harry Croswell, the editor of a paper in the small town of Hudson, New York, called *The Wasp*, and a federalist to the marrow. The Sedition Act might no longer exist, but seditious libel remained an offense as defined by law.

The Wasp's motto, emblazoned on the masthead, was "To lash the rascals naked through the world," and Croswell had come to believe that Jefferson was as deserving of lashes as anyone in public life at the time, primarily because of his continued refusals to admit the truth of his relationship with Callender. Croswell scoffed at Jefferson's claims that the president had given him money solely for "charitable" reasons. Jefferson's true motive, Croswell argued in *The Wasp*, was the opposite, to compensate Callender for writing as uncharitably as possible about Adams and his fellow federalists. Callender, Croswell charged, "is precisely qualified to become a tool, to spit the venom and scatter the malicious poisonous slanders of his employer. He, in short, is the very man that a dissembling patriot, pretended 'man of the people,' would employ to plunge the dagger or administer the arsenic." Callender's employer, that "man of the people," was, of course, Jefferson.

In a later article, Croswell was more specific. "Jefferson paid Callender for calling Washington a traitor, a robber, and a perjurer; for calling Adams a hoary-headed incendiary; and for most grossly slandering the private characters of men whom he well knew were virtuous. These charges, not a democratic editor has yet dared, or ever will dare, to meet in an open and manly discussion."

Jefferson was as upset by Croswell's *Wasp* as Washington had been by Bache's *Aurora*. He had once explained that the "moral evils" of newspapers "must be submitted to, like the physical scourges of tempest, fire." But now that Jefferson was the highest-ranking official in the land, he began to believe that he no longer needed to submit. Harry Croswell would stand trial as soon as the authorities could inform him of the charges and hustle him into a courtroom.

And who should elect to defend him, of all the attorneys in the state of New York, of all the experts on and practitioners of journalistic mayhem, but the president's most devoted rival (despite his recent, although watery, backing of Jefferson's candidacy)—who, indeed, but the former secretary of the treasury. It is an even more remarkable turn of events than it seems. In one corner, Thomas Jefferson, who had once glorified freedom of the press as if it were divinely ordained and then laid it aside for no other reason than personal pique and political expediency. In the other corner, Alexander Hamilton, who had promoted the Sedition Act, however reluctantly, a few years earlier, and who had then urged that it be brandished not only against the Connecticut editor Charles Holt for calling attention to Hamilton's adultery but against the editor of another paper, the *Argus*, for claiming that Hamilton had been the brains behind a scheme to buy the *Aurora* and then put it out of business. This very same Alexander Hamilton was now affirming that sedition on the page was protected by the Constitution, perhaps even encouraged by it.

❖

Hamilton began his defense of Croswell by arguing that one person cannot libel another unless he is willfully false and malicious. He argued that if the content of a newspaper story was true, there "is a reason to infer that there was no design to injure another." He argued that libel cases must be decided by a jury, not "a judge appointed by the executive branch, lest the American judiciary revert to the tyranny of the Star Chamber [a notorious British tribunal abolished in the seventeenth century, known for deciding cases without a jury and according to the Crown's whim]."

Summing up, he said to the court, "I never did think the truth was a crime," and this was especially so, Hamilton believed, although he did not say it on this occasion, when the truth could act as a rein on republicans in their attempts to impose tyranny on America. "To watch the progress of such endeavours is the office of a free press. To give us early alarm and put us on our guard against the encroachment of power. This then is a right of the utmost importance, one for which, instead of yielding it up, we ought rather to spill our blood."

It was, by all accounts, a masterly performance on the part of attorney Hamilton, "a most extraordinary effort of human genius," said one who witnessed it. Another courtroom observer swore that Hamilton's eloquence "drew tears from his eyes and . . . from every eye of the numerous audience." A third believed he had heard "the greatest forensic effort that [Hamilton] ever made." One suspects these onlookers of certain federalist sympathies.

The jury, too, was impressed, but not enough to side with the defense. It voted against Hamilton's reasoning, which is to say against Croswell's right to publish what he did. But, in a manner of speaking, although Hamilton lost the case, he won the war, as the judge agreed with him that when a newspaper printed the truth, it could not be guilty of criminal behavior, which is the principle that had been affirmed in the Zenger trial more than half a century earlier and acknowledged in the Sedition Act, one of the provisions of which paid lip service to veracity. Some of Hamilton's standards for libel, as outlined in the Croswell case, were incorporated into law in New York a few years after the verdict, after which Croswell was granted a new trial and this time acquitted of all charges against him.

The reasons for Hamilton's losing the case are complex, and even more difficult to analyze two centuries after the fact. Except, that is, for one reason, one that was obvious at the time and is no less obvious today. It seems that a witness Hamilton had wanted to call in Croswell's defense, a man who would have testified that he had been paid by Jefferson for vilifying federalist causes, thereby proving beyond a doubt the truth of Croswell's accusations and perhaps even swaying the jury, was not able to present himself.

❋

IN A SENSE, James Thomson Callender had become two people since his split with Jefferson. One of them went through the motions of life as often and as conventionally as possible, but sometimes, unable to carry on, stood to the side and watched helplessly as the other spun ever more out of control. He had alienated republicans with his charges against Jefferson, but had not won the approbation of federalists, who still resented him for his earlier rants against Hamilton and Washington and now thought of him not as one of their own, which Callender had so frantically hoped, but as a person who could not be trusted by anyone, a person who would manipulate his pen indiscriminately, reviling at whim.

And it seemed at times that he would. Callender accused George Hay, one of the attorneys who represented him at his Sedition Act trial, of malfeasance in a later case. Hay, incensed, hoped for a chance to avenge himself and then stumbled across it one day when he saw Callender walking down the street. Arming himself with a club of some sort, he trailed Callender for a block or two, perhaps getting up his nerve, perhaps just waiting for the right moment. Then the journalist went into a store. Hay entered behind him and struck viciously, beating Callender in the face and on top of his skull, bloodying his forehead and leaving bruises so deep and colorful that they did not heal for weeks. Some of Hay's blows were deflected by the high hat his victim was wearing; Callender told others the hat had saved his life.

His reputation had received a similar clobbering. "Of all the foreigners who were connected with journalism in the United States at the beginning of the century," says one historian, "James Thomson Callender was easily the first in the worst qualities of mind and character . . . a traitorous and truculent scoundrel . . . [t]he most outrageous and wretched scandalmonger of a scurrilous age."

He began to drink even more than before, eventually reaching a point, according to a contemporary, at which "what is called soberness in him, would make any two men constantly drunk. For at his sober periods, he never gets drunk above once a day, which he will do contentedly, by taking a quart of rum, one hour, and get sober in the next." He was sometimes belligerent in such a state, sometimes morbidly quiet. He would lose the thread of conversations, stare into space, try to focus his eyes on something he could not see. He was, on many days, too drunk to pick up his pen.

But it was worse than that. He had no hope for the future, no prospects for employment beyond menial and transitory work, and perhaps not even that. He had nothing to offer his children, no way to provide for them, not even enough self-respect to visit them in Thomas Leiper's care. Many years later, Jefferson would write of Callender: "He was a poor creature, sensible [i.e., oversensitive], hypocondriac [sic], drunken, penniless & unprincipled."

In the early morning hours of a summer Sunday, a few weeks before the Croswell trial began, Callender was seen wandering about Richmond in a highly inebriated state, listing from side to side, muttering to himself, firmly in the grip of his demons. A few times he almost fell, stumbling into the side of a building, or cursed at someone or something. But this kind of behavior had become a fairly common sight of late; no one who saw him paid much attention. Then he disappeared.

Not long afterward, Callender's body was found floating facedown in the James River. What Meriwether Jones had reluctantly prophesied, or devoutly wished, had come true. But how? Why? What path had led Callender from the street to the bottom of the river? Some people wondered whether he had been attacked by supporters of Jefferson, determined that Callender would turn on the president no more. Others wondered whether a republican was responsible, someone who held a grudge against Callender for his earlier writings.

According to a coroner's jury, Callender was his own perpetrator. The jury ruled the drowning was an accident, brought on by intoxication, and there has never been any evidence to the contrary.

After his death, few people had anything to say about Callender, and fewer still anything nice. Meriwether Jones, of all people, might have come closest. "However barefaced [Callender's] falsehoods, or atrocious the calumnies, they were undeniably dictated with an energy of thought, and expressed with a grace of style which was calculated to make an impression, in proportion to the penetration, impartiality or prejudices of the persons who perused them."

Callender was buried the very day his body was found. A brief announcement appeared in the Richmond papers, but no ceremony was conducted, and there is no record of mourners at graveside or even of a clergyman's having officiated at his burial. "It was as if," writes Michael Durey, "the citizens of Richmond could not wait to destroy all evidence of his existence."

Post-*Script*

*B*Y THIS TIME, to the delight of some and the apprehension of others and the surprise of even more, Alexander Hamilton had started his second newspaper. Washington had wanted nothing to do with the press, John Adams became disenchanted with it, Jefferson remained ambivalent when not actually spiteful, and even Franklin and Sam Adams, two of the most enthusiastic journalists among the founders, had gotten out of the business after a time and taken other paths—and here was Hamilton, well into middle age, with a thriving legal practice demanding his time and presence, returning to the field yet again, raising $10,000 to get paper number two off the ground and into the thick of public dialogue.

His first paper, which was still being published, was not what it used to be. The *Gazette of the United States* had lost its founding editor, then lost the editor's son and successor, the young man who had thrown a punch at Benjamin Franklin Bache and later sold the *Gazette* to the first of a series of others; and, most important, it had lost its passion. Its reporting had become uninspired, its federalism diluted. Some people thought it had simply tried to maintain too high a temperature for too long and, with age, could not help but turn lukewarm.

In truth, though, it was not a good time for any federalist publication. It was not a good time for federalism, period. As Jefferson's election to the presidency had signaled, Americans were beginning to question Hamiltonian notions of centralized power and financial control and industrial growth and planning. And, as Susan Dunn observes, there was a further problem for federalism as the nineteenth century dawned. "The Sedition Act had backfired," she notes, and as a result, "new Republican newspapers were springing up at the grass roots all over the country, from New Hampshire to North Carolina and beyond, openly trumpeting their party loyalty with names like *Herald of Liberty*, *Tree of Liberty*, *Genius of Liberty*, *Rights of Man*, and *Republican Atlas*. There were now two-thirds more Republican newspapers than before the Sedition Act."

Look again at their names; they sound like rallying cries, cheers from the throng at a republican gathering, rather than mere words composing a masthead. No wonder Hamilton felt outmanned and decided that he needed a new journalistic fiefdom, one that would stir the populace at the beginning of the new century as the *Gazette of the United States* had stirred it at the end of the old. So when William Coleman approached him with the idea for the *New-York Evening Post*, Hamilton promised his full support, just as he had done earlier with John Fenno.

Asked to describe his relationship with Hamilton, Coleman replied even more deferentially than Fenno might have. "Whenever anything occurs on which I feel the want of information," he said, "I state matters to [Hamilton], sometimes in a note. He appoints a time when I may see him, usually a late hour in the evening. He always keeps himself minutely informed on all political matters. As soon as I see him, he begins in a deliberate manner to dictate and I to note down in shorthand. When he stops, my article is completed."

Like Hamilton, Coleman was a lawyer with a growing practice and a sound reputation, an intelligent man with a busy schedule but commitment to spare, and he was said to be such a Hamiltonian in outlook that he would one day be referred to by a rival journalist as "the Field Marshall of Federal Editors." His paper would come to be known as "the strongest arm of the Federalist Party." The *New-York Evening Post* published its first issue in November 1801, promising in a front-page prospectus that it would cover only those stories worthy of coverage.

Gazettes, it is seriously to be feared, will not long allow room to any thing that is not loathsome or shocking. A newspaper is pronounced to be very lean and destitute of matter, if it contains no account of murder, suicides, prodigies or monstrous births. Some of these tales excite horror, and others disgust; yet the fashion reigns like a tyrant to relish wonders, and almost to relish nothing else.

The *Evening Post* would relish more substantive matters. It would not be a forerunner of the tabloid press of the nineteenth century's end.

Then Coleman continued in a blaze—or phrase—of disingenuousness.

Persuaded that the great body of the people of this country only want correct information, to enable them to judge of what is really best; and believing that nothing will so directly conduce to this desirable end, as candid and liberal discussion; this paper shall be equally free to all parties. All Communications, therefore, shall be inserted with equal impartiality. . . .

Equal impartiality? Equally free to all parties? Correct information? It was a ringing endorsement of the principles of sound and responsible journalism as we understand them and so appreciate them today, principles that could be emblazoned on the portals of a journalism school or recited as an oath by those entering the field, as physicians recite the Hippocratic Oath.

But Coleman did not really mean it. Such lofty ideals stood no chance against the fundamental and pragmatic ideals he had expressed a few lines earlier, when he admitted that "we openly profess our attachment to that system of politics denominated FEDERAL, because we think it the most conducive to the welfare of the community, and the best calculated to ensure permanency to our present form of government." It would be *un*equal impartiality, equal freedom to *some* parties, correct information *only* when appropriate. It would be, in other words, a typical newspaper of its time.

Coleman would not try to seek a rapprochement between republicans and federalists, as some journals claimed they were doing, their editors believing there was so much hostility between the parties as to make efficient governance impossible. Rather, he would try to restore brotherhood among various factions of the federalists, who had begun to quarrel with one another in the wake of Jefferson's having banished them from the President's House.

> It has been long since observed, that the cause of FEDERAL-ISM has received as much injury from the indiscreet contentions and bickerings among those who profess to be its friends, as from the open assaults of its enemies. . . . With sincerity then the Editor declares that it will always be his wish and endeavor to promote a spirit of harmony and conciliation among those who, forgetful of party distinctions, little rivalships, or unessential shades of opinion, are disposed to unite in their exertions to maintain the CONSTITUTION and LAWS.

It is not certain how much Hamilton wrote for the *New-York Evening Post*, but his articles must have made his old nemesis, the president, look back at the Sedition Act with longing. Hamilton seemed even more vexed by Jefferson now than he had been in the past; he was certainly as dedicated as ever to expressing his frustrations in print. To some extent, one supposes, the explanation for his renewed zeal is jealousy. Once equals in Washington's cabinet, Hamilton was now a lawyer in private practice while Jefferson held the highest office in the land; Hamilton stood on the periphery of events as Jefferson, the captain of the ship of state, steered its course and charted its goals; Hamilton had represented Harry Croswell in court, whereas Jefferson had invoked the law that led to the trial in the first place. It was enough to make old grievances feel new again, and make them fester even more than before. Hamilton could not help but express them.

Signing himself Lucius Crassus, he helped launch the *New-York Evening Post* by writing an eighteen-part series, a virtual encyclopedia, in response to Jefferson's first presidential message to Congress, seeming to find ignorance or treachery or worse in every topic the president raised, and in the process turning out a document far longer than the one it was intended to refute.

Hamilton claimed that Jefferson could not protect the nation should war arise: "The Message of the President, by whatever motives it may have been dictated, is a performance which ought to alarm all who are anxious for the safety of our Government, for the respectability and welfare of our nation. It makes, or aims at making, a most prodigal sacrifice of constitutional energy, of sound principle, and of public interest, to the popularity of one man."

Hamilton swore that Jefferson did not care about the interests of the shopkeeper: "But who and what are the merchants when compared with the patriotic votaries of whiskey in Pennsylvania and Virginia?"

Hamilton declared that Jefferson had been in office too short a time to be making pronouncements of any kind on public policy: "To attempt, therefore, to draw important inferences from the short experience hitherto had, is worse than puerile."

Hamilton believed that Jefferson should just give up and turn the President's House over to a federalist, or at least a more erudite republican, if there was such a thing: "But vain will be the attempt to add lustre to the dim luminary of a benighted administration!"

In a number of its early issues, the *New-York Evening Post* published letters that provided their own criticisms of the president, not only encouraging such correspondence but soliciting it. The following, addressed to Jefferson and originally appearing in a Georgia paper, had nothing to do with the concerns of men and women in New York. But since it opposed one of the president's judicial appointments, the *Evening Post* was pleased to reprint it.

SIR

So much has been written on the inconsistency of your conduct, that it is unpleasant to add any thing more, but your appointment of William Stephens to the office of District Judge for the District of Georgia, is such an indelicate procedure . . . that I cannot but enquire whether in the filling of this office, "time was taken, information was sought, and such obtained as could leave no room to doubt of his fitness."—Sir, until you return to that state of things, when the only questions concerning a candidate shall be, is he honest, is he capable, is he faithful to the constitution? and while you are lessening private distress by extending your correctives to anti-revolutionary adherence to our enemies, it is proper you should be in this manner informed [reminded] of the public characters of men, that you put in office, and their delinquency. . . .

Where Jefferson was concerned, Hamilton seemed possessed by the spirit of the late, unlamented James Thomson Callender.

❁

BY THE STANDARDS OF THE TIME, the *New-York Evening Post* was an influential paper; in fact, it is the only journal of the early nineteenth century that is still publishing today, although it long ago dropped the "evening" from its name. But the standards of the time were different from what they had been a few decades earlier—when the Stamp Act was passed, when more than 300 chests of tea were dumped into Boston Harbor, when the shots were fired at Concord and Lexington. Which is to say that influence was not so influential anymore—not influence of the journalistic variety, at any rate. As the United States was becoming a larger and more powerful nation, the importance of its newspapers was beginning to shrink.

It might have been that the crucial issues of the day, such as the role of a national bank in America's future and the terms of westward expansion, were more nuanced than they had been earlier, not as clearly defined in terms of Whigs versus Tories and thus not lending themselves as readily to simplification and bombast by the press. It might have been that with the government more settled, more of a reliable institution than it had been a decade earlier, those same issues appeared less in the control of journalists now and more in the hands of legislators. It might have been, with the nation seeming almost daily to be adding new industries and pastimes, new states and territories, new institutions and traditions—in other words, with changes coming so rapidly and dramatically that Americans could not be assured of their own places in their own country anymore—they had less time for journalism now; like the men and women of ages past, they were consumed by the goals and interests and fears of their own, not those of the broader society. Or it might have been that with an expanding population moving westward at so frantic a pace, newspapers could not keep up; as the populations they served kept shifting, the impact of any given paper on any given community could not help but be weakened.

It would not be until much later in the century, when men like Joseph Pulitzer and James Gordon Bennett Jr. and William Randolph Hearst were the nation's press barons and their journalism was a bright and shocking yellow, a catalog of crimes unspeakable and lust uncontrollable, of violence and hardship and aberration, of derring-do and villainy, of freaks of nature and freaks of occurrence, of the very kinds of stories that the *New-York Evening Post* had promised to eschew—not until then would Americans again pay attention to their papers as they had in the years leading up to and following their independence from Britain, although now they would be amusing themselves, seeking distraction more than information, entertainment more than a grounding and currency in public affairs.

❁

THE PAPERS CHANGED WITH THE TIMES, but slowly. Some of them began to separate fact and opinion, or to attempt to do so, but the process would not be complete for many years, and some would argue that it remains incomplete today. Some papers began to publish more often; some added more pages; some made themselves more appealing to the eye, dolling themselves up with more illustrations, more styles and sizes of type. Some would run ads that were larger and more compelling than they used to be, small works of art in themselves. Some hired additional reporters, giving them areas of specialization: the police beat, the local government beat, the shipping and trade beat. Some occasionally sent their reporters abroad to cover a war or a coronation and thus get their foreign news firsthand. As the technology of printing improved, a few papers began to turn a decent profit, some of them turning large profits, enabling a printer who owned one paper to buy another, and then more after that. And some began to broaden their scope, to devote space to the popular culture as well as to politics and crime and foreign affairs. Benjamin Franklin would surely have approved.

Hamilton's *New-York Evening Post*, for instance, became one of the first American papers to review plays on a regular basis. An early review considered *Fortune's Frolic*, in which a certain Mrs. Hodgkinson "filled the character of Amelia with much Success." As for Mr. Martin, another cast member, he "made a very decent Minister, but rather a cold Lover." And then there was Mr. Tyler, who, "had he been perfect in his part, wou'd have claimed much approbation." A month later, the paper sent its arts man to a concert, where he found a certain Mr. Gautier worthy of "particular mention: The piece he chose was, indeed, charming, and his execution astonishing. When he came to the *adagio*, we saw 'the tear of rapture on the cheek of beauty.'"

American newspapers continued, of course, to report the major events of the day, the stories that would end up in the history books. In the first few decades of the nineteenth century, they told of the

Louisiana Purchase and the first voyage of Robert Fulton's steamboat on the Hudson River and the War of 1812 and the Missouri Compromise. They told of the Monroe Doctrine and the removal of Indian tribes from the eastern United States to encampments west of the Mississippi River and the construction of the Erie Canal. And they told, in sometimes wondering detail, of Andrew Jackson's presidency, which was the end of the old Massachusetts-Virginia aristocracy in American politics, and of Jackson's campaign against the Bank of the United States, which seemed to many the final repudiation of Alexander Hamilton's brand of federalism.

And, earlier in the century, much earlier, the newspapers had reported another important story, one that would have fit as nicely into the sensationalized journalism of the century's end. The federalist press reported it with more feeling than the republican journals, and the *New-York Evening Post* reported it with the most feeling of all. Yet it was a story the *Evening Post* did not want to report and was in fact astonished to report, a black-bordered story that appeared the day after Alexander Hamilton, whose son had died in a duel a few years earlier, and Aaron Burr stood facing each other on a bluff in New Jersey. They overlooked the Hudson River, their seconds standing by. They waited for a signal.

For a number of reasons, both political and personal, the two men had never cared for each other. Hamilton's efforts on behalf of Jefferson rather than Burr in the presidential campaign of 1800 might have been the last straw. Which is to say that Hamilton's single show of support for the man who was otherwise his most consistent and vexing enemy may well have gotten him killed.

The signal came. Hamilton and Burr fired their pistols. The *Evening Post* told the story as best it could.

With emotions that we have not the hand to inscribe, have we to announce the death of ALEXANDER HAMILTON. He was cut off in the 48th year of his age, in the full vigor of his faculties, and in the midst of all his usefulness.

We have not the firmness to depict this melancholy, heart-rending event. Now—when death has extinguished all party animosity, the gloom that over spreads every countenance, the sympathy that pervades every bosom, bear irresistible testimony of the esteem and respect all maintained for him, of the love all bore him; and assure us that an impression has been made by his loss which no time can efface. . . .

As soon as our feelings will permit, we shall deem it a duty to present a sketch of the character of our ever-to-be-lamented patron and best friend.

Alexander Hamilton's death was a landmark in the history of American journalism, one that has gone largely unacknowledged. It took the soul out of the federalist press and the animus out of the republican, the one having lost its guiding spirit and the other its most frequent and influential target. There was no man of similar stature to replace Hamilton as the dark prince of all things republican, no foe so worthy of invective, no scourge so deserving of eradication in print. In fact, it was to some extent because of Hamilton that the republican press existed in the first place, as a response to the federalist press, which he also helped bring into being.

And so, however indirectly, however inadvertently, however tragically, Hamilton's death led to yet another change in the journalism of the United States: a less contentious, more civil tone. It was, like the separating of fact and opinion, the most gradual of processes, with a good many false steps or backward steps and roaring exceptions. But a more civil tone came in time and remains with us to the present, no matter how inclined we are to think otherwise when we read certain newspapers or Web sites, when we watch certain all-news talk shows, or when we listen to certain verbal mud wrestlers on the radio. Alexander Hamilton's passing was the beginning of the end of an era.

For the most part, we Americans have thrived on what the

Founding Fathers left us. We have accepted the ideals of the Declaration of Independence, the structures and guidelines of the Constitution, the code of conduct that is the Bill of Rights. And we have appreciated the examples that the founders provided, examples that have not been the focus of the present volume, but which are in many ways noble and admirable: Washington's dignity and leadership, Franklin's charm and practicality and ecumenical erudition, Hamilton's ambition and farsightedness, Jefferson's eloquence and love of learning, John Adams's sense of duty and firmness of purpose.

But we have not adopted their style of journalism. We do not, in most of our print and broadcast news sources, impugn character as they did. We do not, except in extraordinary cases, use the kind of language they did. We do not, except on well-publicized and well-punished occasions, make up the news to suit our ideology. It is a rare example of our turning our backs on the Founding Fathers, finding them unworthy, rejecting their legacy.

We are to be commended.

EPILOGUE

Renewed Subscriptions

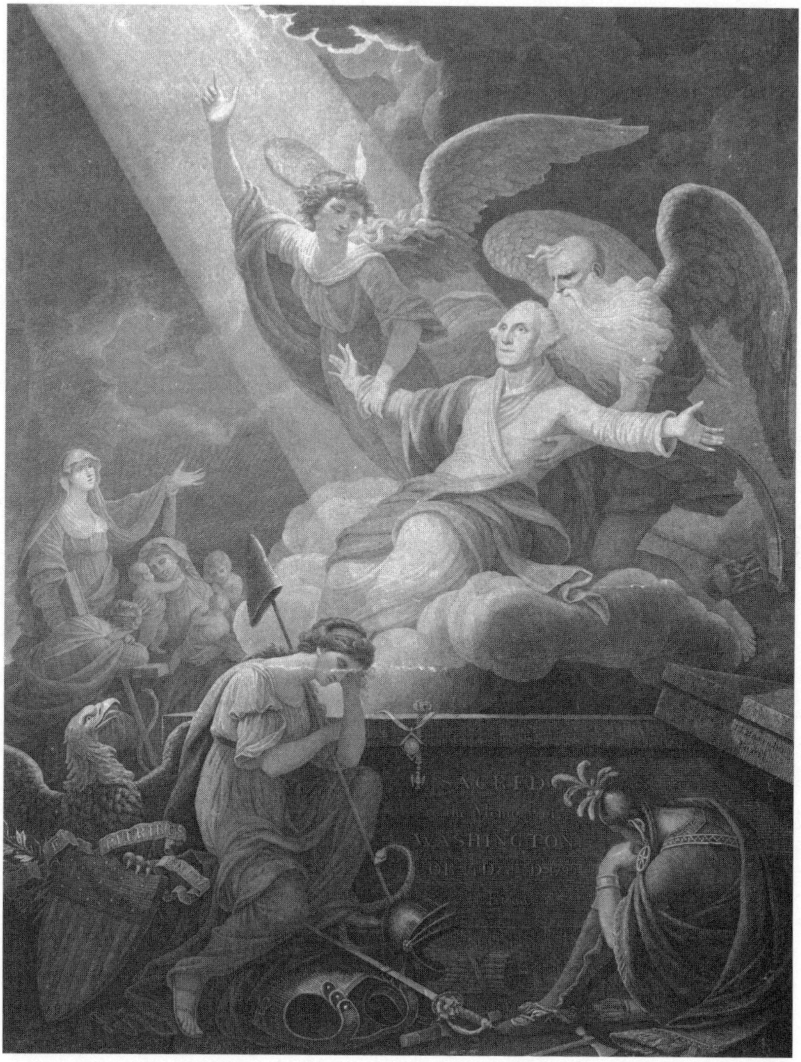

*T*HE MOST FAMOUS OF THE FOUNDERS, the first to be stretched across the rack of American journalism and feel the rollers turn, and perhaps the only one who never wrote a word specifically intended for a newspaper, had died five years before Hamilton.

It was an "afflicting" event, said the *Gazette of the United States* about George Washington's passing; a "melancholy event," said *Russell's Gazette*; and cause for "poignant grief," according to the *Massachusetts Mercury*. It must be considered a "calamity," wrote the *Columbian Centinel*, which then went on to acknowledge "that vast debit of gratitude due to the late pre-eminently, illustrious Deceased." The following week, the *Centinel* declared that Washington's death "filled the hearts of all virtuous people in the *United States* with the sincerest affliction."

And the *Aurora*, with one final chance to look back on Washington's career and repudiate all that he stood for, chose instead to publish a last, and lasting, and perhaps even to some extent sincere, tribute: "As we can offer no higher Eulogium to the memory of a character elevated by fortune, talents, and the voice of his country to so high a station among the benefactors of mankind—we confine ourselves to that alone, recommending the principles for which he fought with so much honor to himself and his fellow citizens, and to the freedom of his country to the careful and stedfast conservation of those who survive him."

❀

WASHINGTON'S LIFE WAS DIFFERENT after returning to his Mount Vernon estate in 1787. He had worked hard, just as he had as a soldier and a statesman, but there were no political upheavals on a farm. He had worked long, but there were no journalists peeking over fences to critique him, demanding a greater crop yield or more production from his herds, questioning his treatment of his field hands and the motives behind it. And he had worked productively, concentrating on matters directly at hand; after all, it no longer fell to him to monitor the behavior of Hamilton and Jefferson, to try to keep them either silent or apart. He had yearned for Mount Vernon during his days as commander in chief and president, and now that he was back, he had determined never to subject himself to the scrutiny of public life again.

Most mornings Washington would rise with the first rays of the sun. After breakfast, he would inspect his grounds on horseback, tending to all manner of chores: "ordering drainage ditches to be widened, inspecting the operation of a new distillery he had recently constructed on the premises, warning poachers that the deer on his property had become domesticated and must not be hunted, inquiring after a favored house slave who had recently been bitten by a mad dog."

By midafternoon he was once again at the main house and dressed for dinner, usually served at three. There was always company. Sometimes he and his family were joined by friends, and more often than not by a small contingent of strangers who had appeared at his gate without invitation, men and women and children who regarded Washington as a tourist attraction and were hoping for a glimpse or even an opportunity to thank him for all he had done for the nation. Washington would invite them in, allow them to stay. It was considered common courtesy at the time. If people had made a journey to express their gratitude, perhaps standing outside for several hours waiting for admittance, Washington believed he could do no less than offer his hospitality.

After eating, he would remain with his visitors for a while, perhaps showing them some of the military medals he had won over the years and giving them details of the battles, perhaps just strolling with them through the house and outbuildings and along the banks of the Potomac—a tour guide at his own residence. The conversation was not animated, not particularly stimulating; talking had never been what Washington did best. But people wanted to know what he thought, whether about a decision of his presidency or a choice he had made more recently about which of his acres to devote to which crops. And they did not care how expressive he was; they just wanted to hear the sound of his voice, the tones that had once commanded an army and a nation, and had inspired a free press to respond so freely.

By late afternoon, Washington had said good-bye to his guests and would spend the next two hours or so tending to his correspondence, writing letters to friends or creditors, or, as Joseph J. Ellis informs us, "reading one or more of the ten newspapers to which he subscribed."

The number must have surprised even Washington. On first retiring, he had canceled all his subscriptions; he wanted no more journalism either in his abode or on his mind, no more challenges to his contentment or to his reputation. For a few months, he seems to have been pleased.

Although Washington might not have had the desire to manage events anymore, neither did he care to be ignorant of them. He could not rely on his visitors, who were always a random grouping, to keep him up-to-date on what was happening in the world, nor on his correspondents to know which of those happenings were of most interest to him. For all of the press's imperfections, all of its distortions, all of its rancor and rowdyism and bias, there seemed no choice but to start the papers coming again, despite the fact that, according to John Tebbel and Sarah Miles Watts, he "found them as irritating, partisan, and unreliable as ever."

Then: Tea at seven, some time with his wife and perhaps a close friend or two at eight, bedtime at nine.

❁

DECEMBER 12, 1799, was a day like most of the others in his retirement, except for the weather: there were ice-crusted mounds of snow on the ground when he awoke, and a cold sleet had begun to fall and would not let up as the day wore on and the sky turned ever grayer. Washington should have stayed inside; he did not. At the least, he should have changed his routine; he did not do that either. Instead he rode for five hours, from one end of his property to the other, and then returned to the house, where he did not do something else he should have done: go immediately to his room for some dry clothes. Instead, he sat for dinner; his guests were already at the table and he did not think it polite to make them wait.

The next day was as cold and icy as its predecessor. "Morning snowing and about three inches deep," Washington wrote in his journal. "Wind at northeast and mercury at 30. Continuing snowing till one o'clock, and about four it became perfectly clear." At that point, Washington went outside, dispensing with his usual rounds but still spending an hour or two marking some trees that he wanted chopped down. He had awakened with a thick head and a hoarse throat; when he got back to the house, he was feeling worse. A servant summoned Washington's doctor, who in turn called for the assistance of two other physicians.

But the trio was stumped. Did their patient have pneumonia, acute tonsillitis, a severe inflammation of the throat? Was it something else that they could not even identify? They knew only that what had laid Washington low was serious, and a serious attempt at a cure was required. So they withdrew their blades from their bags and started bleeding him. According to one account, more than five pints of blood were taken from the patient that day; the doctors hoped they contained all of what ailed him.

Later, William Cobbett, the Porcupine, would hear of the doctors' actions and, horrified, write that they were "in precise conformity to *the practice of Rush*!"

❁

GEORGE WASHINGTON WOULD DIE on the night of December 14. But the previous evening, somehow managing to rally, he had sat up talking with his wife, Martha, and a few friends, among them his secretary, Tobias Lear. Shortly before he went to bed, Lear would later write, Washington was "reading the papers. He was very cheerful; and when he met with anything which he thought diverting or interesting, he would read it aloud as well as his hoarseness would permit."

More often, though, what he found did not please him. He grimaced at what he believed to be the journalists' misunderstanding of events, shook his head at what he thought of as the papers' misrepresentation of a good man's deeds, perhaps even stifled a curse or two at the press's continuing encouragement of ill will and abiding resentment.

After a while, Martha excused herself for bed. Washington, also tiring, indicated that he would soon join her. In the meantime, he asked Lear to read him an article from one of the papers that told of Monroe's intention to become a senator and Madison's attempts to help him. It was the last brush with journalism that George Washington would ever have and, said Lear, he was not pleased; in fact, he "spoke with some degree of asperity." He did not think much of Monroe. He did not approve of Madison's support for him. He wondered why the journalists who wrote about them did not know the men as he did, did not realize both their strengths and shortcomings, the occasional narrowness of their visions.

He could not understand, in other words, not on this penultimate day of his life and after so many years of trying, why infamous scribblings continued to fill the columns of America's newspapers, deceiving all who read them and frustrating the purposes of those who attempted to govern wisely.

NOTES

❀

Introduction: Inappropriate Behavior

3   "taking a line," Ellis, *Excellency*, p. 231.

4   "sublime terms," and "radiance of virtue," quoted in *Aurora*, March 13, 1798.

5   "plantations of religion," *Religion and the Founding of the American Republic*, "Part I. America as a Religious Refuge: The Seventeenth Century," Library of Congress, http://www.loc.gov/exhibits/religion/rel01.html.

5–6   "a moral sanction," *Religion and the Founding of the American Republic*, "Part III. Religion and the American Revolution," Library of Congress, http://www.loc.gov/exhibits/religion/rel03.html.

5–6   "sacred cement," and "*Families* are the *Nurseries*," quoted in Schlesinger, *Birth*, p. 17.

6   "usually an indigent widow," ibid., pp. 148–9.

7   "between 1640 and 1700," and "is estimated to have run, Postman, *Amusing*, pp. 31–2.

7   "mental furniture," "enormities of the times," and "the delightful pursuit of knowledge," quoted in Burns, *Joy*, p. 137.

7   "But above all," quoted in ibid., p. 138.

7   "read a considerable amount," and "hardly light fare," Chernow, p. 110.

7   "five books—military," quoted in Flexner, *Forge*, p. 335.

8   "the graceful motion," quoted in *International Encyclopedia of Dance*. New York: Oxford University Press, 1988.

8   "healthy exercise," quoted in Burstein, p. 93.

8   "foul-mouthed impertinence," quoted in Schlesinger, *Prelude*, p. 134.

8   "Tom S**t," *New-York Journal*, September 20, 1787.

9   "It was mass calamities," Schlesinger, *Birth*, p. 115.

11   "were very rough," Fisher, p. 97.

11   "incendiary, prostituted," *Newport Mercury*, November 22, 1774.

11   "If ever a nation," *Aurora*, December 23, 1796.

12 "[t]he memory of this scoundrel," quoted in Tebbel, p. 68.

12 "*Influenced neither by,*" and "*the most impartial accounts,*" quoted in Schlesinger, *Prelude*, p. 188.

12 "Free and impartial," quoted in ibid., p. 214.

12 "Professions of impartiality," and "crafty and lecherous," *Porcupine's Gazette*, March 4, 1797.

14 "Here various news we tell," *Connecticut Bee*, March 26, 1800.

Chapter One: The End of the Beginning

20 "there was the broadside," Ackroyd, p. 174.

20 "running patterers," and "take up positions," ibid., p. 175.

20 "public noises," quoted in Darnton, p. 27.

21 "the 'pitilesse' Sir John Fites," and "Split, split," Stephens, p. 2.

21 "Renaissance blackmailer," Brookhiser, *Hamilton*, p. 159.

21 "produced a regular series," Postman, *Bridge*, 59.

24 "Medieval man could eat," Durant, *Faith*, p. 622.

25 "threaten to overwhelm," Simon, Linda, p. 46.

25 "[t]rade, commerce and industry," Kobre, *American*, p. 6.

26–27 "In the early days," Kobre, *Colonial, p. 3.*

28 "He was a bigot," Tebbel, p. 12.

28 "a rabid anti-Catholic," Stephens, p. 184.

28 "mercury in his blood," quoted in Kobre, *Colonial*, p. 13.

28 "the worst man in the world," quoted in Payne, p. 14.

29 "[I]t is safe to say," Tebbel, p. 12.

29 "*Indians* and *French*," and "The chief discourse," *Publick Occurrences*, September 25, 1690.

30 "Memorable Occurents," and "*Circumstances of Publique Affairs,*" *Publick Occurrences*, ibid.

30 "*[t]hat some thing may be done,*" ibid.

30 "malicious raiser," and "*It is Suppos'd,*" ibid.

30 "*if any Glut of* Occurrences," ibid.

30 "The Christianized *Indians*," ibid.

31 "the kidnapping of two children," ibid.

31 "miserable Salvages," ibid.

31 "Two *English Captives*," and "cut the faces," ibid.

31 "having newly buried his wife," and "But one evening," ibid.

31 "used to lie with," ibid.

31 "did not like [their] tone," Kobre, *Colonial*, p. 16.

32 "The Governour and Council," quoted in Copeland, p. 5.

33 "stands out as the first," Solomon, p. 14.

33 "is so far from," quoted in Tebbel, p. 14.

33 "spent his last years," Mott, p. 10.

Chapter Two: Publishing by Authority

36 "[t]here is none," and "timid," Payne, p. 26.

36 "puny and uninteresting," ibid., p. 27.

36 "terse and drab," Kobre, *American*, p. 18.

36 "designed more to survive," Stephens, p. 184.

36 "a monument of dullness," Solomon, p. 15.

36 "Boston's sour-faced Scottish postmaster," Tebbel, 15.

37 "shipping and governmental news," Kobre, *American*, p. 16.

38 "Letters from great *Poland*," and "Letters from *Turkey*," *Boston News-Letter*, April 24–31, 1704.

38 "Popish ministers," quoted in Kobre, *Colonial*, p. 19.

39 "*Philadelphia, May 3d*," *Boston News-Letter*, May 7–14, 1705.

39 "the great industry," ibid., October 15–22, 1705.

39 "The entire contents," Mott, p. 11.

40 "The Humble Address," *Boston News-Letter*, May 8–15, 1704.

40 "twopence a copy," Mott, p. 12.

40 "This News-Letter," *Boston News-Letter*, May 1–8, 1704.

41 "Your Majesties," ibid., May 8–15, 1704.

41 "under the thumb," Kobre, *American*, p. 16.

42 "I thank God," quoted in ibid., p. 6.

42 "Lost on the 10.," "several sorts," and "a very good Fulling-Mill, *Boston News-Letter*, May 1–8, 1704.

43 "*a young man named* William Rogers," ibid., April 23–30, 1705.

43 "Two Negro Men," ibid., May 22–29, 1704.

43 "a likely Negro Boy and Girl," *Boston Gazette*, May 15, 1750.

43–44 "a Negro Man Servant," ibid., November 24, 1747.

44 "I have reason to suspect," ad reprinted in Rice, p. 93.

45 "shippers who had room," Kobre, *American*, p. 14.

45 "offered a remedy," quoted in Solomon, pp. 21–22.

46 "supplied them conscientiously," *Boston News-Letter*, August 10, 1719.

46 "the tendency to exalt," Payne, p. 28.

47 "I pity the reader," *Boston News-Letter*, December 28, 1719.

47 "small, simple, and bland affairs," Wood, p. 20.

47 "It is hard to know," ibid., p. 21.

47 "*Letters from Moscow*," quoted in Bowen, p. 4.

50 "We Desire those Gentlemen," *American Weekly Mercury*, February 23, 1720.

50 "We have little News," quoted in Mott, p. 56.

51 "Criticized by an anti-Methodist," Solomon, p. 22.

51 "Brings Men of Merit," quoted in Schlesinger, *Prelude*, pp. 59–60.

Chapter Three: Defying Authority

54 "out of kindness," *New England Courant*, August 7–14, 1721.

54 "dull vehicle of intelligence," and "that nothing here shall be inserted," ibid.

54 "Jack of all Trades," *Boston News-Letter*, August 21–28, 1721.

55 "the first fighting, rebellious periodical," Kobre, *American*, p. 21.

55 "a searing indictment," Bailyn, p. 36.

55 "is now very much abated," *Publick Occurrences*, September 25, 1690.

56 "Profane and Promiscuous Dancing," quoted in Grant, p. 19.

56 "While displaying the neatness," Silverman, p. 8.

56 "reprov[ed] smutty talk," ibid., p. 198.

57 "received a prick," Grant, p. 47.

57 "drew up an address," Silverman, p. 338.

58 "by teaching and practicing," "the practice," and "profoundly ignorant," *New England Courant*, August 7–14, 1721.

58 "Impostumations," ibid., August 14–21, 1721.

59 "James Franklin knew," Brands, p. 24.

59 "wicked Libel," *Boston Gazette*, January 24, 1721.

59 "Notorious, Scandalous paper," "Flagicious and Wicked Paper," and "full-freighted with Nonsence," *Boston News-Letter*, August 28, 1721.

60 "*many curses,*" and "*The Lord will smite,*" quoted in Silverman, p. 358.

60 "This heinous Charge," and "to make me an Object," *New England Courant*, November 27–December 4, 1721.

60 "COTTON MATHER," quoted in Silverman, p. 350.

61 "Thanks be to GOD," *Boston Gazette*, July 31, 1721.

61 "precocious, curious, and special," Isaacson, *American*, p. 82.

63 "'Tis thought he will sail," and "This Pride of Apparel," *New England Courant*, June 4–11, 1722.

63 "I had the management," Franklin, p. 27.

64 "Wonder on the Stupidity," *New England Courant*, July 23–30, 1722.

64 "They have the Blaze," January 7–14, 1723.

64 "The highest Pitch," and "the greatest Ignorance," ibid., June 15–22, 1723.

64 "to mock religion," and "James Franklyn, the printer," quoted in Brands, p. 31.

65 "BOSTON: Printed and sold," *New England Courant*, February 4–11, 1723.

66 "The February 11, 1723, issue," Brands, p. 31.

Chapter Four: The Sounds of Silence Dogood

68 "readily obey," "shall not commit," and "procure and provide," *This Indenture*. Philadelphia: The Franklin Court Printing Office and Bindery, 2004.

68 "obscure," Franklin, p. 7.

68 "gave up all the coins," Isaacson, *American*, p. 17

68–69 "was employed in cutting Wick," Franklin, p. 11.

69 "Bookish Inclination," ibid., p. 17.

69 "was either generally," and "Tho' a brother," ibid., p. 26.

72 "was employ'd to carry," ibid., p. 25.

72–73 "The New-Year verses," *Pennsylvania Gazette*, January 1, 1772.

73 "proposed for London," Isaacson, *American*, p. 26.

74 "It is my Custom," quoted in Ross, ed., p. 172.

74 "perfected," and "His prose style," *Benet's Reader's Encyclopedia*. New York: Harper & Row, 1987, p. 9.

74–75 "he reproduced pages," Bowen, p. 18.

75 "By comparing my work," Franklin, p. 21.

75 "There is no Humour," quoted in Stephens, p. 13.

76 "Will you hear of a bloody battle," quoted in Brands, p. 23.

76 "wretched Stuff," Franklin, p. 19.

77 "It may not be improper," *New England Courant*, April 2–9, 1722.

77 "untainted with vice," ibid.

77–78 "took a more than ordinary delight," "enable[d] the mind," "all sorts of needle-work," and "spending my leisure," ibid.

78 "that he liked to do his writing," Bowen, p. 19.

78–79 "I am apt to fancy," *New England Courant*, June 25–July 2, 1722.

79 "[N]one were named," Franklin, p. 26.

79 "Without freedom of thought," *New England Courant*, June 25–July 2, 1722.

80 "It has been for some time," ibid., July 23–30, 1722.

80 "fraternal tyranny," quoted in Morgan, p. 17.

80 "probably with reason," Franklin, p. 26.

80 "extreamly amiss," ibid., p. 26.

81 "ought to be remembered," Isaacson, *American*, p. 22.

81 "set an example," and "was the most important," ibid., p. 34.

81 "When he found," Franklin, pp. 28–9.

82 "I sold some of my books," ibid., p. 29.

82 "James Franklin, printer in Queen Street," *New England Courant*, September 23–30, 1723.

Chapter Five: Science, Sex, and Super Crown Soap

84 "physically striking," Isaacson, *American*, p. 37.

84 "I was in my Working Dress," Franklin, p. 34.

84–85 "several Gentlemen," and "had so wretchedly performed," *Pennsylvania Gazette*, October 1, 1728.

85 "is not so easy an Undertaking," ibid.

86 "what *they think* their right," quoted in Wright, p. 75.

86 "*Algebra*, or the Doctrine of Equations," *Pennsylvania Gazette*, October 1, 1728.

86 "that the material cause," ibid., December 15, 1737.

86 "a Monster which has introduced," ibid., July 11, 1729.

86 "to join the rationalists," Kobre, *American*, p. 32.

87 "caught napping," *Pennsylvania Gazette*, June 17, 1731.

87 "made an agreement," ibid., June 24, 1731.

87 "We are credibly informed," ibid., July 29, 1731.

87 "rather raunchy young publisher," Isaacson, *Reader*, p. 64.

87–88 "Of their Chloes," quoted in ibid., p. 123.

88 "Can it be a crime," quoted in ibid., p. 128.

88 "The Duty of the first," quoted in ibid., p. 129.

88 "induced one of her Judges," quoted in ibid., p. 128.

91 "scraps of fire," *Pennsylvania Gazette*, February 4, 1731.

91–92 "scurrilous and defamatory," and "To determine whether I should publish," quoted in Isaacson, *American*, p. 67.

92 "chemical and galenical medicines," and "two young likely Negro men," quoted in Brands, p. 118.

93 "JUST IMPORTED," quoted in ibid., p. 60.

93–94 "UNDERSTANDING 'tis a current Report," *Pennsylvania Gazette*, December 30, 1736.

94 "drew up typically detailed procedures," Isaacson, *American*, p. 157.

94 "not to discourage the Spreading," Boorstin, *Colonial*, p. 338.

95–96 "Being frequently censured," *Pennsylvania Gazette*, June 10, 1731.

Chapter Six: The End of Authority

98 "a lazy, lecherous, dissolute man," Tebbel, p. 23.

98 "He was mean spirited," quoted in Putnam, p. 23.

100 "a Fort, impregnable," *New-York Weekly Journal*, November 5, 1733.

100 "public display," ibid., p. 23.

101 "[t]he Liberty of the Press," *New-York Weekly Journal*, November 12, 1733.

101 "monkeys," "spaniels," quoted in Alexander, James, p. 9.

101 "directed a stream," Tebbel, p. 24.

102 "Some have said," *New-York Weekly Journal*, December 10, 1733.

102 "SCHEMES OF GENERAL OPPRESSION," "INSTRUMENTS OF PUBLICK RUIN," and "have generally at once," ibid., January 28, 1734.

102 "Cosby *the Mild*," *New-York Gazette*, December 31, 1732–January 7, 1733.

103 "a Nullity of Laws," and "The Support of Government," *New-York Weekly Journal*, September 23, 1734.

103 "Scandalous, Virulent, and Seditious Reflections," quoted in Payne, p. 50.

103 "Wicked Authors," quoted in Putnam, p. 61.

104 *"To all my Subscribers,"* *New-York Weekly Journal*, November 25, 1734.

105 "In the height of summer," Putnam, p. 70.

105 "seditious Libels," quoted in Mott, p. 33.

105 "legal and oratorical brilliance," Kobre, *Colonial*, p. 66.

106 "The Greater the Truth," quoted in ibid., p. 66.

106 "[a]nd that is a matter of law," quoted in Putnam, p. 116.

106–107 "The question before the Court," quoted in Payne, p. 53.

107 "Power may be justly compared," quoted in Mott, pp. 36–7.

107 "the best cause," quoted in Payne, pp. 54–5.

108 "The reception of the verdict," Putnam, p. 116.

108 "[T]he jury having taken," *New-York Weekly Journal*, August 18, 1735.

109 "so greedily read," *Pennsylvania Gazette*, May 11, 1738.

109 "he was saluted," *New-York Weekly Journal*, August 18, 1735.

110 "The independence of the jury," Wishman, p. 206.

Chapter Seven: Severing the Snake

116 "Party-disputes," "Accounts of Remarkable Trials," "Collections and Abstracts," and "As several Colonies," *American Magazine, or A*

Monthly View of the Political State of the British Colonies, February 1741.

117 "as entertaining and useful," *General Magazine and Historical Chronicle for all the British Plantations in America*, February 1741.

117 *"Brief Historical," "Proceedings in the Parliament,"* and *"Account of the Export,"* ibid.

118 "the *New York Journal* had 1500," and "the *Massachusetts Gazette*," Schlesinger, *Prelude*, p. 303.

119 "'Tis truth," *New York Gazette, or, The Weekly Post-Boy*, April 16, 1770.

119 "Our services," *New-York Journal*, April 19, 1770.

121 "many more French," "the present disunited State," and "JOIN OR DIE," *Pennsylvania Gazette*, May 9, 1754.

123 "assessed a halfpenny," Schlesinger, *Prelude*, p. 68.

123 "fatal *Black-Act*," quoted in Stephens, p. 187.

123 "the sums involved," Bailyn, p. 100.

124 "daze and indecision," Schlesinger, *Prelude*, p. 69.

124 "had not only a respect," quoted in Ferling, *Leap*, p. 27.

124 "I think [the Stamp Act] will affect," quoted in Schlesinger, *Prelude*, p. 69.

124 "The Stamp Act wholly cancels," quoted in Bobrick, p. 75.

124 "taking from the poorer sort," quoted in Bailyn, pp. 101–2.

125 "[t]he Stamp Act engrosses," quoted in Bobrick, p. 76.

125 "A New York crowd," Ferling, *Leap, p. 35.*

125 *"I must die,"* *New Hampshire Gazette*, October 31, 1765.

125 "AWAKE!—Awake, my countrymen," *Boston Gazette*, October 7, 1765.

125 "Alas! What have we done," *New York Mercury*, October 28, 1763.

126 "Saturday last," *Boston Evening-Post*, November 4, 1765.

126 "without certain Destruction," *New York Gazette, or, The Weekly Post-Boy*, December 12, 1765.

126 "[i]f a newspaper were published," Tebbel, pp. 35–6.

126 *"No Stamped Paper to be had,"* quoted in Schlesinger, *Prelude*, p. 78.

126–127 "EXPIRING: IN THE HOPES," *Pennsylvania Journal*, October 31, 1765.

127 "[a]n Apparition," quoted in Mott, p. 74.

128 "every falshood," quoted in Schlesinger, *Prelude*, p. 72.

128 "the many Seditious," quoted in ibid., p. 75.

128 *"excluded every thing,"* quoted in ibid., p. 76.

128 "GLORIOUS NEWS," quoted in Kobre, *Colonial*, p. 112.

128 "the inexpressible Joy of all," *Boston Post-Boy & Advertiser*, May 26, 1766.

129 "His Majesty seemed," *Newport Mercury*, May 19, 1766.

129 "There is no doubt," *Virginia Gazette*, May 23, 1766.

129 "[t]he press hath never done," *New Hampshire Gazette*, April 11, 1766.

130 "once again placing itself," Davis, p. 46.

131 "Duty on Tea," quoted in Ferling, *Leap*, p. 87.

131 "Miss Grace Coit," *New London Gazette*, June 16, 1769.

131 "a very inoffensive man," ibid., January 23, 1767.

131 "ascended to the skies," *Rivington's New-York Gazetteer*, April 22, 1773.

131–132 "letters in the sense," McDougall, p. 219.

132 "one of the few," Ferling, *Leap*, p. 69.

132 "I have looked over," Dickinson (Letter II), pp. 13–16.

132 "an innovation," ibid., (Letter II), p. 18.

132 "to convince the people," ibid., (Letter III), p. 29.

132 "[n]o free people ever existed," ibid., (Letter IX), p. 87.

133 "For my part," ibid., (Letter XII), pp. 145–6.

133 "were gathered and issued," Ferling, *Leap*, p. 70.

133–134 "The colonists lived," Kobre, *Colonial*, p. 102.

134 "strike while the iron is hot," quoted in Schlesinger, *Prelude*, p. 192.

134 "patriarch of liberty," quoted in ibid., p. 219.

Chapter Eight: "The Weekly Dung Barge"

136 "*the killing of Wolves*," and "shall be intitled," *Boston Gazette*, December 25, 1753.

136 "the most radical newspaper," quoted in Alexander, John K., p. 28.

137 "[T]hose trumpeters of sedition," quoted in Tebbel, p. 38.

137 "spit their venom," quoted in Canfield, p. 10.

137 "The Weekly Dung Barge," quoted in Tebbel, p. 38.

137 "were to destroy," Kobre, *American*, p. 75.

138 "whether it be lawful," quoted in Tindall, p. 182.

139 "had no trouble separating," Langguth, p. 32.

139 "an impressive sum," Alexander, John K., pp. 3–4.

140 "the steps of the law," quoted in Beach, p. 60.

140 "assailed the royal governor," Langguth, p. 33.

140 "the germ of the ideas," Miller, John C., p. 21.

140 "engaging Manners," quoted in Alexander, John K., p. 15.

141 "Containing the freshest Advices," *Boston Gazette*, July 15, 1765.

141 "iron Hand of Tyranny," ibid., October 5, 1772.

142 "Black List," quoted in Miller, John, p. 104.

142 "[t]hat the Boston mob," ibid., p. 104.

142–143 "Is it not," and "Just published," *Boston Gazette*, July 15, 1765.

144 "Every dip of his pen," quoted in Canfield, p. 1.

145 "an indignant band," and "Liberty, property and no stamps!" quoted in Lewis, p. 44–5.

145 "a tall, slender, fair-complexioned," *Boston Gazette*, January 31, 1763.

146 "hellish crew," "split down the door," "was obliged to retire," and "Nothing remained," quoted in Ferling, *Leap*, p. 39.

146–147 "Such horrid scenes," "rude fellows," "heating themselves," "hellish fury," "a great Number," and "committed . . . Outrages," *Boston Gazette*, September 2, 1765.

147 "*detestable*," and "the ruin of the most glorious Empire," ibid., October 2, 1769.

148 "some of the most effective propaganda," Kobre, *Colonial*, p. 122.

148 "piping hot atrocities," quoted in ibid., p. 122.

148 "If Adams and his fellow journalists," Kobre, *Colonial*, p. 122.

149 "a typical Superpower response," Davis, p. 46.

149 "arbitrary power," and "as yet unsubdued," *Boston Gazette*, December 5, 1768.

150 "swung his musket," Langguth, p. 133.

150 "It is very odd," quoted in Brands, p. 424.

150 "Shouting, cursing," McCullough, *Adams*, p. 65.

151 "detestable murderers," quoted in Brands, p. 424.

151 "imprudent and fool-hardy," *Boston Gazette*, August 13, 1770.

151 "bloody butchery," quoted in McCullough, *Adams*, p. 66.

151 "this fatal maneuvre," *Boston Gazette*, March 12, 1770.

151 "*Permit me thro' the Channel of your paper*," ibid., March 12, 1770.

152 "To be sold by EDES and GILL," ibid., March 26, 1770.

152 "Special emphasis," Forbes, p. 153.

152–153 "For some days," "a most unfortunate affair," and "*We decline at present*," *Boston Chronicle*, May 5–8, 1770.

153 "*His Majesty's most gracious SPEECH*," and "distemper among the horned cattle," ibid., May 15–19, 1770.

153 "there must be an abridgement," quoted in Kobre, *Colonial*, p. 124.

154 "that all is in *anarchy* here," and "yet remains to compleat," quoted in Miller, John C., p. 281.

154 "plan of slavery," quoted in ibid., p. 282.

154 "seven eighths of the people," quoted in Schlesinger, *Prelude*, p. 130.

154 "What was the Consequence," *New York Gazette*, April 2, 1770.

155 "would push the continent," quoted in Schlesinger, p. 131.

156 "closed extremely well," and "[p]retty good distinctions," quoted in Grant, p. 98.

156 "greedily licking human Blood," *Boston Gazette*, December 10, 1770.

156–157 "The *furor brevis*," ibid., December 17, 1770.

157 "*SOMEBODY*, in Mr. Draper's paper," ibid., December 24, 1770.

158 "a solemn and perpetual Memorial," ibid., May 11, 1771.

158 "not . . . the result," quoted in Ferling, *Leap*, p. 77.

158 "hirelings, pimps," and "abandoned and shameless ministry," *Boston Gazette*, October 14, 1771.

160 "likely longshoremen," Ferling, *Leap*, p. 106.

160 "Well, boys, you have had," quoted in Bobrick, p. 90.

160 "Boston's harbor," Langguth, p. 182.

161 "[W]ith gratitude," *Boston Gazette*, December 20, 1773.

161 "RULES," "to all ministers," "to consider," "To make your taxes," and "Redress no grievance," *Massachusetts Spy*, December 16, 1773.

161 "At length, Sir," ibid., December 23, 1773.

161–162 "But outside New England," Schlesinger, *Prelude*, pp. 181–2.

162 "carrying Matters to such Extremity," quoted in ibid., p. 182.

163 "UNITE OR DIE," *New-York Journal*, June 23, 1774.

163 "Rise just indignation," *South-Carolina Gazette*, June 13, 1774.

163 "How will you feel," *Newport Mercury*, June 13, 1774.

163 "*Our sister colonies*," *Boston Gazette*, May 16, 1774.

163 "a plan of despotism," and "has incessantly been pursued," *Boston Gazette*, May 23, 1774.

163 "Your Excellency," *Pennsylvania Journal*, June 29, 1774.

163–164 "to settle and dwell," "shall be void," "that on the birth," "paid by the Mother," and "shall be applied," *Pennsylvania Journal*, June 29, 1774.

165 "an affront to the common sense," *Massachusetts Gazette*, December 23, 1773.

165 "the line of decorum," quoted in Schlesinger, *Prelude*, p. 190

165 "Your Old and unvaried Friend," quoted in Alexander, John K., p. 219.

166 "the helmsman," quoted in ibid., p. 219.

166 "calumniated for," and "without the least shadow," quoted in ibid., p. 221.

166 "great," and "glorious," quoted in ibid., p. 157.

167 "The fashion of allowing," Chernow, p. 397.

168 "suffered from nervous disorders," Canfield, p. 129.

168 "The entire country," Lewis, p. 390.

168 "the consistent," "our *political parent*," and "the undeviating friend," quoted in Alexander, John K., p. 221.

168 "always for softness," quoted in Canfield, p. 129.

168 "truly a great man," quoted in Burstein, p. 49.

169 "It would be the Glory," quoted in Alexander, John K., p. 223.

169 "Truth was his first victim," Hallahan, p. 240.

Chapter Nine: The Tory Dung Barge

172 "A Married Lady," *New-York Journal*, December 29, 1768.

172 "Clues to the reliability," Stephens, p. 188.

173–174 "A little after ten o'clock," quoted in Tebbel, p. 42.

174–175 "You have read," quoted in ibid., p. 43.

176 "one of the handsomest," Kobre, *Colonial*, p. 142.

176 "a rich purple velvet coat," quoted in Mott, p. 85.

176 "to submit to their unreasonable," *Rivington's New-York Gazetteer*, April 13, 1775.

177 "to assure the public," ibid., February 23, 1775.

177 "dirty," and "malicious," *Boston Gazette*, January 16, 1775.

177 "JUDAS," *Massachusetts Spy*, December 29, 1774.

177 "either an ignorant impudent pretender," quoted in Chernow, p. 68.

177 "a most wretched," *Newport Mercury*, April 10, 1775.

177 "Solomon Saphead," *Rivington's New-York Gazetteer*, March 30, 1775.

177 "a most infamous," "most traiterously [sic] declaring," "repugnant to the laws," and "the preposterous enormity," *Rivington's New-York Gazetteer*, November 9, 1775.

178 "Lying Gazette," quoted in Payne, p. 123.

178 "Twistifications," and "false colourings," quoted in Schlesinger, *Prelude*, p. 224.

178 "misled by dangerous," "various disorderly acts," and "traitorously preparing," *Rivington's New-York Gazetteer*, November 9, 1775.

178 "execrable mobs," and "treasonable associations," ibid., March 2, 1775.

178–179 "injected partisan bias," Schlesinger, *Prelude*, p. 222.

179 "that the people," and "fully to forewarn," *Rivington's New-York Gazetteer*, November 9, 1775.

179 "a number far beyond," quoted in Schlesinger, *Prelude*, p. 222.

179 "Up and down the coast," ibid., p. 222.

180 "In politics," quoted in ibid., p. 225.

180 "to every person," quoted in Payne, p. 123.

181 "The Printer is bold to affirm," *Rivington's New-York Gazetteer*, April 20, 1775.

181 "rode into the city," ibid., p. 124.

181 "ark of refuge," Schlesinger, *Prelude*, p. 227.

181 "We hope," *Pennsylvania Journal*, May 17, 1775.

182 "however wrong and mistaken," quoted in Schlesinger, *Prelude*, p. 227.

182 "Morris urged," Brookhiser, *Gentleman*, p. 24.

183 "Long months of pent-up resentment," Hallahan, p. 30.

Chapter Ten: The Shot Spread 'Cross the Page

186–187 "I early became," quoted in Payne, p. 81.

187 "emerged from a lifetime," Tebbel, p. 39.

188 "bastard sone," and "had been prostituted," quoted in Hallahan, p. 215.

188 "few men, perhaps," quoted in Tebbel and Watts, p. 8.

188 "YE Sons of Sedition," *Rivington's New-York Gazetteer*, August 25, 1774.

188 "sat in the belfry," Tebbel, p. 40.

189–190 "AMERICANS!" and "We have the pleasure," *Massachusetts Spy*, May 3, 1775.

190 "[t]he *whigs* call no man," *Massachusetts Spy*, May 10, 1775.

190 "the most sanguinary," "the most profligate," and "a venal and corrupt majority," ibid., May 17, 1775.

190 "Americans!" ibid.

190 "Twice he was threatened," Marble, p. 85.

190 "BLOODY NEWS," quoted in Schlesinger, *Prelude*, p. 232.

191 "Cruelty was not less brutal," *Essex Gazette*, April 25, 1775.

191 "The kind intentions," *New-York Journal*, May 25, 1775.

191 "to stop the further effusion," *Pennsylvania Gazette*, August 2, 1775.

191 "repent of your villainies," *Boston Gazette*, June 5, 1775.

191 "[t]he shattered Remains," *New York Gazette and Weekly Mercury*, December 16, 1775.

192 "*Rags taken in*," *The Freemen's Journal or New-Hampshire Gazette*, March 24, 1778.

193 "a noble Cause," quoted in Ellis, *Excellency*, p. 80.

193 "I have it in express," *Virginia Gazette*, April 24, 1778.

194 "There is no evidence," Flexner, *American Revolution*, p. 533.

194 "that neither BLOOD nor TREASURE," *Pennsylvania Gazette*, August 2, 1775.

194 "His Excellency General WASHINGTON," *The Freemen's Journal or New-Hampshire Gazette*, March 24, 1778.

195 "Printer to the King's," *Rivington's New York Royal Gazette*, November 1, 1777.

196 "James Rivington *Has brought*," and "for weighing gold," ibid., November 1, 1777.

196 "An Historical Account," ibid., February 21, 1778.

197 "If Rivington is taken," quoted in Schlesinger, *Prelude*, p. 295.

198 "Our old acquaintance," *Rivington's New York Royal Gazetteer*, August 6, 1780.

Chapter Eleven: Uncommon Prose

201 "Pamphlets have madden'd," quoted in Mott, p. 55.

201 "Gothic irregularity," Tyler, vol. 1, p. 39.

201 "We have every thing good," Otis, p. 80.

202 "gained wider currency," Malone, *Virginian*, p. 182.

202 "The wretched condition," Adams, p. 194.

203 "His eye, of which the painter," quoted in Hawke, p. 14.

204 "In 1772," ibid., p. 185.

204 "Besides two letters," Liell, p. 16.

205 "perhaps in homage of Dr. Franklin," ibid., p. 82.

205 "patriotic fervor," Ellis, *Excellency*, p. 88.

205 "nothing more than simple facts," Paine, *Common Sense*, p. 20.

205–206 "Men of passive tempers," ibid., p. 26.

206 "a single advantage," ibid., p. 20.

206 "another of the self-educated," Johnson, pp. 152–3.

206–207 "Were a manifesto," Paine, *Collected Writings*, pp. 45–6.

207 "A few more," quoted in Schlesinger, *Prelude*, p. 256.

207–208 "Conservatively, between January and July," Ferling, *Leap*, p. 151.

208 "Is this *common sense*," *New York Gazette and Weekly Mercury*, April 8, 1776.

208 "Into an atmosphere," Liell, p. 106.

208 "Whether we ought," quoted in ibid., p. 114.

208–209 "I saw, or at least thought I saw," Paine, *Collected Writings*, pp. 701–2.

209 "had signed over the copyright," Bobrick, p. 341.

Chapter Twelve: A Sword of a Different Kind

212 "The grand, the alarming," *Massachusetts Spy*, July 10, 1776.

212–213 "a number of patriotic gentlemen," ibid., July 24, 1776.

214 "We have thought," ibid., October 23, 1776.

215 "By the Morris-Town post," *Boston Gazette*, April 28, 1777.

215 "HAIL! Glorious chief," *The Freemen's Journal or New-Hampshire Gazette*, March 10, 1778.

216 "received with as much joy," *Boston Gazette*, May 18, 1778.

216 "His Majesty having been informed," *The Freemen's Journal or New Hampshire Gazette*, June 2, 1778.

216–7 "General Ash's division," *Boston Gazette*, May 10, 1779.

217 "While the enemy," *Pennsylvania Gazette*, July 5, 1780.

217 "crimson coloured curtain," and "dreadful TRAGEDY," quoted in Lutnick, p. 187.

217–218 "Cornwallis taken," and "glorious Conquest," *Boston Gazette*, October 26, 1781.

218 "I have the honour," *Pennsylvania Journal*, October 24, 1781.

218 "shattered the breathless hush," Ferling, *Leap*, p. 241.

219 "animated with an equal desire," *Newport Mercury*, January 3, 1784.

219 "to forget all past misunderstandings," *Pennsylvania Journal*, December 3, 1783.

219 "would have been our ally," quoted in Lutnick, p. 195.

220 "It was by means," quoted in Schlesinger, *Prelude*, p. 284.

220 "Among other Engines," quoted in ibid., pp. 284–5.

220 "Nature had adorned him," Ramsay, p. 608.

221 "In establishing American independence," ibid., p. 634.

Chapter Thirteen: The Passionate Decade

227 "far-sighted as always," and "with an extraordinary plan," McDougall, p. 182.

227 "we shall gradually consume," *South Carolina Gazette*, June 20, 1754.

229–230 "With the national government," Ferling, *Adams*, pp. 39–40.

231 "Though we readily admit," *Boston Gazette*, June 11, 1787.

232 "The American war is over," quoted in Dunn, p. 10.

233 "artful ambiguities," Ellis, *Excellency*, p. 179.

233 "Should the citizens," *Boston Gazette*, June 30, 1788.

234 "most of the people," Davis, p. 90.

235 "[I]t is to be remarked," *The Federalist Papers*, No. 10.

235–236 "heresies," "In place of," and "timid men," quoted in Malone, *Ordeal*, p. 267.

236 "Attention! Citizens of Philadelphia," *Aurora*, October 14, 1800.

239 "one of America's most passionate decades," Ferling, *Adams*, p. 57.

239–240 "*Christianity* in the morning," and "A despicable impartiality," quoted in Dunn, p. 140.

240 "A typical issue," Chernow, pp. 396–7.

240 "The highest price," *Gazette of the United States*, May 4, 1795.

241 "Political leaders," Kobre, *American*, p. 110.

243 "Jefferson accused Hamilton," Ellis, *Excellency*, pp. 215–6.

244 "[Aaron] Burr and his henchmen," Allen, p. 93.

245 "pleasures of society," and "who have been intimate," quoted in Ferling, *Adams*, pp. 105–6.

Chapter Fourteen: The Not-So-Unlikely Target

248 "America's secular saint," Ellis, *Excellency*, pp. 147–8.

248 "For some writers," Wills, p. 28.

249 "fine Broad Cloath," quoted in Ellis, *Excellency*, p. 25.

249 "a Conduct so novel," and "the greatest man," Ferling, *Leap*, p. 255.

249 "afraid to use power," Wills, p. 18.

249 "as a thing that might be destroyed," Brookhiser, *Father*, p. 131.

251 "had not been paid," Ellis, *Excellency*, p. 128.

251 "Certain I am," quoted in ibid., p. 127.

252 "a gambler," Brookhiser, *Founding Father*, p. 115.

252 "treacherous," "mischievous," "inefficient," "stately journeying," "ostentatious professions," "a frail mortal," and "a spoiled child," quoted in Tebbel and Watts, p. 16.

252 "a tyrannical monster," quoted in Ellis, *Excellency*, p. 245.

252 "posterity will in vain," and "put off your suit," quoted in Tebbel and Watts, p. 16.

252–253 "the patron of fraud," and "whether you are an apostate," ibid.

253 "It is much to be wished," quoted in Tebbel, p. 56.

253 "Newspaper Accounts," Abbot, p. 41.

253–254 "I have Such a number," ibid., p. 54.

254–255 "spontaneous effusions," and "Hail, thou auspicious day, *Gazette of the United States*, April 25, 1789.

254 "unpracticed in the duties," and "inherit[ed] inferior endowments," quoted in Flexner, *Nation*, p. 184.

255–262 "the extravagant," and "equally extravagant," quoted in Tebbel, p. 57.

255 "the most notorious model," Ellis, *Excellency*, p. 37.

255 "outrages on common decency," and "arrows of malevolence," quoted in Dunn, p. 38.

255 "buffited in the public prints," quoted in Wise, p. 313.

256 "grossest and most insidious," and "indecent terms," quoted in ibid.,
p. 70.

257 "some of the Gazettes," quoted in Tebbel and Watts, p. 17.

257 "Having learnt," quoted in Tebbel, p. 57.

258 "invented," Flexner, *Anguish*, p. 291.

258 "Orders or advertisements," quoted in Tebbel, p. 59.

259 "Aides to Treasury Secretary," Smith, p. 439.

259 "We have some infamous Papers," quoted in Tebbel, p. 63.

Chapter Fifteen: The Gazette . . .

262 "a man without a biography," Payne, p. 154.

264 "such a contemptible creature," *Independent Chronicle*, August 3,
1795.

264 "*He that is not for us*," quoted in Dunn, p. 111.

264 "more than nine-tenths," quoted in Durey, pp. 92–3.

264–265 "Virtue was ne'er confin'd," *Gazette of the United States*, August 1, 1792.

265 "an host within himself," quoted in Ferling, *Adams*, p. 66.

265 "have been urged," and "weakening the confidence," *Gazette of the
United States*, March 13, 1793.

266 "pretensions of Thomas Jefferson," "most dangerous," "on our guard,"
"demagogue," "*garb of patriotism*," and "*language of liberty*," ibid., October 20, 1796.

266 "a few comments," and "will place in just light," ibid., October 15,
1796.

266 "a paper of pure Toryism," quoted in Malone, *Rights*, p. 424.

267 "for the purpose," quoted in Payne, pp. 154–5.

267 "adoring in his treatment," Chernow, p. 395.

268 "was even listed," ibid., p. 395.

270 "been daily hoping," *Aurora*, June 29, 1795.

270–271 "Jay's desertion," and "Jay's capitulation," Callender, *Prospect*, vol. 1,
p. 66.

271 "claimed he could have walked," Ellis, *Excellency*, p. 227.

271 "the omnipotent director," and "thundered contempt," quoted in
Tebbel, p. 64.

272 "is a most dangerous one," *Gazette of the United States*, September
12, 1795.

272–273 "Mr. Fenno, In your Gazettes," ibid., September 8, 1792.

274 "Sir, I am informed," ibid., May 5, 1795.

274–275 "THE POTATOE, a rhapsody," ibid., June 25, 1795.

Chapter Sixteen: . . . versus the Gazette

278 "Were I to undertake," in Foley, John P., ed. *The Jefferson Cyclopedia: A Comprehensive Collection of the Views of Thomas Jefferson* [book-on-line] (New York: Funk & Wagnalls Company, 1900); available at http://etext.lib.virginia.edu/etcbin/ot2wwwfoley?specfile=/texts/english/jefferson/foley/public/JefCycl.o2w&act=surround&offset=1464883&tag=1073.+CALUMNY,+Newspaper.+—+&query=Were+I+to+undertake&id=JCE1073.

278 "a man of genius," Malone, *Rights*, p. 424.

279 "Yes—wait," Freneau, "To Mr. Blanchard, the Celebrated Aeronaut in America," *American Poetry*, p. 8.

279 "In spite of all," Freneau, "The Indian Burying Ground," http://earlyamerica.com/review/fall96/freneau.html.

279–280 "Fair flower," Freneau, "The Wild Honeysuckle," quoted in Austin, p. 70.

280 "was a good hater," Tyler, vol. 1, p. 173.

280 "To the king," Freneau, "Rivington's Last Will and Testament," quoted in Austin, p. 134.

281 "stupid, suspicious, licentious," *National Gazette*, December 22, 1792.

282 "With his pass key," Randall, *Hamilton*, p. 402.

282 "cannot otherwise than have," *National Gazette*, August 15, 1792.

284 "conferred a *sinecure* office," *Gazette of the United States*, October 21, 1796.

285 "sad effects," "numerous evils," "pregnant with every mischief," "baneful," and "as unjust in its operation," *National Gazette*, March 15, 1792.

285–286 "Can wits or serious sages," *National Gazette*, March 29, 1792.

286 "intriguer," quoted in Burstein, p. 204.

286 "a womanish attachment," "to occupy themselves," and "destructive of morality," quoted in Simon, James F., p. 33.

287 "mutual forebearances," quoted in McCullough, *Adams*, p. 436.

287 "a fraternal spat," Ellis, *Excellency*, p. 215.

287 "As to the merits," quoted in Tebbel, p. 61.

287–288 "critical of Mr. Jefferson's conduct," and "So far, then," *National Gazette*, December 12, 1792.

288 "I am aware," ibid., June 5, 1793.

288 "adverted to a piece," quoted in Tebbel, p. 62.

289 "The President was much inflamed," quoted in ibid., pp. 62–3.

289 "Who will deny," *National Gazette*, February 27, 1793.

289 "Political Christmas," *Aurora*, March 7, 1797.

289 "assist in establishing," ibid., February 21, 1795.

290 "The *unity* of your conduct," *National Gazette*, January 12, 1793.

290 "With the present number," *National Gazette*, October 26, 1793.

292 "The sun's in the west," quoted in Tyler, vol. 2, p. 274.

Chapter Seventeen: Dark Whispers on the Page

294 "prophesied much of post–Civil War America," quoted in Chernow, p. 374.

295 "a woman called at my house," and "a seeming air of affliction," Hamilton, p. 27.

295 "to apply to my humanity," and "her situation," ibid., p. 28.

295 "wavy chestnut brown hair," Brookhiser, *Hamilton*, p. 1.

295 "a small supply of money," Hamilton, p. 28.

296 "I put a bank bill," ibid., p. 28.

297 "extreme anxiety," quoted in Chernow, p. 367.

297 "a great sacrifice," quoted in Brookhiser, *Hamilton*, p. 98.

298 "that [Reynolds] had frequently enjoined," quoted in ibid., p. 366.

298–299 "Ben Sick all moast Ever," quoted in Randall, p. 408.

301 "Sir, I am very sorry to find," quoted in Hamilton, p. 80.

301 "wounded honor," quoted in ibid., p. 81.

301 "A plain statement," Brookhiser, *Hamilton*, p. 99.

302 "Faced with Hamilton's wrath," Chernow, p. 416.

304 "no political impropriety," "the most delicate sentiment," and "one of the most illiberal," *American Daily Advertiser*, December 31, 1792.

305 "in the scale of just calculation," Callender, *Progress*, p. 6.

306 "Callender had a repressed," Durey, p. 2.

306 "a complex and contradictory character," ibid., p. 2.

306 "Such is the in-born baseness," quoted in ibid., p. 23.

306 "arrogant pedantry," and "covetous and shameless prolixity," Callender, *Deformities*, p. 88.

307 "invidious and revengeful remark," ibid., p. 11.

307 "None has discovered more contempt," ibid., 12.

307 "one of the most famous diatribes," quoted in Durey, p. 95.

307 "If ever a nation was debauched," *Aurora*, December 23, 1796.

308 "very much agitated," "totally false," and "Colo. Monroe," quoted in Ammon, p. 159.

309 "dark whispers," quoted in ibid., p. 529.

309 "We now come," Callender, *History*, p. 204.

310 "see this great master," ibid., pp. 205–6.

310 "So much correspondence," quoted in Rosenfeld, p. 33.

310–311 "The result of all these measures," ibid., pp. 227–8.

310–311 "I dare appeal," and "however natural," Hamilton, pp. 6–7.

311 "My real crime," "is not made," and "I can never cease," ibid., p. 14.

311 "[t]he public too," ibid., p. 15.

311 "If you have not seen it," quoted in Durey, p. 103.

311 "Tom S**t," *New-York Journal*, September 20, 1787.

312 "In the name of justice," and "sufficient slander on our country," *Gazette of the United States*, April 24, 1798.

312–313 "The volunteer acknowledgement," and "Throughout the whole," *Aurora*, September 19, 1797.

Chapter Eighteen: "The Arising Vapour"

317 "turbulent and fractious," quoted in Isaacson, *American*, p. 379.

317 "a base and unnatural miscreant," "impudent dog," "outraged every principle," "hollow-cheeked," and "filth," quoted in Tagg, p. ix.

317 "malignant industry," quoted in Rosenfeld, p. xv.

317 "malice & falshood," quoted in Tagg, p. ix.

317 "this fountain head," *Massachusetts Mercury*, May 8, 1798.

318 "of abilities and of principles," quoted in Rosenfeld, p. 28.

318 "was not entirely a bad paper," Tebbel, p. 63.

318 "the most formidable check," quoted in Tagg, p. ix.

319 "didactic little essays," Isaacson, *American*, p. 379.

319 "live comfortably," and "are poor and dirty," quoted in ibid., p. 379.

319 "had a philosopher," quoted in Tagg, p. ix.

320 "French pay," *Massachusetts Mercury*, May 8, 1798.

320 "notorious hireling," *Porcupine's Gazette*, April 10, 1798.

320 "It is time," *Aurora*, April 11, 1794.

321 "principally calculated," "may be regarded," and "would be dangerous," ibid., July 28, 1795.

321 "like a volcano," ibid., August 21, 1795.

321 "the benevolence of the good man," ibid., August 22, 1795.

321–322 "The House of Representatives," ibid., April 11, 1796.

322 "rewarded the people," ibid., August 22, 1795.

322–323 "Tall and imposing," quoted in Rosenfeld, p. 484.

323 "Will not the world," *Aurora*, October 23, 1795.

323 "You seem to have entered," ibid., October 21, 1795.

324 "mauls," quoted in Tagg, p. 222.

324 "portrayed Washington," ibid., p. 283.

324 "damn," quoted in Rosenfeld, p. 28.

324–325 *"Retire immediately,"* *Aurora*, November 20, 1795.

325 "The valuable legacy," ibid., September 23, 1796.

325 "all the misfortunes," quoted in Tagg, p. 285.

326 "the final stage," ibid., p. 284.

326 "It is even said," quoted in Rosenfeld, p. 32.

326 "conservative," Schiff, p. 5.

327 "an illustrious descent," and "Noble blood," *Gazette of the United States*, May 15, 1790.

328–329 *"We have no partiality,"* *Columbian Centinel*, August 1, 1798.

329 "saved us from perdition," and "one half the United States," *Aurora*, April 4, 1798.

330 "The prejudices, which have been excited," ibid., March 6, 1798.

330 "The chance of truth," *Gazette of the United States*, April 4, 1798.

330 "It may be debated," Callender, *Prospect*, vol. 1, p. 131.

330 "By sending these ambassadors," ibid., p. 141.

331 "the vile calumnies," *Gazette of the United States*, April 24, 1798.

331 "This AMERICANS," *Porcupine's Gazette*, June 20, 1798.

332 "Lightning Rod, Jr.," quoted in Schiff, p. 406.

332–333 "Few issues," Tagg, p. 132.

333 *"adulterous confessions,"* and "wonted malice," *Aurora*, September 19, 1797.

333 "by many it is shrewdly suspected," *Aurora*, November 8, 1794.

333–334 "The *Gazette* panegyrick," ibid., February 11, 1794.

334 "were usually as unenlightening," and "Having begun," Tagg, p. 228.

334 "swinish multitude," *Aurora*, June 2, 1794.

334 "incendiary faction," *Gazette of the United States*, February 24, 1794.

334 "Men bred in the schools," *Aurora*, February 24, 1794.

335 "shall diffuse," ibid., November 8, 1794.

335 "emblematic of the vapour," *Gazette of the United States*, November 25, 1794.

335 "the dirty tool," quoted in Weisberger, p. 206.

336 "a sound rap or two," quoted in Tagg, p. 349.

336 "Beating up editors," Brodie, p. 367.

336 "ironically, but with underlying earnestness," Mott, p. 147.

336 "to leave the liberty," quoted in ibid., p. 147.

Chapter Nineteen: Cobbett's Quills

338 "a self-tutored English farm boy," Weisberger, p. 207.

338 "sitting on the edge," Kobre, *American*, p. 119.

339 "a whole system of army graft," ibid., p. 119.

339 "your rapacious Officers," Cobbett, p. 15.

339 "have not been content," ibid., p. 9.

340 "My *politics*," *Porcupine's Gazette*, March 4, 1797.

340 "a rallying point," and "may speak their minds," ibid.

340 "a war of words," *Porcupine's Gazette*, ibid.

341 "a newspaper controversy," *Aurora*, March 7, 1797.

341 "a vehicle of lies," *Porcupine's Gazette*, March 4, 1797.

341 "Methinks I hear," *Aurora*, March 4, 1797.

341 "my sweet," and "[W]hat end," *Porcupine's Gazette*, March 4, 1797.

341 "nothing but contempt, *Aurora*, March 7, 1797.

341 "I assert," *Porcupine's Gazette*, March 4, 1797.

341–342 "all the world knows," ibid., March 17, 1798.

342 "a brilliant series," *Aurora*, April 1, 1797.

342 "No man is bound," *Porcupine's Gazette*, April 20, 1798.

342 "not a bad thing," quoted in Rosenfeld, p. 40.

342 "might do more good," quoted in Brookhiser, *Hamilton*, p. 160.

342–343 "It is hardly necessary," quoted in Foley, John P., ed. *The Jeffersonian Cyclopedia: A Comprehensive Collection of the Views of Thomas Jefferson* [book on-line] (New York: Funk & Wagnalls Company, 1900); available at http://etext.lib.virginia.edu/etcbin/ot2wwwfoley?specfile=/texts/english/jefferson/foley/public/JefCycl.o2w&act=surround&offset=229445&tag=9.+ABUSE,+Newspaper.+—+&query=It+is+hardly+necessary&id=JCE0009.

343 "the equal of," quoted in *Porcupine's Gazette*, January 29, 1799.

343 "should keep and feed," and "and the 'fretful porcupine,'" *Columbian Centinel*, April 10, 1799.

343 "*the Apostle*," "this profligate madman," and "once lodged in Market Street," *Porcupine's Gazette*, March 7, 1790.

344 "till the Patient," quoted in Silverman, p. 407.

344 "The ultimate proof," Boorstin, *Colonial*, p. 214.

344 "pounded away at the man," Brodsky, p. 338.

345 "Wanted, by a physician," "is a man," and "And so is a *musquito*," quoted in Butterfield, L.H., p. 1215.

345 "The times are ominous indeed," *Porcupine's Gazette*, September 19, 1797.

345 "he bestowed with impartiality," Brodsky, p. 279.

346 "So much was the Doctor," *Porcupine's Gazette*, October 7, 1797.

346 "genius for savage journalistic satire," quoted in Brodsky, p. 338.

346 "to ignore Porcupine," ibid., p. 341.

347 "Including the cost," ibid., p. 342.

348 "told me when dying," quoted in Burstein, p. 22.

348 "self-justifying tone," and "must be partly attributed," Butterfield, L.H., p. 1218.

349 "That this man," *Porcupine's Gazette*, January 13, 1800.

Chapter Twenty: Sedition

352 "Cooking up Paragraphs," quoted in Grant, p. 80.

352 "cannot be preserved," quoted in McCullough, *Adams*, p. 60.

353 "I arnt book larnt enuff," *Boston Evening-Post*, June 20, 1763.

353 "It is a pleasant thing," "I cant hardly beleeve," and "I love to see," ibid., September 5, 1763.

353 "finery gentlefolks," and "Lunnun," ibid., June 20, 1763.

353 *"A Free Press,"* quoted in Dunn, p. 108.

354 "a person without patriotism," quoted in Dunn, p. 103.

354 "man of incorruptible integrity," and "equal to the duties," quoted in Ferling, *Leap*, p. 405.

354 "old, bald," quoted in Dunn, p. 103.

355 "terrorism," quoted in Stephens, p. 199.

355 "disgraced and degraded," quoted in Wise, p. 313.

355–356 "That if any person," "An Act in Addition to the Act, Entitled 'An Act for the Punishment of Certain Crimes Against the United States,'" http://www.yale.edu/lawweb/avalon/statutes/sedact.htm.

357 "the federal constitution," Callender, *Prospect*, vol. 1, p. 122.

357 "If ever there was," quoted in Tagg, p. 372.

357 "so diametrically opposed," and "To laugh at," *Aurora*, July 3, 1798.

358 "declares what is unconstitutional," quoted in Tagg, p. 373.

359 "the Friend of Government," *American Minerva*, December 9, 1793.

359 "time to stop newspaper editors," quoted in ibid., p. 506.

359 "Let us not be cruel," and "Let us not establish," quoted in Ferling, *Adams*, p. 111.

360 "an experiment on the American mind," quoted in Rosenfeld, p. 235.

360 "the late lawless," "the sanguinary," "diabolical designs," and "To prevent the effects," *Aurora*, August 3, 1798.

361 "Are our young officers," quoted in Weisberger, p. 216.

361 "A meaner, more artful," quoted in Grant, p. 408.

362 "a native American," and "ungraceful aspersions," *Sunbury and Northumberland Gazette*, July 13, 1799.

362 "all-around incompetence," Grant, p. 408.

363 "imbued with rather more impudence," quoted in Tebbel and Watts, p. 26.

363 "Is there anything evil," quoted in ibid., p. 26.

363 "if these papers fall," quoted in Tagg, p. 395.

364 "was under arrest," ibid., p. 396.

364–365 "escaped the affliction," *Aurora*, September 7, 1798.

365 "a man inflexible," quoted in Tagg, p. 397.

365 "The Jacobins are all whining," *Russell's Gazette*, September 21, 1798.

366 "Died, last evening," and "long and sincerely," *Porcupine's Gazette*, September 16, 1798.

366 "William Duane," *The Wasp*, July 7, 1802.

367 "he committed or was charged," Payne, p. 180.

367 "matchless effrontery," quoted in ibid., p. 181.

367–368 "false, defamatory," quoted in Dunn, p. 172.

368–369 "the passage of," Payne, p. 175.

369 "power had been easily transferred," Dunn, p. 11.

369 "Should the infidel Jefferson," *Hudson Bee*, September 7, 1802.

369–370 "Do you believe," *Connecticut Courant*, October 6, 1800.

370 "embark[ed] upon," and "aiming at," *Gazette of the United States*, July 3, 1800.

370 "is an enemy," and "considers all the merchants," ibid., August 1, 1800.

370 "THE GRAND QUESTION STATED," ibid., September 16, 1800.

370 "the crooked character," and "insatiable ambition," et al., *Columbian Centinel*, September 20, 1800.

371 "the report of Mr. Jefferson's death," *Gazette of the United States*, July 2, 1800.

372 "some *compassionate* being," *Connecticut Courant*, July 7, 1800.

372 "is by far not so dangerous," and "far more cunning than wise," quoted in Chernow, p. 632.

372 "a circumstance much regretted," *Gazette of the United States*, December 16, 1800.

373 "YESTERDAY EXPIRED," *Columbian Centinel*, March 4, 1801.

373 "bear a striking," *The Recorder*, September 1, 1802.

Chapter Twenty-One: Master and Mistress

376 "barbarity and brutality," "to wallow in filth," and "to perish," *The Examiner* (Richmond), September 25, 1802.

377 "in his customarily toxic style," Ferling, *Adams*, p. 136.

377 "exhibit the multiple corruptions," Callender, *Prospect*, vol. 1, p. 3.

377 "Mr. Adams has laboured," ibid., pp. 30–1.

377 "designed to do," ibid., p. 141.

377 "was distinguished by," ibid., p. 157.

377 "Mr. Adams has mistaken," ibid., p. 168.

377 "In Pennsylvania," ibid., p. 24.

378 "Such papers," quoted in Brodie, p. 320.

378 "abuse and scandal," quoted in Dunn, p. 168.

378 "And once she found out," Brodie, p. 321.

378 "exceeded his lawful powers," Callender, *Prospect*, vol. 1, p. 100.

378 "another topmast of absurdity," ibid., p. 101.

378 "Thousands, and twenties of thousands," ibid., p. 55.

378 "wishing to preserve the peace," ibid., p. 33.

379 "mockery," Payne, p. 194.

379 "probably the most violent partisan," quoted in Mott, p. 150.

379 "interrupted Callender's," Payne, p. 194.

380 "When the minutes," Brodie, p. 322.

380 "And so the day's our own," *The Examiner* (Richmond), January 6, 1801.

380 "James Thomson Callender, who looks" quoted in ibid., p. 142.

381 "absurd," Callender, *Prospect*, vol. 2, p. 125.

381 "flock of harpies," ibid., p. 31.

381 "jumble of impertinence," ibid., pp. 146–7.

382 "According to one Federalist account," Ellis, *Jefferson*, p. 218.

383 "I am really mortified," and "mere motives of charity," McCullough, *Adams*, p. 578.

383 "apostasy, ingratitude," quoted in ibid., p. 578.

384–385 "It is well known," *The Recorder*, September 1, 1802.

386 "*Of all the damsels,*" quoted in McCullough, *Adams*, p. 579.

386 "When a person is desirous," and "in his original nakedness," *The Recorder*, September 29, 1802.

386 "Will the *damnable lie,*" ibid., September 29, 1802.

387 "has determined not to disgrace," *National Intelligencer*, September 29, 1802.

387 "Mr. Jefferson has been a bachelor," *The Examiner* (Richmond), September 25, 1802.

387 "Oh! could a dose," ibid., November 3, 1802.

387 "a tin can," Ellis, *Jefferson*, p. 217.

388 "The basis of our government," quoted in Foley, John P., ed. *The Jefferson Cyclopedia: A Comprehensive Collection of the View of Thomas*

Jefferson [book-on-line] (New York: Funk & Wagnalls Company, 1900); available at http://etext.lib.virginia.edu/etcbin/ot2www-foley ?specfile=/texts/english/jefferson/foley/public/JefCycl.o2w&act=sur-round&offset=6912489&tag=5950.+NEWSPAPERS,+Government+a nd.+—+&query=The+basis+of+our+government&id=JCE5950.

389 "unauthorized," quoted in Mott, p. 152.

389 "is precisely qualified," quoted in Chernow, p. 668.

389 "Jefferson paid Callender," quoted in Malone, *First Term*, p. 232.

389 "moral evils," quoted in Tebbel and Watts, p. 33.

390 "is a reason to infer," quoted in Chernow, p. 669.

390 "a judge appointed," ibid., pp. 669–70.

390–391 "I never did think," and "To watch the progress," quoted in ibid., p. 670.

391 "a most extraordinary effort," "drew tears from his eyes," and "the greatest forensic effort," quoted in ibid., p. 670.

392 "Of all the foreigners," quoted in Durey, p. 173.

393 "what is called soberness," quoted in ibid., p. 170.

393 "He was a poor creature," quoted in Burstein, p. 117.

394 "However barefaced," quoted in Durey, p. 171.

394 "It was as if," ibid., p. 171.

Chapter Twenty-Two: Post-Script

396 "The Sedition Act," and "new Republican newspapers," Dunn, pp. 139–40.

396 "Whenever anything occurs," quoted in Chernow, p. 650.

396 "The Field Marshall," quoted in ibid., p. 649.

396 "the strongest arm," Kobre, *American*, p. 114.

397 "Gazettes, it is seriously to be feared," *New-York Evening Post*, November 16, 1801.

397 "Persuaded that the great body," ibid., November 16, 1801.

397 "we openly profess," ibid., November 16, 1801.

398 "It has been long since observed," ibid., November 17, 1801.

399 "The Message of the President," ibid., December 17, 1801.

399 "But who and what," ibid., December 24, 1801.

399 "To attempt, therefore," ibid., December 29, 1801.

399 "But vain will be the attempt," ibid., February 3, 1802.

400 "SIR, So much has been written," ibid., March 3, 1802.

402 "filled the character," "very decent Minister," and "had he been less perfect," ibid., November 18, 1801.

402 "particular mention," ibid., December 30, 1801.
403–404 "With emotions," ibid., July 13, 1804.

Epilogue: Renewed Subscriptions

407 "afflicting," *Gazette of the United States*, December 19, 1799.
407 "melancholy event," *Russell's Gazette*, January 2, 1800.
407 "poignant grief," *Massachusetts Mercury*, January 24, 1800.
407 "calamity," and "that vast debt," *Columbian Centinel*, December 28, 1799.
407 "filled the hearts," ibid., January 6, 1800.
407 "As we can offer," *Aurora*, December 19, 1799.
408 "ordering drainage ditches," Ellis, *Excellency*, p. 242.
409 "reading one or more," ibid., p. 243.
409 "found them as irritating," Tebbel and Watts, p. 18.
410 "Morning snowing," quoted in Flexner, *Anguish*, p. 456.
410 "in precise conformity," *Porcupine's Gazette*, January 13, 1800.
411 "reading the papers," quoted in Tebbel and Watts, p. 18.
411 "spoke with some degree," quoted in ibid., p. 19.

BIBLIOGRAPHY

❂

Newspapers and Magazines

American Daily Advertiser (Philadelphia)
American Magazine, Or A Monthly View of the Political State of the British Colonies (Philadelphia)
American Minerva (New York City)
American Weekly Mercury (Philadelphia)
Aurora (Philadelphia)
Boston Chronicle
Boston Evening-Post
Boston Gazette
Boston News-Letter
Boston Post-Boy & Advertiser
Columbian Centinel (Boston)
Connecticut Bee
Connecticut Courant
Essex Gazette (Massachusetts)
The Examiner (Richmond, Virginia)
The Freemen's Journal or New-Hampshire Gazette
Gazette of the United States (New York City, Philadelphia)
General Magazine and Historical Chronicle for all the British Plantations in America (Philadelphia)
Hudson Bee (New York State)
Independent Chronicle (Boston)
Massachusetts Gazette
Massachusetts Mercury
Massachusetts Spy
National Gazette (Philadelphia)
National Intelligencer (Washington)
New England Courant (Boston)
New Hampshire Gazette
New-York Evening Post
New York Gazette
New York Gazette and Weekly Mercury

New York Gazette, or, The Weekly Post-Boy
New York Journal
New York Mercury
New-York Weekly Journal
Newport Mercury (Rhode Island)
Pennsylvania Gazette
Pennsylvania Journal
Porcupine's Gazette (Philadelphia and Bustleton, Pennsylvania)
Publick Occurrences Both Foreign and Domestick (Boston)
The Recorder (Richmond, Virginia)
Rivington's New-York Gazetteer
Russell's Gazette (Boston)
South Carolina Gazette
Sunbury and Northumberland Gazette (Pennsylvania)
Virginia Gazette
The Wasp (Hudson, New York)

Books and Pamphlets

Abbot, W.W., ed. *The Papers of George Washington, Confederation Series: April 1786–January 1787*. Charlottesville, Virginia: University Press of Virginia, 1995.

Ackroyd, Peter. *London: The Biography*. New York: Doubleday, 2000.

Adams, Charles Francis, ed. *The Works of John Adams*, vol. 4. Boston: Charles C. Little and James Brown, 1851.

Alexander, James. *A Brief Narrative History of the Case and Trial of John Peter Zenger*. Cambridge, Massachusetts: Harvard University Press, 1963.

Alexander, John K. *Samuel Adams: America's Revolutionary Politician*. Lanham, Maryland: Rowman & Littlefield, 2002.

Allen, Oliver E. *New York, New York: A History of the World's Most Exhilarating and Challenging City*. New York: Atheneum, 1990.

American Poetry: The Nineteenth Century, vol. 1, *Philip Freneau to Walt Whitman*. New York: The Library of America, 1993.

Ammon, Harry. *James Monroe: The Quest for National Identity*. New York: McGraw-Hill, 1971.

Austin, Mary S. *Philip Freneau: The Poet of the Revolution, A History of His Life and Times*. New York: A. Wessels Company, 1901.

Bailyn, Bernard. *The Ideological Origins of the American Revolution*. Cambridge, Massachusetts: The Belknap Press of Harvard University, 1992.

Beach, Stewart. *Samuel Adams: The Fateful Years, 1764–1776*. New York: Dodd, Mead & Company, 1965.

Bobrick, Benson. *Angel in the Whirlwind.* New York: Simon & Schuster, 1997.

Boorstin, Daniel. *The Americans: The Colonial Experience.* Norwalk, Connecticut: Easton Press, 1987.

———. *The Americans: The Democratic Experience.* Norwalk, Connecticut: Easton Press, 1992.

———. *Hidden History: Exploring Our Secret Past.* New York: Harper & Row, 1987.

Bowen, Catherine Drinker. *The Most Dangerous Man in America: Scenes from the Life of Benjamin Franklin.* Boston: Atlantic–Little, Brown, 1974.

Brands, H.W. *The First American: The Life and Times of Benjamin Franklin.* New York: Doubleday, 2000.

Brodie, Fawn M. *Thomas Jefferson: An Intimate History.* New York: W.W. Norton & Company, 1974.

Brodsky, Alyn. *Benjamin Rush: Patriot and Physician.* New York: St. Martin's Press, 2004.

Brookhiser, Richard. *Alexander Hamilton: American.* New York: Free Press, 1999.

———. *America's First Dynasty: The Adamses, 1735–1918.* New York: Free Press, 2002.

———. *Gentleman Revolutionary: Gouverneur Morris: The Rake Who Wrote the Constitution.* New York: Free Press, 2003.

———. *Founding Father: Rediscovering George Washington.* New York: Free Press, 1996.

Burns, Eric. *The Joy of Books: Confessions of a Lifelong Reader.* Amherst, New York: Prometheus Books, 1995.

———. *The Spirits of America: A Social History of Alcohol.* Philadelphia: Temple University Press, 2003.

Burstein, Andrew. *Jefferson's Secrets: Death and Desire at Monticello.* New York: Basic Books, 2005.

Butler, Vera Minnie. *Education as Revealed by New England Newspapers Prior to 1850.* Philadelphia: Majestic Press, 1935.

Butterfield, L.H. *Letters of Benjamin Rush,* vol. 2, *1793–1813.* Princeton, New Jersey: American Philosophical Society, 1951.

Butterfield, Roger. *The American Past: A History of the United States from Concord to the Great Society.* New York: Simon and Schuster, 1976.

Callender, James Thomson. *Deformities of Dr. Samuel Johnson, Selected from His Works (1782).* Los Angeles: Augustan Reprint Society, Williams Andrews Clark Memorial Library, University of California, Los Angeles, 1971.

———. *The History of the United States for 1796; Including A Variety of Interesting Particulars Relative to the Federal Government Previous to That Period.* Philadelphia: Snowden & McCorkle, 1797.

———. *The Political Progress of Britain: Or, An Impartial History of Abuses in the Government of the British Empire, In Europe, Asia, and America: From the Revolution in 1688, to the Present Time: The Whole Tending to prove the Ruinous Consequences of the Popular System of Taxation, War, and Conquest.* Philadelphia: Wrigley & Berriman, 1794.

———. *The Prospect Before Us, Volume I.* Richmond, Virginia: M. Jones, S. Pleasants, Jun. and J. Lyon, 1800.

———. *The Prospect Before Us, Volume II.* Richmond, Virginia: M. Jones, S. Pleasants, Jun. and T. Field, 1800.

Canfield, Cass. *Sam Adams's Revolution: With the Assistance of George Washington, Thomas Jefferson, Benjamin Franklin, John Adams, George III, and the People of Boston.* New York: Harper & Row, 1976.

Chernow, Ron. *Alexander Hamilton.* New York: The Penguin Press, 2004.

Cobbett, William. *The Soldier's Friend; or, Considerations on the Late Pretended Augmentation of the Subsistence of the Private Soldiers.* [London?: s.n.], 1793.

Copeland, David A. *Debating the Issues in Colonial Newspapers: Primary Documents on Events of the Period.* Westport, Connecticut: Greenwood Press, 2000.

Darnton, Robert. *George Washington's False Teeth: An Unconventional Guide to the Eighteenth Century.* New York: W.W. Norton & Company, 2003.

Davis, Kenneth C. *Don't Know Much About History: Everything You Need to Know About American History but Never Learned.* New York: Crown, 1990.

Dickinson, John. *Letters From A Farmer in Pennsylvania, to the Inhabitants of the British Colonies.* New York: The Outlook Company, 1903.

Dos Passos, John. *The Shackles of Power: Three Jeffersonian Decades.* Norwalk, Connecticut: The Easton Press, 1988.

Dunn, Susan. *Jefferson's Second Revolution: The Election Crisis of 1800 and the Triumph of Republicanism.* Boston: Houghton Mifflin Company, 2004.

Durant, Will. *The Age of Faith: The Story of Civilization: 4.* Norwalk, Connecticut: The Easton Press, 1992.

Durant, Will and Ariel. *The Age of Reason Begins: The Story of Civilization: 7.* Norwalk, Connecticut: The Easton Press, 1992.

Durey, Michael. *"With the Hammer of Truth": James Thomson Callender and America's Early National Heroes.* Charlottesville, Virginia: University Press of Virginia, 1990.

Earle, Alice Morse. *Home Life in Colonial Days.* New York: The Macmillan Company, 1902.

Ellis, Joseph J. *After the Revolution: Profiles of Early American Culture.* New York: W.W. Norton & Company, 1979.

———. *American Sphinx: The Character of Thomas Jefferson.* New York: Alfred A. Knopf, 1997.

———. *Founding Brothers: The Revolutionary Generation.* New York: Alfred A. Knopf, 2000.

———. *His Excellency, George Washington.* New York: Alfred A. Knopf, 2004.

Estes, Todd. "Shaping the Politics of Public Opinion: Federalists and the Jay Treaty Debate." *Journal of the Early Republic,* Fall, 2000, pp. 394–422.

The Federalist Papers by Alexander Hamilton, James Madison and John Jay. New York: Bantam Books, 1982.

Ferling, John. *Adams Vs. Jefferson: The Tumultuous Election of 1800.* Oxford, England: Oxford University Press, 2004.

———. *A Leap in the Dark: The Struggle to Create the American Republic.* Oxford, England: Oxford University Press, 2003.

Fisher, Sydney Geo. *Men, Women, & Manners in Colonial Times, Volume I.* Philadelphia: J.B. Lippincott Company, 1897.

Flexner, James Thomas. *George Washington and the New Nation, 1783–1793.* Boston: Little, Brown and Company, 1969, 1970.

———. *George Washington: Anguish and Farewell, 1793–1799.* Boston: Little, Brown and Company, 1969, 1972.

———. *George Washington in the American Revolution, 1775–1783.* Boston: Little, Brown and Company, 1967, 1968.

———. *George Washington: The Forge of Experience, 1732–1775.* Boston: Little, Brown and Company, 1965.

Foley, John P., ed. *The Jeffersonian Cyclopedia: A Comprehensive Collection of the Views of Thomas Jefferson.* New York: Funk & Wagnalls Company, 1900. Online. Available: http://etext.lib.virginia.edu/jefferson/quotations/foley/. December 22, 2004.

Forbes, Esther. *Paul Revere and the World He Lived In.* New York: Book-of-the-Month Club, Inc., 1942.

Fowler, William M. *Samuel Adams: Radical Puritan.* New York: Longman, 1997.

Franklin, Benjamin. *The Autobiography of Benjamin Franklin.* Norwalk, Connecticut: The Easton Press, 1976.

Furnas, J.C. *The Americans: A Social History of the United States, 1587–1914.* New York: G.P. Putnam's Sons, 1969.

Galvin, John R. *Three Men of Boston.* New York: Thomas Y. Crowell Company, 1976.

Gelb, Norman. *Less Than Glory: A Revisionist's View of the American Revolution.* New York: G.P. Putnam's Sons, 1984.

Grant, James. *John Adams: Party of One.* New York: Farrar, Straus and Giroux, 2005.

Hallahan, William H. *The Day the American Revolution Began.* New York: William Morrow, 2000.

Halliday, E.M. *Understanding Thomas Jefferson.* New York: HarperCollins, 2001.

Hamilton, Alexander. *Observations on Certain Documents Contained in No. V & VI of "The History of the United States for the Year 1796," In Which the Charge of Speculation Against Alexander Hamilton, Late Secretary of the Treasury, Is Fully Refuted. Written by Himself.* New York: Hamilton Club, 1865.

Hannaford, Peter, ed. *The Essential George Washington: Two Hundred Years of Observations on the Man, the Myth, the Patriot.* Bennington, Vermont: Images from the Past, Inc., 1999.

Hawke, David Freeman. *Paine.* New York: Harper & Row, 1974.

Hibbert, Christopher. *Florence: The Biography of a City.* London: The Folio Society, 1997.

Hudson, Frederic. *Journalism in the United States from 1690 to 1872.* New York: Harper & Row, 1969.

Isaacson, Walter. *Benjamin Franklin: An American Life.* New York: Simon & Schuster, 2003.

————, ed. and annotator. *A Benjamin Franklin Reader.* New York: Simon & Schuster, 2003.

Johnson, Paul. *A History of the American People.* New York: HarperCollins, 1997.

Jones, Howard Mumford and Bessie Zaban Jones. *The Many Voices of Boston: A Historical Anthology, 1630–1975.* Boston: Little, Brown and Company, 1975.

Jones, Michael Wynn. *A Newspaper History of the World.* New York: William Morrow & Company, 1974.

Ketcham, Ralph. *James Madison: A Biography.* New York: The Macmillan Company, 1971.

Kobre, Sidney. *Development of American Journalism.* Dubuque, Iowa: W.C. Brown Company, 1969.

————. *The Development of the Colonial Newspaper.* Gloucester, Mass.: P. Smith, 1960.

Langguth, A.J. *Patriots: The Men Who Started the American Revolution.* Simon and Schuster, 1988.

Lerner, Max. *America as a Civilization: Life and Thought in the United States Today.* New York: Simon and Schuster, 1957.

Lewis, Paul. *The Grand Incendiary: A Biography of Samuel Adams.* New York: Dial Press, 1973.

Liell, Scott. *46 Pages: Thomas Paine,* Common Sense, *and the Turning Point to Independence.* Philadelphia: Running Press, 2003.

Lutnick, Solomon: *The American Revolution and the British Press, 1775–1783.* Columbia, Missouri: University of Missouri Press, 1967.

Malone, Dumas. *Jefferson and the Ordeal of Liberty*. Boston: Little, Brown and Company, 1962.

———. *Jefferson and the Rights of Man*. Boston: Little, Brown and Company, 1951.

———. *Jefferson the President: First Term, 1801–1805*. Boston: Little, Brown and Company, 1970.

———. *Jefferson the President: Second Term, 1805–1809*. Boston: Little, Brown and Company, 1974.

———. *Jefferson the Virginian*. Boston: Little, Brown and Company, 1948.

Marble, Annie Russell. *From 'Prentice to Patron: The Life Story of Isaiah Thomas*. New York: D. Appleton-Century Company, 1935.

McCullough, David. *John Adams*. New York: Simon & Schuster, 2001.

———. *1776*. New York: Simon & Schuster, 2005.

McDougall, Walter A. *Freedom Just Around the Corner: A New American History, 1585–1828*. New York: HarperCollins, 2004.

Miller, John C. *Sam Adams: Pioneer in Propaganda*. Stanford, California: Stanford University Press, 1967.

Miller, Nathan. *The Founding Finaglers*. New York: David McKay Company, Inc., 1976.

Morgan, Edmund S. *Benjamin Franklin*. New Haven, Connecticut: Yale University Press, 2002.

Mott, Frank Luther. *American Journalism, A History: 1690–1960* (Third Edition). New York: The Macmillan Company, 1962.

Nagle, Paul C. *Descent from Glory: Four Generations of the John Adams Family*. New York: Oxford University Press, 1983.

Otis, James. *The Rights of the British Colonies Asserted and Proved*. Boston: Edes and Gill, 1764.

Paine, Thomas. *Collected Writings*. New York: The Library of America, 1995.

Payne, George Henry. *History of Journalism in the United States*. Westport, Connecticut: Greenwood Press, 1970.

Postman, Neil. *Amusing Ourselves to Death: Public Discourse in the Age of Show Business*. New York: Viking, 1985.

———. *Building a Bridge to the Eighteenth Century*. New York: Alfred A. Knopf, 1999.

Purvis, Thomas L. *Colonial America to 1763*. New York: Facts on File, Inc., 1999.

Putnam, William Lowell. *John Peter Zenger and the Fundamental Freedom*. Jefferson, North Carolina: McFarland & Company, 1997.

Ramsay, David. *The History of the American Revolution, Volumes I and II*. Indianapolis: Liberty Fund, 1900.

Randall, Willard Sterne. *Alexander Hamilton: A Life*. New York: HarperCollins, 2003.

————. *Thomas Jefferson: A Life*. New York: Henry Holt, 1993.

Rice, Kym S. *Early American Taverns: For the Entertainment of Friends and Strangers*. New York: Fraunces Tavern Museum, 1983.

Rosenfeld, Richard N. *American Aurora: A Democratic-Republican Returns: The Suppressed History of Our Nation's Beginnings and the Newspaper That Tried to Report It*. New York: St. Martin's Press, 1997.

Ross, Angus, ed. *Selections from The Tatler and The Spectator of Steele and Addison*. Hammondsworth, Middlesex, England: Penguin Books, 1982.

Schiff, Stacy. *A Great Improvisation: Franklin, France, and the Birth of America*. New York: Henry Holt and Company, 2005.

Schlesinger, Arthur M. *The Birth of the Nation*. New York: Alfred A. Knopf, 1969.

————. *Prelude to Independence: The Newspaper War on Britain, 1764–1776*. New York: Alfred A. Knopf, 1958.

Silverman, Kenneth. *The Life and Times of Cotton Mather*. New York: Harper & Row, 1984.

Simon, James F. *What Kind of Nation: Thomas Jefferson, John Marshall, and the Epic Struggle to Create a United States*. New York: Simon & Schuster, 2002.

Simon, Linda. *Dark Light: Electricity and Anxiety from the Telegraph to the X-Ray*. Orlando, Florida: Harcourt, 2004.

Singleton, Esther. *Social New York Under the Georges, 1714–1776, Two Volumes*. Port Washington, New York: Ira J. Friedman, Inc., 1969.

Smith, Hedrick. *The Power Game: How Washington Words*. New York: Random House, 1988.

Solomon, Louis. *America Goes to Press*. New York: Crowell-Collier Press, 1970.

Stephens, Mitchell. *A History of News: From the Drum to the Satellite*. New York, Viking, 1988.

Stewart, Donald Henderson. *The Opposition Press of the Federalist Period*. Albany, New York: State University of New York Press, 1969.

Tagg, James. *Benjamin Franklin Bache and the Philadelphia Aurora*. Philadelphia: University of Pennsylvania Press, 1991.

Tebbel, John. *The Compact History of the American Newspaper*. New York: Hawthorn Books, 1969.

————, and Sarah Miles Watts. *The Press and the Presidency: From George Washington to Ronald Reagan*. New York: Oxford University Press, 1985.

Tindall, George Brown. *America: A Narrative History, Volume 1*. New York: W.W. Norton & Company, 1984.

Tyler, Moses Coit. *The Literary History of the American Revolution, 1763–1783, Volumes I and II*. New York: G.P. Putnam's Sons, 1897.

Vidal, Gore. *Inventing a Nation: Washington, Adams, Jefferson.* New Haven, Connecticut: Yale University Press, 2003.

Weisberger, Bernard A. *America Afire: Jefferson, Adams, and the Revolutionary Election of 1800.* New York: William Morrow, 2000.

West, Thomas G. *Vindicating the Founders: Race, Sex, Class, and Justice in the Origins of America.* Lanham, Maryland: Rowman & Littlefield, 1997.

Whitehill, Walter M. and Norman Kotker. *Massachusetts: A Pictorial History.* New York: Charles Scribner's Sons, 1976.

Wills, Garry. *Cincinnatus: George Washington & the Enlightenment, Images of Power in Early America.* Garden City, New York: Doubleday & Company, 1984.

Wise, David. *The Politics of Lying: Government Deception, Secrecy, and Power.* New York: Random House, 1973.

Wishman, Seymour. *Anatomy of a Jury: The System on Trial.* New York: Times Books, 1986.

Wood, Gordon S. *The Americanization of Benjamin Franklin.* New York: The Penguin Press, 2004.

Wright, Esmond. *Franklin of Philadelphia.* Cambridge, Massachusetts: The Belknap Press of Harvard University Press, 1986.

ACKNOWLEDGMENTS

❖

I COULD HAVE WRITTEN this book without the assistance of Debbie Celia, of the Westport Public Library in Westport, Connecticut, but I would still be on chapter 4. It was she who answered the questions I could not answer myself, or told me where the answers could be found when I had no idea where to look, or convinced me that a question had no answer and I needed to think along other lines. She was prompt and tireless, cheerful and accurate. I am very grateful.

Sometimes, though, she would need a break. On those occasions, fellow librarians Marta Campbell and Beth Dominianni filled in graciously. Then they needed breaks.

Their coworker, Susan Madeo, arranged my interlibrary loans, gathering books from all over the country, and she did not complain when I asked for extensions or returned a volume only to ask for her to ship it back to me a few weeks later.

And I could have written this book without the assistance of Peter Hoffer, professor of history at the University of Georgia, but it would be marred by errors of both fact and interpretation. Surely some of them remain, despite my best efforts to the contrary. But Professor Hoffer, who may fairly be called the conscience of contemporary historical scholarship, helped me eliminate mistakes from the sections of the book that he reviewed. My sincere thanks to him as well.

I read hundreds of issues of colonial newspapers in the process of researching *Infamous Scribblers*. The two best collections I found are in the microfilm rooms at Harvard University's Widener Library and Yale University's Sterling Memorial Library, and for long stretches of time I visited one or the other almost every weekend. Without exception, the staffs, almost all of them students, were knowledgeable and patient, with the latter quality being especially evident after my repeated requests for help in all matters mechanical: operating the microfilm reader or the printer attached to it or the machine that adds money to the cash card. Perhaps they assumed it was inevitable that a Luddite would be drawn to the distant past.

Another Harvard library, the Lamont, houses a few early American journals of its own. Thanks to Sydney Owens, who fought her way to work through a blizzard one day, I was able to get copies of some relevant pages faxed to my home in Connecticut, where I was stranded by the same blizzard. The weather was better when I called upon Jennie Rathbun, of Harvard's Houghton Library, and she was no less willing to provide me with needed information.

The microfilm room at the New York Public Library's main branch also has an extensive collection of eighteenth-century periodicals; it is a busy place, and Alice Dowd helped me make efficient use of it.

From Columbia University's Butler Library I needed to see but a single page of a single edition of a single publication; my niece, Barnard student Lizzie Wade, was my research assistant here for a few hours one day, and I appreciate her efforts, especially since she was studying for midterms at the time.

Another college student, Chris Winkler of Yale, also chipped in for a day, saving me a trip and clarifying an important point. He and I are not related but are forever bound: in 2001, when Staples High School in Westport, Connecticut, was the best baseball team in the state, Chris was a star pitcher, my son the catcher.

James Grant, author of *John Adams: Party of One*, answered a few questions I had about the most obscure paper cited in the preceding pages, the *Sunbury and Northumberland Gazette*; Philip Lampi, of the American Antiquarian Society's Newspaper Project in

Worcester, Massachusetts, was kind enough to provide a copy of one of the few remaining editions.

As far as I know, only one print shop from the colonial era still exists, although as a museum, not a business. It is the Franklin Court Printing Office in Philadelphia, which is run by the National Park Service under the auspices of the Department of the Interior, and it looks today as it looked almost 300 years ago, when Benjamin Franklin learned his trade in a very similar setting.

Chuck Kokolsky, the ranger on duty the morning I visited, was as knowledgeable as the print shop's original owner would have been. He slipped on a leather apron and took me through the shop's operations step by step. He showed me the types and the composing sticks and the chases, the ink beaters and the hanging racks on the ceiling, the supplies of paper and the vats for dampening it. He told me how the ink was mixed. He demonstrated the workings of the press, and the physical effort it required. Thanks to Chuck, I was able to appreciate—and, I hope, to convey to readers—the hardships of a day in the life of a colonial printer and, more specifically, the greater hardships of Ben Franklin as a young apprentice.

There are more people to thank. Some of them helped me find articles I could not track down on my own, in most cases because they were written anonymously or under the cover of a pseudonym; or they are people who provided me with a better understanding of the context of articles I had already located. They are editor Greg Lint and associate editor Maggie Hogan, of the John Adams Papers, Massachusetts Historical Society; Karen Duval, associate editor of the Papers of Benjamin Franklin, Yale University; Mary A. Hackett, associate editor of the James Madison Papers, University of Virginia; and Anna Berkes, research librarian at the Thomas Jefferson Library at Monticello.

My gratitude also goes to those who made photocopies of pamphlet pages for me, documents that were too rare and ancient and brittle to circulate; or who, in a few cases, enabled me to see the pamphlets themselves, although first insisting that I either wash

454 | Acknowledgments

my hands or slip on a pair of cotton gloves; or who simply pointed me in the right direction for one pursuit or another: Bill Luebke at the Library of Virginia; Nora Costello at the Mashantucket Pequot Museum and Research Center in Connecticut; Dan Snydacker, executive director of the Pequot Library in Connecticut, whose Special Collections room is a small and little-known treasure; Elise Bochinski of Special Collections at the Fairfield University Library, also in Connecticut; and Anne Dodge of the John Hay Library at Brown University.

The highest praise an author can give to his editor is to say that he made the book better, and David Patterson did just that. In fact, he did more. He and fellow PublicAffairs editor Clive Priddle were at least as responsible as I for the very notion of a volume about colonial journalism, and David's suggestions on improving the manuscript were thoughtful and perceptive and accurate.

John J. Guardiano is the most meticulous copy editor I have ever worked with. He is probably more of a pedant than I am, and he knows I say that with envy.

I would like to thank Peter Osnos, founder and editor-at-large at PublicAffairs, and Susan Weinberg, publisher, for publishing—and supporting—this book.

Also at PublicAffairs, I thank publicity director Gene Taft, managing editor Robert Kimzey, marketing director Lisa Kaufman, art director Nina D'Amario, and production editor Melissa Raymond. All made significant contributions to this book; all made me hope we can work together again.

Finally, I salute my agent Tim Seldes, not only for bringing this project to PublicAffairs, but for the man he is and, even more, the literary tradition he represents.

Index

✿

PUBLICAFFAIRS is a publishing house founded in 1997. It is a tribute to the standards, values, and flair of three persons who have served as mentors to countless reporters, writers, editors, and book people of all kinds, including me.

I. F. STONE, proprietor of *I. F. Stone's Weekly,* combined a commitment to the First Amendment with entrepreneurial zeal and reporting skill and became one of the great independent journalists in American history. At the age of eighty, Izzy published *The Trial of Socrates,* which was a national bestseller. He wrote the book after he taught himself ancient Greek.

BENJAMIN C. BRADLEE was for nearly thirty years the charismatic editorial leader of *The Washington Post.* It was Ben who gave the *Post* the range and courage to pursue such historic issues as Watergate. He supported his reporters with a tenacity that made them fearless, and it is no accident that so many became authors of influential, best-selling books.

ROBERT L. BERNSTEIN, the chief executive of Random House for more than a quarter century, guided one of the nation's premier publishing houses. Bob was personally responsible for many books of political dissent and argument that challenged tyranny around the globe. He is also the founder and was the longtime chair of Human Rights Watch, one of the most respected human rights organizations in the world.

.   .   .

For fifty years, the banner of Public Affairs Press was carried by its owner Morris B. Schnapper, who published Gandhi, Nasser, Toynbee, Truman, and about 1,500 other authors. In 1983 Schnapper was described by *The Washington Post* as "a redoubtable gadfly." His legacy will endure in the books to come.

Peter Osnos, *Founder and Editor-at-Large*